A Young Mind
in a Growing Brain

A YOUNG MIND
IN A GROWING BRAIN

Jerome Kagan
Harvard University

Norbert Herschkowitz
University of Bern

With the collaboration of
Elinore Herschkowitz

LEA LAWRENCE ERLBAUM ASSOCIATES, PUBLISHERS
2005 Mahwah, New Jersey   London

Lawrence Erlbaum Associates, Inc., Publishers
10 Industrial Avenue
Mahwah, New Jersey 07430
www.erlbaum.com

Cover design by Sean Trane Sciarrone

Library of Congress Cataloging-in-Publication Data

Kagan, Jerome.
　　Young mind in a growing brain / Jerome Kagan, Norbert Herschkowitz, Elinore Herschkowitz.
　　　　　p.　cm.
Includes bibliographical references and index.
ISBN 0-8058-5309-X (cloth : alk. paper)
ISBN 0-8058-5425-8 (pbk. : alk. paper)
1. Child psychology. 2. Infant psychology. 3. Brain—Growth. 4. Cognitive neuroscience.　I. Herschkowitz, Norbert.　II. Herschkowitz, Elinore.　III. Title.
BF721.K18　2005
155.4'3—dc22　　　　　　　　　　　　　　　　　　2005040052
　　　　　　　　　　　　　　　　　　　　　　　　　　　　CIP

Books published by Lawrence Erlbaum Associates are printed on acid-free paper, and their bindings are chosen for strength and durability.

Printed in the United States of America
10　9　8　7　6　5　4　3　2

Science tells us what we can know, but what we can know is little and if we forget how much we can not know we become insensitive to many things of very great importance.

—Bertrand Russell, *A History of Western Philosophy*.
1945, New York: Simon & Schuster.

The question always to ask when exaggerated, dogmatic assertions are made is: What is actually true in this? Or again: In what case is that actually true?

—Ludwig Wittgenstein, *Culture and Value*.
1980, University of Chicago Press.

Contents

Preface

The stunning discoveries by neuroscientists, behavioral biologists, developmental psychologists, and pediatricians over the last half century have brought the broad boundaries of these disciplines into initial points of contact. These advances are a cause for celebration and an invitation to those with the time and passion to search for an initial set of integrative propositions that unite the phenomena these disciplines probe. Such a synthesis occurred in biology over 60 years ago when scholars recognized the complementary contributions of genes and ecology to animal evolution. A second, equally fruitful, synthesis is forming as molecular biologists and protein chemists collaborate in attempts to elucidate the mechanisms that allow the estimated 30,000 genes to manufacture more than 100,000 proteins.

This book summarizes some initial conclusions that follow simultaneous examination of the psychological milestones of human development during the first decade and what has been learned about brain growth. However intriguing, these correlations in timing between changes in brain and psychological competence cannot prove that the former caused the latter, and it is not possible at present to map in any detail the psychological phenomena on the biological events.

Although we argue that the biological events enable the new psychological properties, we do not assume a one-way maturational model. Brain growth is shaped by the interactions of genes, gene expression, and experience. A brain deprived of stimulus input will have a compromised structure; hence, an infant isolated from social experience will show anomalous growth of brain, as well as delayed development of behavior, emotion, and cognitive ability. Our discussion assumes a healthy infant developing in a world that contains objects, people, animals, sounds, smells, and opportunities to locomote and to manipulate objects.

Many excellent books and technical articles have described either the biology, the psychology, or both, for a limited interval of time, but few writers have attempted to link the two domains over a longer era. We restricted the discussion to the first 8 years because the biological information was richer for this interval than for the adolescent years. Future discoveries will permit others to elaborate, and to revise, many of our claims, for all descriptions of nature are temporary and vulnerable to refutation. To paraphrase Montaigne, we seek the truth, rather than to lay it down.

The dominant beliefs of a culture and the consensual premises of the scientific community have mutual influences on each other. If industrialization had not created cities with large numbers of poor families, Malthus might not have thought about populations outstripping food supplies. As a result, Darwin might not have invented the notion of natural selection, which influenced late 19th-century views on the utility of competition and self-interest as ways to promote progress. If Europeans had not developed an elaborate set of railway connections between its major cities, they would not have been motivated to guarantee that the clock time in Berlin would be perfectly coordinated with the times in Paris, London, and Copenhagen, and inventors would not have submitted proposals to meet this demand. Because they did, Einstein, studying the many submitted clock designs, turned his imaginative mind to the meaning of time, which eventually led to relativity theory and society's questioning of absolutes in domains outside of physics.

Western culture has always preferred a materialistic view of nature in which the origins of observed phenomena are assumed to be discrete entities—atoms, molecules, neurons, spines, and lobes. Thus, once powerful methods to study the brain had been developed, it was not surprising that bright young men and women seeking a career in science would be attracted to the neurosciences. The new facts they discovered led psychologists, psychiatrists, and their patients, to view most psychopathological profiles as disturbances of brain and to seek pharmacological cures for symptoms that ignored different etiologies and the therapeutic effects of experience.

The argument that a select set of human psychological properties cannot appear until certain maturational events have occurred bothers a number of American and European social scientists. We understand their resistance to the suggestion that there are natural restraints on the time of emergence of some human competences. Western society values freedom of action and the continual contribution of experience to biological structures. However, the earliest descriptions of infants and young children are very similar to those written today, despite very different living conditions in ancient Greece and suburban California.

There is also the hint of paradox in the fact that many psychologists who deny biological determinism in the first stages of development favor determinism for early environmental events. No one, including the authors, denies that experiences have a profound influence on brain development. However, no scientist claims that a 6-month-old would be able to speak if one arranged the proper regimen of experiences. We also distinguish between the substantial effects of experience on variation in a psychological property and its effects on the first display of a competence. All children, except a few with biological compromise, or subjected to extreme isolation, will speak by their third birthday, but the extraordinary variation in vocabulary size is due primarily to variation in experience. Thus, we are not indifferent to the profound influence of experience on both brain and psychological growth. This book focuses on those aspects of early development for which this influence is less potent, but not impotent.

We have restricted discussion of the psychological phenomena to those that might benefit from the facts of neuroscience, and omitted consideration of a wealth of biological and psychological evidence that could not be reasonably related to psychology, at least at the present time. With the exception of human temperaments and a few clinical syndromes, there is no discussion of the obvious variation among children in the timing of the milestones or their level of competence, much of which is attributable to experience. Neuroscience and developmental psychology are still young disciplines and future scientists have much to discover.

Every natural phenomenon is a whole, but scholars from distinct disciplines carve each gestalt into fragments that are described in the language of their discipline. When neuroscientists use the psychological term *fear* to describe a brain state in a rat, it is not obvious that the meaning of the word is synonymous with the meaning of the same word used by a patient or her therapist. We have tried to be sensitive to this semantic problem.

The aim of this book, written primarily for neuroscientists, psychologists, psychiatrists, pediatricians, and their students, is to acquaint those who do not regularly read psychological journals with what has been learned about human psychological development, and to acquaint those who do not read the neuroscience literature with the biological evidence, hoping that each group will gain a richer appreciation of both knowledge corpora. Thus, this book is neither a textbook in child development, nor a summary of the extensive literature on the relations between variation in experience—either experimentally induced or naturally occurring—and brain or behavioral growth.

It is critical that readers understand that the current state of knowledge does not permit persuasive propositions that link psychological competences to specific maturing brain functions. Every one of our claims for a relation between the change in brain and the emergence of a psychological phenomenon is a hypothesis. Given this permissiveness, readers might wonder why we devoted so much effort to this mission. We did so because we believe that simultaneous descriptions of the behavioral and biological features of a stage of growth should generate fruitful questions for both developmental psychology and neuroscience, although each group will feel the frustration that attends partially complete explanations.

The idea for this volume was born in 1993 when the authors, a psychologist and a pediatrician, met for the first time and recognized the complementarity of their backgrounds and the potential fruitfulness of a collaboration. The reception of our first two journal articles motivated this more ambitious attempt to synthesize the information covering a longer developmental era. We have learned a great deal over the past decade and hope that our enthusiasm provokes an equally intense curiosity in our readers.

ACKNOWLEDGMENTS

We are grateful to the Rockefeller Foundation for permitting us a month of residence in the fall of 2002 at the Villa Serbelloni in Bellagio where the first full draft of this book was prepared, and to the Bial Foundation for partial support of this work.

We also thank Nancy Snidman, Vali Kahn, Laura Gibson, and Paula Mabee for help in preparing the manuscript, and thank Charles Nelson, Steven Reznick, Pasko Rakic, Lazlo Seress, John Volpe, Oskar Jenni, Jay Giedd, Peter Huttenlocher, Harry Chugani, Karl Zilles, and Katrin Amunts for comments on parts of this book. The efforts of Elinore Herschkowitz are acknowledged on the title page.

—*Jerome Kagan*
Norbert Herschkowitz

1

Brain and Behavioral Development

How Close a Relation?

The assumption that psychological phenomena originate in brain activity was not obvious to the wisest ancients. It took over two millennia to arrive at the hypothesis that the timing of the milestones that define human psychological development was partially dependent on the maturation of neuronal circuits. These insights required the invention of machines and methods that permitted scientists to observe phenomena that were completely hidden a hundred years ago.

The chemistry of the synapse, myelination, and profiles of neural activation accompanying psychological activity has led to reasonable speculations regarding the contribution of neurophysiology to psychological events and deepened our understanding of thought, feeling, and behavior, because two sources of evidence are always better than one. The discovery of bacteria permitted better explanations of disease, the discovery of microwave radiation enriched conceptualizations of the origins of the universe, and research on brain development enhances our comprehension of developing psychological phenomena.

Correlations between the profile of neural activity at a particular time—which we call a *brain state*—and a mental or behavioral product are most obvious in infancy and early childhood because the young brain's structural immaturity limits the psychological properties that can be actualized. Hence, there should be a closer tie between the developmental stage of the nervous system and the age when the first psychological competences of our species appears. Two hundred years ago, almost 70% of

1

American children lived in two-parent farm families, saw both parents regularly, and, of course, did not enjoy radio, television, or airplane travel. Today, almost 70% of American children live with one parent, or in families in which both parents work in separate places in nonagricultural jobs, and the child has access to radio, television, and occasional travel. Nonetheless, the ages when language, inhibition of prohibited acts, and the assumption of responsibility first appear have changed very little over the past two centuries (Rogoff, 1996). The evidence to be summarized affirms the brain's modulation of psychological growth, although a detailed knowledge of the mechanisms that mediate the modulation remain mysterious.

There was so little information on human brain growth a quarter century ago, it was impossible to map the sequential changes in behavior and abilities on a maturing brain. As a result, it was easy for psychologists to argue that experience was the primary determinant of new actions, cognitive abilities, and moods. Piaget (1950) argued that infants' actions in and on the world created psychological structures that made it possible for 8-month-olds to reach toward the location where an adult had hidden an attractive toy seconds earlier. We now believe that the successful retrieval of the hidden toy requires the maturation of the hippocampus, medial temporal lobe, prefrontal cortex, and their interconnections. No amount of sensory–motor experience would permit a 4-month-old to reach to the correct location.

The degree of determinacy in the relation between a psychological product and a pattern of neural activity is controversial and the debate on this issue has some of the features of a culture war. Some neuroscientists believe that, given access to the total pattern of brain activity in a person at a particular moment, they could, in principle, predict exactly what thought or feeling would be experienced, or what behavior might be implemented in the next moment. An equal number of more skeptical biologists see only probability distributions defining the relations between brain and psychological states. The probability of an eye blink occurring to a puff of air applied to the cornea (the puff activates neurons that project to eye muscles) is very high. But the probability of a facial grimace to a drop of lemon juice placed on the tongue (due to activation of the neurons that project to the muscles of the face) is lower. Lower, still, is the probability that a child will become immobile on seeing a large spider on a table (due to activation of the amygdala) because the child's prior history with spiders, and related expectations, determine whether the prefrontal cortex will or will not modulate the amygdala's projections to brain stem sites.

Experience could make one person's semantic network for "chocolate chip cookies" emphasize the semantic nodes for "mother," "oven," and "dinner," whereas the primary nodes for another might be "a friend," "restaurant," and "lunch." But the neuronal ensembles underlying these two different networks could involve exactly the same neurons in temporal and other cortical associational areas. Thus, a neuronal ensemble can represent different psychological forms in different individuals. This possibility implies that psychological structures have some autonomy and cannot be discovered with neuroscience evidence alone. One needs, in addition, information on the individuals' past history.

When future neuroscientists can measure the electrochemical events occurring in a pair of synapsing neurons they will probably discover that these microprocesses are loyal to the assumptions of quantum mechanics. Should this prediction prove valid, there will be a necessary indeterminacy at every synapse, and, therefore, lack of perfect predictability between the brain's reaction to a particular incentive and a psychological outcome (Lau, Roger, Haggard, & Passingham, 2004).

Many social scientists resist the strong form of determinism found in the writings of some neuroscientists because they know that each agent's prior experiences—both recent and from the distant past—play a critical role. It is always necessary to state the conditions under which a relation between brain activity and a psychological outcome holds. The amplitudes of the sequential event-related potential (ERP) waveforms to the same olfactory stimulus changed when participants were tested three times over a 12-day interval (correlations ranged from 0.4 to 0.7) because their expectations on the second and third sessions were different from those on the first session (Welge-Lussen, Wille, Renner, & Kobal, 2003). Neurons in both the anterior and posterior portions of the orbitofrontal prefrontal cortex become active when a person receives a squirt of chocolate milk. However, the anterior neurons stop responding when the person has been sated on the chocolate milk and finds its taste unpleasant, although the posterior neurons continue to respond (Kringelbach, O'Doherty, Rolls, & Andrews, 2003).

If the brain's reactions to olfactory and taste stimuli are affected by past experience, we can be certain that this influence is more dramatic for complex events with a rich network of associations. For example, the brain generates a distinct negative waveform at 170 msec to a human face (called the N170 because it has a negative polarity and usually occurs with a latency of 170 msec), but not to a pair of black dots enclosed within a circle. However, the N170 does occur if the pair of black dots is presented after the participant has seen a series of schematic faces and, therefore, anticipates the presentation of a face.

There is no consensus on how to conceptualize a psychological property, like a competence or an emotion. One position conceives of a psychological property as a permanent brain state always ready to influence behavior, much like a hand that is always capable of picking up an object.

The less popular view regards a psychological property as a temporary state whose actualization depends on the context and the brain state at the moment. This difference is captured by the different meanings of the following two sentences:

1. Mary is an anxious person.
2. Mary has the capability for feeling anxious if criticized by a stranger.

Because an agent's expectations are a function of life history, and it is usually impossible to know that history, there is some indeterminacy in the relation between an incentive, on the one hand, and the brain's reaction and subsequent psychological product, on the other. Therefore, the verb "enable" is more appropriate than "cause" when we think about the relation between brain activity and a psychological reaction. Even as vocal a defender of biological determinism as E. O. Wilson (1999) agreed that, "There can be no simple determinism of human thought . . . because the individual mind can not be fully known . . . the self can go on believing in its own free will" (p. 131). This book assumes neither a fixed determinism between brain activity and a psychological product nor the equally extreme view that psychological development is independent of brain growth. We recognize that the middle ground is rarely popular in most controversies, but urge readers to maintain a tolerance for ambiguity as they reflect on the extensive corpus of facts scientists have discovered.

How to Conceptualize Brain and Behavior

We can select at least four different ways to structure the phenomena that define biological and behavioral development. The most desirable relies on theory as a guide. Physicists work with that advantage because they possess rigorous theory describing functional relations among concepts like mass, electron, energy, force, magnetism, and entropy. Thus, the organization of physics textbooks is determined by the nature of the theoretical relation, and the phenomena of friction and heat are separate from the quantum events of photons and quarks.

Unfortunately, neither neuroscientists nor developmental psychologists possess robust theory. Both disciplines are still trying to understand how brains enable human thought, feeling, and behavior. As a result, scholars exploit three other guides for organization: (a) comparison with an ideal, (b) shared features, and (c) a common history.

Ideal Forms. Most scientists, including psychologists and neuroscientists, hold notions of ideal forms. The neuroscientists often write as if the brain of the 20-year-old possesses optimal properties. For example, they note that the sensory areas of 3-month-olds contain 150% of the number of synapses of the 20-year-old. Psychologists, too, assume the young adult is the ideal when they claim that a 5-year-old has a poorer retrieval memory and less control over action than a college student.

This perspective assumes that the child and the elderly are less perfect forms. Although 19th-century biologists assumed that humans were the acme of evolution, most contemporary biologists acknowledge that the human species happens to have some qualities that are more, and some that are less, adaptive for their niche.

Shared Properties. Neuroscientists and psychologists often exploit a second strategy which relies on shared observable features. The former group considers neurons with the same shape (for example, pyramidal neurons), same class of receptor, or same location, as belonging to a common category. The psychologist is more slavishly devoted to this rule because of the inability to measure brain states in natural settings. Thus, all acts that mimic another are called imitation, all acts that hurt another are called aggressive, and all acts that help another are called altruistic. Unfortunately, psychologists are prone to use performance on one procedure as the basis for a broad category of competence. One of the most egregious errors made in clinical settings is to categorize the child as having "impaired memory functioning" simply because of a low score on the digit recall scale of the Wechsler Intelligence Scale. The correlations among recall memory for numbers, recognition memory for scenes, and implicit memory for words are so low it is a mistake to treat performance in any one situation as representing a child's memorial talents.

One serious problem with treating similarity in a single feature as a basis for a common category is that acts that are similar in appearance often have different antecedents and, therefore, different meanings. A 2-day-old infant will protrude his or her tongue when an adult, bending over the infant, displays that action. But this newborn response should not be placed in the same category with a 4-year-old's attempt to bake a cake alongside her mother. An infant's striking a parent should not be classified with an adolescent's murder of a peer at a street corner, or a mouse biting an intruder. Similarly, most physiological events are due to different antecedent conditions; for example, high vagal tone in a laboratory could be the product of restlessness, a relaxed mood, or an extreme degree of attentiveness to events in a testing room.

Because a particular behavior can be derived from different biological states, there are fewer classes of behavior than classes of brain states. This asymmetry is present in our language. Behaviors are described with predicates and there are fewer predicates with distinctive meanings than words for different agents or contexts. A person bites a cookie when eating, a thread when sewing, and a cellophane wrap when opening a gift. The word "bite" has different meanings in these three contexts because the intention and the brain state are distinct. Thus, the sentences, "the mouse bit the intruder animal" and "the infant bit her mother" have different meanings. But because English has only one predicate for this act, the word "bite" is used to describe both events.

Neuroscientists often borrow words intended originally to describe human psychological states and apply them to animals, with the tacit assumption that important features of the word's meaning remain unchanged. For example, some scientists attribute "fear" to a mouse who stays in a dark area and does not enter a brightly lit one, but would not attribute "love" to a pair of copulating mice, or "pride" to a bird who had completed construction of a nest. Fear, love, pride, and a host of other words intended to describe human emotional states should not be indiscriminately applied to animals. New terms must be invented.

The understandable desire to minimize the psychological differences between humans and other animals serves the rational desire to use the evolutionary principle of inclusive fitness to explain human behaviors and social institutions. For example, some primatologists believe that capuchin monkeys understand the semantic concept "inequity" because they behave in a distinct way when they receive less tasty food than another animal a few feet away (Brosnan & de Waal, 2003). However, differential behavior to two distinct events is insufficient evidence to infer a semantic concept as abstract as "inequity." Otherwise, scientists should award male monkeys possession of the semantic concept "estrus" because the animals behave in different ways when a female is or is not sexually receptive. Although many human sensory, motor, and physiological competences have legitimate analogs in other animals, unique properties often occur in evolution—flight in birds and internal fertilization in mammals are two examples.

There are at least three reasons why many scientists search enthusiastically for animal behaviors that seem to share essential features with human language, morality, inference, and consciousness. The usual argument is that all vertebrates have strings of DNA on their chromosomes that are responsible for the proteins that comprise the tissues and organs that many species share. Hence, it is reasonable to assume that the neural bases for the behaviors of mice and rats will resemble those that mediate behaviors serving similar functions in humans. A second legitimate argument is that scientists can perform experiments with animals that are impossible with humans and the results of this work might illuminate the human condition. Harry Harlow's (1966) research with isolated infant monkeys was celebrated because the abnormal development of infant rhesus separated from their mothers and placed with inanimate objects implied that a similar outcome would hold for human infants. This discovery provided support for the popular assumption that human infants required intimate contact with their adult caretakers.

A less rational, but nonetheless attractive, reason for generalizing from animals to humans is that this view rationalizes the human qualities of aggression, selfishness, and multiple sex partners. These, and other ethically questionable tendencies, provoke a little guilt in some humans. However, if humans and chimpanzees share a common biology and psychology, perhaps humans should not feel ashamed or bothered by these motives and actions.

Finally, the assumption of biological proximity lends tacit support to the strong wish for a seamless unity among all living things. Many adults in contemporary societies would like to believe that humans could be a band of brothers and sisters, sharing common motives, values, emotions, and talents. Because the current strife across the world frustrates this idealistic hope, it is reassuring to believe that humans, chimpanzees, and monkeys might be "brothers under the skin." However, it is worth noting that biologists who study varied bird species have not tried to find the anlage of flight, imprinting, or seasonal migration in crocodiles, snakes, or lizards because they know that these characteristics are novel evolutionary features that have no analogue among reptile species.

The human brain has a number of sufficiently distinct features to suggest that the relations between brain and behavior in rats, monkeys, and humans are not the same for many psychological processes. Even rats and cats behave differently during a 3-min delay between the appearance of a conditioned stimulus signaling food and food delivery (Bos, Meijer, Van Renselaar, van der Harst, & Spruijt, 2003). Flax is a poor model for Mendelian genetics, the spider is a poor model for mammalian reproductive physiology, and the mouse and monkey may not be useful models for all human properties. This claim is especially valid for language, inference, consciousness, and morality.

Although classification of forms based on a single feature remains a frequent strategy, individuals who share a single characteristic are usually heterogeneous with respect to other qualities that should be added to the shared feature. One of the most useful sources of supplementary information comes from the individual's past.

Shared History. Shared history is a useful criterion to guide organization. The cladists in evolutionary biology use common ancestor forms to classify a contemporary animal group. Terriers and wolves are classed together because the former evolved from the latter. Terriers and Siamese cats are not placed in the same category, although they are more similar in size, tameness, and usual location.

Neuroscientists rely on origins when they study the derivatives of the neural crest cells, which have different final functions and locations in the newborn. Psychologists group together all adults who had been securely attached infants, abused children, or grew up in poverty, on the assumption that the members of each of these groups share significant features. The danger in this strategy is to ignore the differences between adults who share a contemporary feature but have different histories. For example, depressed adults whose first episode occurred before age 20 differ from those whose first bout of depression occurred after that age. The depressive mood of the former group is more chronic and responds less favorably to drug treatment (Stewart, Bruder, McGrath, & Quitkin, 2003).

Multiple Criteria.   Ideal states, shared features, and common histories have both advantages and disadvantages as criteria. Hence, neuroscientists and psychologists exploit two or all three. The biological concept of species, for example, rests on similarity in contemporary features as well as evolutionary history. The classification of neurotransmitters relies on similarity in molecular structure, as well as their effects on psychological states. We have chosen this strategy; hence the primary organization of this text is a chronological description of historical changes in organization.

The principle that forms and functions of an early structure do not always resemble those of advanced stages is general because mature forms often swallow their nascent beginnings. The brain of a 6-year-old ready for school provides no clue as to how that brain was formed, and 19th-century scientists could have imagined many different ways nature might have constructed this organ.

The Vocabulary of Brain and Psychological Processes.   We argue that, at least at present, descriptions of brain states and their emerging psychological products require two distinct vocabularies; hence, scientists should not use the words that name a psychological property to describe a brain state. To illustrate, adolescents can compare two different semantic networks simultaneously (e.g., the network for snakes and the network for danger). Some scientists have suggested that the anterior prefrontal cortex—the frontal pole—makes a significant contribution to this cognitive ability. Although this suggestion may be valid, one should not write that neuronal ensembles "compare different semantic networks." No biologist would write that the proteins that give rise to heart muscles can be deprived of blood (and provoke a heart attack). No physicist would suggest that molecules of air and water can destroy a coral reef (as happens in a typhoon). A heart attack and the destruction of a coral reef are emergent events enabled by their constituent structures, but not isomorphic with them. The phenomena we call "human consciousness" require particular brain states, but consciousness is not a property of neuronal ensembles.

Significance of Context

The evidence on brain and psychological growth reveals the significance of the context in which measurements are taken. The conceptualization of every incentive and subsequent response must be combined with its context, and never treated as an entity that has the same essential properties across varied contexts. Remember, an electron is neither a wave nor a particle, but has the potential to appear as either depending on the experimental context in which it is measured; a gene can contribute to a neuron in the cortex or a pigment cell in the skin depending on its location.

At least four contrasting contexts must be specified: (a) the location is familiar or unfamiliar, (b) the agent is alone or with familiar or unfamiliar conspecifics, (c) the context is challenging or presents no challenge, and (d) the context does or does not contain an incentive for a desired goal state. Most experiments with animals are performed in an unfamiliar place, the animal is alone, and the context presents either a challenge or contains an incentive for a goal. The context in most studies of children is unfamiliar and challenging, the child is usually with an unfamiliar adult, and there is often no salient goal state that the child desires.

Consider some examples of the influence of context. Seven-month-old infants are likely to cry to an approaching stranger if they are in an unfamiliar place but less likely to cry if the stranger approaches when they are at home. The behavioral consequences of an injection of cocaine in the brain of a rat depend on whether the animal is in a familiar home cage or in an unfamiliar location.

Whether one bonobo chimp dominates another depends on whether the two animals form a dyad, or a third chimp is present (Vervaecke, DeVries, & Van Elsacker, 1999). Further, whether a monkey injected with corticotropin releasing factor does or does not develop behavioral signs of depression depends on whether the animal has been caged alone or has been housed with other animals in a laboratory (Strome et al., 2002). Elephants are seriously influenced by the age and sex of the individuals in their local territory. Young males experience periodic surges in testosterone that are accompanied by increased aggressive and sexual behavior. This state, called *musth*, which usually lasts a few weeks, can last as long as 6 months if no adult males are present. However, the duration of a musth episode is much shorter if older male elephants are introduced into groups of wild young males (Slotow, Vandyk, Poule, Page, & Klacke, 2000).

The size of a city predicts whether a person will or will not help a stranger who appears hurt or blind. When the population density reaches about 1,500 people per square mile, adults are less likely to help a stranger in obvious need; hence, Americans from large cities are less helpful than those who live in smaller cities or towns (Levine, 2003).

The social class of the child's family represents a continual context for psychological development. The family's position, which must always be viewed in relation to others in the society, is one of the best predictors of the adolescent's cognitive abilities, school performance, vocational choice, and psychopathology. Indeed, the heritability estimate for the I.Q. scores of 7-year-olds is close to zero for children growing up with very poor families and increases linearly as social class rises (Turkheimer, Haley, Waldron, D'Onofrio, & Gottesman, 2003). Social class possesses this power because the skills, values, and beliefs promoted by most societies are congruent with those held by citizens with the most education and wealth and adaptation is facilitated if children acquire these properties.

Adults who grew up in economically disadvantaged families are at higher risk for a psychiatric illness, compared with those reared in middle-class homes (Melzer, Fryers, Jenkins, Brugha, & McWilliams, 2003). The city of Warsaw, Poland, razed at the end of World War II, rebuilt its homes and schools following a policy that required families of different educational and professional training to live together in the same apartment building and to send their children to the same school. Despite the absence of residential segregation by social class, which is so common in America and Europe, there was a linear relation between the social class of a child's family and his scores on a standard test of cognitive ability (Firkowska, Ostrowska, Sokolowska, Stein, & Susser, 1978). Siblings born with perfectly healthy nervous systems develop distinct personalities and talents if one grows up with parents who never graduated from high school and the other with parents who have professional degrees (Schiff et al., 1978).

In the dirt poor Mayan Indian village of San Marcos, located on the shores of Lake Atitlan in northwest Guatemala, all homes were of crude adobe without running water or electricity when one of us worked there 30 years ago (Kagan, Klein, Finley, Rogoff, & Nolan, 1979). But the children of families who owned the quarter acre on which their small home stood performed better on a variety of cognitive tests than the children of families who did not own any land. Further, the residents of this village felt inferior to those in a larger town 2 km away because the former did not have a resident priest, running water, electricity, and regular mail delivery. The children in the small village were cognitively and behaviorally different from those in the larger town.

Among many ancient societies, and a few isolated groups today, each child's name announced his family, birthplace, and the ethnic origins of his parents and grandparents. Among the Berbers of Morocco the name

"David u Said n'ait Yussif" means that a boy named David is the son of Said and a member of the peoples of Yussif. Most peasants in medieval England gave their children one-syllable names, whereas the nobility used two-syllable names—Bearn versus Edward (Orme, 2001). The names given most American children hide their familial and class roots so that each child will be judged by his or her personal characteristics rather than by their ethnic or class origin.

The particular psychological symptom or symptoms displayed by a patient with a particular biological diathesis is also a function of the cultural setting. Consider, as an example, the rituals and intrusive obsessions of patients with obsessive-compulsive disorder (OCD). The frequent washing of hands and concern with dirt are primary symptoms in industrialized cultures where socialization of cleanliness is emphasized. However, Balinese patients with OCD are obsessed with the need to know the details of the people in their social network because social relationships have a priority (Lemelson, 2003). Many adults in America and Europe who work long hours every day of the week, and accept the description "workaholic," might be regarded as having OCD. Most of these individuals do not seek treatment, or regard themselves as having a psychiatric symptom, because their behavior is accompanied by enhanced status and income, and is celebrated by the society. Physical symptoms, like a fever due to malaria or diarrhea due to a bacterial infection of the gut, are the same across cultures. However, psychological symptoms involve an interpretation of one's feelings and, for that reason, can vary across cultural context.

An entity's position in a context, whether the spatial location of a cell, relative social status of a family in a community, one culture among many, or a particular DNA sequence on a chromosome, exerts a potent force. The cell's fate is determined by chemical gradients linked to its original spatial position and migratory path. An individual's education, vocation, and health are controlled, partly, by their social class position.

Early 20th-century biologists thought that each gene was an autonomous unit with the power to transmit a specific trait. This view was replaced when scientists learned that the products of a gene are determined by neighboring stretches of DNA; that is, by the local context. If we let a word serve as a metaphor for a gene, the traditional view was that the products of a gene might be likened to the meaning of a word like "ale." The new view suggests that the letter string "ale" could appear in the sequence bale, pale, whale, valet, salesman, talent, calendar, or baleful; each has a different meaning (Dillon, 2003; Nijhout, 2003).

The importance of the context increases with development because one of the significant functions of the prefrontal cortex is to select the most appropriate response from several alternatives. Thus, as the prefrontal cortex matures, the person's knowledge of the context assumes increasing importance. The newborn reacts in relatively stereotyped ways to a stimulus because the influence of the prefrontal cortex is minimal. The reactions of 8-year-olds are more dependent on context because the prefrontal cortex, acting as an executive, integrates past with present to permit the child to select the most adaptive response.

The Importance of Procedure. Every laboratory procedure is a distinct context. Hence the validity of every conclusion must be evaluated in light of the specific method that produced the evidence. The estimate of the evolutionary relation between two species depends on whether fossils, internal anatomy, proteins, or DNA are used to index the degree of genetic relatedness. The processes attributed to the brain are invisible and scientists must rely on special apparatus to generate observations that are indirect signs of the phenomena of interest. Each procedure produces information representing only a part of the whole event scientists wish to comprehend and it is often necessary to combine methods to obtain a fuller and, hopefully more accurate, view of the phenomenon. These stubborn facts mean that many generalizations about infants' perceptual, memorial, or emotional functions are limited to the particular measure quantified. For example, different measures assumed to index an infant's ability to recognize a novel event are often unrelated (Rose, Feldman, & Jankowski, 2003), and maternal descriptions of a child's timidity can be independent of behavioral observations of the child (Kagan, 1994).

An examiner tells a 4-year-old that if she points to the location where a piece of candy is hidden, an adult stranger and not she will get the sweet. However, if she points to the other location, she will enjoy the candy. If an examiner tells the child to use her finger to point, she is honest and informs the stranger of the candy's correct location. However, if given a rod as the indicator, she points to the other location and takes the candy for herself (Hala & Russell, 2001).

Simultaneous recordings of psychological and biological measures often lead to different inferences. For example, most 10-year-olds shown pictures of children they had played with in preschool 4 to 5 years earlier, along with pictures of unfamiliar children, had a poor recognition memory for the former playmates when asked to say whether they had ever seen the child in the photo, for they recognized only 21% of their former friends correctly. However, many children who did not recognize a former peer displayed a galvanic skin response to photos of children they had played with earlier, but not to strangers (Newcombe & Fox, 1994). Thus, the answer to the question, "Can 10-year-olds recognize former playmates after a 4-year interval?" is, "It depends on the method."

ERPs often yield results at variance with behavioral data. Six-month-old infants look longer at an inverted than at an upright face because the former is discrepant from their schemata for faces, but show equivalent ERP waveforms at 170 msec to upright and inverted faces. It is not until 12 months that the waveforms are larger to the inverted faces. Thus, the answer to the question, "Can 6-month-olds discriminate between upright and inverted faces?" depends on whether fixation time or the ERP supplies the evidence (DeHaan, Pascalis, & Johnson, 2002). And ERP waveforms can lead to inferences different from those drawn from functional brain scan evidence (fMRI) (Tsivilis, Otten, & Rugg, 2003).

This frustration is not restricted to the study of humans. Mice from a genetically homogeneous strain who enter and explore an open section of a circular area divided into quadrants do not necessarily enter and explore a large open field, although the two testing contexts are very similar (Cook, Bolivar, McFayden, & Flaherty, 2002). Rats normally spend more time exploring the two dark rather than the two brightly lit arms of an apparatus called the elevated plus maze. But they spend equivalent exploratory times if all the arms are dark or all the arms are brightly lit because the animals are responding to the contrast between dark and light and not to the absolute amount of light (Salum & Roque-da-Silva, 2003).

A major historical change in the referential meaning of psychological concepts, like "reward," "fear," "memory," and "emotion," has been the replacement of behaviors with brain events. A half century earlier, the word "reward" was defined as any event that increased the probability of a behavior (for example, food for a hungry rat increased the probability that a rat would press a bar to get the food). Changes in dopamine concentration in select areas of the nucleus accumbens, striatum, and cortex have become a primary referent for reward. This semantic substitution alters the sense and theoretical meaning of reward in a major way for some events that lead to an increase in dopamine in the above sites do not increase the probability that a rat will work to attain those events.

Psychologists use the concept "reward" to explain the acquisition of behaviors that can range from a rat striking a bar to receive food to a child memorizing the multiplication tables to receive praise. But neuroscientists, who can measure the circuits activated when animals behave, have discovered that the pattern of brain activation to a rewarding event varies with the nature of the rewarding event and the response being acquired. Although psychologists regard novelty, cocaine, and sexual stimulation as rewarding events, the circuits activated when a rat hits a lever to receive cocaine are different from those activated when a rat leaves one compartment to enter another containing unfamiliar objects, or a receptive female.

A leading cosmologist asked to estimate the age of the universe replied that any number he might suggest was neither interesting nor important, because it would change over time. What was of interest was the procedure that generated the estimate. The use of brain measurements to define psychological terms like reward leads to theoretically different understandings of the meaning of the word.

Splitters Versus Lumpers.   There is a serious asymmetry in the level of abstraction of most biological, compared with psychological, concepts. The neuroscientists' procedures usually produce evidence that constrains the positing of broad, abstract concepts and motivates investigators to be splitters. A complex cascade of neurochemical events occurs when an animal acquires an association between stimuli. However, the nature of the cascade varies with the events being associated and the behaviors measured. Unfortunately, many psychologists, who are lumpers, ignore this variety and use a broad concept like "learning" to refer to all acquired associations, regardless of the species, behavior, or conditions producing the association.

The problem with the psychologists' strategy is the overly permissive assumption that a term for a function or process does not change its meaning when the class of agent or the context is altered. Everyday conversation between people usually contains this extra information. The statements that follow contain the word "anxious" but their meanings are not the same because the different agents and the contexts in which the emotion occurred imply distinct feelings:

1. I was anxious over my newborn's premature birth.
2. My husband said he was anxious after being fired by his supervisor.
3. My 4-year-old child is anxious with large dogs.

Yet, many psychologists and psychiatrists continue to use the term anxious to describe rats, infants, adolescents, and adults confronting different situations and assume that a core meaning of the term is preserved.

Biologists often, although not always, restrict the meaning of a process to a particular entity in a specific context. Meiosis, for example, refers to germ cells dividing within a gonad to produce gametes. The term *meiosis* cannot be applied to any other biological object. Thus, if Mach, Poincaré, and Bohr are correct, and all scientists ever know are the relations between, or among, observed phenomena, we need one construct for the state that explains the relation between an ERP waveform to a discrepant tone that is perceived consciously and another construct to explain the state when the same waveform appears but there is no conscious awareness of the changed tone.

Methods of Analysis.   The varied methods of analysis also influence the conceptualization of phenomena. When investigators use the standard heritability equation to study the genetic contribution to intelligence in twin pairs, they are forced to assume that genetic and environmental contributions are additive, although most biological functions are not additive. When psychologists use analysis of covariance to control for social class differences on the relation between a child's vocabulary and adult vocational choice, they must assume that the influence of social class on vocabulary is linear and of similar magnitude across all vocabulary levels.

The preference for assuming linear, rather than nonlinear, relations between variables is due, in large measure, to the fact that the statistical procedures used most often by social scientists require this assumption. An analysis of variance performed on changes in facial response in newborns to different frequencies, loudnesses, and rise times of an auditory stimulus revealed neither a significant main effect nor an interaction. However, a specific combination of frequency, loudness, and rise time (which happened to match the profile of the human voice), produced eye opening in the infant (Kearsley, 1970). The relation of the three features of the sound to newborn behavior was nonlinear.

Because functional concepts like the perception of loudness, memory span for numbers, or speed of recognition dominate psychological theory, psychologists are prone to assume that every distribution of values should be treated as a continuum, with the mean representing the most valid index of a construct. By contrast, neuroscientists often quantify peak or extreme values of a neural profile, rather than the mean; for example, the maximal amplitude of an evoked potential with a particular latency at a particular site. One of us found no difference in mean heart rate between two different temperamental categories of infants following the placement of lemon juice on the child's tongue. However, one temperamental type attained a single interbeat interval during the 10-sec episode that was significantly smaller than the smallest interval displayed by the other group (Kagan, 1994).

Each class of evidence biases an investigator to select a description that favors either qualitative or continuous phenomena. That is why Mendel, who saw either wrinkled or smooth peas, disagreed with Darwin who assumed blending in heredity because he saw continuous variation in the beak size of finches and the coloring of tortoises.

The ascendance of molecular biology and genetics has been accompanied by a shift in descriptions of pathological moods and actions from continuous to qualitative phenomena. Several decades ago, psychologists described a bout of depression as a process due to a quantitative increase in guilt or feelings of helplessness. Psychiatric geneticists searching for the alleles that are the diathesis for depression assume a unique set of genes, and an accompanying neurochemistry, and regard depression as a state qualitatively different from the sadness that occasionally penetrates human moods. Of course, the preference for, and utility of, continua versus categories always depends on the question being asked. Categories are more useful if the concern is with etiology; continua provide a more fruitful approach if the interest is with the therapeutic effect of a drug.

Thus, contemporary scientists shuffle between the yang of qualitative structure and the yin of continuous processes. Most natural phenomena, however, are like the ambiguous figure seen in psychology textbooks that, depending on the features selected for attention, can be perceived as an old or a young woman, but not both simultaneously. An observer can restrict his or her attention to the sudden appearance of the white crest that forms as the sea approaches the shore, and conceive of a wave as a qualitative event, or expand his or her gaze to include the continuous movement of water that began 20 yards from the beach, and only gradually became a stretch of white water for a few seconds before disappearing in the sand. An infant's reach toward a hidden object, for example, is a qualitatively discrete event that emerges from a prior set of more continuous brain events, which, in turn, is a derivative of activity in discrete brain structures, which, in turn, is derived from continuous variation in neurotransmitters. And so we descend through alternating layers of qualitative structure and continuous process until we strike a dark wall of ignorance.

Human feeling, perception, memory, thought, and action cannot be simpler than the brain states that permit those functions to be actualized. The number of fundamental concepts in the natural sciences is smaller than the many derivatives that emerge from those foundations. One exception to this rule is the current imbalance between many brain states and the small number of psychological functions, a fact that should provoke suspicion that a theoretical error is being made.

Are There Stages in Development?   The conceptualization of change is now, and has always been, a perennial node of debate. The essential issue is whether to treat change as continuous, or as a sequence of qualitatively different stages with brief or prolonged transitions between them. When a quarterback throws a football to a receiver down the field, there is an interval when the ball is ascending, an instant when ascent turns into descent, an interval when it is descending, and a final interval when the ball is still, either in the receiver's arms or on the ground. Should we conceptualize this 8-sec event as continuous or as composed of four stages? Nature must smile every time scholars brood on whether they should select one or the other description.

The attraction to stages is understandable because the human mind is exquisitely sensitive to contrast. The ascending ball is perceptually and semantically distinguishable from the descending one. Therefore, parsing an event into stages seems to be loyal to experience. Archaeologists and anthropologists regard the change from hunter–gatherer bands to sedentary agricultural groups, around 10,000 years ago, as a new stage in human social structure. Evolutionary biologists are concerned with this question, for each species "appears" to be qualitatively distinct. There are dogs and wolves, rather than a graded series of animals between these two species. Darwin favored small, gradual, continuous changes in anatomy and physiology over the last 3.5 billion years. However, many biologists who followed him have argued that some mutations or recombinations of genes, when accompanied by geographic and reproductive isolation of a species, can produce relatively large changes in biological structures or functions in a short time. Gould and Eldredge (1977) argued that there can be long periods in the life of a species characterized by little change, interrupted by a natural event—like an earthquake—that produces a discontinuous change in a relatively short time.

It is easy to see stages in brain growth. Three days after fertilization the zygote is an almost homogeneous sphere called the blastula. Only 3 weeks later, the spherical blastula has become the more heterogeneous gastrula. The form at day 21 is so different from the form on day 3 that it is hard to avoid the inference that these changes are stage-like, although there is continuous change between the prior and the later phenomenon.

The argument for stages in psychological development is only a little less persuasive. The placement of a finger in the palm of a newborn produces an immediate grasp reflex. Three months later, the grasp fails to appear because the establishment of synapses from cortical axons on spinal motor centers inhibits the brain stem reflex. The 4-month-old cannot remember that her mother left the house 30 minutes earlier to buy a bottle of milk; the 4-year-old asks the mother if she brought cookies with the milk when the parent returns. These differences are so stark investigators are tempted to favor stage-like descriptions of psychological development, although the underlying brain growth can be conceptualized as gradual and continuous (Courage & Howe, 2002).

But, surprisingly, some scientists resist the possibility of discontinuities in psychological growth. For example, some want the language of the 2-year-old to be continuous with that of the adult so that they can apply the formal rules applicable to adults to the speech of children. Piaget (1950) also hoped to see the forerunner of adult logic in the reactions of 18-month-olds. But no anatomist would claim that the structure of the adult brain could be seen in the appearance of the neural tube. And no molecular biologist would suggest that the structure of a neuropeptide was recognizable in the DNA that represented its origin. It is unlikely that there is any psychological structure in 4-month-old infants that contains an early form of adult grammar, morality, or anxiety over failure.

However, acceptance of psychological stages does not imply an instant of transition, as is true of the football. We attribute a stage to psychological growth when a correlated cluster of features (or properties) displayed in a class of context changes its pattern of organization. But it always takes time for all the components to assume the new organization and to generalize to a broad range of situations. That is why most developmental scientists prefer the word *phase* to *stage*; for the former implies that the process of transformation was gradual and continuous. However, once we acknowledge that time is required to pass from one form of organization to another, the words stage and phase become almost synonymous, and we shall use the word transition to refer to a change in developmental phase.

It is understood that variation in experience across families or cultures guarantees that the phases will not occur at the same age in all children. Nonetheless, no 1-year-old feels responsible for a mistake, whereas all 10-year-olds do. During most of human history, parents did not keep a record of the birthdays of their many children and could not be certain of a child's exact age. Yet ethnographies reveal that parents in most societies expected their children to conform to simple requests by the third birthday and to assume simple responsibilities by their 7th year. These judgments were generally correct.

Scientists have discovered many transitions in development; many more remain undiscovered. We shall describe phases during fetal development, as well as during the first year, second year, preschool, and the early school years. The corresponding stages in brain development are marked by spurts of growth in neurons and dendritic spines, enhanced connectivity of neuronal ensembles across sites, and the appearance of neurotransmitters and neuromodulators. We suggest that the bases for the psychological phases include, first, a shift from sensory input as a main determinant of action and emotion to the power of schema during the first year. A second important phase occurs in the second year when semantic representations emerge to supplement schematic structures. A third phase, which appears after age 4, involves the ability to relate each event in the perceptual field to acquired knowledge and to the broader context.

FUNCTIONS OF BRAIN AND MIND

Three seminal psychological functions shared by all animals and humans, in addition to perceiving and creating representations of the environment and satisfying physiological needs, are: (a) detection of and reacting to change, (b) the establishment of associations between the representations of events and between these representations and behavioral or physiological reactions, and (c) the inhibition of inappropriate responses. These functions are as critical to psychology as the physical functions that relate force, mass, and acceleration to a missile's flight.

Detecting Change

The brain is biologically prepared to detect an event that is a change in the sensory surround, to compare an event to the immediate past and long-term knowledge, and, if necessary, to create a new representation that combines the event with existing representations. The brain reacts to the physical properties of an event, as well as to its unfamiliarity. The infant's smile to a sweet tasting liquid (or frown to a sour taste) is a function of both the sensory properties of the liquid, and the degree to which it was, or was not, expected. Infants stop smiling after several administrations of sugar water. The fact that every event that animals or humans attend to, or approach, loses this power after successive repetitions (although it can gain it on another occasion) means that almost all psychological reactions to an incentive are a joint function of both its inherent features and degree of unfamiliarity. We should not attribute the influence of an incentive only to its intrinsic features.

The sequence of waveforms in the EEG evoked by varied events (ERPs) reveals at least four classes of neuronal reactions. Waveforms that appear in the first 100 msec reflect the brain's response to the energy inherent in a sensory event; scientists call these forms exogenous. A second class of waveforms, between 200 and 250 msec, reflects the brain's reaction to a sensory event that is different from those that occurred in the immediate past. For example, humans display a negative waveform when a tone of 1500 Hz occurs after the person has heard identical tones of 1000 Hz over the past few seconds; this waveform is called mismatch negativity or MMN. The third waveform, which typically occurs between 300 and 500 msec, reflects the brain's reaction to an event that differs from representations that are part of the person's store of knowledge; for example, hearing a voice say, "the ice cream fell on the century," or seeing a camel sitting in a high chair. The fourth class of waveforms, occurring between 500 and 1000 msec, reflects the brain's attempt to assimilate the unfamiliar events that evoked the preceding waveform.

These waveforms should be described with a vocabulary that does not imply a psychological state because the first three waveforms can occur in animals and humans who are sleeping. Further, the MMN waveform to a vocal sound can occur although the individual does not consciously detect any change in sound pattern. Hence, we should not use the word *surprise* to describe the brain state, for this term implies a conscious psychological state. We suggest that the phrases (a) detection of sensory energy, (b) detection of change, (c) detection of discrepancy, and (d) detection of features shared with existing knowledge are useful ways to describe the four waveforms noted earlier.

The adaptive function of a readiness to detect change, present in the fetus, is obvious. A sudden sound piercing the silence, or a moving object with an unfamiliar shape, might signal a predator and the need to alter current behavior. Equally significant is the fact that a change in the stimulus surround or an event that is discrepant from acquired knowledge recruits an agent's attention and makes it more likely that a new association or cognitive structure will be established.

Establishing Associations

A second function of the brain is the establishment of a new association between representations of two events. The association can be between two stimuli—based on the brain states created by the two stimuli—which is called S-S learning. The association can also be between a state created by a stimulus and a biological or behavioral response—called S-R learning. In a common class of conditioning called Pavlovian, one of the stimuli, called the unconditioned stimulus (US), automatically elicits a particular behavioral or bodily reaction (e.g., a startle to a loud sound). The stimulus that becomes associated with the US, called the conditioned stimulus (CS), acquires the ability to evoke the response originally elicited by the US. For example, an investigator presents an animal with a light CS that is followed immediately by a brief electric shock to the feet (US) that automatically causes a rise in heart rate. The light and the subsequent shock alert the animal and produce changes in the basolateral nucleus of the amygdala that represents a link between the light and the electric shock. As a result, subsequent presentation of the light alone, without the shock, produces a rise in heart rate as a conditioned reaction. The newborn sucking response to the tactile stimulus of a nipple can be provoked by the conditioned stimulus of seeing an approaching nipple on a bottle or breast.

On some occasions, the brain state produced by a CS can resemble the state created by spontaneous neuronal activity. Under these conditions, the response that had been conditioned to the original CS can be elicited by the spontaneous brain activity. For example, most American children have learned to feel uncertain when their hands are very dirty, because of parental socialization; hence washing them became a conditioned reaction to this state. It has been suggested that OCD patients with a hand-washing compulsion possess unusually excitable basal ganglia. It is possible that the brain state created by spontaneous discharge of neurons in the basal ganglia resembles the brain state created by recognizing one's hands are dirty and, as a result, the former can elicit hand-washing. Social phobics avoid strangers because they create a state of uncertainty. If spontaneous activity in limbic sites created a brain state similar to the one generated by interacting with strangers, that neural activity, too, could elicit avoidant behavior. Despite the fact that these examples are speculative, it remains possible, even likely, that the varied brain states created by spontaneous activity in distinct neuronal ensembles could acquire the ability to elicit behaviors that had been linked to different, but similar, brain states.

The specific brain sites recruited by Pavlovian conditioning depend on the nature of the conditioned stimulus (for example, whether light, tone, or touch), the unconditioned stimulus (whether shock, an unpleasant odor, loud noise, or food), and the unconditioned response (whether immobility, startle, escape behavior, orienting, increase in heart rate or salivation). If the conditioned stimulus is a tone, the unconditioned stimulus electric shock, and the conditioned response an increase in heart rate, the amygdala and the hypothalamus are important participants. But if the conditioned stimulus is a light, the unconditioned stimulus a loud sound, and the conditioned response a bodily startle, the amygdala and brain stem nuclei are important participants.

Instrumental conditioning recruits a different circuitry because the behavior is not a biologically prepared reaction to an unconditioned stimulus and must be acquired. The response might be a rat's striking a lever with a paw to receive a food reward, or a child learning to play finger games. Some scientists have suggested that Pavlovian conditioning relies more on dopaminergic projections from the ventral tegmental area in the brain stem, whereas instrumental conditioning relies more on dopaminergic projections from the substantia nigra (Dayan & Balleine, 2002). Pavlovian conditioning of an eye blink reflex to the US of a puff of air applied to the cornea is mediated by a circuit different from the one activated by an instrumentally conditioned voluntary wink to a friend.

A third form of association, unique to humans, involves the spontaneous creation of links among semantic representations that have similar meanings. If a child has acquired on separate occasions semantic associations between "mother" and "food," and between "mother" and "love," semantic representations of love and food will become linked spontaneously, without any additional experience. All metaphors rely on this class of association.

Surprisingly, American children as young as 4 years of age acquire, without conscious awareness, associations between certain phonological sequences in English and a person's gender. Contemporary, English-speaking, American parents are likely to give names to their sons that are either (a) a single syllable (for example, Mark); (b) two syllable names with an accent on the first syllable (for example, Robert); or (c) two syllable names that end in a "stop consonant" (for example, Edward). By contrast, parents are likely to give their daughters names that are either (a) three syllables (for example, Jennifer); (b) two syllable names with an accent on the second syllable (for example, Louise); or (c) two syllable names that end in a vowel (for example, Ella). Four-year-old children, as well as adults, presented with pseudo names that have these phonological qualities, and asked to decide whether the names were more appropriate for a male or a female doll, used these rules to make their decision. Manufacturers occasionally exploit these rules to name products used differentially by men and women. One popular brand of kitchen toweling and one of flour, used primarily by women, are named "Bounty" and "Wondra," whereas American made computers and trucks, more often associated with men, are named "Dell" and "Ram." It is interesting, however, that the Japanese often choose names for cars that have a female symbolism in English (for example, Toyota Camry; Cassidy, Kelly, & Sharoni, 1999).

Conscious awareness is such a salient human feature that psychologists are tempted to exaggerate the amount of knowledge acquired through directed, conscious attention, and to minimize the knowledge that is gained implicitly without awareness. It is not clear, for example, what processes must be invented to explain how neural ensembles register and retain the less than perfect correlations between the sound pattern of a person's first name and his or her gender. We have to assume that the brain creates a prototype, or average representation, of the multiple associations—a topic discussed in chapter 4. It is likely, but not proven, that these prototypes are more easily formed for experiences that are psychologically distinctive, like a person's gender, and less likely for the colors of doors. The circuits mediating this implicit learning are probably different from those that mediate explicit conscious learning (Reber, Gitelman, Parrish, & Mesulam, 2003).

In addition, the probability of establishing an association between two events is generally greater when one or both events represent an unexpected change in the perceptual surround, or are discrepant from the individual's experience, because unexpected or unfamiliar events create a state conducive to the establishment of an association (Schultz, 2000). Adults commuting to work might pass two different houses next to each other 10 times a week for 10 years but fail to establish any association between them because neither dwelling was distinctive enough to recruit attention to its features.

We note in chapter 4 that the basolateral and central nuclei of the amygdala play an important role in this process. Every time an unexpected or discrepant event occurs, the basolateral area is excited and, in turn, activates the central nucleus which sends projections to varied brain stem sites (for example, the locus ceruleus and ventral tegmentum), resulting in the release of neurotransmitters that create a psychological state, described as attention, vigilance, or surprise, that increases the probability that an association will be formed. Individuals are most likely to establish associations between experiences that are distinctive, and less likely if they are not. The events that scientists call rewards are often those that are distinctive or violate expectancies (Kagan, 1984).

Inhibition of Inappropriate Responses

A third function of the brain is to inhibit responses that are inappropriate in a particular context. One form of inhibition is seen in the automatic habituation of brain reactions to repeated stimulation. A second, different form involves voluntary behavior. Individuals possess a set of behavioral potentialities for most situations, and usually one response is most appropriate for a particular situation. For example, each person possesses many possible reactions to the sight of a cup. One response is appropriate if the cup is full of coffee, another if the cup is to be emptied into the sink, and a third if it is to be rinsed and put in a cupboard. The person inhibits all but the appropriate one.

The ability to detect a change in sensory stimulation, and to establish associations between events, are present in an early form before birth. The inhibition of inappropriate voluntary responses develops later because this competence involves the prefrontal cortex, and it is not until the last quarter of the first year that the brain reliably mediates the first forms of this function.

The above three functions are present in all mammals. The primate brain adds three more complex functions: (a) the ability to hold the present and representations of past events in a working memory circuit for periods as long as 30 sec while the agent attempts to relate them, (b) the seeking of new experiences that are neither potential threats nor ones for which the agent has no appropriate response, and (c) maintaining representations of a distant future state, despite distracting stimuli or competing incentives, while a goal is being pursued.

Six additional competences, which may be unique to humans, and emerge in an initial form in children between 2 and 8 years, are: (a) states of consciousness; (b) application of the concepts of good and bad to self, other people, and events; (c) the capacity for shame and guilt following violation of a standard; (d) the ability to infer a variety of thoughts, intentions, and feelings in others; (e) a generative language consisting of semantic networks and syntax; and (f) the ability to remember the time and place of a past experience (called episodic memory). Each function is part of a hierarchy with executive functions controlling or modulating each one. The same principle holds for genes; the Hox genes act on target genes to determine, for example, the segmentation of an insect's body.

Although we frequently cite research on other primates, we rely much less on the extensive literature on rodents because this book emphasizes the psychological qualities of humans, rather than those possessed by all mammals.

THE PHASES OF DEVELOPMENT

Prenatal Era

The sequence of the development of brain structures follows a strict time-table. There are brief temporal windows when a particular brain site is especially malleable to change if a particular molecule (or molecules) is present. Some stressful events during gestation can affect the embryo or fetus. The postnatal sexual maturation of the offspring for example can be influenced by placing a pregnant vole with another unfamiliar pregnant vole three times a day for only 10 min on three successive days (during days 13–15 of gestation; Marchleska-koj, Kruczek, Kaposta, & Pochron, 2003).

Closing one eye of a kitten during the first 3 postnatal months has a permanent effect on development in the visual cortex while closing one eye at 12 months of age does not. These facts invite a rejection of the traditional question, "How much of development is nature, and how much is nurture?" and a replacement with, "What is the course of development for a particular system or a feature?" When the question is asked this way, the flaw in the assumption of a competition between nature and nurture becomes clear.

Some chapters contain discussions of particular syndromes appropriate to the developmental phase being discussed. Chapters 3, 5, and 6, for example, describe syndromes that have a major impact on some children. Study of the cause(s) of these diseases, and investigating the cascades leading to the clinical symptoms, provides information that aids prevention, might ameliorate the condition, or generate insights into the factors that modulate the maturational events.

The First Year

The first year consists of two important transitions: one occurs at 2 to 3 months, and a second at 7 to 12 months. The products of the first year invite a distinction between biologically prepared and less prepared psychological properties. The former require only the experiences present in most environments, as long as the brain has attained the appropriate level of growth. A newborn's biologically prepared reactions are almost automatic to particular classes of stimuli. The infant sucks a finger inserted in the mouth, grasps a finger placed in the palm, and fixates a black line on a white background.

The less prepared reactions, like playing peek-a-boo with a stranger, require special conditions. Biologically prepared functions dominate the first year. The ability to detect the difference between moving and stationary objects is a highly prepared competence; the ability to detect the difference between a maple and an oak tree is not. Older children find it easier to learn the contrast between one and many objects than between several and many, between up and down than between right and left, and between in and on than between near and far.

Because experience influences all psychological properties, scientists must decide how to conceptualize experience and its products. This issue is controversial. We suggest in chapter 3 that the psychological representations of events be called *schemata*. Infants establish schemata in every sensory modality, including bodily feelings, called visceral schemata. The sense meaning of a schema is a representation of the patterned features of an event, where pattern refers to the relations among the features of an event, and an event is a segment of experience sliced out of the continuous flow whose features capture the child's attention. The 3-month-old's schema for a human face is represented by a particular arrangement of eyes, nose, and mouth. If those elements are rearranged within an oval boundary, young infants do not activate their schema for a face, although all the elements are present. Sometimes it is easy to guess the event (for example, a red rattle is moved slowly in front of the infant); sometimes it is difficult to know the event with certainty (for example, the mother and father are looking down at the infant while talking and smiling with exuberance).

A schema is the first psychological structure to emerge from the neuronal activity provoked by an event, as an amino acid is the first product of the activity of DNA and messenger RNA within a cell. The vocabulary that describes schemata is different from that used to describe its neural foundations. The former contains terms like *symmetry, motion, color, contour,* and *curvature* that are inappropriate descriptors for neurons or circuits. A schema for the symmetrical placement of the oval shape of a parent's blue eyes has a corresponding neuronal pattern, but symmetry, circularity, and hue are not properties of neuronal ensembles. Hence, scientists should use different words to name the schema and the biological substrate for the schematic representation.

The fatigue of the asthmatic patient supplies an analogy. The feeling of fatigue is due to a compromise in the availability of oxygen because of the constriction of the smooth muscles of the respiratory tract in response to an antigen. But the vocabulary that best describes the quality of fatigue is different from the vocabulary that describes the cascade of biological reactions within the respiratory tract.

We suggest that infants develop schemata for "events-in-a-context," rather than representations of individuated objects. The term *object* is a philosophical concept that implies preservation of properties, or permanence, over time. The phrase "event-in-a-context" does not have that connotation. We are not certain that a 3-month-old staring at a moving red rattle in a parent's hand "knows" that the rattle is a permanent object with a stable size, color, and shape. This notion will require at least 12 to 18 months of additional development. Two-year-olds show surprise when a rattle suddenly disappears from sight because they expected the rattle to persist; 3-month-olds are not surprised. Some birds migrate each spring to the same location, often thousands of miles away, but no scientist suggests that these animals know that the places toward which they are flying are permanent geographical areas.

There is, at present, a lively controversy between developmental scholars who believe that young infants are biologically prepared to infer agency and intentions to humans, causality to events, numerosity to object arrays, and impossibility to certain physical events (for example, a ball penetrating a solid wood barrier). An equally large group of scientists is more skeptical of these claims. The disagreement centers on the abstractness of the psychological structures infants can create from encounters with the world. An infant sees a rolling red ball strike a toy animal and the latter moves a few inches following contact. Does the infant infer that the ball "caused" the toy to move, or does the child create a schema for that temporal sequence? The movements of honeybees returning to the hive following a visit to some flowers vary with the distance of the flowers from the hive. But that fact does not mean that the bees compute the distance that they flew. We consider this issue in detail in chapters 3 and 4.

Two psychological products of brain growth across the first year are: (a) liberation from automatic alerting to events that have certain physical attributes (for example, motion and contour) to a greater reliance on, and attraction to, events that are transformations of the infant's knowledge; and (b) an ability to retrieve schematic representations of the past without a relevant clue in the immediate present. These competences require maturation of the hippocampus, parahippocampal region, as well as prefrontal structures and their reciprocal connections.

The ability to retrieve the immediate past and to compare it with the present in a working memory circuit renders 8-month-olds vulnerable to a state called fear of the unfamiliar. The 8-month-old is able to detect that a present event is discrepant from the past, but not mature enough to assimilate the discrepant event to available knowledge. As a result, the infant becomes uncertain and is liable to cry. Crying to a stranger and to separation from a caretaker are illustrations. The 8-month-old who sees a stranger walk toward her compares the face and form of the stranger with retrieved schemata of her parents and other familiar adults. The infant is able to hold both sources of information in a working memory circuit that includes hippocampus, medial temporal cortex, amygdala, and prefrontal cortex. The fact that pyramidal neurons in the cortex and hippocampus show a spurt of differentiation during the second half of the first year contributes to the improvement of retrieval memory at this time. The infant perceives that the stranger is physically different from familiar adults but cannot relate the schema of the stranger to those of the familiar caretakers. The reaction following the failure of assimilation is often overt distress.

However, infants vary in their vulnerability to this state of uncertainty. This variation is called temperamental if it is due to an inherited biology. A stable psychological profile associated with an inherited biology is the contemporary definition of a temperament. Because the number of biological states is large, there will be a great many temperamental types. The discovery that closely related strains of animals raised under identical laboratory conditions behave differently to the same intrusion is one reason why the concept of temperament has returned to scientific discussions after five decades of exile during the first half of the last century. Because species differ in their neurochemistry, they differ in the ease with which they will display particular behaviors and affects. The temperamental differences among children in "degree of uncertainty to the unfamiliar" probably have a partial foundation in neurochemical profiles; this topic is considered in chapter 4.

The Second Year

The milestones of the second year differ from those of the first 12 months. One significant novelty of the second year is the addition of semantic structures to the schematic representations that dominate the first year. The brain honors the distinction between schematic and semantic representations which have different structures and are represented differentially in the two hemispheres. Semantic structures organize experience in unique ways in networks whose seminal feature is a hierarchical organization of concepts linked to a context. The 6-month-old, without language, has schemata for bottles, crackers, and the pureed cereal he is fed each day. But after the child learns the words "food" and "eat," the representations of these physically different objects become members of a common semantic category.

The notion of essences is a second feature that language adds to mind. The infant without language only has schemata for events. For example, a schema for a pet beagle is a pattern of features. If the animal's ears and tail were removed, a different schema would be formed. However, the 2-year-old who has learned the word "dog" assumes there is an invisible essence that is the proper referent for the word, and all dogs, even one without ears, fur, and a tail, is still a dog.

Infants and animals judge the similarity between events on the basis of physical features like shape, size, movement, texture, color, sound, taste, and smell. After language emerges, similarity in semantic meaning is added to this list. Although words are arbitrary human inventions, this habit leads humans to group events that share no physical features into a common category. One 4-year-old girl, who noticed that her dresses were close together in the closet, said to her mother, "Look, my dresses are friends." The girl invented this metaphor because the word "close" describes the emotional relations between people, as well as the spatial relations between objects. This uniquely human process is evaluated on intelligence tests. One subscale of the Wechsler Intelligence Test, called "similarities," requires the older child to answer questions like, "How are a fly and a tree alike?" The 10-year-old answers correctly because she has learned the meanings of the words "alive," "living," "life," "grow," and "die."

An initial appreciation of the concept of punishable acts, a second advance in the second year, prepares the child for acquiring the semantic concepts of right, wrong, good, and bad. These representations are the first component of a moral sense that, by adolescence, will be the basis for one of the strongest human desires; namely, the wish to regard the self as possessing signs of virtue—a seminal component of human morality. This initial stage of conscience derives from the 1-year-old's sensitivity to the unexpected adult chastisements that occur when the child violates a family's standard on cleanliness, destruction of property, disobedience, or aggression. The 2-year-old reacts to the adult chastisement with a feeling of uncertainty because he infers the adult's evaluation of the child and his action. The linking of that feeling to the schematic and semantic representations of the parent's admonition, which is mediated, in part, by the orbitofrontal prefrontal cortex, and to the action that produced it, become part of the semantic networks for "good" and "bad."

This psychological milestone cannot be attained until the child is able to infer some of the thoughts of adults, and especially, thoughts that evaluate the child. The first sign of this competence emerges by the middle of the second year. A fourth feature of the second year is the initial conscious awareness of self as an agent with intentions, feelings, and actions. This awareness is the first phase of what will become adult consciousness.

Brain growth in the second year involves accelerated growth of spines on the pyramidal neurons of layer 3, which receive information from callosal projections connecting the two hemispheres and from association-al fibers linking cortical areas of one hemisphere. We suggest as a fruitful hypothesis that the four psychological qualities of the second year profit from, and are partially dependent on, more efficient communication of information between the right and left hemisphere. When layer 3 neurons in the prefrontal cortex mature, schematic information from the right hemisphere is integrated more effectively with relevant semantic information in the left. Children acquire schemata for objects, people, and animals during the first year. Although the infant has heard the words "cup," "mother," and "dog," he or she has not integrated those words with the appropriate schemata for those objects. This integration usually begins by the first birthday. As a result, when the child sees a cup on a table, activation of the schema for this object in the right hemisphere is integrated with the lexical information in the left and the child is likely to speak the appropriate name.

When an 18-month-old feels uncertain because the mother has chastised her for spilling food on her dress, the representation of that feeling, elaborated more fully in the right hemisphere, is integrated with the semantic representations for the action in the left, and a moral standard begins to form.

Self-awareness could rest on a similar mechanism. The feeling component of body tone is more fully represented in the right hemisphere. When this information is integrated with the semantic network for self (for example, the child's name, intentions, and anticipations), the child becomes aware of self as an agent.

Years 2 Through 8

The period from 2 to 8 years is characterized by many psychological transitions. One significant phenomenon is the more automatic integration of past with present. The 4-year-old, but not the 2-year-old, relates an event in the perceptual field, or a thought, with a schema or a semantic representation of events experienced in the past. The behaviors of 2-year-olds, who live in the present moment, are determined primarily by features in the current situation and the habits conditioned to that situation. The 5-year-old, freed from this limited time horizon, can relate the present to a richer documentation of the past.

Once the child automatically relates her action to a prior intention, request, or incentive, she generates reasons for why she had behaved in a particular way. The bored 6-year-old in a kindergarten classroom who can rehearse the reasons for her presence in school will remain attentive. The

6-year-old also relies more frequently on semantic categories to represent experience, and is sensitive to the quasi-logical relations among semantic categories, especially the relations that define antonyms and the nesting of taxonomic categories. The 6-year-old knows that he cannot be both a boy and a girl, tall and short, asleep and awake, smart and dumb. This semantic bias makes possible identifications with family, gender, and ethnic group. The words for these categories imply, simultaneously, what social categories the child belongs to as well as the categories to which she does not belong. If a child knows she is Hispanic, she cannot be African American; if she is a girl, she cannot be a boy; if she is a member of the Jones family, she cannot belong to the Smith family. The child cannot avoid the conviction that only one member of each of the above category pairs is appropriate, and will experience a feeling of uncertainty if any information implies that she is a member of the wrong category.

The uncertainty requires an integration of semantic knowledge with the consequences of neural activity in the orbitofrontal prefrontal cortex. This activity adds a conscious feeling component to the knowledge. The complex semantic networks that grow over this era generate a uniquely human property; namely, the power to experience a distinct state of uncertainty when there is semantic inconsistency among the nodes of the child's network for self.

Finally, the 6- to 8-year-old can detect relations shared by semantic categories for dissimilar events. For example, the 8-year-old child is able to recognize the semantic feature "least" shared by the smallest of three cups, the softest of three voices, and the slowest of three arm movements. The psychological changes that characterize this era are accompanied by equally significant biological changes that include attainment of 90% of adult brain size, peak metabolic activity, and synaptic density; massive pruning of synapses; and a shift in blood flow from the right to the left hemisphere.

Although the products of the human genome ensure that these psychological functions emerge in most children in a relatively fixed sequence, the specific contents of a child's schemata, semantic networks, and motor skills are monitored primarily by the child's experiences. The capacity for guilt following violation of a moral standard is universal; however, 16th-century 10-year-olds from middle-class German families felt guilty if they refused their parents' insistence that they leave home to be apprenticed to a skilled craftsman. Ten-year-old boys in contemporary Germany feel guilty if they do not conform to peer standards on how to dress. Thus, each psychological capacity is a set of possibilities, only some of which will be actualized, not unlike the wood from a pine tree that could become a desk, bench, cupboard, or fence, but not a bicycle, oven, or computer.

SUMMARY

Temporal correlations between changes in the brain, on the one hand, and a behavior, mood, or cognitive process, on the other, are insufficient to infer causality. Although the neurons of the prefrontal cortex mature at about the same time that the infant's working memory improves, it remains possible that the two phenomena are not causally related. Each reader will have to judge the persuasiveness of our arguments.

Moreover, lawful relations among psychological phenomena can be described without reference to the brain; for example, all infants show a fear reaction to adult strangers during the second half of the first year because of the enhancement of working memory. However, an understanding of the maturational events in the brain that enable this phenomenon allows the pleasure that accompanies a richer appreciation of nature's plan.

We acknowledge, with most psychologists, the profound effect of experience on brain structure and function and the extraordinary plasticity of brain growth (Greenough, Black, & Wallace, 1987). Adults who practice juggling three balls over a 3-month period showed a significant increase in gray matter in the midtemporal area and the left posterior intraparietal sulcus. However, after 3 months of little or no juggling activity, the amount of gray matter had decreased and approached baseline values (Draganski et al., 2003). The profile of beliefs, values, emotions, and skills possessed by most 8-year-olds in an 18th-century French village would differ from the profiles of contemporary French children; therefore, the detailed synaptic patterns of the two groups will vary. However, this book has a more limited scope. It describes what has been learned about the growth of the brain and argues that many universal psychological properties cannot emerge until the relevant circuitry has been established. The brains of 1-month-old infants cannot support speaking, walking, or the feeling of guilt.

Nonetheless, we reject a strict determinacy between the maturational state of the brain and the psychological properties of the developing child. An infant restricted to a bare room, although fed on a regular schedule, will be retarded in both brain growth and behavior. The changes in the brain that occur at the end of the first year and the beginning of the second year are necessary for speech, but children will not speak if not exposed to any language. Seven-year-olds living in an isolated Mayan village in northwest Guatemala do not show consistent signs of concrete operational thought until they are 12 to 13 years old, 6 years later than children in Paris or Chicago. Experience is a necessary participant in almost all behaviors.

However, despite the contribution of experience, over 90% of 1-year-olds in every village, town, and city across the world will smile to the approach of the caretaker, remember and reach toward the place where an adult hid a toy, cry occasionally to an approaching stranger, and imitate some parental behaviors. Further, 90% of 8-year-olds will appreciate the antonymic relation between word pairs in their language and integrate past with present, despite an extraordinary variety of rearing conditions. Our basic premise is that the maturation of the brain constrains the time of emergence of the universal psychological characteristics of our species. This book summarizes the evidence that supports this assumption, while acknowledging our inability to prove cause–effect relations between the events in the two domains.

Prenatal Development

It is unlikely that the wisest 18th-century scholar, with unlimited time and an extravagant reward for the correct solution, would have imagined the details of brain development that have been discovered over the past quarter century. This corpus of information contains many surprises. For example, the cortex is composed of six layers, each with a distinct function, that develop in an inside-out fashion. The second surprise is that although the axonal tracts that mediate motor behavior develop before those that mediate sensation, the newborn can see, hear, feel, taste, and smell, but has relatively poor motor coordination. Perhaps the most counterintuitive discovery is that the 8-month-old infant has many more synapses in the visual cortex than the 8-year-old. A brilliant 18th-century scholar in a mood of exuberant originality would have rejected this idea as bizarre if it occurred on a sunny June morning.

Although the brain is built in accord with genetic instructions, expression of the genetic information requires both the activity of molecules during particular time frames as well as extrinsic events. Hence, the interactions of genes and environment begin at the moment of conception.

The Foundations of the Nervous System

The 40 prenatal weeks, about 1% of an expected lifetime in this century, shape the human brain. The place where the sperm penetrates the egg coincides, in most cases, with the equator of the first cell division and the top–bottom axis of the future embryo. One cell of the first pair of cells usually becomes the embryo, and the other becomes the placenta and supportive tissues. Thus, the first cell division determines the fate of the succeeding cells (Pearson, 2002).

Only 3 days after fertilization—called PFD—the embryo consists of 16 cells, which, a day later, become a hollow sphere that is called the blastula. Scientists prefer to use PFD to date the age of the embryo, because the older term *gestational age* could refer to the time since the last menstruation, or the time of ovulation, fertilization, or implantation (O'Rahilly & Müller, 1999).

The cells on the inside of the blastula, called embryonic stem cells, have the potential to form an entire embryo. However, these cells lose their early pluripotentiality as they develop, and soon become committed to specific functions (Gage, 2000). Three days later—the sixth PFD—the embryo, with about 100 to 200 cells, becomes attached to the uterine wall—a process called *nidation*. This event has recently acquired legal implications. German law defines the beginning of life as the moment of fertilization; British law defines life as beginning 6 days later, at the time of nidation. The British definition has the advantage of permitting researchers to use the omnipotent stem cells of the blastula for therapeutic purposes. Sixteen days following fertilization (PFD), when the embryo is only 0.4 mm long, or about the size of this dot (.), the primordial anlage of the future brain can be detected, and the blastula has been transformed into a gastrula, consisting of ectoderm, mesoderm, and endoderm.

The endoderm gives rise to the trachea, bronchi, lungs, liver, pancreas, intestines, and bladder. The mesoderm is the origin of the connective tissue, muscles, vascular system, spleen, and skeleton. The ventral part of the ectoderm becomes the epidermis and the nails; the dorsal portion develops into the neural plate which is the precursor—or *anlage*—of the nervous system.

NEURONAL INDUCTION AND NEURULATION

Diffusable molecules originating in the underlying mesoderm induce the uncommitted ectoderm lying above it to form a neural plate (see Fig. 2.1; Jessell & Sanes, 2000). The fusion of the neural plate to the neural tube begins around 28 PFD when the edges of the neuroectoderm form an arch that covers the surface of the neural tube. The neural tube closes first in its middle portion, and later in the rostral and caudal sections until, at 32 PFD, it closes completely (O'Rahilly & Müller, 1999). If closure of the anterior part of the neural tube is incomplete, the embryo is anenecephalic and the pregnancy is usually terminated. Incomplete closure of the caudal portion of the tube leads to a syndrome called *myeloschisis* in which the infant is often stillborn (Volpe, 1995).

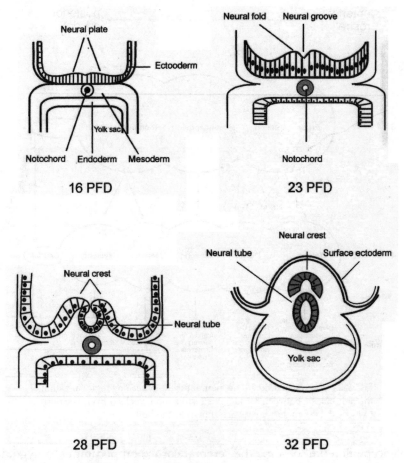

FIG. 2.1. Neural induction and neurulation—Four stages of neurulation from 16 to 32 postfertilization days (PFD).

Regionalization of the Neural Tube

By 3 to 4 weeks following fertilization (PFW), three bulges appear in the neural tube: the prosencephalon (anlage of the forebrain), mesencephalon (midbrain), and rhombencephalon (hindbrain; see Fig. 2.2). This tripartite differentiation, along rostro-caudal and dorso-ventral axes, is believed to be the result of cell–cell interactions that are intrinsic to the neural tube (Kandel, 1995).

One to two weeks later, as a result of proliferation and migration of cells, the neural tube has six divisions: telencephalon, diencephalon, mesencephalon, metencephalon, myelencephalon, and the caudal section. These six areas form the architecture of the brain and spinal cord. The

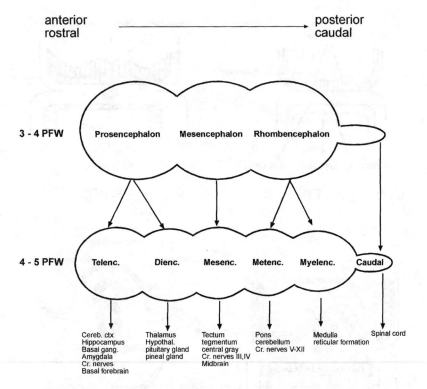

FIG. 2.2.   Regionalization of the neural tube—Increasing regionalization of
the neural tube between 3 and 5 postfertilization weeks (PFW). The derivatives of the six main regions are shown at the bottom.

telencephalon will become the cerebral cortex, hippocampus, amygdala,
basal forebrain, and basal ganglia. The diencephalon will become part of
the midbrain. The mesencephalon is the origin of the inferior and superior
colliculus, substantia nigra, bed nucleus, central gray, and the cranial
nerves involved in auditory and vestibular functions, facial expressions,
and eye movements. The metencephalon will become the pons, cerebellum, and the remaining cranial nerves, and the myelencephalon will give
rise to the medulla oblongata and reticular formation. The last three components form the brain stem. The caudal portion of the neural tube becomes the spinal cord.

Neural Crest

A small population of cells located in the dorsal region of the neural tube
begins to migrate by 4 to 6 weeks after fertilization (PFW) to form a crescent of cells called the neural crest (see Table 2.1). Some of these cells dif-

TABLE 2.1
Neural Crest Derivatives

- Sensory spinal ganglia.
- Autonomic ganglia; parasympathetic and sympathetic nervous systems.
- Schwann cells: peripheral myelin.
- Adrenal medulla.
- Thyroid.
- Pigment cells of the dermis, melanocytes.
- Head: skeletal and muscle components, mesenchymal and connective tissue.
- Aortic arch.

---

ferentiate as they migrate and eventually become the peripheral sensory and autonomic nervous system, pigment cells, thymus, medulla of the adrenal gland, part of the aortic arch of the heart, and a component of the respiratory system. Other neural crest cells migrate into the mesenchyme to affect the shape of the skull and the facial bones and contribute to the factors that create a broad or a narrow face. During this period the brain, face, and heart should be regarded as a single morphogenetic field because of interactions among these components (Hutson & Kirby, 2003). The secretion of thyroxine from the mother's thyroid gland appears to influence the migration of neural crest cells (Minugh-Purvis & McNamara, 2002).

Neural crest cells can migrate long distances with the help of molecules in both the intercellular space and the basal membranes of the cells that provide scaffolding. The developmental fate of each neural crest cell depends on its original location and the chemical gradients through which it migrates. The developmental options of each cell become restricted and their functional capacities become enhanced as migration proceeds (Wood, 2002) and these cells lose their pluripotentiality. For example, when the crest cells from quail were transplanted into duck hosts, the resulting chimeras had beaks that resembled quail rather than ducks or an intermediate form. The opposite outcome occurred when crest cells from the duck were transplanted into the quail hosts (Schneider & Helms, 2003).

Proliferation

Most cells of the newborn's future nervous system are generated between 6 and 20 PFW in a structure called the ventricular zone lying inside the neural tube. Initially, before 6 weeks, each cell divides perpendicular to the ventricular zone to produce two identical, but still uncommitted, progenitor cells that continue to divide. This process is called symmetric division (Alvarez-Buylla & Garcia-Verdugo, 2001; Anderson, Gage, & Weissman, 2001; de Velis & Carpenter, 1999; Gage, 2000; Uylings, 2001;

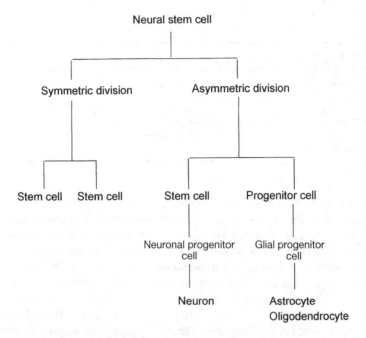

FIG. 2.3.   Neural cell lineage—Neural stem cells reside in the ventricular zone. The neural stem cell is self-renewing and can divide either symmetrically—producing two neural stem cells—or asymmetrically—producing one copy of itself and one progenitor cell, which migrates from the ventricular zone postmitotically. Various neurotrophic factors induce progenitor cells during migration to become either neurons or glial cells.

Vaccarino, 2000; van der Kooy & Weiss, 2000; van Praag, Kempermann, & Gage, 2000).

However, after 6 PFW, cell division in the telencephalon becomes increasingly asymmetric. Now some progenitor cells divide parallel, rather than perpendicular, to the ventricular zone to give rise to one uncommitted progenitor cell, which remains in the ventricular zone to divide further, and a second, postmitotic progenitor cell that leaves the ventricular zone to migrate to the cortical plate (see Fig. 2.3; Chenn & McConnell, 1995; Rakic, 2000). These migrating, committed cells become either neurons or glia. Trophic molecules, outside the cell, aid differentiation of the original stem cells, first into progenitor cells, and later into neurons, astrocytes, or oligodendrocytes (Rakic, 2000; Vaccarino, 2000).

Progenitor cells in the ventricular zone possess receptors responsive to the inhibitory neurotransmitter GABA, and kainate receptors responsive to the excitatory transmitter glutamate (Ghosch & Greenberg, 1995). Cells exposed to excessive GABA or kainate decrease their rate of DNA synthesis, associated with reduced proliferation that, if extreme, can lead to microcephaly (Chenn, Braisted, McConnell, & O'Leary, 1997). The period of cell proliferation is vulnerable to environmental disturbances, especially infection, irradiation, and other toxic factors that reduce the final number of neurons.

Because cell division proceeds exponentially, a small increase in the total duration of cell division (about 120 days in humans), and therefore in the number of cell cycles, has a dramatic impact on the final number of neurons. For example, fewer than four extra cycles of symmetric cell division over a period of 3 days can produce a tenfold difference in the final cortical surface between humans and monkeys. The larger number of cell divisions in humans than in monkeys explains why humans have about 100 billion and monkeys only about 10 billion neurons (Rakic, 2000; Vogel, 2002).

Surprisingly, the size of any one brain area is correlated with total brain size (with the exception of the olfactory bulb) across a variety of mammalian species. This fact means that the size of any one area is dependent on the rate and duration of cell division during the proliferation phase (Finlay & Darlington, 1995). One implication of this fact is that the selection of any one of the adaptive psychological functions of humans (for example, language) might require enlargement of all brain areas, and not only those involved in comprehending speech or talking. This suggestion is in accord with the belief that the neocortex is not rigidly specialized and can participate in many psychological competences.

Cell Death

Two main forms of cell death occur during brain development. One is caused by damage to the cell; the second is guided by intrinsic processes. The first type is due to insults to the nervous system, for example, a lack of oxygen (Nelson et al., 2001; Oppenheim, 1999). The genetically regulated death of neurons, or their precursors, is referred to as Programmed Cell Death (PCD), which occurs most often in a phenomenon called *apoptosis*. Apoptosis is characterized by cell shrinkage and fragmentation of the nucleus, followed by the removal of the dead cell by phagocytes. As many as 50% of the neurons generated in the monkey cerebral cortex are eliminated in this manner during development. Although PCD is a universal feature of the prenatal and postnatal development of the central nervous system, it occurs predominantly during the prenatal period.

PCD occurs first in the ventricular zone of the neural tube and the ganglionic eminence to affect the final number of cortical neurons. PCD during the later fetal period, characterized by differentiation and synaptogenesis, affects neuronal circuitry. PCD helps to establish appropriate

relations between the number of projection and target neurons and proba-
bly between glial cells and neurons as well (Hunot & Flavell, 2001;
Lagercrantz & Ringstedt, 2001; Rakic & Zecevic, 2000; Simonati, Tosati,
Rosso, Piazzola, & Rizzuto, 1999; Sperandio, de Belle, & Bredesen, 2000).

PCD had been regarded as autonomous; that is, not dependent on signals from other cells. However, Marin-Teva et al. (2004) have shown recently that selective elimination of microglial cells greatly reduced the
apoptosis of Purkinje cells in the cerebellum. Superoxide ions, produced
by microglia, play a major role in this form of cell death. These experiments suggest that microglia function not only as phagocytes in the removal of dead cell material, but also provoke the death of developing
neurons.

Migration

The process of migration has been studied most extensively in the cerebral cortex; hence, we concentrate on this phenomenon. The first phase
of migration occurs at 8 PFW when postmitotic neurons leave the ventricular zone to move radially toward the dorsal (pial) surface of the
brain. Most of these cells will become glutamergic, excitatory, pyramidal
neurons. This migration is aided by glial cells that act as scaffolding by
extending their processes from the ventricular zone to the pial surface, as
well as by proteins produced by genes. Some proteins in the vicinity of
the optic chiasm repel, whereas others attract, an approaching neuron
from the retina, as a function of their original location in the retina
(Hatten & Maron, 1990).

By contrast, cells originating in the ganglionic eminence, a derivative of
the ventral region of the telencephalon, first migrate tangential to the ventricular zone and then change direction by 90 degrees or more to migrate
radially to the cortex. Most of these cells become GABA-ergic, inhibitory,
local circuit interneurons (see Fig. 2.4; Letinic, Zoncu, & Rakic, 2002;
Nadarajah & Parnavelas, 2002; Tan et al., 1998).

The combination of the radially migrating excitatory neurons and the
tangentially migrating inhibitory interneurons is crucial for maintaining a
balance between excitation and inhibition in the central nervous system.

It is not surprising that any disturbance in cell migration can have serious functional consequences (Hatten, 2002; Rorke, 1994; Ross & Walsh,
2001). For example, calcium ion channels help to control the rate of migration. Low calcium concentrations cause a decrease, whereas higher concentrations lead to an increase, in the rate of migration. Deviations in migration, caused by genetic mutations, adverse exogenous factors, or a
combination of both (Akbarian et al., 1993; Roberts, 1991; Ross & Pearlson,
1996; Ross & Walsh, 2001; Royston & Roberts, 1995), can result in children

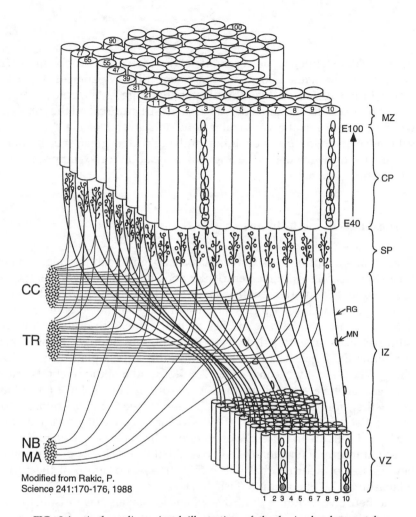

Modified from Rakic, P.
Science 241:170-176, 1988

FIG. 2.4. A three-dimensional illustration of the basic developmental events and types of cell–cell interactions during early stages of cortico-genesis, before formation of the final pattern of cortical connections. The figure emphasizes the radial mode of migration which underlies its elaborate columnar organization in primates. The cohorts of neurons generated in the ventricular zone (VZ) traverse the intermediate zone (IZ) and subplate (SP) containing "waiting" afferents from several sources (cortico-cortical connections, CC; thalamic radiation, TR; afferents from nucleus basalis of meynert, NB; brainstem monoamine system, MA) and finally pass through the earlier generated deep layers before settling in at the interface between developing cortical plate (CP) and marginal zone (MZ). The relation between a proliferative mosaic of the VZ and corresponding protomap within the SP and CP is preserved during cortical expansion by transient radial glial scaffolding (for details, see Rakic, 1988). One goal is to determine the role of specific molecules that mediate recognition of migratory pathways and provide substrate for cell motility during this complex process (courtesy of P. Rakic).

41

susceptible to epilepsy or cerebral palsy (Girard & Ryaybaud, 1992; Iannetti, Spalice, Atzei, Boemi, & Trasimeni, 1996; McConnell, 1992).

The brains of some schizophrenic patients suggest anomalous migration of neurons that originated in a transient structure called the subplate, which lies between the ventricular zone and layer 1 of the cortex. The subplate expanded during evolution and attained its greatest elaboration in humans in an area that is the origin of association cortex, hippocampus, and related structures.

Cortical Layers and Columns

The establishment of the six-layered cortex begins with the migration of Cajal–Retzius cells from the ventricular zone into future layer 1 of the cerebral cortex. Soon after, another layer of cells located between the ventricular zone and layer 1 forms a transient subplate, noted earlier, which reaches maximum width at 30 PFW, with the thickest portion below the future association cortex. New cells now migrate through the subplate, but below the Cajal–Retzius cells, to form the cortical plate. The cortical plate will eventually become layers 2, 3, 4, 5, and 6 of the cerebral cortex, but these layers are established in reverse order. That is, layer 6 is established first, followed by layers 5, 4, 3, and 2 (see Fig. 2.5; Lavdas, Grigoriou, Pachnis, & Parnavelas, 1999). Recent research suggests that after the layer 1 cells are in place, the progenitor cells in the ventricular zone express a transcription factor, called Foxg1, that results in the production of new classes of neurons that will establish layers 5 and 6 of the cortex (Hanashima, Li, Shen, Lai, & Fishell, 2004).

The neurons within each of the six cortical layers have distinct functions and project to specific targets or receive afferents from specific sources. Layer 2 neurons participate in short cortico-cortical connections. Layer 3 neurons participate in longer cortico-cortical, as well as callosal, connections between the two hemispheres. Layer 4 is the target of fibers from the thalamus. Layer 5 is the origin of projections to subcortical structures, and Layer 6 neurons project from the cortex back to the thalamus. Very little is known about the connectivity of the neurons in layer 1. The superior colliculus, thalamus, cerebellum, olfactory lobe, and the hippocampus also have a laminar architecture, but one that differs from that of the cerebral cortex.

In addition to the layers, the visual, somatosensory, and prefrontal cortices possess a vertical arrangement of cylindrically shaped columns of neurons. These columns, which vary in diameter and are perpendicular to the cortical layers, are interconnected by the short axons of interneurons, permitting excitation to spread horizontally across contiguous columns

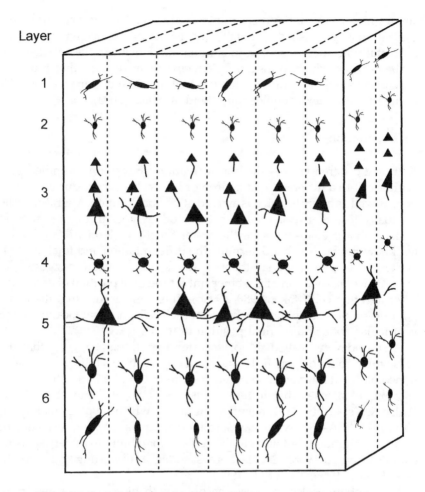

FIG. 2.5.   Cortical layers and columns—Neurons are positioned in horizontal layers and vertical columns (adapted from Churchland, 1998).

(Grinvald, Slovin, & Vanzetta, 2000). The number of columns determines the size and form of the future cortical areas.

Each column functions as an input–output module (Churchland, 1986), and both excitatory and inhibitory connections are present in each column. Neurons within a particular column respond to input from the same set of contiguous sensory receptors to form an elementary functional unit. Axons from the thalamus, which make contact with interneurons, transmit their signals within the column to the pyramidal neurons located at various layers. It is believed that these interneurons enhance the incoming signal by reducing noise. The output of the neurons within a column usually terminates in contiguous columns. Although the basic columnar organization is established prenatally, most synaptic connectivity develops postnatally in direct response to stimulation. However, the subplate described earlier, which forms a transient circuit between the thalamus and the cortex, is required for the establishment of ocular dominance columns in the visual cortex (Kanold, Kara, Reid, & Shatz, 2003).

Differentiation

Neuronal differentiation—the transformation from an uncommitted progenitor cell to a differentiated neuron or glial cell—occurs during migration, as well as after the cell has arrived at its final location. Migrating cells gradually lose their potential to become other types through structural changes that prepare them for their later functions (Rakic, 2000). We do not know the factors that determine the differentiation and final location of these cells. The protomap theory, proposed by P. Rakic, suggests that the ventricular zone contains a blueprint for the final position of each radially migrating cell (Rakic, 1988, 1995b). This view argues that there is a point-to-point correspondence between each cell's original location in the ventricular zone and its final position in the cortex.

A second view, called the protocortex hypothesis, suggests that the cells with a common genetic background do not always follow a predetermined path but migrate tangentially to different locations, as a function of environmental cues that influence their final fate (Chenn et al., 1997; Walsh & Cepko, 1992). Tangential migration, which involves mainly inhibitory, GABA-ergic cells, may permit greater plasticity and correction of errors of migration, but adds to the cell's vulnerability to adverse perturbations (Monk & Webb, 2001). There is evidence supporting both hypotheses (Rakic, 1995a; Tan et al., 1998).

Differentiation also involves the outgrowth of axons and dendrites, synapse formation, and the synthesis and activity of neurotransmitters. Axonal movement toward a target is under the control of extracellular molecules, often proteins under genetic control, that attract or repel the growth cone of the axon (de Velis & Carpenter, 1999; Gage, 2000; Vaccarino, 2000).

Axonal growth into the transient subplate has implications for later sensory functions. Afferents from the thalamus arrive at the subplate between 17 and 25 PFW and remain there for several weeks before growing upward into the cortical plate between 26 and 32 PFW (see Fig. 2.6; Mrzljak, Uylings, Kostovic, & Van Eden, 1988; Mrzljak, Uylings, Van Eden, & Judas, 1990). This latter phase is accompanied by a rapid increase in the elongation and arborization of dendrites and the emergence of dendritic spines, probably due to an increase in afferent thalamo-cortical

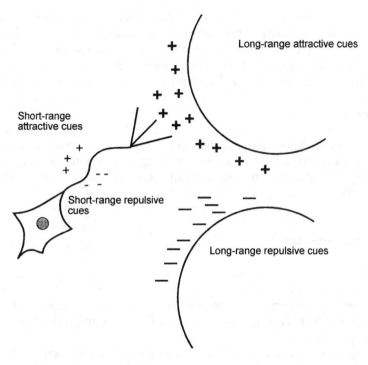

FIG. 2.6. Axonal guidance—Growing axons are guided by both short and long-range attractive and repulsive cues (adapted from Jessell & Sanes, 2000).

stimulation (Mrzljak, Uylings, Kostovic, & Van Eden, 1992). The transient connections between the subplate and the thalamus may be necessary to match thalamic input to specific primary sensory cortical areas (Ghosch & Shatz, 1992; McConnell, 1992). Spontaneous activity in the lateral geniculate nucleus of young ferrets, which occurs before the eyes open and before any visual experience occurs, may play an important role in the formation of columns within the visual cortex (Katz & Shatz, 1996; Weliky & Katz, 1999).

Establishing Contacts

Establishment of contact after an axon has reached its target neuron can be either direct or indirect. In direct contacts, which mediate more rapid transmission, there is a cytoplasmic continuity between the two cells because the axon of one neuron terminates on the outer membrane of the other. Indirect contacts, which are slower than direct ones, assume the form of a synapse between two cells with a synaptic cleft between the two neurons ranging in width from 20 to 40 micrometers. Electrical activity in a presynaptic neuron causes the release of a neurotransmitter into the synaptic cleft. The transmitter molecule, stored in presynaptic terminal vesicles, crosses the synaptic cleft to bind to specific receptors on the postsynaptic membrane of the proximal neuron—these are unidirectional connections.

The temporal delay between the arrival of an impulse on the presynaptic neuron and the activation of receptors on the postsynaptic neuron can range from 0.3 to 0.5 msec or longer. Because the overwhelming majority of contacts in the brain are indirect—that is, synaptic—we concentrate on this category.

Neurotransmitters

The biochemical differentiation of neurons is accompanied by an increasing ability to synthesize neurotransmitters and their appropriate receptors. Neurotransmitters are present before synapses are formed when they probably play a trophic role in influencing migration and other neuronal processes.

Noradrenergic, dopaminergic, serotonergic, and cholinergic neuronal systems, located in the brain stem, emerge before the third PFW and are the first to form. GABA-ergic neurons, which influence proliferation, migration, differentiation, synapse maturation, and cell death, appear later. Glutamate, the most common transmitter, and excitatory, is produced by over one half of the brain's 100 billion neurons, compared with about 10,000 that produce dopamine (Lagercrantz & Ringstedt, 2001; Owens & Kriegstein, 2002). Glutamate receptors appear around the fourth PFM.

Neuroactive peptides, a class of neurochemicals with trophic functions synthesized in neurons, act directly on neurons, blood vessels, and glands. One function is to regulate blood flow in the upper layers of the cerebral cortex; for example, vasoactive intestinal polypeptide (VIP) is a potent vasodilator, whereas Neuropeptide-Y (NPY) is a potent vasoconstrictor.

The peptide cholecystokinin appears in cortical neurons at 11 PFW, NPY occurs at 14 PFW, and Substance-P in the hippocampus at 16 PFW. Vasopressin is detected in the hypothalamus at 18 PFW, and somatostatin receptors appear in the cerebellum at 20 PFW (Del Fiacco, Diana, Floris, & Quartu, 1990; Delalle, Evers, Kostovic, & Uylings, 1997; Dorn, Schmidt, Schmidt, Bernstein, & Rinne, 1985; Murayama, Meeker, Murayama, & Greenwood, 1993; Yu, 1993).

Myelination

As axons elongate and their terminals form synaptic contacts, a special class of glial cell, called oligodendrocytes, wrap their membrane processes concentrically around the axon to form a multilaminar myelin sheath that insulates and separates one axon from another (see Fig. 2.7; Demerens et al., 1996). The appearance of myelin on an axon is an indication of neural activity and the more efficient transmission of action potentials (Zalc & Fields, 2000).

Myelination increases the speed of axonal conduction by a factor of 20. To achieve a conduction speed that fast without myelin, the spinal cord would have to possess a diameter of almost 3 yards. Myelination proceeds

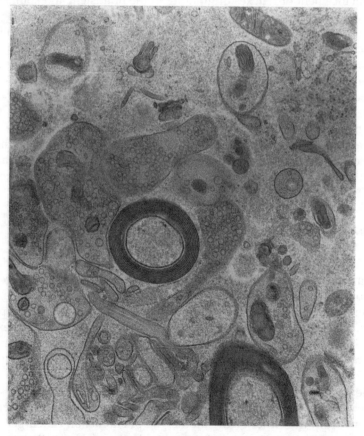

FIG. 2.7. Myelinated axon—Cross-section of myelinated axon shown under electron microscopy at a magnification of 55,000. Courtesy of Peter Eggli, University of Bern.

first from the spinal cord to the forebrain, and from dorsal to ventral areas. Fiber tracts mediating sensory input to the thalamus and cortex are myelinated before the tracts that mediate motor or association pathways (Grodd, 1993).

Although most myelination occurs postnatally, some occurs prenatally. Motor and sensory roots of the spinal cord develop signs of myelin at 4 to 5 PFM (postfertilization months). The medial lemniscus (relevant to touch), the lateral lemniscus (relevant to hearing), and the statoacoustic system (relevant to body position as well as hearing), show myelination at 6 PFM.

The subcortical-spinal pathways myelinate between 24 and 30 PFW and the cortico-spinal pathways at 28 to 34 PFW. Despite their immaturity, these pathways mediate passive muscle tone, resting postures, and the enhancement of reflexes originating in the brainstem and spinal cord that include sucking and swallowing. Myelination of the innervating cranial nerves is linked to the appearance of slow eye movements at 16 PFW and rapid eye movements at around 23 PFW (Brody, Kinney, Kloman, & Gilles, 1987; Kinney, Brody, Kloman, & Gilles, 1988). Axons connecting the cerebellum and basal ganglia myelinate at 7 to 8 PFM; the fornix of the hippocampus myelinates at 8 to 9 PFM.

The pathway from the inner ear to the brainstem is almost fully myelinated by 29 PFW, but this process continues through the first postnatal year (Moore, Perazzo, & Braun, 1995). The pathway from the inferior colliculus to the medial geniculate nucleus of the thalamus, which is the gateway to the cerebral cortex and the amygdala, myelinates around 22 PFW.

Phases of Prenatal Brain Development

The sequence and timing of prenatal brain development are genetically determined and regulated by trophic molecules. Although this process is susceptible to exogenous factors, it is a little less vulnerable to such interventions during the first trimester than during the remainder of the pregnancy. An approximate timetable for the growth of the cerebral cortex appears in Table 2.2; the development of the hippocampus, basal ganglia, amygdala, hypothalamus, thalamus, brainstem, cerebellum, and spinal cord follow a comparable timetable.

Scientists have discovered that the differential expression of some genes that affect brain growth depends on whether the embryo inherited the gene from the father or the mother—a phenomenon called genomic imprinting. The current understanding of this process claims that methylation of the cytosine nucleotide in the promoter region of a gene supresses expression, whereas unmethylated nucleotides are expressed. Experiments with zygotes of mouse chimeras created by the union of two sperm,

TABLE 2.2
Development of the Neocortex

Phases	5–8 PFW	9–12 PFW	13–24 PFW	25–38 PFW	Newborn
Proliferation	++	+++	++	+/–	(+)
Migration	+	+++	+++	+	(+)
Axonal growth					
(dendrites, axons)	–/+	++	+++	+++	+
Synapse formation	–/+	+	++	++	+++
Apoptosis	+/–	+	+	++	+
Myelination	–	–	+	++	+++

Note. PFW = postfertilization weeks. Number of + indicates speed and intensity of the histogenic process. The neocortex is the latest part of the cerebral cortex to appear in evolution. In humans, it comprises 90% of the cerebral cortex. The remaining areas include the paleocortex (olfactory system) and the archicortex, containing parts of the limbic system (Kostovic, 1990).

two egg pronuclei, or a single diploid egg, reveal that cells from zygotes containing two sperm inserted into a normal blastocyst make little or no contribution to the development of the cortex, whereas blastocysts containing two egg pronuclei or a diploid egg are expressed more completely in the developing brain, especially in the frontal lobe (Goos & Silverman, 2001).

The sequence begins with cell proliferation and migration, followed by differentiation, including the outgrowth of axons, dendrites, and synapse formation (see Table 2.2). These stages are accompanied, or followed, by apoptosis and then myelination. Postnatal changes that fine-tune the systems and life-long brain plasticity are omitted from Table 2.2.

FROM STRUCTURE TO FUNCTION

We now turn to a discussion of the emerging functions of the fetal brain, which includes motor activity, the internal regulation system, and the processing and registration of sensory signals.

The Motor System

The first signs of activity in the motor system, observed with ultrasound at 4 PFW, are isolated muscle twitches reflecting the spontaneous activity of the contractile proteins that compose the muscle fibers (see Fig. 2.8). One to two weeks later, twitching movements of the head and trunk are observed (Drife, 1985). The first large limb movements, lasting only 1 to 2 sec, are seen at 7 PFW. Examples include startles and abrupt simultaneous

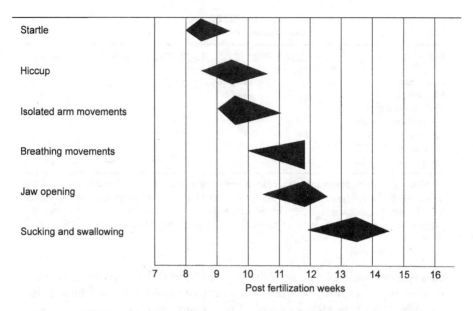

FIG. 2.8.   Variation in the emergence of specific fetal movements.

flexion and extension of arms and legs (DeVries, 1991). In addition, movements of the head, trunk, and extremities accompany changes in fetal position. The establishment of neuromuscular connections to the diaphragm, thorax and abdomen make hiccups possible between 8 and 11
PFW. The classes of motor movements follow a sequence; for example, the
fetus hiccups and opens its jaws before it swallows. It is of interest that
mouth movements, which increase from 16 to 20 PFW because of the
growth of axons to the perioral region, appear earlier in female than in
male fetuses (Hepper, Shannon, & Dornan, 1997).

Fetal mobility affects brain circuitry. Movements of the body and limbs
(touching the uterine wall or the fetus's own body) provide sensory input
to the brain. Individual differences in the time of appearance, as well as
the frequency and quality of motor actions, are probably due to both genetic differences and to variation in maternal health and psychological
state. The axons of cortical pyramidal cells reach their targets in the brain
stem and spinal cord to form the basis for cortical motor control (Marin-
Padilla, 1970a, 1970b, 1990).

The cortico-spinal tract, which links the motor cortex to the motor neurons in the spinal cord, precedes the development and myelination of the
major sensory projections. The establishment of synaptic connections
from motor cortex to the motor neurons in the spinal cord permits the cortex to modulate spinal motor centers.

Spines on apical dendrites of neurons in the motor cortex, which appear between 20 and 28 PFW, provide synaptic sites for afferent axons from the thalamus and basal ganglia. Excitatory pyramidal neurons and inhibitory interneurons form close connections within the cortical columns, achieving a balance between excitation and inhibition. The syndrome called cerebral palsy, once thought to be caused by complications during the birth process, is now believed to be due to prenatal disturbances in the development of the cortico-spinal motor system (Croen, Grether, Curry, & Nelson, 2001; Eyre, Miller, Clowry, Conway, & Watts, 2000; Moster, Lie, Irgens, Bjerkedal, & Markestad, 2001; Paneth, 2001). It is believed that excessive levels of the neurotransmitter glutamate can produce anomalous growth.

The fetus shows cycles of spontaneous movements during the second half of gestation that occur with a periodicity of 1 to 10 min. This activity occurs in a number of vertebrate species and is believed to be essential for neuronal development of muscles, bones, and joints. The most frequent fetal activities are touching the uterine wall or the fetus's body.

Regular and irregular breathing movements are first observed at 11 PFW; by 24 PFW, their frequency increases from less than 5% to over 30% of the time (de Vries, Visser, & Prechtl, 1982; DeVries, 1991). The increased movements are correlated with innervation of the diaphragm by the phrenic nerve. Prospective parents should appreciate that maternal ingestion of alcohol can affect the frequency of these respiratory movements; for example, drinking 0.25g/kg of alcohol (approximately one drink) can suppress fetal breathing movements for periods up to 3 hours (Patrick, 1982).

Laterality of Movements

Fetuses older than 10 PFW show a bias for moving the right rather than the left arm, a preference present in 83% of one group of fetuses studied longitudinally from 12 to 27 PFW (Hepper, McCartney, & Shannon, 1998; McCartney & Hepper, 1999). There is also a bias for sucking the right over the left thumb, revealed by ultrasound recordings, from 12 PFW to birth. The ratio of sucking the right, rather than the left, thumb increased from 7:1 at 15 to 21 PFW to 11:1 between 36 PFW and birth (Hepper, Shahidullah, & White, 1991; McCartney & Hepper, 1999). The early occurrence of lateralized motor action at a time when cortical control over the spinal cord motor neurons is not yet established suggests that some aspects of laterality have a genetic origin related to muscle or spinal control. It is possible that asymmetric gene expression influences the development of asymmetries in neuronal ensembles or muscles resulting in lateralities of motor acts and asymmetries in EEG activity (McCartney & Hepper, 1999).

Lateralized motor behavior and the preference for one hand or foot over the other may be preserved for a lifetime (Amunts, Schlaug, Schleicher, Steinmetz, & Dabringhaus, 1996; McCartney & Hepper, 1999). Observations of adult couples (from three different countries) kissing in public places (airports, beaches, and parks) revealed that 64% of the couples turned their heads to the right rather than the left as they embraced (Gunturkun, 2003).

However, the observed asymmetry of fetal movements is not necessarily permanent because changes in lateralization can occur following damage to a specialized brain region. This fact has been demonstrated for language functions in patients who suffered early brain lesions or the removal of a single hemisphere (Thal et al., 1991). Right-handedness is usually associated with a left-sided location for language. Right-handed children who underwent a left hemispherectomy late in life—12 to 13 years or later—showed a recovery of language functions, accompanied by the retaining of their earlier personality and sense of humor (Thal et al., 1991; Vining et al., 1997).

Sensory Systems

The functional capacity of prenatal sensory systems, which are partially functional before birth, is studied by observing changes in bodily activity following the presentation of an external stimulus. For example, display of a body startle, or change in body movement or heart rate, to a stimulus indicates that the fetus detected the incentive event. However, failure to respond to a stimulus does not necessarily mean that the fetal brain did not detect it. It is always possible that the fetus was not aroused by the stimulus or that the relevant sensory neurons were not yet connected to motor or autonomic targets.

The Auditory System

Over 75 years ago, Albrecht Peiper (1925) challenged the widely accepted view that the fetus and newborn could not perceive sound. Peiper's carefully planned experiments showed that during the last weeks before birth, the fetus reacted to the sound of a car horn with a change in body movement. To avoid frightening the mother with the car horn, Peiper first presented a "preparatory" quiet sound. A direct correlation between the sound and the fetal movement indicated that the fetus perceived the sound or the vibrations produced by the sound (Peiper, 1925). He also observed that the fetal movements to a sound decreased during repeated presentations and concluded that the fetus had created a "memory trace" for the sound (Peiper, 1925). Contemporary scientists say that the fetus habituated to the stimulus.

Contemporary studies of auditory functioning, which use varied stimuli and indexes of detection, including changes in movement, heart rate, or eye-blinks, suggest that a reaction to sound can appear as early as 12 to 16 PFW (Drife, 1985; Hepper, White, & Shahidulla, 1991).

The fetus can detect a broad spectrum of sound frequencies, ranging from 83 to 3000 Hz. Hepper and Shahidullah (1994) presented fetuses, 19 to 35 PFW, with sounds through a loudspeaker placed on the maternal abdomen, and recorded fetal movement with ultrasound. Most fetuses first responded to the 500 Hz tone at 19 PFW; by 27 PFW, 96% responded to the 250 and 500 Hz tones, but not to tones of 1000 or 3000 Hz. Responsiveness to these very low or high tones was first observed at 33 and 35 PFW, respectively. The use of magnetoencephalography revealed evoked responses to a 1000-Hz tone burst sometime after 33 PFW (Eswaran, Lowery, Robinson, Wilson, & Cheyne, 2000).

Some scientists writing a half century ago believed that the fetus heard nothing because sounds coming from the maternal heartbeat and digestive system (borborygmi) should have masked all external sounds. However, the frequencies of maternal heartbeat and gut movements (less than 32 Hz) are too low for the fetus to detect (Hepper & Shahidullah, 1994).

Introduction of microphones into the uterus near the fetus's head following the rupture of the amniotic membranes permits an estimate of the sound intensity within the uterus during gestation (Drife, 1985). This evidence suggests that the fetus hears the mother's voice, which is about 24 decibels (dB) louder than the internal uterine background, and louder than any outside voice, which is only 8 to 12 dB above the background level within the uterus. The mother's voice is transmitted to the fetus directly through vibrations of membranes and body liquids; outside voices must pass through the maternal abdomen and amniotic fluid. As a result, the mother's voice will be more salient than most outside voices allowing the fetus to register and store the prosody of the mother's voice, but probably not individual words. This possibility is affirmed by the fact that newborns prefer the sound of their mother's voice to that of others when the sounds are "filtered" to resemble the signals the fetus would have heard while in the uterus (Lecanuet & Schaal, 1996).

Auditory Pathway

The auditory pathway, as well as the adult size of the inner ear, are established at birth. The sensory receptor cells on the basilar membrane that detect varied sound frequencies show intensive differentiation between 9

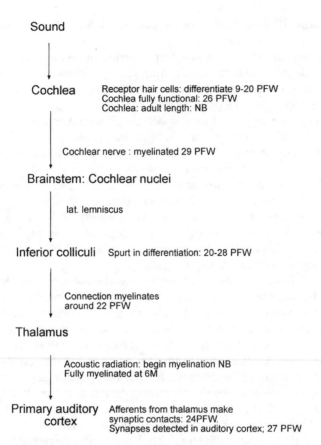

FIG. 2.9.   Auditory pathway.

and 20 PFW (see Fig. 2.9; Lavigne-Rebillard & Pujol, 1990). Auditory stimuli are transmitted by the cochlear nerve to cochlear nuclei in the brain stem, where a partial crossing takes place. These impulses reach the inferior colliculi, where a tonotopic pattern of axonal endings is preserved. The inferior colliculi are capable of integrative, multimodal, functions comparable to those of the superior colliculi in the visual system (Lecanuet & Schaal, 1996; Moore & Guan, 1998). Neurons in the colliculus show an intensive spurt of differentiation between 20 and 28 PFW, when axons from the lower auditory structures grow into the colliculi and axonal branches make contact with the dendrites (Moore & Guan, 1998; Sie, van der Knaap, Wezel-Meijler, & Valk, 1997; Sininger, Doyle, & Moore, 1999). It is possible that spontaneous activity in this system helps to shape the circuitry.

Afferent axons from the thalamus grow into the primary auditory cortex to make synaptic contacts at 24 PFW, and synapses can be detected at 27 PFW.

Somatosensory System

The somatosensory system, which functions early in gestation, processes sensory changes in touch, pain, proprioception (position of limbs), and temperature. Touch receptors in the skin appear first in the perioral region at 8 to 9 PFW, spread to the rest of the face, palms of the hands, and soles of the feet by 11 PFW, to the trunk and limbs by 15 PFW, and finally to all cutaneous and mucous surfaces by 20 PFW (Lecanuet & Schaal, 1996).

The first synapses between sensory fibers and interneurons in the spinal cord appear at 6 PFW, when unmyelinated sensory fibers grow into the cord (Glover & Fisk, 1999). Specific neurotransmitter sites in the spinal cord are found prior to 14 PFW and are complete by 30 PFW. Afferents from the thalamus reach the cortex to make synaptic contacts between 20 and 26 PFW—a prerequisite for the sensation of pain. Myelination of nociceptive and touch tracts to the brainstem and thalamus occur before 30 PFW. The thalamo-cortical pain fibers in the posterior limb of the internal capsule and corona radiata myelinate around 37 PFW, permitting more rapid transmission of impulses and a faster pain response.

Two tactile systems are formed simultaneously: one pathway for punctate touch and another for broad tactile input (i.e., stroking of a large area). The punctate touch sensations terminate in the somatosensory cortex; the broad tactile pathway ends in the insula, part of the limbic system, and may mediate a hormonal response to touch. This latter pathway does not depend on myelinated axons and could be the neural basis for the observation that stroking often soothes infants (Olausson et al., 2002; Sie et al., 1997).

Chemosensation

Distinct sensory systems for smell and taste operate simultaneously and respond prenatally to molecules in the surrounding amniotic fluid. Olfactory receptors are located in the upper nasal cavity; taste receptors are on the tongue, in the buccal cavity, and at the back of the throat. The cells of the olfactory bulb differentiate between 10 and 20 PFW, olfactory afferents mature at around 30 PFW, and nasal chemosensitivity is present by 25 to 28 PFW. The first taste buds appear at around 5 PFW, differentiate at 15

PFW, and gustatory responses can be elicited by 20 PFW (Hudson & Distel, 1999; Winberg, 1998).

The fact that a 3-day-old newborn has a selective preference for the odor of its own amniotic fluid, compared with the amniotic fluid of others, means that the fetus can detect and store the unique chemosensory information in its prenatal environment (Hudson & Distel, 1999; Schaal, Marlier, & Soussignan, 1998).

The Internal Regulation System (Responses to Stressors)

The internal regulation system, important for survival, controls visceral, endocrine, and behavioral functions and maintains an optimal internal environment. The internal regulation system allows the organism to react to internal or external challenges and to return to a baseline level (homeostasis). The network of the internal regulation system encompasses components derived from all six segments of the neural tube.

Investigators had assumed that a response of the internal regulation system to an intrusion, and the subsequent return to baseline levels, was driven solely by the mother's system (Gitau, Cameron, Fisk, & Glover, 1998; Taddio & Katz, 1997). However, blood samples from the intrahepatic vein of fetuses at 20 PFW were compared to blood samples taken from the placental cord, which reflects maternal blood. An increase in cortisol occurred in fetal blood, but not in maternal blood, following piercing of the trunk of the fetus. This result suggests that the fetus can mount a cortisol reaction to an invasive procedure independent of the mother's response (Gitau, Fisk, Teixeira, Cameron, & Glover, 2001). There is a surge in circulating fetal cortisol just before birth which is essential for the initiation of parturition. However, moderate malnutrition of the mother (in sheep) is associated with a precocious surge of cortisol in the fetus and with premature birth (Bloomfield et al., 2003).

Fetal Learning

The fetus can acquire a representation of a sensory event (for example, the mother's voice), and can associate two events that occur close together in time (that is, temporally contiguous). The concept of "representation" has a biological and a psychological meaning. The former is contained in a description of the pattern of neuronal activation produced by an event. The psychological meaning is captured by the words that describe the pattern of features in the event. The psychological representation of the mother's voice, for example, consists of the modal pattern of frequencies, rise times, tempos, and loudnesses that characterize a mother's speech. And newborns preferentially orient to the sound of their mother's voice compared with the voice of a stranger. These properties are not easily translated into sentences that describe neurons and their functions (DeCasper & Fifer, 1980).

The issue of fetal learning has been a target of curiosity for centuries. The British philosopher John Locke suggested in *Essay Concerning Human Understanding* that the fetus was capable of forming ideas, although Rousseau regarded the fetus as a "witless tadpole" (Hepper, 1989, 1992). It is not clear how long prenatal representations are preserved (Hepper, 1997a, 1997b). Scientists use two methods to study prenatal acquisition of representations and each awards a distinct meaning to the concept. One method involves habituation–dishabituation; the other relies on classical conditioning.

Habituation–Dishabituation

Habituation is defined as a decrement in response, usually a motor reaction, following repeated presentation of a stimulus. The decrement in responsivity is not due to fatigue because fetuses respond if the experimenter changes the stimulus. The reactivation of a response, called dishabituation, implies that the fetus must have created a representation of the repeated event and detected the difference between it and the novel event (Hepper, 1992; Rizzo, 2001).

Hepper (1997a, 1997b) used ultrasound imaging to assess fetal reactions to sound. Fetuses, 36 PFW, were exposed to 250-Hz pure tone sine waves played through a loudspeaker. Fetal movement habituated after 10 to 15 repetitions of the sound, but increased when the frequency of the tone was changed from 250 to 500 Hz. The fetuses were then habituated again to repeated presentations of the 500-Hz tone, and dishabituated to the original 250-Hz tone. However, this second habituation (to the 500 Hz tone) required fewer repetitions, indicating that the fetuses had stored a representation of the tones over the brief period of the experiment.

Classical Conditioning

The index of fetal learning that relies on classical conditioning procedures involves the presentation of a conditioned stimulus (CS) (for example, a pure tone) followed by an unconditioned stimulus (US) (for example, a vibroacoustic stimulus that usually evokes a motor reaction). The CS alone does not elicit any response initially; only the US elicits the movement. If a CS is followed by a US for a number of trials, presentation of the CS alone elicits a conditioned motor reaction in 3rd-trimester human fetuses (Hepper, 1997a, 1997b). Conditioned reactions acquired during fetal life can be preserved through the early postnatal months. A chimpanzee fetus experienced a 500 Hz tone CS followed by a vibroacoustic US that provoked movement, over 150 trials over a 30-day period. Presentation of the CS alone 58 days after birth provoked a conditioned motor response (Kawai, Morokuma, Tomonosa, Horimoto, & Tanaka, 2004).

THREE PRINCIPLES

The study of early brain development reveals three principles that apply to both biological and psychological phenomena over a life span. The first principle is specificity. The facts of prenatal brain growth imply that nature uses a very large number of highly specific rules, rather than a few broad, generalized ones, to create the fetal nervous system. One set of proteins moves the migrating progenitor cell toward its proper destination; a different set of proteins removes the neuron from its glial shaft. One set of progenitor cells grows radially; another set migrates tangentially. Some genes are expressed early; others are expressed later. Later chapters describe the differences between the specificity of biological phenomena and the psychologist's attraction to broad, highly generalized concepts to describe cognitive and affective phenomena.

The exquisite balance between excitation and inhibition, or between reactivity and regulation, represents a second principle. The complementary relation between glutamergic and GABA-ergic neurons has an analog in the symmetry of atomic phenomenon and in the ancient Chinese concepts of *yang* and *yin*. The fetal movements created by the initial presentation of a vibroacoustic stimulus (a result of excitatory processes) are gradually reduced following repeated presentation by inhibitory processes. We shall see in later chapters that enhancement of the inhibitory psychological processes of restraint, coping, and regulation is a seminal feature of psychological development.

The third principle emphasizes the importance of location. The specific location of the radially migrating progenitor cells produced in the ventricular zone determines each cell's final location. The path of the tangentially migrating cells is affected to a greater degree by the chemical gradients encountered on their journey. But in both cases, each cell's future fate is influenced by its location and the time of its birth. The specific location of an embryo in the uterus can influence brain development and future behavior. Although most humans have single births, many small mammals, especially mice, give birth to large litters. A pregnant mouse can have as many as 12 developing embryos in her two uterine horns. Hence, a female embryo can lie between two males, between a male and a female, or between two females. A female embryo developing between two males is influenced by the testosterone secreted by the two surrounding males and these females develop differently from females surrounded by two female embryos. For example, the masculinized females have a longer distance between the genital and the anus—called the anogenital distance. Males have larger distances than females. In addition, as adults, these females have lower reproductive success and wander further from the natal area (Vandenbergh, 2003). Analogously, the ratio of the second to the fourth digit in humans (the index to the ring finger) is correlated with the amount of exposure to prenatal testosterone. Most infant boys have a smaller ratio than girls (that is, a smaller index than ring finger) and women with more masculine interests have ratios that resemble males rather than females (Csatho et al., 2003; Manning, 2002). The significance of context applies throughout development, for most behaviors are dependent on the situation in which a child acts.

3

Birth to 6 Months

This chapter and the next, which consider the correspondences between postnatal brain growth and psychological development during the first year, are not detailed reviews of all that has been learned. The emphasis in this chapter is on the changes that occur during the transition between 2 and 3 months; chapter 4 focuses on the transition between 7 and 12 months. The behavioral clusters that define these two transitions are linked to maturational changes in brain organization, suggesting, but not proving, that the alterations in anatomy and physiology are important foundations for the behavioral phenomena. We assume that these maturational processes occur in healthy infants exposed to the objects, events, and people that are characteristic of most environments.

The young brain is biologically prepared to perceive and to create representations of events, like voices, shadows, and moving hands, that are present in all but the most abnormal environments. William Greenough called these events *experience expectant*. Less common events, like picture books and swimming pools, are called *experience dependent* (Greenough et al., 1987). Analogously, some responses—like smiling and reaching—develop without effort because their circuits are inherent in brain organization; others, like typing and soccer, have to be acquired with considerable effort.

The biologically prepared perceptual and motor functions are prominent in the first year. The ability to detect the difference between the faces of the parents is a highly prepared competence; the ability to discriminate male from female cats is not. The newborn's biologically prepared reactions are almost automatic to particular classes of stimuli. The infant sucks a finger inserted in the mouth, grasps a finger placed in the palm, and fixates a black line on a white background.

Two important psychological products of brain activity during the first year are (a) liberation from an automatic alerting to events with certain physical attributes to greater reliance on, and attraction to, events that are transformations of the infant's knowledge; and (b) the ability to retrieve schematic representations of the past without relevant clues in the immediate present. These competences require maturation of sensory systems, the hippocampus, prefrontal structures, and their reciprocal connections.

Although the focus in this chapter is on the transition at 8 to 12 weeks, it is useful to consider first the properties of the newborn, an era that, by convention, refers to the first 7 postnatal days, as well as the competences observed during the 8 weeks prior to the transition.

BIRTH TO 8 WEEKS

Arousal and Alertness

Most newborns are alert and physiologically stable during the initial hours following a medically uncomplicated delivery. The patterns of sleep, activity, and attention are less predictable over the next 2 or 3 days when the most obvious features are distinct shifts in state, from quiet sleep to alert attention, and from alert attention to intense crying, followed, eventually, by a return to a sleep state. After self-regulatory systems become organized by the third or fourth day, these functions regain a modest degree of stability (see Appendix A; de Vries et al., 1982).

The newborn's behavioral states are influenced by physiological profiles created by variations in brain chemistry. For example, changes in the concentration of norepinephrine and serotonin, synthesized in the brain stem by the locus ceruleus and raphe nucleus, respectively, as well as the density of their receptors, modulate lability and intensity of arousal. The locus ceruleus projects to many brain structures, including two classes of nuclei in the thalamus. The sensory relay nuclei send information to layer 4 of the cortex which receives stimulation from sensory surfaces. The diffuse nuclei of the thalamus, on the other hand, project to all cortical layers inducing a general state of arousal (Marrocco, 1994).

SENSORY FUNCTIONS

Vision

The newborn detects information in all sensory modalities and discriminates among select features in each modality. We consider the visual system in great detail because more is known about this system at the present time.

CHAPTER 3

Anatomy

The photoreceptors in the retina are the rods and cones, which absorb light waves, translate that energy into electrical impulses, and transmit them to ganglion cells within the retina (see Fig. 3.1). The rods, located in

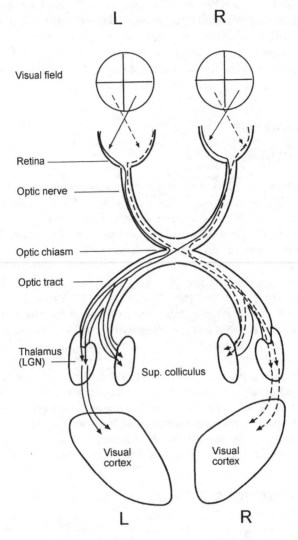

FIG. 3.1. Visual pathway from the retina to the visual cortex—Light from the temporal half of the visual field falls on the nasal half of the retina, whereas light from the nasal half of the visual field falls on the temporal half. This arrangement means that the right field of vision is projected to the left hemisphere and the left visual field to the right (Carpenter, 1991).

the periphery of the retina, are extremely sensitive to the dimmest levels of light but have a relatively slow latency and are relatively poor at detecting motion, shape, and color.

The cones, concentrated in the central foveal area of the retina, are less developed than the rods at birth and require more intense light, but have a faster latency and are able to detect motion, fine details of objects, and color (Boothe, Dobson, & Teller, 1985; Hendrickson & Drucker, 1992). By 3 months, the balance between rod and cone signals in response to moving gratings resembles the profiles of adults (Chien, Teller, & Palmer, 2000). The postnatal development of cones continues to about age 5; the rods continue to develop until age 13, although visual acuity and contrast sensitivity appear to reach a plateau by 5 years of age (Boothe et al., 1985; Ishigaki & Miyao, 1994; Zilles, Werners, Buesching, & Schleicher, 1986).

The signals from the photoreceptors are transferred to ganglion cells in the retina. These cells are specialized for processing a particular feature of the visual image, for example, contrast, rapid change in intensity, detailed features of a stimulus, movement, and color. The ganglion cells belong to two main classes, called — and P-cells. The M-cells have large receptive fields, due to extensive dendritic arbors, and are responsive primarily to large objects and movement. The more numerous P-cells have smaller receptive fields and are sensitive to form and color. A spurt in dendritic growth occurs earlier in M-cells than in P-cells. This might explain why newborns detect motion more accurately than form (Wadhwa & Bijlani, 1988).

The increase in visual acuity in the first postnatal month may be due to increased lateral inhibition of the ganglion cells that improve the contrast between stimulus and surround (Rusoft & Dubin, 1977). Visual acuity is usually assessed by presenting pairs of stimuli with black and white stripes differing in thickness. If infants look longer at one set of stripes than another, investigators conclude that they must have discriminated between the two stimuli. The evidence based on this method suggests that the thinnest black and white stripes a healthy 1-week-old can differentiate are about one tenth of an inch viewed from 1 foot away—a level of acuity that is 30 times poorer than that of a normal adult. The apparently poor acuity is due to the immaturity of the fovea, poor coordination of the eyes, incompletely developed visual cortex, and less mature lateral inhibition in ganglion cells (Hendrickson & Drucker, 1992). (See Fig. 3.2.)

During the first few months after birth, the cones in the fovea and neurons in the visual cortex develop, muscle control improves, and there is increased lateral inhibition of the specialized ganglion cells (Rusoft & Dubin, 1977).

The axons of the ganglion cells leave the retina to form the optic nerve which links the retina to the lateral geniculate nucleus (LGN) of the

FIG. 3.2.   Newborn acuity—Illustration of the finest stripe width a newborn can detect from 1 foot away.

thalamus. Animal experiments reveal that ganglion cells in the retina are spontaneously active before the rods and cones develop and, therefore, prior to any visual experience (Galli & Maffei, 1988; Meister, Wong, Baylor, & Shatz, 1991; Shatz, 1996).

Spontaneous activity in retinal ganglion cells, producing waves of excitability across the retina, might stimulate connections between the retina and the thalamus. When ganglion cell activity is blocked by a chemical, specific connections to the LGN do not form (Mooney, Penn, Gallego, & Shatz, 1996). Although this spontaneous activity seems to be necessary for refinement of these connections, it is not sufficient to establish the usual connections between the retina and thalamus. Sensory experience is required for this outcome (Penn & Schatz, 1999).

The axons in the optic nerve originating from the medial, or nasal, half of the retina cross (decussate) in a structure called the optic chiasm to join the uncrossed axons originating in the temporal (or lateral) half of the retina of the other eye to form the optic tract. Information in the child's right visual field, which strikes the right nasal retina, ends up in the left hemisphere, whereas information in the left visual field striking the left nasal retina ends up in the right hemisphere.

The majority of axons in the optic tract terminate in the lateral geniculate nucleus, the main relay site on the path to the visual cortex. Each neuron in the LGN has a retinotopic representation in the contralateral visual field. The representation in the LGN is not a point-for-point reflection of the image on the retina. The fovea, the area of the retina with the greatest acuity, occupies a proportionately larger area in the LGN than the periphery of the retina.

The lateral geniculate nucleus is composed of six layers. Two layers contain the large magno cells, whose main input comes from the M-cells in the retina; the other four layers contain smaller parvo cells that receive their main input from the P-cells in the retina. These cells comprise separate pathways to the primary visual cortex.

Visual evoked potentials from infants from birth to 1 year to two spatial frequencies presented at four contrast levels revealed a developmental dissociation between the underlying magno and parvo pathways. This evidence suggests that the former is functional earlier and matures faster than the latter during the first year (Hammarrenger et al., 2003), although some parts of the parvo pathway are functional during the early months, for 4-month-olds use this pathway to detect color (Thomasson & Teller, 2000).

Some axons in the optic tract terminate in the midbrain; some in the superior colliculus and others in the tectum. The superior colliculus has a laminar structure resembling the cortex. Visual information terminates in the top three layers, whereas information from the spinal cord and ascending somatosensory and auditory systems terminates in lower layers. This arrangement allows reflexive guidance of head and eye movements and enables the infant to integrate information from different sensory modalities. Simultaneous visual and auditory stimulation produces patterns of activity in the superior colliculus that are different from those produced by input from either modality alone (Meredith & Stein, 1986). It is likely that the simultaneous processing of the face and voice of a parent tending the infant creates a special brain state that facilitates creation of a firmer representation of the adult. Three-month-olds can create a firmer schema for the tempo of a brief event if both visual and auditory information are presented simultaneously. A representation is less firm if the event is presented only in the visual mode without any sound, or only in the auditory mode without any visual input (Bahrick, Flowm, & Lickliter, 2002).

It is also possible that the superior colliculus or the visual cortex has an optimal level of activation and young infants prefer a degree of collicular or cortical arousal that is neither too low nor too high. Four-month-olds, seated in front of a panel, saw one light flashing at 2 Hz and another flashing at 4 Hz. When both lights were flashing at their respective frequencies, the infants either heard nothing or they heard the sound of a cymbal beating at 2, 3, 4, or 5 Hz. When the room was silent, the infants looked longer at the 4- than at the 2-Hz light, but they looked longer at the 2-Hz light when they heard any sound from the cymbal. This result suggests that the

4-Hz light was too arousing, and, perhaps, aversive, when a sound was also present in the perceptual space (Moore, 1988).

The colliculus projects to the lateral geniculate nucleus, tectal area, reticular formation, cranial nerves modulating eye movements, and the facial muscles. The colliculus contributes to the coordination of eye and head movements and the reflex tracking of moving objects which declines between 6 and 12 PFW, suggesting that the subcortically guided action is replaced by cortical control (Bronson, 1994; Hamer, 1994; Johnson, 1996).

Primary Visual Cortex

The primary target of axons from the LGN is layer 4 of the visual cortex which consists of four "sublayers." Information about motion and location terminates in the upper half of layer 4; form and color information terminate in the lower half. Readers will recall from chapter 2 that the separate pathways from each eye are organized in vertical columns with each column responding to a single axis of orientation. In addition, a set of ocular dominance columns permits the perception of depth. Each ocular dominance column receives information from one eye, and a pair of columns, one from each eye, alternates with horizontal connections linking the paired columns. Initially, axons from the LGN send several collaterals to terminate in overlapping contiguous columns. Later in development, after some synapses have been pruned, the stimulation from one eye only innervates the columns serving that eye.

Impressive changes in the primary visual cortex occur during the first 4 to 8 postnatal months. The number of synapses (per mm) doubles between 28 PFW and birth, and by 8 months, this number has increased by a factor of 11 (Huttenlocher, deCourten, Garey, & van der Loos, 1982). Synaptic density in layer 4 of the visual cortex peaks at around 4 months, a little before peak density in cortical layers 2 and 3.

The peak density of spines on apical dendrites of pyramidal neurons in layer 3 of the primary visual cortex, attained at 5 months, is followed by a decrease until the adult level of about 50 spines per segment is reached by the second birthday (Michel & Garey, 1984). Although spines can form in rodent brains in the absence of afferent stimulation, preliminary human data suggest that spine formation follows synapse formation and, therefore, afferent input (Segal, Korkotian, & Murphy, 2000).

Information from the primary visual cortex is conveyed to adjacent areas of the occipital cortex and to parts of the temporal and parietal cortex. The dorsal pathway contains information about the location of an object—the "where" path. The ventral pathway mediates the recognition of the shape of an object—the "what" path. The integration of these two pathways occurs in the temporal and prefrontal cortex (Rao, Rainer, & Miller, 1997). Both paths were activated when adults performed an integrated visuospatial task in which they had to attend to form and location simultaneously. But activation of the "where" pathway appeared earlier, peaked later, and lasted longer than activation of the "what" pathway (Okabe et al., 2003; Rao, Zhou, Zhuo, Fan, & Chen, 2003).

Developmental Processes Driven by Spontaneous Neural Activity. We noted that spontaneous neuronal activity plays a crucial role in development. The ganglion cells in the rodent retina show spontaneous waves of activity before the development of retinal photoreceptors. This activity is necessary for partitioning the LGN (Galli & Maffei, 1988; Meister et al., 1991; Shatz, 1996), and forming ocular dominance columns in the visual cortex (Rakic, 1976). Spontaneous activity is also present in the auditory system, cortex, hippocampus, cerebellum, thalamus, superior colliculus, and locus ceruleus. However, we should not view the endogenous activity as operating at exclusive times in development (Penn & Schatz, 1999).

Influence of Sensory Input. Hubel and Wiesel demonstrated that postnatal deprivation of visual experience, produced by suturing one eye of a kitten so that the animal received no visual information through that eye, disturbed the formation of the ocular dominance columns in the primary visual cortex. The connections from the normal eye, which received visual input, dominated the columns, whereas the columns that served the closed eye lost some of their connections within a week (Hubel & Wiesel, 1970; LeVay, Wiesel, & Hubel, 1980; Wiesel & Hubel, 1965). However, despite the absence of visual input to the closed eye, ocular dominance columns in the relevant sites in cortex continued to form, although more slowly, because retinal ganglion cells remained active. Loss of visual input does not abolish all activity in the ganglion cells of the retina.

The dramatic consequences of closing one eye are restricted to a narrow period in development, called a *critical period.* Disruption of expectant sensory experience during a critical period can affect cortical anatomy permanently (Hubel, 1982; Wiesel, 1982; Wiesel & Hubel, 1965). A similar phenomenon occurs in children born with a congenital cataract of the lens that impairs vision in the affected eye. If the cataract is not removed within the first 3 months, the ability to use both eyes for depth vision can be permanently lost. However, not all consequences of events during a critical period are irreversible. Continuous exposure to white noise during postnatal days 12 to 30 in the infant rat seriously disturbs the functioning of the auditory cortex. But exposure to a normal auditory environment in adulthood is followed by recovery of normal auditory function (Chang & Merzenich, 2003).

Neuronal Activity and Gene Expression.   Repeated neurotransmitter activation of the synaptic transmembrane receptors leads to the translocation and binding of CREB (cyclic-AMP an acronym for adenosine 3'5' cyclic monophosphate-response element-binding protein; see Fig. 3.3) to the promoter region of the gene, which controls the timing and intensity of the gene's activity. This binding induces the structural sector of the gene (exon) to transcribe and to express coded messenger RNA (mRNA). The mRNA is released from the nucleus and captured by ribosomes in active, "tagged," dendrites, where the mRNA is translated, leading to local protein synthesis and the incorporation of proteins into cellular structures. This process is the basis of the brain's plasticity. The mechanisms by which specific synapses are targeted for protein synthesis remain unresolved (Martin & Kosik, 2002). An impressive example of cortical plasticity is the brain's ability to exploit alternative sensory areas in the absence of normal sensory input. This phenomenon occurs in individuals who were born deaf, or who suffered a loss of hearing early in life, and learned sign language. These adults showed activity in the auditory cortex to the visual signals of sign language, suggesting that their auditory cortex processed visual events (Finney, Fine, & Dobkins, 2001).

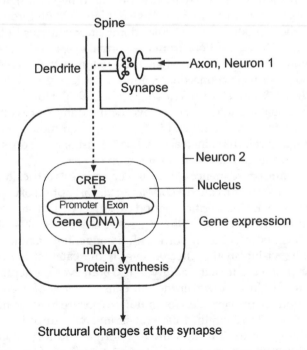

FIG. 3.3.   Synaptic activity leads to gene expression, protein synthesis, and structural changes.

INFANT PERCEPTION

Salient Visual Features

The number and nature of the biologically prepared, psychological functions represent a central, but still unresolved, issue. Observers of infants have either minimized or exaggerated the presence of perceptual and cognitive biases that require little or no experience to be actualized. A defense of either extreme is inconsistent with the evidence (Newcombe, 2002).

The neuronal ensembles of animals from different families, genera, or species often differ in their responsivity to stimuli in each sensory modality. Size is so salient a property for chimpanzees it is difficult to teach them to pick the smaller of two arrays of a desirable food to receive a food reward, although choosing the larger array prevents them from getting the food (Boysen, Berntson, & Mukobi, 2001). These biases are not surprising for the members of each taxon have to adapt to particular ecologies. The brain of the human infant is especially prepared to respond to contour and motion in visual events, and to particular frequencies, loudnesses, and rhythms in auditory events (Feigenson, Carey, & Spelke, 2002). The primacy of motion helps explain why children make a sharp distinction between living and nonliving things.

The Salience of Contour. Contour, the most salient feature of a visual event after motion, always recruits the newborn's attention (Haith, 1980). Haith (1980) has posited four rules that guide the newborn's eye movements: (a) if awake and alert and the light is not too bright, open the eyes; (b) if in darkness, maintain a controlled search of the environment; (c) if there is light, but no object, search for edges by broad, jerky sweeps of the visual field; and (d) if an edge is found, stop scanning and remain in the vicinity of the edge. It is of interest that spontaneous neural activity in the visual cortex of anesthetized cats (with no visual input because their eyes are closed) fluctuates between states that resemble those recorded when the animal is looking at vertical or horizontal stripes. This intriguing fact suggests that the visual cortex cycles in its receptivity to contours that differ in orientation (Kenet, Bibtchkov, Tsodyks, Grinvald, & Arieli, 2003).

Although some investigators claim that infants can create a representation of the number of elements in a visual array, because they look longer at an array of five dots after being familiarized on an array of three dots— or vice versa—the infants are actually responding to the differing amount and density of contour in the three and five dot displays rather than to the "number" of dots (Feigenson et al., 2002). Six-month-old infants do not look longer at a display of four objects after familiarization with one containing two objects when contour density is controlled (Xu, 2003). Because infants can discriminate an array of 8 dots from one containing 16 dots, they are perceiving some difference between the elements in the two arrays although their brains are not "counting" the number of elements. We need to invent a construct, other than "numerosity," to explain the data. Although it has been suggested that the intraparietal sulcus is biologically prepared to process number, this cortical area is also activated when adults decide if a number on a screen is darker or larger than a comparison number (Kadosh et al., 2003).

The factors that influence the dance of a bee returning to the hive after a foraging mission are relevant to this issue for the dance is a function of the distance of the hive from the foraging site. This intriguing fact tempted scientists to assume that the bee's brain was computing distance. However, the critical factor determining the bee's dance following return to the hive was the frequency and density of the contoured objects that passed in front of the bee's visual receptors. In a natural environment, this metric is highly correlated with distance. However, scientists can separate distance from density of optical flow, by placing bees in tunnels of different lengths that vary in the density of contoured lines painted on the tunnel's inner surface. These experiments revealed that optical flow, not distance, controls the bee's dance. The rate at which visual information enters the visual system creates a brain state that, in turn, influences the duration and nature of the dance (Esch, Zhang, Srinivasan, & Tautz, 2001).

This discovery has implications for the claim that young infants process and represent the numerosity of a display. As with the bee's dance, it is not necessary to assume that the brain represents the number of dots in an array. The brain is excited by the total amount and density of contour in a display, and the brain state created by five dots is different from the state created by three dots. Thus, after being familiarized on three dots, the presentation of five dots leads to prolonged attention because of the altered brain state. There is no need to assume that the brain "counts" the number of objects (Mix, Huttenlocher, & Levine, 2002). Even 3-year-old children use total amount of contour, rather than number, to differentiate pairs of stimuli (Rouselle, Palmers, & Noel, 2004).

A similar critique applies to claims that infants perceive "human speech." The human voice has a characteristic acoustic pattern and neurons in auditory cortex are especially responsive to sounds with the acoustic properties of the human voice. Hence, newborns should be able to discriminate human vocal sounds from those that do not share all the features of the human voice, and might attend longer to the former than to the latter because the human sounds preferentially excite neurons in the auditory cortex. Preliminary evidence confirms this intuition. Infants only a few days old discriminate between the acoustic envelope produced by single words spoken by a human and an envelope characterized by very similar sounds not produced by the human voice. But the conclusion that "the acoustic properties of the human voice have special properties" is not identical in meaning to the statement "newborns can discriminate speech from nonspeech."

Newborns can discriminate a pair of horizontally placed dark circles enclosed within a circular boundary—and therefore suggestive of a face—from a scattered arrangement of straight lines with the same amount of contour. This competence can be described in two ways. On the one hand, scientists can write that the newborn is biologically prepared to discriminate circular forms from straight lines or, on the other, to conclude that the infant is biologically prepared to recognize a human face. Some psychologists prefer the latter description because the pair of horizontal circles within a boundary resembles a face. But because the newborn does not "know" that the stimulus is a face, it seems more accurate to use the former description. Otherwise psychologists might be tempted to state that infants recognize *happiness* and *sadness* when they discriminate a face with the mouth turned up from a face with the mouth turned down; or they recognize *animacy* when they discriminate a moving from a stationary sphere. The incentives for infants during the first postnatal days are not faces, numbers, emotions, or speech, but the physical features of those events. The former will become psychological representations after infants have had additional experience and attached schemata to the sensory events.

Although the newborn's ability to perceive the major colors remains controversial, most 4-month-old infants appear to have excellent color vision, and look longer at a red than at a blue sphere. The perceptual boundaries between color categories are more distinct than equivalent wavelength differences within a particular hue (that is, the difference in wavelength, in nanometers, between orange and red, is perceptually more salient to infants than an equivalent difference in wavelength between pink and crimson).

Young infants also habituate more quickly to simple than to complex colors, where a simple color is the central wavelength of a particular hue. The crimson color on Christmas cards is a simple hue; the wavelength that corresponds to the border between red and orange—the color of a peach—is complex (Bornstein, 1981). However, initial perceptual preferences can be altered by experience. Some older children prefer the color blue to the color red. Analogously, all infants prefer sweet over bitter tastes, but many adults prefer the taste of martinis and hot peppers to chocolate cake and ice cream.

The infant is also preferentially attentive to curved over linear segments. Thirteen-week-olds were shown pairs of similar patterns; one member of the pair was composed of curved arcs and the other of straight lines. The infants looked longer at the former patterns; for example, a bull's-eye composed of arcs was studied longer than a bull's-eye composed of straight-line segments (see Fig. 3.4; Ruff & Birch, 1974). Further, infants showed a greater increase in attention when they saw a curved segment following habituation on a line segment than when the situation was reversed and they were dishabituated on a straight line following habituation on a curved arc (Hopkins, Kagan, Brachfeld, Hans, & Linn, 1976).

Vertical symmetry (that is, symmetry around a vertical plane) is a fourth salient feature for infants (Bornstein & Krinsky, 1985; Fantz, 1965; Slater & Morison, 1985; Super, Kagan, Morison, Haith, & Wieffenbach, 1972). One-week-old infants were presented with a pair of black and white photographs of female faces. Adults had judged one member of each pair as attractive and the other as unattractive. The infants looked longer at the attractive faces, suggesting a sensitivity to vertical symmetry because vertical symmetry is a critical component of the judged attractiveness of female faces (Bornstein & Krinsky, 1985; Slater et al., 1998). However, older infants, 5 to 8 months old, looked longer at less symmetric faces, probably because they were discrepant from their acquired schemata for faces (Rhodes, Geddes, Jeffery, Dziurawiec, & Clark, 2002).

The salience of vertical symmetry may explain why older infants show increased attention when two horizontally placed black circles enclosed in a larger circle are replaced with two vertically placed black circles, but show no increase in attention when the pair of horizontal circles is replaced with a pair of horizontal squares, although infants can discriminate circles from squares.

In addition to motion, contour, color, curvilinearity, and vertical symmetry, visual stimuli that form good gestalts (for example, triangles and squares that have symmetry and continuity of contour) possess salience and infants form firmer representations of them than of events that are poor gestalts. Three- and four-month-olds were first familiarized on pairs of identical squares composed of small black dots that formed a good ge-

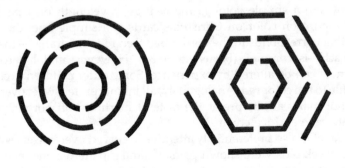

FIG. 3.4.   Patterns shown to 13-week-old infants.

stalt, and then shown one of these squares alongside a different design. They discriminated between the old and new stimulus. However, they failed to discriminate the familiar event from the novel one if initially familiarized on a pair of identical black dot arrays that were not good gestalts (the arrays had neither symmetry nor continuity of contour; Quinn, Bhatt, Brush, Grimes, & Sharpnack, 2002).

The behaviors of male and female vervet monkeys provide an example of the inferential error that can occur if the investigator leaps to a conceptually abstract interpretation of a behavior that can be more parsimoniously explained by the physical qualities of the event. Adult female vervets spent more time than males in contact with a doll and a pot—toys that most girls prefer—than with four other toys. Although some scientists might leap to the conclusion that female monkeys understand something about their gender, the investigators were wise enough to note that the two toys the female monkeys played with were the only ones with a red and pink coloration. Because infant monkeys display this coloration, adults might be biologically prepared to be attracted to objects with this color (Alexander & Hines, 2002).

Although adult chimpanzees easily discriminate between familiar and unfamiliar objects, that observation does not mean that they possess the concept "unfamiliarity." Highly-trained chimps presented with two unfamiliar and one familiar object could not learn to place the two unfamiliar objects on one tray and the familiar one on another tray because they were unable to create a conceptual representation of *unfamiliarity* (Tanaka, 1995).

The important point is that discriminating between two events, inferred from the fact that infants look longer at one stimulus than at another, does not imply possession of the semantic concept the investigator imposed, a priori, on the stimuli, whether the concept is number, *in* versus *on*, or *tight fit* versus *loose fit*. Seven-month-old infants shown photos of morphed faces that varied in the degree of a "happy" compared with a "fearful" expression looked longer at faces that had at least 60% of the elements of the fearful expression (Kotsoni, de Haan, & Johnson, 2001). However, the more fearful faces had larger eyes and a smaller mouth opening than the faces containing more happy components. Young infants usually look longer at faces with larger, rather than smaller, eyes, independent of the emotional expression on the face (Geldart, Maurer, & Carney, 1999). Thus, the infants might not be responding to the emotional expression on the face, but rather to the size of the eyes, and perhaps the mouth opening as well. Monkeys and young infants can discriminate between closed figures composed of three or eight sides of equal length, but that fact does not mean that they possess the concepts "triangle" and "octagon."

A thought experiment reveals the logical flaw in interpreting differential attention to two events as implying possession of a semantic concept. Imagine a psychologist who, believing that 8-month-old infants understood the concept "causal action at a distance," first habituated infants on a sequence in which one red ball moved a few inches to strike a second green ball which moved on impact. The psychologist then presented infants with two test stimuli: one was the familiarization sequence and the other was a novel event consisting of a stationary red ball on the left and a moving green ball on the right. Infants would look longer at the novel event than at the familiarized one. But that preference does not imply that the infant understood "causal action at a distance." Nonetheless, some psychologists have used differential attention to claim that infants comprehend this notion (Schlottmann & Surian, 1999).

Perception of Faces. The hypothesis that newborns are biologically prepared to perceive a human face remains controversial. On the one hand, most newborns track a moving schematic representation of a face longer than a moving stimulus with the same amount of contour that bears no resemblance to a face. However, most investigators fail to find differential attention to a face and a nonface stimulus with an equivalent amount of contour when the stimuli are static. It is possible that the newborns in the former study had sufficient postnatal experience with adult faces during the opening day or two of life to establish a schema for a human face, or the moving facial stimulus facilitated more alert attention and aided discrimination (see Fig. 3.5; Haaf & Brown, 1976; Maurer & Barrera,

FIG. 3.5. Three schematic faces of equivalent contour but differential facelike quality shown to 1-month-olds who showed equivalent attention to the three stimuli.

1981). Although newborns can discriminate between a regular schematic face and one with the facial features scrambled, they devote equivalent attention to both events, suggesting no special preference for the normal facial pattern (Easterbrook, Kisilevsky, Muir, & Laplante, 1999).

One reason why newborns might look longer at stimuli that resemble a face is that they usually attend for a longer time to any bounded stimulus with contoured elements in the upper part of the visual field than to stimuli containing the same elements in the lower part of the visual field. Thus, newborns look longer at stimulus A than stimulus B, but look equally long at stimulus C and D although D is more face-like than C (see Fig. 3.6; Turati & Simion, 2002). That is why infants look longer at an array of five contoured elements that form the shape of an upright T than at the five elements forming an inverted T (Turati, 2004).

A second reason for doubting the newborn's ability to recognize a face as a distinct pattern is that infants younger than 6 weeks focus on the contour defining an outline, and fail to scan the features within an outline (see Fig. 3.7). Young infants can discriminate a triangle from a square, and a square

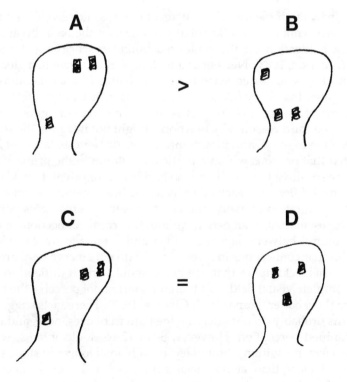

FIG. 3.6. Four patterns shown to infants.

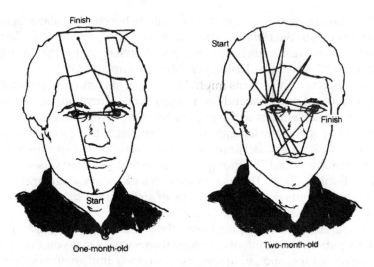

FIG. 3.7.   Patterns of fixation in 1- and 2-month-old infants to a human face
(Fogel & Melson, 1988). Courtesy of A. Fogel and G. F. Melson.

from a circle. But if the triangle, square, or circle is enclosed in a larger circle, infants do not attend differentially to one over the other because they
focus their attention on the contoured boundary enclosing the stimuli
(Fogel & Melson, 1988). Newborns look longer at a change in a global feature with low spatial frequency than at a change in a local feature with
higher spatial frequency (Cassia, Simion, Milani, & Ulmilta, 2002).

The immature connectivity between and among contiguous cortical
columns is a third reason why newborns might not integrate the separate
features of eyes, nose, and mouth into a holistic representation of a face.
We noted that neurons within a particular column in the primary visual
cortex are sensitive to stimuli with a specific axis of orientation. Contiguous columns differ from each other by about 10 degrees in axis of orientation. The integration of many columns to create hypercolumns permits a
fuller representation of an event. Although vertical connections within a
single column between layers 2 and 3 and 5 emerge by 29 PFW, the
intercolumnar connections in layers 2 and 3 do not emerge until around 4
months. This fact implies that newborns should find it difficult to represent a complete visual field, and therefore, might not perceive the pattern
of a face (Burkhalter, Bernardo, & Charles, 1993). These facts suggest that
newborns probably do not integrate the pattern of eyes, nose, and mouth
into a unified perception. However, 8- to 12-week-old infants, who do
scan the elements within a boundary, usually look longer at static stimuli
resembling faces than at nonfacial stimuli with the same amount or
density of contour.

Auditory Pathway. The peripheral auditory system is anatomically functional at birth, and newborns can detect changes in the frequency, loudness, and timbre of the human voice, as well as differences between certain vowel sounds, and the acoustic envelope of a voice speaking single words and a nonvocal event with a similar, but not identical, acoustic profile. Infants can discriminate their own cry from the cry of another infant and show more distress to the latter (Dondi, Simion, & Caltran, 1999; Molfese & Molfese, 1985). This competence is probably the result of hearing their own cry during the first hours of postnatal life. Young birds that have been deafened before they sing fail to develop the song characteristic of their species because they cannot hear their own sounds or the sounds of other birds.

Young infants also have a biologically prepared preference for consonant over dissonant musical chords. Four-month-old infants heard a consonant and a dissonant version of two different, unfamiliar melodies. The infants were quieter and looked longer at the speaker transmitting the consonant rather than the dissonant melody, although many adults prefer Stravinsky's dissonant music to Mozart's consonant symphonies (Zentner & Kagan, 1996). However, infants in the first year do not show differential EEG or heart rate reactions to excerpts from symphonies that, in adults, provoke a sad, fearful, or joyous emotion because infants have not learned the relevant symbolism (Schmidt, Trainor, & Santesso, 2003).

Older infants—8 to 12 months—can discriminate among varied rhythms. Infants heard brief tones (each 47 msec in duration) presented in varied patterns. For example, one pattern consisted of a single tone, a pause of 200 msec, followed by two tones (e.g., T—TT). A second pattern consisted of two tones played only 90 msec apart, a delay of 200 msec, followed by a third tone (TT—T). Infants familiarized on one of the aforementioned patterns showed increased attention to the unfamiliar rhythm (Demany, McKenzie, & Vurpillot, 1977). However, newborn infants have difficulty detecting a deviant or discrepant auditory stimulus if the delay between the last familiar and the presentation of the discrepant event is as long as 1.5 sec (Cheour et al., 2002).

The two hemispheres assume different functions when sensory information contains substantial variation in its frequency components. The right hemisphere, especially the dorsal stream of axons, more often elaborates the lower frequency component of a particular pattern, whereas the left hemisphere, especially the ventral stream, elaborates the higher frequency information (Ivry & Robertson, 1998). However, these biases are not absolute and are always modulated by the salience of the features and the relative difference between the lower and higher frequency components of a particular event. Nonetheless, this bias implies that the right hemisphere processes more completely the changing prosody of a sentence, whereas the left hemisphere is biased to process the rapidly moving stream of phonemes in the same vocal signal (Dehaene-Lambertz, 2000).

This last claim finds elegant support in the fact that 2- to 3-month-olds, whether awake or asleep, show equivalent activation in the left temporal lobe (specifically, the angular gyrus) to speech, whether read forward or backward. This evidence implies a biologically prepared substrate in the left temporal lobe for processing rapidly occurring auditory signals, of which speech represents one type (Dehaene-Lambertz, Dehaene, & Hertz-Pannier, 2002). The outside sounds that fetuses hear are predominantly low frequency sounds, typically less than 400 Hz, that should be processed more fully by the right than by the left hemisphere. This asymmetry might contribute to the precocious development of the right over the left hemisphere during the fetal period.

Taste and Olfaction. The three distinct chemosensory systems of newborns—olfaction, taste, and trigeminally mediated sensation—work together to create a single perception in adults; for example, the olfactory and taste qualities of garlic. Olfactory receptors are located in the upper nasal cavity; the taste receptors are on the tongue, in the buccal cavity, and at the back of the throat. Nerve endings from the trigeminal nerve innervate both the nasal and buccal mucosa.

Newborns can discriminate among select tastes and show distinct reactions to sweet, sour, and bitter tastes, as do monkeys and rats (Berridge, 2003). When a food or liquid that has a neutral or slightly sweet taste is warmed, the resulting sensation is sweeter than if it is cooled, suggesting that the practice of warming milk creates a sweeter taste experience (Cruz & Green, 2000). These reactions are mediated, in part, by the orbitofrontal prefrontal cortex and the spatially contiguous nucleus accumbens (Berridge, 2003).

The neurons of the anterior portion of the orbitofrontal prefrontal cortex (OBPFC) are sensitive to the state of satiety, for neuronal activity to a taste is reduced after an individual is sated on a food with that taste. However, the neurons of the posterior OBPFC are relatively insensitive to the state of deprivation, for they remain equally active whether or not the person has been sated on a particular food (Kringelbach et al., 2003). This principle holds for all sensory modalities; some cortical neurons are activated by a stimulus independent of the person's psychological state, whereas other neurons in the same region are sensitive to the momentary psychological state.

Newborns can discriminate among select olfactory stimuli, for they grimace to substances that adults regard as foul (rotten eggs, for example), and smile to olfactory stimuli adults regard as pleasant (honey, for example). Infants less than a week old can detect the olfactory properties produced by a lactating woman, for they orient more reliably to the mother's breast pad than to the breast pad of another woman (Porter & Winberg, 1999; Schaal et al., 1998; Varendi, Porter, & Winberg, 1996).

MOTOR SYSTEM

The human newborn, like all mammalian infants, enters the world with a number of reflexes, each preferentially released by a particular class of stimuli (see Appendix B). An awake newborn turns his or her head toward a visual, auditory, or tactile stimulus; for example, when the newborn's lips contact the nipple of the mother's breast or when an adult touches the newborn's perioral area. But the infant will not orient if his or her own finger is the tactile stimulus applied to the mouth because an inhibitory circuit is activated when the infant touches his or her own perioral area (Rochat, 1998).

The palmar grasp is activated when a finger or an object is placed on the newborn's palm (see Fig. 3.8). The thumb and forefingers automatically close around the finger to form a fist. The sensory information ema-

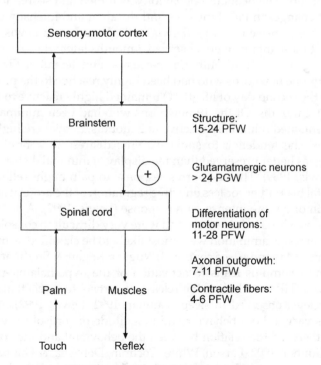

FIG. 3.8.   Newborn palmar grasp reflex.

nating from the object on the surface of the palm is transmitted via the spinal cord to the brainstem and then to the motor nuclei that produce the muscular contractions of the grasp. Newborns show a variety of other motor movements of limbs. But there is considerable individual variation in the frequency and intensity of these movements.

THE NEWBORN'S RESPONSE TO STRESSORS

Pain, cold, heat, and hunger provoke internal regulatory systems that initiate varied response profiles followed by a return to baseline values. For example, newborns usually cry and show an autonomic response (increase in blood pressure, heart rate, respiration, or pupil dilation) to the pain created by blood sampling or circumcision (Gunnar, 1992). However, most healthy newborns have some capacity for regulation and return to a baseline state within a short period of time.

Lewis and colleagues investigated the stability, over the first 2 months, of the newborn's behavioral reaction to pain. The heel of the newborn was pricked with a lancet to collect a few drops of blood used to detect metabolic disorders. The neonate's behavior was filmed and scored for the intensity of changes in facial muscles and duration and intensity of crying over successive 5-sec intervals (Lewis, 1992; Worobey & Lewis, 1989).

Some of these infants were observed 2 months later when each was inoculated against DPT (diphtheria, pertussis, and tetanus). Eighteen of the twenty-one newborns who had been highly reactive to the prick of the lancet on the second day of life (86%) remained highly reactive to the inoculation at 2 months. Of the 19 newborns who had been minimally reactive, 10 remained minimally reactive at 2 months, but 9 were highly reactive. Thus, the tendency to show extreme distress to a brief, painful stimulus was better preserved than the display of minimal distress (Worobey & Lewis, 1989). The newborn's response to pain might reflect a temperamental bias either for less effective regulation of the arousal accompanying pain or a more intense pain response (Lewis, 1992). A small group of newborns who cried intensely and were very difficult to console during a psychological examination were most likely to be classified as high reactive infants at 4 months (see chapter 4; Nugent, Kagan, & Snidman, 2002).

A painful stimulus leads to activation of the hypothalamic-pituitary-adrenal axis (HPA) including the release of cortisol to levels that can be 5 times the level observed in sleep (Gunnar, 1992; Lewis, 1992). Although newborns vary in both behavior and magnitude of cortisol secretion to a "stress," there is little relation between the behavioral and the cortisol response (Gunnar, 1992; Larson, White, Cochran, Donzella, & Gunnar, 1998). For example, some newborns show minimal crying, but a large increase in

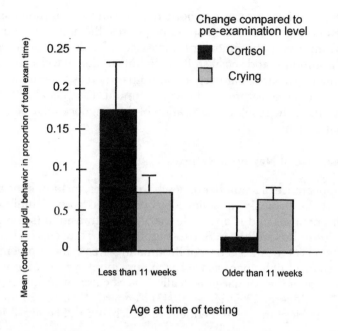

FIG. 3.9.   Cortisol and behavioral responses to routine examination in infants below and above 11 weeks.

cortisol. The reverse relation is more common later in the first year, when an intense behavioral response need not be accompanied by a large release of cortisol because of cortical modulation of the HPA-axis. The daily handling of an infant produces an increase in salivary cortisol in newborns, but not in 3-month-olds, due to maturation of a process that restrains the HPA-axis (see Fig. 3.9). Indeed, the rising plasma cortisol levels in rhesus monkey infants over the first 90 days (comparable to the first 9 months in human infants) seem to be more seriously affected by maturation than by form of rearing. Infant monkeys raised without their mother, but with other monkeys, showed the same rise in cortisol over the first 3 months as normally reared animals (Davenport et al., 2003; Gunnar, 1998).

THE TRANSITION AT 8 TO 12 WEEKS

Emergence of Cortical Control

The transition at 8 to 12 weeks is characterized by the emergence of several phenomena that are due, in part, to the maturation of the cerebral cortex and its influence on the brain stem. The most prominent changes include the disappearance of newborn reflexes and endogenous smiling, decreased crying, reduction of stress responses, the appearance of circadian rhythm, recognition memory, increased saccades to varied components of a stimulus, and social smiling. Infants under 10 weeks tend to remain fixated on a particular part of a stimulus whereas older infants make saccades across the features of the same stimulus (Taga et al., 2002). This change is likely the result of maturation of the magnocellular pathway in the visual system.

Disappearance of Newborn Reflexes

The disappearance of a number of newborn reflexes, including the palmar grasp and the Babinski, is believed to be due to cortical inhibition of brainstem neurons and is a reliable mark of the transition (see Fig. 3.10; Brodal, 1981; Rosenblith & Sims-Knight, 1985; Touwen, 1976; Volpe, 1995). Lesions of the mesial part of Brodmann's area 6, the supplementary motor area in adult humans as well as mature monkeys, are followed by a reappearance of the palmar grasp called *forced grasping* (Addie & Critchley, 1927; Goldberg, 1985; Hines, 1943; Kennard, Viets, & Fulton, 1934; Lawrence & Hopkins, 1976; Penfield & Welch, 1951). See Fig. 3.10.

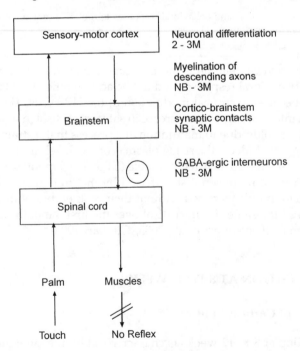

FIG. 3.10.   3 to 7 months—Cortical inhibition of newborn palmar grasp reflex.

Projections from the supplementary motor cortex to the brainstem and spinal cord, via the pyramidal tract, inhibit brainstem neurons (Bates & Goldman-Rakic, 1993; Galea & Darian-Smith, 1995; Kuypers & Lawrence, 1967; Luppino, Matelli, Camarda, & Rizzolatti, 1993; Matelli, Luppino, & Rizzolatti, 1991; Pandya & Kuypers, 1969; Ralston, 1994; Smith, Bourbonnais, & Blanchette, 1981; Wiesendanger & Wise, 1992; Zilles, Schlaug, Matelli, Luppino, & Schleicher, 1995). Although descending axons from the supplementary motor area reach the brainstem and spinal cord targets prenatally, actual synaptic contacts do not appear until 2 to 3 months postnatally (de Vries et al., 1982; Fitzgerald, 1991; Kostovic, 1990). Further, myelination of the pyramidal tract is absent prenatally, and the corticobrainstem tract, which contains the descending fibers from the supplementary motor area, does not show enhanced myelination until 3 to 4 months (Brody et al., 1987; Galea & Darian-Smith, 1995; Kinney et al., 1988).

Finally, several neurochemical processes, including GABA-ergic and glycinergic inhibitory spinal interneurons, show enhanced development during the first 3 postnatal months (Akert, 1994; Brody et al., 1987; Fitzgerald, 1991; Kinney et al., 1988; Kuypers & Lawrence, 1967; McEwen, 1987; Ralston, 1994). Excitatory glutamergic axons from the motor cortex could activate the inhibitory spinal interneurons to produce a reflex inhibition by acting on GABA-ergic inhibitory interneurons.

The suggestion that the disappearance of the spinal reflexes is due to cortical inhibition is not consensual. Heinz Prechtl believes that the disappearance of the palmar grasp is due to a different set of maturational processes within the brainstem and peripheral nerves (Prechtl, 1981, 1984, 1986).

Smiling and Crying

The transition is also marked by an obvious reduction in crying. Descending fibers from both frontal and cingulate cortex modulate sites in the brainstem that coordinate the laryngeal and respiratory movements needed for crying, especially the reticular formation, central gray, nucleus solitarius, and parabrachial nuclei (Akert, 1994; Berger, Mitchell, & Severinghaus, 1977; Fitzgerald, 1991; Jürgens, 1986; Zilles & Rehkämper, 1994). The decrease in crying is correlated with an increase in face-to-face communication and contact between mother and infant during the second month (Lavelli & Fogel, 2002; Lohaus, Keller, & Voelker, 2001).

There is also a sharp increase in social smiling. Four infants were observed weekly, at home, from 2 to 65 weeks of age. Despite week-to-week variability in each infant's behavior, all four showed a clear decrease in crying and an increase in social smiling to stimulation between 10 and 14 weeks (de Weerth & van Geert, 2002). The increased smiling is so reliable that Navaho Indian parents expect every infant to begin to smile between 2 and 3 months. The person who first makes an infant smile gives a feast called the "First Laugh Ceremony" (Chisholm, 1996).

When infants smile there is a subtle asymmetry in the side of the mouth showing a larger aperture. When adults speak, the right side of the mouth opens more than the left, reflecting left hemisphere dominance. It is of interest that when 5- to 12-month-old infants smile, the left side of the mouth opens more than the right, suggesting a larger right-hemisphere contribution to the brain state that produced the smile (Holowka & Petitto, 2002).

The fact that endogenous smiling (that is, smiling without an obvious provocation) disappears at 2 to 3 months in both blind and normal infants implies the influence of brain maturation. The endogenous smile of the first 8 weeks appears to be mediated by the pontine tegmentum and does not require the cerebral cortex. Two anencephalic infants, with largely intact brainstems but no higher structures, displayed endogenous smiles (Harmon & Emde, 1972; Luyendijk & Treffers, 1992). As with the disappearance of the grasp reflex, cortical inhibition of brainstem nuclei probably contributes to the decrease in endogenous smiling (Emde & Harmon, 1972).

Sudden Infant Death Syndrome

Although cortical inhibition of the brainstem is an important phase in development, it can pose a risk to some infants. Sudden Infant Death Syndrome (SIDS), which occurs in approximately 1 per 1,000 live-born infants, is defined as the sudden death of an infant without obvious provocative circumstances or a pathology attributable to a prior health history.

The peak age of SIDS is between 3 and 4 months (Herschkowitz, Kagan, & Zilles, 1997). Some SIDS patients have smaller nuclei in the brainstem circuits participating in cardiorespiratory control, and the total number of neurons is reduced. This fact could be due to abnormal migration of neurons to the brainstem during gestation (Ansari, Sibbons, & Howard, 2001; Harper, 2001; Kinney, McHugh, Miller, Belliveau, & Assmann, 2002; Macchi, Snenghi, De Caro, & Parenti, 2002; Matturri, Biondo, Suarez-Mier, & Rossi, 2002; Schechtman, Lee, Wilson, & Harper, 1996). Other SIDS infants show reduced myelination of tracts linking cortical areas to the brainstem. If brainstem mechanisms controlling respiration are compromised or immature, the increased cortical inhibition of the brainstem at 2 months could place some infants at risk for respiratory failure (Herschkowitz et al., 1997). This hypothesis is supported by a prospective study of four pairs of twins, born prematurely and assessed as newborns, in which one member of the pair died of SIDS between 2 and 5 months of age. The twin with SIDS, compared with the co-twin, was less motorically active when awake, but more reactive to the presentation of a highly contoured bull's-eye. Because cortical projections to the brainstem mute reactivity to highly contoured visual events, this result implies less effective cortical control by SIDS patients (Riese, 2003).

CIRCADIAN RHYTHM

Although the fetus shows a cyclical pattern of rest and activity during the few months before birth, the regularity of this pattern disappears at birth and does not reemerge until the transition at 8 to 12 weeks (Glotzbach & Edgar, 1994). The fetal rhythm is regulated primarily by the mother's physiology (Davis, 1997); hence, the postnatal infant must reestablish his own circadian rhythm. This requires maturation of the retinal-thalamic projection to the suprachiasmatic nucleus (SCN) in the hypothalamus and the pineal gland. The SCN, the brain's clock in the anterior hypothalamus, and changes in melatonin synthesis in the pineal gland, are the most important mechanisms for reestablishing a circadian rhythm (Kennaway, Goble, & Stamp, 1996; Lieberman, 1986; Sandyk, 1992; Swaab, Goudsmit, Kremer, Hofman, & Ravid, 1992). Photons of light striking the retina are transformed into electrical signals that travel along the optic tract to the SCN and eventually induce neurons to adopt an approximate 24-hr light–dark cycle. The SCN of the newborn contains only 10% to 15% of the number of neurons in the adult (about 20,000). But the number of neurons and the volume of the pineal gland increase during the transition at 8 to 12 weeks.

Changes in external light modulate the rate of synthesis of melatonin. When light is increasing, melatonin secretion is inhibited; when light is decreasing, melatonin synthesis is increased. Melatonin is synthesized from its precursor, serotonin, with the aid of the rate-limiting enzyme N-acetyl-transferase (whose activity increases postnatally; Attanasio, Rager, & Gupta, 1986; Li & Borjigin, 1998). During the evening hours, as the light fades, activity of the enzyme N-acetyl-transferase, which contributes to the synthesis of melatonin, is increased and induces sleep in a process that is accelerated between 1 and 3 months. The periodicity of the day–night cycle of melatonin concentration in the serum is established by 3 months (Kennaway et al., 1996).

Melatonin is a potent molecule for it slows cell division and increases the sensitivity of the HPA-axis to negative feedback. One implication, not mentioned in chapter 2, is that embryos conceived in the Northern Hemisphere during August and September, when the light is decreasing, would be subject to increasing levels of melatonin from the mother. The brain development of embryos or fetuses with a particular genome might be affected by the increase in melatonin in ways that could affect their future behavior. It is relevant that one sample of patients with anorexia were more likely than bulimic patients to be conceived between July and September (Waller et al., 2002).

Changes in rapid eye movement during sleep (called REM sleep) are also observed between 2 and 3 months. The newborn spends almost one half of her total sleep time in REM and enters REM sleep soon after her eyes close. However, by 3 months, REM sleep accounts for only 30% of sleep time, and the initial sleep period is free of REM, a pattern characteristic of adults (Attanasio et al., 1986; Kennaway et al., 1996; Sandyk, 1992).

Finally, it is probably not a coincidence that alpha frequencies in the EEG (4 to 8 Hz) and a clearer ERP waveform to a novel sound also appear at the transition. These phenomena imply enhanced synchronization of pyramidal neurons in occipital, parietal, and temporal areas (Kushnerenko, Ceponiene, Balan, Fellman, & Naatanen, 2002; Thomas et al., 1997).

THE CHANGE IN BASES FOR ATTENTION

The bases for the recruitment and maintenance of behavioral indexes of attention (that is, prolonged orientation to an event) are altered after the transition. We noted earlier that, during the first 8 weeks, duration of attentiveness is influenced primarily by the physical features of the event, especially variation in contour and motion in the visual modality and frequency, intensity, and rhythm in the auditory mode. After the transition, duration of attention is modulated to a greater degree by the relation between the event and the infant's acquired schemata for that class of event; that is, by features in the event that are shared with features in the infant's cognitive representation. This fact is true for family-reared as well as institutionalized infants (Fantz & Nevis, 1967).

THE CONCEPT OF SCHEMA

One important reason why recruitment of attention to a discrepant event is not automatic before the transition is that infants must relate the present event to an acquired schema. This process is fragile during the first 2 months because of the structural immaturity of the connections between the entorhinal and perirhinal cortex and hippocampus (structures that evaluate the relation of an event to acquired knowledge), on the one hand, and the frontal cortex, which directs and sustains attention to the event, on the other (Geva, Gardner, & Karmel, 1999). The most fundamental psychological structures acquired during the first year are: (a) perceptual schemata for events that originate in vision, audition, and touch; (b) visceral schemata for taste, smell, pain, posture, and other bodily states; (c) sensory–motor schemes; and (d) associations that link external events and brain states with behaviors (for example, babbling to the sight of the mother).

A perceptual schema consists of a pattern of features that vary in essentialness, where essentialness is defined as the probability of recognizing the event when that feature is present. Thus, the eyes are more essential features of the schema for a face than the chin or ears. Perceptual schemata differ from visceral schemata in important ways. Perceptual schemata originate in patterns of distinct elements in space or time. For example, the representation of a table set for dinner contains a variety of distinct objects in a spatial pattern; the visceral schemata for the taste of honeyed sweet potatoes is a gestalt representing an unanalyzed sensation. Further, perceptual schemata are more easily retrieved from memory than visceral schemata. Most children can retrieve schemata for a circus clown seen 6 years ago, but cannot retrieve as easily the taste of a chocolate bar eaten an hour ago. One reason for this difference is that visceral schemata have a weaker link than perceptual schemata to semantic structures. Bodily activity synapses on the corticomedial and central areas of the amygdala; visual, auditory, and tactile stimuli synapse on the lateral area. Reciprocal connections between the lateral nucleus and cortical association areas containing semantic forms are richer than the connections between the corticomedial and central areas of the amygdala and association cortex. Hence, associations between visceral schemata and language are less well elaborated. That is probably why all human languages have fewer words to describe the sensations that originate in smell, taste, or internal bodily activity, than words for varied shapes, sizes, textures, and sound qualities. This limitation means that humans find it difficult to describe their feelings.

Schemata represent the first psychological forms to emerge from the brain activity evoked by an event, but the vocabulary describing schemata should not be used to describe the neuronal activity that is the foundation of the psychological form. For example, the repeated presentation of a tone (of a specific frequency) followed by a brief electric shock led to a shift in the tuning frequency of the receptive fields in the sensory neurons of an animal's auditory cortex, suggesting that these neurons had acquired a representation of the relation between the tone and shock (Weinberger, 2003). However, the change in tuning frequency in these neurons should not be called a schema because the same change in tuning frequency occurs if the shock is omitted, and the tone is followed by direct electrical stimulation of the basal nucleus of Meynert. The schema that represents the tone–shock sequence is different from the schema that represents the sequence of a tone followed by activity in the basal nucleus of Meynert.

This position is not without controversy. One leading neuroscientist, who defined a representation of experience as "a neural event that represents some cause in the sensorium," left the term *cause* vague because he appreciated that events that produce different neural patterns could create the same schematic representation (Friston, 2002). A 3 × 5 in. black and white and 5 × 8 in. color photograph of the same face would create different neural patterns in the occipital lobe, but might create the same perceptual schema. Adults listening to repetitions of a consonant–vowel combination, for example, "ba," do not consciously detect the appearance of a slight variation in this sound because they assimilate it to their schema for "ba," although their brain displays a distinct ERP wave form at 200 msec to the slight acoustic variation. The perceptual schema for "ba" was unchanged by the slight variation, but the brain detected it. That is why the vocabulary that describes the brain activity that is the foundation of a schema must be different from the vocabulary that describes the psychological representation.

It will be useful to invent one construct to explain the relation between an event and a subsequent brain state, but a different construct to account for the relation between the same event and a subsequent psychological state. This argument is not a defense of Cartesian dualism, which, for good reasons, frustrates scientists. We do not argue for two qualitatively distinct forces in nature, only for different vocabularies to describe the structures and processes that represent psychological, compared with neurobiological, events. Readers will recall that adults display a negative wave form at 170 msec to pictures of faces, but not to a pair of small black dots enclosed in a circle. However, if the adults first see a series of schematic faces, they show the negative waveform at 170 msec to the pair of small black dots. This fact requires positing a schema for faces to explain the absence of the waveform when the participants saw only the black dots, but the presence of the waveform when they saw the schematic faces before the encircled black dots, although the evocative stimulus was identical in both cases.

Although we define a schema as a psychological representation of an "event," some eminent developmental scholars have suggested that infants create schematic representations of "objects" (Kellman & Spelke, 1983; Spelke, 1994). Although the difference in meaning between event and object may seem like semantic nit-picking, the distinction has theoretical implications. One empirical basis for the claim that young infants perceive objects is that infants looked longer at a disconnected than at a connected rod after first being familiarized on a rod partially covered with an occluder that moved back and forth in front of them. Because infants usually look longer at unfamiliar than at familiar events that have no affective associations, the investigators assumed that the infants "inferred" the presence of a continuous object behind the occluder. They looked longer at the disconnected rod, assumed to be the less familiar of the two events. However, 4-month-olds look longer at a vertical arrangement of a series of disconnected bars that form a grating after first being habituated on this grating that had an occluder across the middle of the stimulus. Although one could argue that the grating of many bars was perceived as a unitary object, it is equally reasonable to suggest that the disconnected bars of the grating recruited more attention because they had greater contour density than the series of connected bars (Kawabata, Gyoba, Inoue, & Ohtsubo, 2001). A second argument for assuming the perception of objects is the observation that infants are more likely to reach toward a solid object that is graspable than toward a pile of sand or cranberry juice in a bowl.

This issue turns on the distinction between the processes of "perception" and those of "inference." All investigators agree that infants can perceive the differences among a ball, a pile of sand, and a bowl of cranberry juice. It is less obvious, however, that they "infer" that the clearly bounded contour of a ball means it is a stable "object." It might mean only that it invites being grasped.

The brains of humans and animals are biologically prepared to display very particular responses to certain classes of events. Frogs protrude their tongue to a fly that passes in front of the eyes. Newborns suck a plastic nipple placed in their mouth, protrude their tongue to a nipple slowly approaching their face but retreat to a nipple approaching at a fast velocity, and close their fingers over a nipple placed in their palm. These automatic motor reactions do not require any inference about the object status of the nipple. Thus, there is a subtle, but theoretically important, difference in meaning between the following two sentences:

1. The infant grasped the ball.
2. The infant perceived the ball as an object.

The first sentence is an empirical observation; the second sentence is a hypothesis. The imaginative suggestion that young infants create representations of objects is a potentially important hypothesis with some empirical support. Future research will determine the validity of this seminal idea.

Distinctiveness of Features

The distinctiveness of a feature that is a component of an event refers to the probability that it will recruit attention and be preserved as a component of a schema. Motion is almost always a distinctive feature. However, the distinctiveness of a feature is rarely absolute and is usually a function of the event in which it is a component, as well as the particular discrimination the agent is making. A shout is maximally distinctive in a forest, but not on a city street.

Five-month-olds looking at video clips of different women performing distinctly different acts (for example, brushing their teeth or combing their hair) preferentially attend to the actions, rather than the facial features, of the women. However, when the event is a static scene, infants preferentially attend to the details of the women's faces, rather than the position of their arms (Bahrick, Gogate, & Ruize, 2002).

The oval shape and spatial arrangement of the eyes, nose, and mouth are distinctive features of the human face. However, if psychologists constructed a mask with the eyes placed close to the mouth, the discrepant location of the eyes would be more distinctive than their shape. Infants who were first familiarized on four different toy cats placed in front of them played longer with a toy dog than with a novel instance of a toy cat. But infants of the same age who were familiarized first on four toy dogs did not play longer with a toy cat than with a new dog, suggesting an asymmetry in the relative distinctiveness of toy dogs versus toy cats (Mareschal, Powell, & Valein, 2003).

The relative, rather than the absolute, distinctiveness of the shape of an object was revealed in an experiment in which infants saw a human hand move, over a series of trials, to touch a toy. Infants were more attentive when the shape of the toy changed than when the path of motion changed, suggesting that the toy's shape was more distinctive than the path of motion of the hand. However, when an inanimate rod, rather than a human hand, moved to contact an object, infants were more attentive when the rod changed its path of motion than when the object assumed a different shape (Woodward, 1998). Some psychologists believe that young infants possess a schema for the goal-directed quality of human actions. If this were true, the path of motion of a human hand would not be a distinctive feature whereas the object contacted would be distinctive. If infants did not attribute goals to moving inanimate rods, they should regard a change in direction of motion as more distinctive than the object contacted.

However, infants usually attend to the features of new events that are less, rather than more, frequent—that is, discrepant from their experience. Infants regularly see human hands move toward objects, but rarely see a rod move toward an object. Hence, the latter event is more distinctive and should attract more attention. The behavior of infant chimpanzees (10–32 weeks old) supports the principle that the distinctiveness of a feature depends on the nature of the total event. Chimps looking at different photos of a woman's face looked longer when the two eyes were looking directly ahead rather than when the eyes were averted. But when the photos contained rearrangements of the eyes, nose, and mouth (to create a scrambled facial pattern), the animals did not look longer at the face with the eyes gazing directly at them compared with the one with eyes averted (Yamakoshi, Tomonaga, Tanaka, & Matsuzawa, 2003). The distinctiveness of a feature always depends on the larger context in which it is embedded. That is why neurons in the cat's primary auditory cortex respond with greater activity to a particular tone when it is infrequent than when the same tone is presented frequently (Ulanovsky, Las, & Nelken, 2003).

THE RELATION BETWEEN DEGREE
OF DISCREPANCY AND ATTENTION

Most inferences about an infant's knowledge and cognitive abilities are based on small differences in the duration of behavioral orientation to an event, or in the distribution of orientations to pairs of simultaneously presented events (which psychologists assume covary with a hypothetical state of attention). It is important, therefore, to understand the multiple determinants of duration of orientation.

At least three factors control the distribution and duration of an infant's attention to an event: its physical properties, relation to acquired schemata, and associations with pain or pleasure. We noted that the physical properties of amount and density of contour, circularity, symmetry, curvilinearity, motion, and color in the visual mode, and frequency, rhythm, and loudness in the auditory mode, exert primary control during the first 8 weeks. Although these properties continue to be of some influence, they begin to share power with the degree of discrepancy between an event and the infant's schema for that class of event after the transition.

Every event consists of essential and less essential features from the perspective of a perceiving agent. We noted earlier that the essentialness of a feature is defined by ease of recognition of an event in which it is a component. The distinctiveness of a feature, by contrast, is defined by its ability to alert the infant. A child can be alerted by a distinctive event that it does not recognize (loud sound) and can recognize an event that is not distinctive (for example, the mother's voice). The presence of essential features permits rapid, almost automatic, recognition of an event.

The essential features of a schema that permit recognition of an event also vary with the target of the identification. When the mother and father are simultaneously looking at the infant, the amount and arrangement of hair are more essential features of the mother's face. But when the mother and aunt are looking at the infant, the arrangement of eyes, nose, and mouth become more essential. Thus, the schema for a frequently encountered event contains a large number of features; only some are activated in particular acts of recognition. The same principle holds for sensory motor schemes and, as we shall see, for semantic networks. This principle has an analogy in biology. Every cell in the body (except the germ cells) has the same set of genes; the degree of activation of each depends on the specific tissue in which the gene is located.

Every event bears some relation to the infant's store of schemata. At one end are those events for which the infant possesses no relevant schemata (for example, a golf club). As a result, there is no attempt at assimilation and minimal attention. At the other end are events for which the infant possesses schemata for all the relevant features (for example, a favorite rattle). These events are assimilated quickly with minimal attention. Two broad categories of events lie between these two extremes. One category refers to events that share less essential features, but lack essential ones, and therefore, require an extreme level of cognitive effort to assimilate. Four-month-olds show less prolonged attention to a three-dimensional mask of a human face that has no eyes, mouth, or nose than to a normal face because the featureless mask lacks the essential features of a face. Hence, the young infant's brain-mind detects no relation between the event and its knowledge and does not attempt a comparison.

A second category refers to events that share essential, but not less essential, features with the infant's schema. Although these events require some effort, they are assimilated more easily and infants attend to them for the longest period of time. Four-month-olds display prolonged attention, as well as a smile and a decrease in heart rate, to the mask of a normal human face because it contains the essential features of their schema for human faces, but lacks the less essential features of movement, speech, and an attached body (Kagan, Henker, Hen-tov, Levine, & Lewis, 1966).

Four-month-olds shown the faces in Fig. 3.11 looked longer at the faces with the proper configuration of facial features than at the ones with reorganized features, although the latter are less familiar, because the former lack the less essential features of the three-dimensional faces infants encounter in their daily lives. By 1 year, however, infants devote more attention to the rearranged faces because their schemata for human faces have become firmer. Hence they assimilate the regular faces quickly, and recognize the possible relation of the rearranged faces to their schemata for normal faces.

The significance of the transition at 2 to 3 months is revealed in a study in which 2-, 4-, and 6-month-old infants sat across from an unfamiliar woman who either interacted with the infant as a parent would or sat, with an immobile face, displaying either a neutral, happy, or sad expression. The 4-month-olds looked longer when the stranger was interacting as a parent would than when she was immobile, because the former event

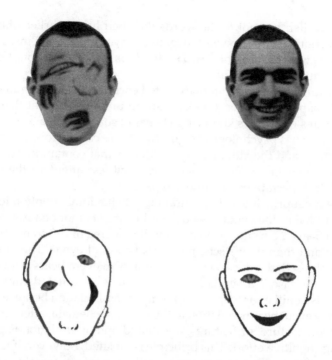

FIG. 3.11.   Set of achromatic two-dimensional faces shown to infants.

shared essential but not less essential features with the infant's schemata. The 2-month-olds were less able to relate the stranger in either posture to their schemata for the humans they had encountered in the past, and therefore, looked equally long at both events (Rochat, Striano, & Blatt, 2002).

Events that lack essential features, but contain less essential ones, elicit a state we might describe as, "What could that be?" Events that contain essential features but lack less essential ones create a state one might regard as, "Aha, I recognize what that is." Adults regard the latter events as more aesthetic (Hekkert, Snelders, & van Wieringen, 2003). ERPs show some promise of differentiating between these two states. Infants 5 to 8 months old showed a positive waveform between 750 and 1600 msec to the unexpected appearance of a stimulus that was familiar to the infant—this is the "aha" reaction. However, they showed a negative waveform with the same latency to the unexpected presentation of a totally unfamiliar stimulus—this is the "what could that be" reaction (Richards & Hunter, 2002).

A strikingly parallel result occurred in adults who saw or heard a long list of familiar words, but were tested with familiar and new words presented only in the visual mode on a screen. The participants showed a larger positive waveform (at about 200 msec) to the familiar words they had seen earlier, but not to the words they had heard earlier (this is the "aha" reaction). They showed a negative waveform (at 400 msec) to the new words, whether seen or heard earlier (this is the "what could that be" reaction; Curran & Dien, 2003).

The distinction between an unexpected encounter with a familiar event (a bar of soap on a dinner plate) versus an unfamiliar event that shares some features with one's knowledge (a bar of soap with black, green, and white stripes) has psychological significance. We call the former a *violation of expectations* and the latter *discrepant*. Events that contain no features of acquired schemata, which we call *novel*, elicit less attention than events that violate expectations or are discrepant.

The seminal principle is that duration of behavioral attention to a neutral event (that is, the event has no prior history of emotionally-tinged experience) bears a curvilinear relation to the degree of difference between the event and the infant's schema for that class of event. This statement can be rephrased; the duration of attention to an event bears a curvilinear relation to the ease of assimilation. If the event is assimilated immediately because it is familiar, or there is no attempt at assimilation because the features of the event bear no relation to the infant's schemata, attention is less than if some feature, or features, are shared and assimilation is possible following cognitive effort. This principle is violated, however, if the event has a prior history of pleasure or pain. Although infants usually pay more attention to an unfamiliar than to a familiar face, this preference can be reversed if an initially unfamiliar person gazing at the infant had given her some sugar water moments earlier. Under those conditions, 3-month-olds look longer at the adult who gave them the sweetened water than at a totally unfamiliar person (Blass & Camp, 2001; Morrongiello, Lasenby, & Lee, 2003). Infants, like adults, are often in conflict between remaining in a place that has been a source of pleasure and seeking a less familiar place.

There is robust support for the claim that infants do not always look longer at an unfamiliar than at a more familiar event. Seven-month-olds looked longer at an object that was moving in synchrony with a sound than at an object that was not synchronized during the initial period of familiarization. When the infants were tested, either after the familiarization, or following a delay of 7 days, they continued to look longer at the synchronously moving object than at the less familiar event. One interpretation is that an event that evokes another representation (because of past experience in home or laboratory) usually recruits more prolonged attention than one without any associations. That is why 7.5-month-old infants looked longer at the vocal source of short sentences containing words they had been familiarized with a day earlier than at the source of spoken sentences speaking totally unfamiliar words (Houston & Jusczyk, 2003). Most studies that use duration of attention as an index of a schema present an originally unfamiliar event that has few or no associations with other schemata. As a result, infants become bored quickly and look longer at a less familiar event on a test trial. Seven-month-olds look longer at a mask of a human face with the proper arrangement of eyes, nose and mouth than at a mask with no facial features because the former elicits associations that maintain attention. Thus, a longer bout of attention to an unfamiliar than a familiar event is most likely to occur when the latter fails to evoke a set of associated representations (see Ghazanfar & Logothetis, 2003, for a similar result in monkeys, and Harley, Putman, & Roitblat, 2003, for dolphins). This principle implies that, following familiarization with a face moving behind an occluder that hid the nose and mouth, infants shown a complete face or a disconnected one would look longer at the former (see the earlier discussion of the issue of whether infants perceive objects versus events).

Support for the curvilinear function relating attention to discrepancy comes from a study in which 7-month-olds were first familiarized with either the sphere (a) or the cylinder (d) illustrated in Fig. 3.12. When the infant struck a bright yellow padded lever, she was allowed a 2½-sec view of either the sphere (or the cylinder). After the child habituated—that is, the child stopped hitting the lever because of boredom—different groups of infants saw one of the four other stimuli in the figure. Infants familiarized on the sphere saw either the pear-shaped object (b), club (c), cylinder (d), or the irregularly shaped styrofoam object (e), whenever they struck the lever. Infants who had been familiarized on the cylinder saw either the club, the pear-shaped object, sphere, or styrofoam object. The patterns of increased attention (dishabituation) revealed a curvilinear function. Infants who were familiarized on the sphere showed their greatest dishabituation to the club, which was moderately discrepant from the sphere. However, infants habituated on the cylinder showed their longest bout of

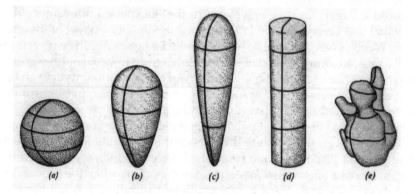

FIG. 3.12. Three-dimensional shapes shown to infants.

attention to the sphere. No group showed their greatest dishabituation to the irregular styrofoam object. Thus, attention to an unfamiliar event was a curvilinear function of the psychological distance between the event and the child's schema (Hopkins, Zelazo, Jacobson, & Kagan, 1976). The curvilinear principle is also valid when the stimuli are novel, multisyllable utterances (Saffran & Thiessen, 2003).

The curvilinear function relating attention to discrepancy, which is a reliable phenomenon by 3 months, also applies to the distribution of attention after language has emerged in the second year. Mayan children from the Yucatan Peninsula and Boston children, 1 to 3 years old, were shown four different masks of a male face (a regular face; a face with the eyes, ears, and nose rearranged; a blank face; and a face with a single eye on the forehead) as well as a meaningless styrofoam form. The 3-year-olds from both cultural settings showed their longest initial bout of attention to the face with the features rearranged, and their shortest bout of attention to the styrofoam form, although the latter was the least familiar object (Finley, Kagan, & Layne, 1972).

The adult judgment that a play, novel, or scientific idea is creative is most likely when the less essential, rather than the most essential, ideas of the community's semantic networks have been altered. That is why Joyce's "Finnegan's Wake" and Monet's paintings were not initially regarded as creative. It took several decades before the public mind was ready for these novel artistic products. The content of the themes dominating the front pages of newspapers from eight societies (including Canada, France, and the United States) was similar over a 300-year interval. Discrepant events had the highest probability of being a front-page story. Murder, suicide, rape, unusual heroism, and abandonment of a family, were the most frequent headline stories (Davis & McLeod, 2003).

The ERP waveforms occasionally, but not always, reflect the curvilinear relation between attention and discrepancy. Six-month-old infants showed a larger negative waveform to the unexpected appearance of a face that had been viewed 6 to 12 trials earlier than to a novel or inverted face (Webb & Nelson, 2001). Adults showed a larger negative waveform at 350 msec to a familiarized object presented in an unusual or unexpected perspective (for example, an umbrella in an open position) than to an unfamiliar object presented in an unusual perspective. The mind-brain automatically related the familiar object in the anomalous perspective to the schema for that object as it usually appeared, and, as a result, was surprised. However, this reaction did not occur to unfamiliar objects (Schendon & Kutas, 2003). It cannot be a coincidence that monkeys showed the largest increases in brainstem secretion of dopamine when the probability of a food reward, signaled by a conditioned stimulus, was between .25 and .75. The increase in dopamine was minimal when the conditioned stimulus signaled either that no reward would be delivered or the probability was 1.0 that the reward would occur (Fiorillo, Tobler, & Schultz, 2003). That is, the amount of dopamine released was an inverted U function of the probability of reward. We noted in chapter 1 that events categorized as rewards are often those that create uncertainty because they are unexpected.

Because scientists are rarely certain of the form or firmness of an infant's schema for an event, they are usually unable to predict which of several discrepant events will recruit the longest bout of attention. For example, 16-month-old infants sat beside an examiner who named a picture on a screen (e.g., "that's a duck") either while the adult looked at the infant or while she looked away from the infant. Most infants who see two objects look longer at the one that an adult names, presumably because the child is trying to assimilate the object to the schema for that object as he or she hears its name. However, the children in this study had two competing incentives for attention: (a) the adult's discrepant posture of looking away from them and (b) hearing the object's name. The infants looked longer at the adult than at the picture on the screen that was named (Koening & Echols, 2003). There is often competition between different incentives in laboratory experiments, and therefore, scientists cannot always be certain as what to conclude from a particular pattern of attention.

In addition, failure to show increased attention to one of two events does not mean that an infant did not discriminate between them. For example, 10-month-old infants can discriminate a pair of dark circles enclosed in a circular form from a pair of dark circles placed outside a circular form, but they do not show greater attention to the latter after being familiarized with the former. The meaning of "no difference in behavioral reaction" to two different events is always equivocal (Kagan, Linn, Mount, & Reznick, 1979). The brain state that accompanies absence of body immobility (freezing) to an event that is not a conditioned stimulus (for example, seeing a stranger) is different from the brain state following extinction of a conditioned freezing reaction to a stimulus that had signaled discomfort. The prefrontal cortex is more active in the latter than in the former condition (Barrett, Schumake, Jones, & Gonzalez-Lima, 2003).

The restriction on permissible inferences from the absence of differential attention to two events limits the generalizability of conclusions regarding an infant's preferences, discriminative abilities, or schematic knowledge. Scientists should include other measurements, for example, heart rate, skin conductance, or ERPs, to arrive at more valid inferences. For example, infants who were familiarized on trios of objects that changed their shape, color, and orientation did not show an increase in attention when shown a pair of objects, but did show a change in the ERP to the two objects (Arriaga, 2001). On the other hand, infants familiarized on stimu-

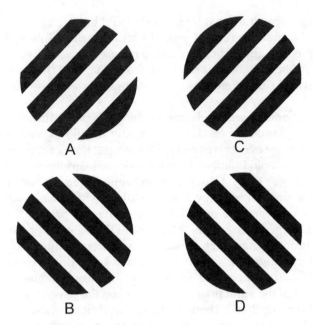

FIG. 3.13.   Stimuli shown to infants in the first 6 weeks, illustrating that differential attention is dissociated from differences in the visual evoked potential.

lus A in Fig. 3.13 looked longer when shown stimulus D, although the visual evoked potentials to A and D were similar. That is, the difference in the behavioral index of attention indicated that the infants discriminated between A and D; the visual evoked potentials implied that they made no discrimination (Slater, Morison, & Somers, 1988). These facts require us to acknowledge that conclusions inferred from brain events can be different from those based on behavior. A saccade can originate in different neuronal profiles (Schall, 2004). Thus, a fixation time of a particular duration can originate in different brain states. Therefore, the occurrence or failure of an increase in attention to a new event does not have an unambiguous meaning.

There are other reasons why a difference of 1 or 2 sec in duration of attention to two events is ambiguous. First, attending to an event for 2 or 3 sec is not the only way infants reveal that they have detected the difference between a new event and a familiarized one. Infants look longer at a speaker baffle playing the babbling of an unfamiliar infant than at a speaker playing their own babbling, but they vocalize more when they hear themselves babble. Both auditory events are discrepant, for infants do not usually hear tape recordings of infant babbling. Prolonged attention appears to reflect the state created by an event that is difficult to assimilate, whereas vocalization reflects the state created by a discrepant event that is easier to match to a schema, and as a result, evokes an emotion we might call excitement. If the infant detects a discrepant event—a neighbor entering the living room—but assimilates it quickly, attention will be brief, but the infant might vocalize. If the event is difficult to assimilate, attention will be prolonged, but there may be no vocalization.

Third, infants sometimes show equivalent attention to a familiar and discrepant event presented simultaneously, but look back and forth several times between the two stimuli. They do not do so when the two stimuli are identical. Other psychologists use instrumental motor behavior, rather than orientation, to measure a schema. For example, Rovee-Collier and colleagues presented an attractive mobile to infants lying supine in a crib and tied a ribbon from each infant's foot to the mobile, so that every time each infant kicked, the mobile moved (Fagen, Morrongiello, Rovee-Collier, & Gekoski, 1984). The investigators returned days or weeks later and placed the same, or a different, mobile above each infant's crib. If the infant kicked, the investigators concluded that the infant recognized the familiar mobile; if the infant did not kick, the investigators inferred a failure of recognition. But conclusions regarding an infant's schema based on the "kicking" evidence often differ from conclusions based on differences in duration of attention.

Fourth, on occasion, smiling can reflect recognition of an event. The new brain organization that makes it possible for 12-week-olds to relate an event to a schema releases a smile when the infant recognizes an event after some effort. That is why 3-month-old infants smile to the face of a stranger. This reaction is not the endogenous smile of the newborn, but the product of a state produced by successfully relating a discrepant event to a schema following some effort in a process called *assimilation*. No smile occurs if assimilation is rapid or impossible. However, as we noted for duration of attention, if the event has a history of reward or punishment, infants will smile more at the event that had been associated with pleasant experiences. For example, they smile more often when the face and voice of the mother are accompanied by a happy, rather than a sad, facial expression (Kahana-Kalman & Walker-Andrews, 2001).

Finally, infants differ in the tendency to display several short fixations to a stimulus versus a single prolonged bout of attention. The former infants are more likely than the latter to show increased attention to a novel event. This observation does not mean that the infants who show a single long fixation do not discriminate between familiar and unfamiliar events.

Duration of attention, vocalization, smiling, shifting attention between two stimuli, instrumental motor responses, and ERPs, reveal different information about the structure and firmness of an infant's schemata for a class of events. One reason is that the brain structures that mediate detection of an unfamiliar event—the parahippocampal region and basolateral nucleus of the amygdala (which are reciprocally connected)—are not the sites that mediate the reaction following detection. The central nucleus of the amygdala is more responsible for motor and autonomic reactions following detection of a discrepancy. It is relevant that the embryological origins of the parahippocampal region and basolateral area are different from the origin of the central nucleus. Thus, the detection of a discrepancy is to be distinguished from the responses like prolonged attention that follow detection. Scientists cannot assume that an infant or animal will show an increase in attention every time it detects a discrepant event, nor assume that no change in attention implies a failure to discriminate two events.

An elegant experiment with monkeys reveals the inferential error possible when scientists use only one measure to evaluate a cognitive structure or ability. Four rhesus monkeys were trained, over many days, to make a simple motor response to a particular human face projected on a screen. After the animals had learned to discriminate this standard face from others, the psychologist altered the features of the standard face to determine the most essential features of the monkey's schema for the standard face. As expected, the monkeys responded more when the size or the location of the eyes was altered, but were less affected by alterations in the nose or chin, suggesting that the size and placement of the eyes were the more essential features of the animal's schema for the standard face. But, surprisingly, some monkeys showed no change in motor response to a face with no eyes at all (Keating & Keating, 1993). This unexpected result invites one reasonable and one unreasonable explanation. The latter implies that monkeys perceive faces in a manner that is qualitatively different from humans, for no child would treat a face with no eyes as equivalent to one with eyes. If this explanation were correct, a great deal of psychological theory would have to be rewritten. Hence, the more reasonable interpretation is that the motor response is ambiguous in meaning and can be evoked by more than one condition. We believe that this is the proper inference, and therefore, urge caution when scientists rely on only one response, whether fixation time or instrumental kicking, to evaluate a perceptual or conceptual representation in an infant. *No behavior has one and only one meaning.*

This state of affairs in infant research shares features with quantum events. The ways photons reveal their presence vary with the procedure used to measure them. Under some experimental conditions, they appear to be wavelike; under other conditions, they appear as particles. A schema for an event, for example, a parent's face, can be revealed in different ways depending on the eliciting conditions. If the parent approaches the infant with a smile, the infant is likely to babble and return the smile. If the parent's face is immobile, the infant is likely to stare or cry. If the parent is wearing ski goggles for the first time, the infant is likely to turn away or frown. The nature of the infant's schema for the mother, like the nature of a photon, is unknowable. The information used for inference, and theory, are phenomena observed under varied experimental conditions. Hence, conclusions about an infant's schema for an event should be tempered if the only evidence is a longer bout of attention to one event rather than another.

Three-year-olds, who are considerably more mature than infants, stare for several seconds when a toy that had rolled down a ramp and struck an occluder suddenly appeared on the other side of the occluder; a physically impossible event. However, the same children fail to search correctly for the toy at the place where the occluder rests. If the prolonged staring meant that the children knew the toy could not be on the other side of the occluder, they should have searched in the correct place. Because they did not do so, it seems a mistake to attribute knowledge about physical impossibility to the "looking time" measure (Hood, Cole-Davies, & Dias, 2003). A single measure rarely reveals everything scientists wish to know about a phenomenon, a conclusion that applies to cognitive structures and emotional states as well.

RECOGNITION MEMORY: HOW LONG IS A SCHEMA PRESERVED?

Although developmental scientists would like to know how long a schema for an event experienced briefly is preserved, this question has no single answer. The duration of preservation of a schema depends on (a) the physical nature and familiarity of the event, (b) the duration of exposure, (c) the length of delay between the original exposure and the time of testing, and (d) the evidence used to decide whether the infant did or did not retrieve a schema for the original event, and of course, the infant's state at the time of testing (Rose et al., 2003). There can be no single number that reflects the length of time a schema is preserved because estimates based on looking time will be different from estimates based on ERPs, changes in heart rate, or instrumental kicking. The estimated age of a human fossil changed dramatically when radioactivity was the source of evidence, and current estimates may be altered when new, as yet undiscovered, methods are exploited in the future. A cosmologist answered a reporter wanting to know the age of the universe by saying that the method used to generate the estimate was of greater interest than the estimated age.

The Visual Paired Comparison Test (VPCT) is one procedure used to test the duration of preservation of a schema. The infant is first shown an attractive object never seen before (for example, a blue sphere) and, after a delay, usually less than 15 sec, is shown two objects: the blue sphere seen earlier alongside an equally attractive, novel object (Diamond, 1990b; McKee & Squire, 1993). (The fact that the two objects are equally attractive is assessed by exchanging the objects used for familiarization and the testing of recognition memory.) One-month-olds are unlikely to look longer at the novel event if the delay is longer than 5 sec, whereas 3-month-olds will do so following delays as long as 10 sec. These facts suggest that the schema for the familiarized blue sphere was preserved for a longer period in the older infant (Kagan, 1984).

Three-and-a-half-month-olds first saw identical pairs of moving events on a monitor. The events were either (a) red and yellow forms appearing sequentially to form a checkerboard pattern, or (b) different colored disks appearing sequentially, first in a clockwise flow to form a wheel and then in a counterclockwise flow. Some infants were familiarized on the moving checkerboard pattern, others on the moving disks. Infants then experienced different delays before their recognition memory was tested by showing them the familiar and unfamiliar events. Some infants were tested after 1 min, some after 1 day, and some after 1 month.

Infants this young required a full 30 sec of familiarization to create a schema sufficiently firm to allow them to look longer at the novel event when the delay between familiarization and test was 1 min. The infants tested after a 1-month delay looked longer at the familiar rather than the novel event because their schema for the original event had lost some of its features over the 30-day period. As a result, the event that had been familiar originally was now perceived as moderately discrepant from the child's original schema (Courage & Howe, 2001).

Five-and-a-half-month-olds saw video clips representing different women performing distinct acts. If they were tested 1 min later, they looked longer at the less familiar scene. But if tested 7 weeks later, they looked longer at the familiar scene because the features of the original schema had faded and the original event was now discrepant (Bahrick, Gogate, & Ruize, 2002).

Infants under 6 months usually require more exposure to establish a schema than older infants, even events as meaningful as an unfamiliar human face. Infants 5, 7, and 12 months old were shown a pair of faces on successive trials. One face always remained the same whereas the other face changed on each trial. The variable of interest was the number of trials required before the infant looked longer at the novel than at the familiar face. The 5-month-olds required 19 exposures to the familiar face before they looked longer at the novel one; the 12-month-olds required only

10 trials (Rose, Feldman, & Jankowski, 2001; see also Richards, 1997). When the measure of preservation is a kicking response that produces movement in an attractive mobile, most 3-month-olds do not kick the familiar mobile when the delay between initial conditioning and test is as long as 1 to 3 days (Boller, Rovee-Collier, Gulya, & Prete, 1996).

The Neural Bases for Recognition Memory

Hippocampus. It is likely that maturation of the hippocampus contributes to, but does not determine, the improved ability of 3-month-olds to recognize an event following a delay because the greatest increase in the velocity of growth of the human hippocampus occurs between 2 and 3 months (Kretschman, Kammradt, Krauthausen, & Sauer, 1986). Specifically, the mossy cells of the hippocampal dentate gyrus, which participate in the formation of schemata, undergo a spurt of differentiation during the 2- to 3-month transition (Seress & Mrzljak, 1992).

Studies of monkeys provide information on the brain structures involved in recognition memory (Bachevalier, 1990; Bachevalier, Brickson, & Hagger, 1993). Because the rate of maturation of the monkey brain is about 3 to 4 times that of the human, a 3-week-old infant monkey is comparable to a 2- to 3-month-old human infant (Diamond, 1990a). Rhesus monkey infants did not show signs of recognition of a familiar event after a delay as long as 10 sec until they were 3 weeks old, comparable to 8 to 12 weeks in the human infant. Further, this ability is lost if the hippocampus and contiguous entorhinal cortex are removed before the monkey is 3 weeks old, but is not lost following early removal of area TE in the inferior temporal lobe. The latter lesion does affect recognition memory in the adult. These facts suggest that maturation of the hippocampus at 2 to 3 months makes an important contribution to the preservation of a schema and to the ability to relate an event to a schema formed 10 to 20 sec earlier (Bachevalier et al., 1993).

VISUAL EXPECTATIONS

The hippocampal maturation at 2 to 3 months might also contribute to the infant's ability to establish a primitive form of expectation (Haith, Benson, Roberts, & Pennington, 1994). Infants lying on their back saw one monitor on their left and a second monitor on their right. Colored pictures of schematic faces, bull's-eyes, checkerboards, stripes, and diamond shapes appeared alternately on each monitor. A picture appeared for 700 msec on one monitor, followed by an interval of 1100 msec when both monitors were dark, after which a different picture appeared on the monitor on the opposite side. This alternation of pictures continued for 1.5 min, or a total of about 40 alternations. Two-month-olds showed no sign of anticipation; that is, they did not look at a monitor before a picture was about to appear at that location. However, about 20% of 3½-month-olds moved their head to the monitor on which a picture was about to appear during the 1100 msec interval when both monitors were dark. These infants, who were close to the transition, behaved as if they expected to see a picture on the darkened monitor. It is likely that a more mature hippocampus contributes to this behavior.

SUMMARY

Five important changes that occur in the first half-year appear to be due to specific changes in the brain, combined, of course, with experience. These changes are: the disappearance of select brainstem reflexes, a decrease in the frequency of endogenous smiles and spontaneous crying, the establishment of a circadian rhythm, increased attention to moderately discrepant events, and enhancement of recognition memory for an event following a delay.

This view is not free of controversy. Johnson has argued effectively for the greater contribution of experience to connectivity among cortical sites and the specialization of neuronal ensembles (Johnson, 2000a, 2000b). Although we agree with Johnson that brain development is activity dependent, and acknowledge the contribution of experience to brain growth and behavior, the evidence from both animal and human infants implies that most of the universal behavioral changes that occur at 2 to 3 months cannot be hastened much by experience because of maturational constraints. No 1-week-old, no matter what her past experience, will display a behavioral or biological sign indicating that she had seen a blue ball rather than a blue block 30 sec earlier.

A key competence emerging at the transition is an enhanced ability to relate an event in the perceptual field to an acquired schema. This ability is aided by growth of the hippocampus and its increasing connectivity to perirhinal, entorhinal, and association cortices. The ability to recognize after a long delay (for example, 2 months) a new event that had been experienced briefly is seriously compromised in infants younger than 6 months. This fragile preservation of a schema could be due to fading of the original schema or an inability to relate the event in a perceptual field to an acquired schema. It is likely that both processes are operative during the first half of the first year. This argument implies that events experienced only once or twice in the first half-year, except those that were unusually salient or emotionally arousing because they were accompanied by extreme pain or pleasure, are lost forever.

The extensiveness of the biologically-prepared properties of young infants remains a major node of controversy. Some stimulus features have a privileged ability to provoke brain activity (for example, motion and contour). There is less agreement, however, on cognitive competences like the representation of stable objects, numerosity, or knowing that an object cannot pass through a barrier. This issue cannot be resolved by sole reliance on duration of behavioral attention because of the curvilinear relation between duration of attention and degree of discrepancy between the features of an event and the infant's schema. Most experiments that have led some investigators to award complex cognitive structures to infants have not adequately controlled for amount, density, or pattern of contour, form of motion, familiarity, and, especially, the fading of the features of a schema following the delay between familiarization and testing. The fact that young infants look longer at one of two events does not necessarily imply that they possess the a priori concept of the scientists who designed the experiment. Otherwise, we must award infants, who can discriminate a person with head bowed from one who is smiling, the ability to understand, or to infer, the emotions of shame and joy. Eminent 19th-century students of development believed that the newborn's immediate grasp of a pencil placed in their palm represented the origins of adult "greed." We need additional evidence in order to evaluate the validity of this bold, but potentially significant, theoretical position.

APPENDIX A

Newborn States of Arousal

State 1.   The eyes are closed, the infant is not moving, respiration is regular, and there are no rapid eye movements.

State 2.   The eyes are closed, but the muscles are more tense. Rapid eye movements are observed, breathing is irregular, and there may be spontaneous body movements, startles, or sucking responses.

State 3.   The eyes cycle between open and closed. There is increased motor activity, more rapid breathing rate, and on occasion, a smile.

State 4.   The eyes are open, and the infant scans the environment. Respiration is more rapid than in the prior states, but the body is relatively still.

State 5.   The eyes are open, there are body and limb movements, but the infant is less likely to show prolonged scanning of an external location or object.

State 6.   The eyes are open. The infant is very active. Breathing is
rapid, and there is crying or distress vocalization.

APPENDIX B

Newborn Reflexes

Body Part	Name	Description
Head and face	Head turning	Place baby face down on a mattress. Baby will turn head to side to free breathing passages.
	Rooting	Stroke baby's cheek gently near the mouth. Baby will turn head to the side that is being stroked.
	Sucking	Place a nipple-sized object in baby's mouth. Baby will start sucking movements.
	Defensive reaction	Cover the baby's nose and mouth with a cloth. Baby will turn head and move arms in an attempt to free breathing passages.
Arms	Tonic neck reflex	Turn the baby's head to one side or the other. The baby's arm will extend in the direction in which the head is turned, and the other arm will flex upward. This is also called the fencer's reflex.
	Moro reflex	Drop the baby's head slightly but abruptly. The baby's arms and legs will spread open and make an embracing movement, as if to grasp hold of something. This is a kind of startle reaction.
Hands	Palmar reflex	Lightly touch the baby's palm, and the fingers will clamp into a fist.
Torso	Swimmer's reflex	While baby is lying on its stomach, gently tap the back along the side and above the waist. The baby will twist its lower extremities toward the side that was touched.
	Crawling	Push against the soles of the baby's feet while the baby is lying on the stomach, and rudimentary crawling movements will result.
Legs	Standing reflex	Hold the baby gently under the arms while the feet touch a table. As you release support slowly, the baby will begin to show some resistance to the weight by stretching the muscles of the legs.
	Walking reflex	Hold the baby under the arms with the baby's feet touching a table and move the baby forward, keeping contact between table and feet. The baby will take "steps."
Feet	Plantar reflex	Similar to the Palmar reflex. The toes will curl inward when the instep is lightly touched.
	Babinski reflex	Gently stroke the outer side of the bottom of the baby's foot. The toes will curl outward like a fan.

4

The Second Transition:
7 to 12 Months

The second transition in the first year, which occurs in most healthy infants between 7 and 12 months, is accompanied by cognitive functions that depend more on the frontal lobe and its enhanced connectivity with other brain sites. Knowledge of the biological changes, without any psychological information, would not permit prediction of the accompanying psychological competences. However, joint appreciation of both the emerging behaviors, especially fear of unfamiliar events and imitation, and the biology, suggest that, after 7 months, infants can retrieve schemata for past events no longer in the perceptual field and hold them and their current perception in working memory while they try to assimilate the latter to the former.

RETRIEVAL OF SCHEMATA
AND WORKING MEMORY

It is important to differentiate among three cognitive processes: (a) the ability to recognize that an event in the perceptual field does or does not share features with an acquired schema, (b) the ability to retrieve a schema for an event that is not in the perceptual field, and (c) the ability to relate or to manipulate the perceptual products of the current situation with retrieved schemata over a restricted temporal interval. Psychologists call the first process recognition memory; the second, retrieval, or recall, memory; and the third, working memory, although some psychologists use the phrase *working memory* to describe both the retrieval of a schema and cognitive manipulations imposed on it. These distinctions are based on theo-retical, as well as methodological, grounds for the evidence used to infer each of these three processes differ. Psychologists most often use changes in duration of attention to infer recognition memory, but usually rely on a reaching response, or a saccade, to infer retrieval or working memory.

Working memory is the seminal process that emerges at this second transition. Four-month-olds can recognize that an event in their percep-tual field was experienced in the recent past, but they cannot retrieve their schema for an event no longer present that was experienced more than 10–15 sec earlier. The difference between a 4- and 8-month-old is analo-gous to the difference between recognition and recall memory in older children.

A longitudinal study of eight infants assessed every 2 weeks from 6 to 14 months revealed the enhancement of working memory. Each infant was administered eight tasks during each session, that varied in the diffi-culty of retrieving schemata for past events and holding them in a work-ing memory circuit for more than a few seconds. In one moderately diffi-cult task, which Piaget (1950) called object permanence, the infants had to retrieve a schema for the place where an adult had hidden an object fol-lowing a short delay between the hiding and the time when the child was permitted to reach for the object. Most infants older than 8 months, but not younger ones, reached toward the correct location, indicating they re-trieved the representation of the correct hiding place.

In a more difficult variation of this task, the examiner hid an attractive object under one of two identical cylinders, but this time placed an opaque screen between the infant and the cylinders for delays of 1, 3, or 7 sec. The examiner then removed the screen and allowed the infant to reach toward one of the cylinders. There was a linear increase with age in the probabil-ity of a correct reach. No 7-month-old reached to the correct location when the delay was as long as 7 sec; most 12-month-olds solved that problem easily (Fox, Kagan, & Weiskopf, 1979). A review of nine independent studies of working memory indicates a linear increase in the delay infants can tolerate; 7-month-olds can tolerate delays of 5 sec; 12-month-olds can tolerate a delay of 12 sec (Pelphrey et al., 2003).

The enhanced duration of working memory after 7 months is also illus-trated in a procedure in which 8-month-olds first successfully retrieve an object from one of two locations on four trials. On the next trial, the exam-iner hides the object at the other location while the infant is watching, and, following a delay, permits the infant to reach. Eight and nine-month-olds usually reach toward the first, incorrect, location, although they may look at the correct location before reaching—Piaget (1950) called this response "the A not B error" (see Fig. 4.1). The incorrect reach is due, in part, to the infant's inability to inhibit the act of reaching to a place where he or she

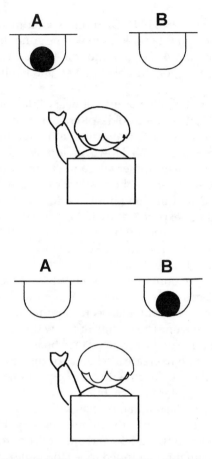

FIG. 4.1.   "A not B task"—Illustration of the Piagetian "A not B task." The child successfully retrieves an object hidden at location A for several trials and then watches the examiner hide the object at location B. As illustrated, many 9-month-old children reach toward location A.

had been rewarded on prior trials. The failure of inhibition, which implies immature frontal lobe function, is one of the three attentional networks called executive control; alerting and orienting are the other two networks (Posner & Petersen, 1990; Swanson et al., 2001).

The more important fact is that the longer the delay between hiding the object and allowing the child to reach, the less likely the infant will reach to the correct location. There was a linear increase with age in the probability of a correct reach as the delay was lengthened. One-year-olds could tolerate a 20-sec delay; most 8-month-olds could not tolerate delays longer than 3 sec. Comparable studies of infant monkeys affirm the age-related improvement in the ability to retrieve an object following increasingly long delays (Diamond, 1985, 1991; Diamond & Goldman-Rakic, 1989). The average age at which infant monkeys make the A not B error is 2 months under a 2-sec delay and 4 months under a 10-sec delay. Two and four months in a monkey are comparable to seven and twelve months in a human infant.

However, as we noted, the validity of every inference depends on the procedure. Recall that 9-month-olds often reach to the previously rewarded location in the A not B procedure, although they saw the examiner place the object at location B. However, infants show behavioral signs of surprise if they see the examiner take a toy from location A and place it at location B, and 6 sec later see the examiner retrieve that toy from location A. The surprise, and the long bout of attention to the event, suggest that the infants did not expect the toy to be at location A, and imply that these 9-month-olds had retrieved their schemata for the toy at location B, although they reached to location A. The evidence from reaching behavior suggests that the infants forgot the location of the toy; the facial expression of surprise and the long bout of attention imply that they had preserved a schema for the object's correct location (Ahmed & Ruffino, 1998).

A longitudinal study of infants, seen monthly from 6 to 11 months, yields the same conclusion. The infants first saw three identical objects (either three ducks or three dolls) arranged on a board in a triangular pattern for 15 sec—long enough to create a schema for the three identical objects. This stimulus was then replaced with a discrepant one, also composed of three objects in a triangular pattern, but the new stimulus replaced either one, two, or all three of the familiar objects with different toys after a delay of either 1 or 7 sec. For example, the infant who saw three ducks initially might see on the test trial two ducks and one doll, one duck and two dolls, or three dolls. Some infants continued to see the same set of three ducks.

The behavior of interest was the frequency with which the infant shifted her attention between any pair of objects. There was a clear increase in the frequency of shifting targets of attention at 8 months. The effect of the 7-sec delay on the frequency of shifting was greatest between 8 and 10 months; the 8-month-olds did not shift their attention between a familiar and unfamiliar object if the delay was as long as 7 sec, suggesting that they failed to retrieve their schema for the original display. By contrast, 11-month-olds shifted attention frequently between the familiar and discrepant objects following a 7-sec delay. This evidence implies that the ability to retrieve a schema of a new event that occurred more than 7 sec earlier is fragile until the child is about 9 or 10 months old (Kagan & Hamburg, 1981).

A different procedure affirms this generalization. The infants first saw on a monitor two curtained windows, A and B. The curtains opened, and a face appeared at either window A or B. A screen then covered the curtains for a delay that varied between 2 and 10 sec. The two windows then reappeared, but this time without any face, and the psychologist noted where the infant directed his attention, to window A or B. The 12-month-olds, but not the 8-month-olds, looked toward the window where the face had appeared earlier, even with a delay as long as 10 sec. The younger infants, however, could not retrieve the prior location of the face under a delay this long. Further, all infants performed less well when the number of windows was increased from two to four, but the delay was held constant at a brief 1.5 sec. This suggests that older infants find it easier to hold a schema for one of two locations for 10 sec than to hold a schema for one of four locations for a much briefer time (Pelphrey et al., 2003).

Six-and-a-half-month-old infants can detect that one of three squares, each appearing on a screen for 500 msec, changed color if there was no delay between successive stimulus presentations. However, if the delay was as brief as 250 msec, the infants appeared unable to detect the color change in one of the squares (Ross-Sheehy, Oakes, & Luck, 2003). This result illustrates the fragile status of a schema for a briefly presented novel event in infants less than 7 months old.

The improved ability to retrieve a schema for a motor act is another feature of the transition. Infants 6, 9, and 12 months old were presented with a box containing a toy train which moved on a track when the infant struck a lever. Following two training sessions, the infants were tested regularly to determine the age at which they forgot the motor response. The "forgetting" was inferred from the infant's failure to hit the lever. Six-month-olds "forgot" the motor response 2 to 3 weeks after the training; 9- and 12-month-olds forgot 6 to 8 weeks after the training (Hildreth & Rovee-Collier, 2002).

Profiles of attentiveness to discrepant events also change at the transition. Children 4 to 36 months old, born to middle-class Boston or to illiterate Mayan Indian parents living in isolated villages in Northwest Guatemala, displayed the same U-shaped relation between age and duration of attention to different masks of human faces. The 4-month-olds from both settings showed prolonged attention to the masks because they were discrepant from the schemata of the faces of familiar people who nurtured them. The 8-month-olds showed much less attention because they had firmer schemata for human faces; therefore, they assimilated the masks quickly. However, the 10- to 36-month-olds showed longer bouts of attention because they retrieved their rich set of schemata for human faces, and compared them with their current perception in working memory. This cognitive activity was accompanied by more prolonged attention (Sellers, Klein, & Minton, 1972).

BRAIN DEVELOPMENT AT THE SECOND TRANSITION

Prefrontal Cortex

The enhancement in working memory is accompanied by a spurt of growth and differentiation in both pyramidal and inhibitory interneurons in the prefrontal cortex between 8 and 12 months. The double bouquet interneurons in layer 3 show a broader distribution of dendrites, and their axons display numerous ascending and descending collaterals (Kostovic, 1990; Mrzljak et al., 1990).

This growth is accompanied by increased synaptic density in the prefrontal cortex and increased glucose uptake (measured by positron emission tomography or PET) in the lateral frontal cortex (from 6 to 8 months) and the dorsolateral prefrontal cortex (from 8 to 12 months; Chugani, 1994; Chugani, Phelps, & Mazziotta, 1987; Huttenlocher, 1974, 1979, 1990, 1994; Kostovic, Skavic, & Strinovic, 1988; Schadé & von Groenigen, 1961). The steepest increase in the density of synapses occurs between birth and 8 months and this period of intensive synapse formation is accompanied by changes in the molecular composition of glutamate receptors (McDonald & Johnston, 1990).

Changes in oxygenated and deoxygenated hemoglobin in the blood supply to the frontal lobe, based on optical scanning, affirm the role of the prefrontal cortex in working memory. A group of infants was assessed for object permanence monthly from 5 to 12 months of age. There was a significant increase in total hemoglobin and oxygenated hemoglobin in the frontal lobe on the session when the infant displayed object permanence, compared with prior sessions when the infant did not reach for the hidden toy. The increase in hemoglobin began as the examiner hid the object under the cloth and peaked 10 sec later (Baird, 2001).

Hippocampus

The entorhinal cortex, a primary source of input to the hippocampus, first establishes synapses on the small granule cells of the dentate gyrus which, in turn, send information to the CA3 region of Ammon's horn. The latter site transfers its information to the CA1 region of the hippocampus which sends efferents back to the cortex. There is an increase in the number of spines and extra-large excrescences on the proximal dendrites of pyramidal cells in the CA3 region of Ammon's horn (postsynaptic sites for the large axon terminals of the mossy fibers of the granule cells) during the first year. These changes should contribute to the enhanced working

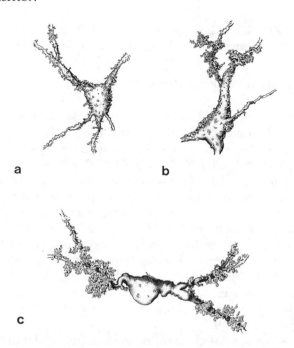

FIG. 4.2.   Mossy cells of hippocampus—Artist's rendition of camera lucida drawing of Golgi-impregnated mossy cells, illustrating the development of large complex excrescences. Somata and proximal dendrites of cells from a (a) newborn, (b) 7-month-old, and (c) 5-year-old child.

memory observed between 8 and 12 months (Seress & Mrzljak, 1992; Witter, 1993). (See Fig. 4.2.)

Although lesions of the monkey hippocampus and parahippocampal gyrus only impaired performance in the A not B task if the delay was longer than 30 sec, the integrity of the prefrontal cortex was necessary for successful A not B performance even with short delays (Diamond, Zola-Morgan, & Squire, 1989). That is why some scientists distinguish between a short-term memory store, which relies on the hippocampus and para-hippocampal gyrus, on the one hand, and working memory, which implies that some cognitive activity is imposed on the information and requires the prefrontal cortex, on the other. Anterograde tracing of the monkey brain reveals that working memory exploits an extensive brain network that includes cortical association regions, anterior cingulate cortex, prefrontal cortex, motor regions, basal ganglia, superior colliculus, hippocampus, and brainstem (Selemon & Goldman, 1988). The monkey brain displays an overproduction of synapses from birth to 2 months, followed by a plateau of synaptic density in the cortex and the dentate gyrus of the hippocampus (Bourgeois, Goldman-Rakic, & Rakic, 1994; Bourgeois

& Rakic, 1993; Rakic, Bourgeois, Eckenhoff, Zecevic, & Goldman-Rakic, 1986; Zecevic, Bourgeois, & Rakic, 1989; Zecevic & Rakic, 1991).

Cellular Basis of Working Memory

The neurons of prefrontal cortex in awake monkeys trained on delayed response tasks become active during the delay between the presentation of a target and the time when the monkey makes a response (Fuster & Alexander, 1971; Kubota & Niki, 1971), suggesting that these neurons participate in working memory. Monkeys were first trained to fixate a central spot on a screen. A target then appeared in the periphery for 0.5 sec but the monkey had to maintain fixation on the central spot during a subsequent delay period that varied between 1 and 6 sec following the disappearance of the peripheral target. When the central fixation spot (on which the monkey was focused) disappeared, the animal received a reward if it made an eye movement to the place where the peripheral target had appeared seconds earlier. Neuronal activity in 288 neurons in the prefrontal cortex was recorded during the delay (Funahashi, Bruce, & Goldman-Rakic, 1989; Goldman-Rakic, 1990).

Activity in a special group of neurons in the caudal dorsolateral prefrontal cortex rose sharply when the target disappeared and remained tonically active during the delay. The activity ceased abruptly when the fixation spot disappeared and the animal made a saccade to the target's location. These neurons, which "hold" the location of the target "online" in working memory, appear to have "spatial memory fields." That is, the same neuron responds to a particular location, suggesting the possibility of a crude topographic mapping of the environment in the neurons of the prefrontal cortex (Goldman-Rakic, 1990, 1994, 1995).

Goldman-Rakic suggested a possible neurobiology underlying this phenomenon. The interaction of glutamergic pyramidal neurons and GABA-ergic inhibitory interneurons is critical for the formation of "memory fields." As the interneurons increase their rate of discharge, nearby pyramidal neurons show decreased activity. The complementarity between these two classes of neurons is modulated by dopamine and serotonin (Arnsten, Cai, Murphy, & Goldman-Rakic, 1994; Brozoski & Brown, 1979; Murphy, Arnsten, Goldman-Rakic, & Roth, 1996; Smiley, Levey, Ciliax, & Goldman-Rakic, 1994; Williams & Goldman-Rakic, 1995). Dopaminergic axons establish synapses primarily on the dendrites of the pyramidal cells, whereas serotonergic axons establish synapses primarily on the inhibitory interneurons (Smiley & Goldman-Rakic, 1996). The density of dopamine receptors in the prefrontal cortex of the rhesus monkey reaches a maximum around 2 months of age, corresponding to 7 to 8 months in the infant.

EEG and ERP

EEG and ERP data from human infants add relevant information. Slow alpha frequencies in the EEG (3 to 5 Hz) appear during the first transition at 2 to 3 months, but faster alpha frequencies (6 to 9 Hz) emerge between 7 and 12 months (Bell, 1998). Further, the amplitude of P2/N2 waveform to a series of click sounds increased in a linear fashion between 1 and 12 months (Ohlrich & Barnet, 1972). Of greater interest is the fact that the 8-month-olds who made their first saccade to the correct, rather than the incorrect, location in a standard object permanence procedure displayed greater alpha power at frontal and pyramidal sites than infants who failed to look at the correct location. The greater the alpha power, implying greater synchronization of cortical neurons, the more likely the child looked at the correct location (Bell, 2002).

The perception of a unified object requires the brain to bind the various features of an object to construct a perceptual unity. Csibra et al. used EEG data to measure oscillatory brain activity in 6- and 8-month-old infants as they viewed a static Kanizsa square (see Fig. 4.3; Csibra, Davis, Spratling, & Johnson, 2000). The Kanizsa square is an illusionary image of a square produced by four correctly-aligned elements. The control stimulus consists of the same four elements, but because they are not aligned, they fail to produce the illusion of a square. Six-month-olds did not, but 8-month-olds did, show a change in gamma activity (30–60 Hz) while viewing a static Kanizsa figure. The control stimulus did not elicit this cortical reaction. The fact that the 8-month-olds showed gamma bursts comparable to those seen in adults presented with the illusory figure implies that the older infants bound the spatially separate elements into a unity. However,

 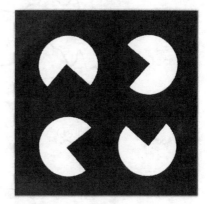

FIG. 4.3.   Kanizsa square—Illusionary image of a square produced by four correctly-aligned elements. The control image consists of the same elements, but not correctly aligned.

4-month-old infants look longer at a Kanizsa square than at a control stimulus if it is in motion, suggesting that younger infants might see the illusory contour under conditions that render the stimulus more salient (Otsuka & Yamaguchi, 2003).

The peak voltages in the sequence of ERP waveforms to an event are produced by the synchronized activity of cortical pyramidal neurons (see Fig. 4.4). Amplification of the dipoles created by the neuronal activity permit recording of the neural excitation in the form of ERPs. The polarity of each waveform, negative or positive, is indicated by the capital letter N or P, followed by a number that signifies the usual latency of the peak magnitude of that waveform following the onset of the stimulus. A dipole, which is a separation of charge in a volume conductor, is generated when an excitatory or inhibitory input from a neighboring neuron alters the charge of the postsynaptic cell. If the input is excitatory, positively charged ions flow into the cell to create a negative charge in the contiguous extracellular space called the *sink*. The positive ions flow through a segment of the neuron and exit back into the extracellular space to create a positively charged area called the *source*. If the synapse is inhibitory, the sink has a positive rather than a negative charge. A disparity in charge between the sink and the source establishes a dipole.

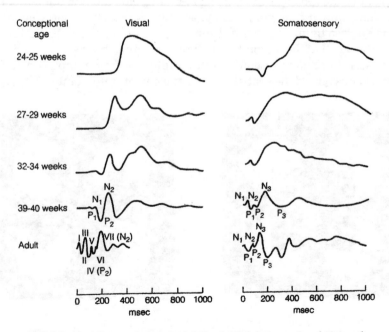

FIG. 4.4.   Age changes in event related potentials between 6 and 10 months compared with adult forms.

Some components of the ERP response to events are present at birth, but their amplitudes increase and their latencies to the peak of the waveforms decrease with age. For example, both newborns and 1-year-olds show the same sequence of waveforms to a simple auditory stimulus, with peaks at about 150, 250, and 450 msec (Kushnerenko, Ceponiene, Fellman, Huotilainen, & Winkler, 2001; Kushnerenko, Cheour, et al., 2001). Equally important, 81% of newborns showed a distinct negative waveform at about 250 msec—called *mismatch negativity*—when a tone with a discrepant frequency was presented following a series of identical tones (Ceponiene et al., 2002).

However, as noted earlier, ERP evidence can occasionally lead to inferences different from conclusions based on behavior. Six- to twelve-month-olds saw a photograph of one face on 70% of the trials, a different face on 15% of the trials, and pictures of unfamiliar objects on the remaining 15% of the trials. As expected, the infants showed their longest bout of attention to the less familiar face, but surprisingly, showed their largest negative ERP waveform to the unfamiliar objects. The behavioral data are in accord with the curvilinear function relating degree of discrepancy to duration of attention because the face that appeared 15% of the time was moderately discrepant from the child's schema for the frequently presented face whereas the novel objects shared no features with the faces. The fact that the ERP data did not conform to the curvilinear principle suggests that ERPs and behavior can reveal different aspects of the processes activated when infants process discrepant events (DeHaan & Nelson, 1997; DeHaan et al., 2002; Thomas & Lykins, 1995; Tsivilis, Otten, & Rugg, 2001).

THE APPEARANCE OF FEARS

The improved working memory permits infants to experience a state of uncertainty following an encounter with an unexpected or discrepant event (Schaffer, Greenwood, & Parry, 1972). If the infant cannot assimilate the unfamiliar event, and, in addition, has no coping response, or is uncertain as to what behavior to display, a state some scientists call *fear of novelty* emerges, and the infant may cry. The psychological state and the cry are far less likely if the infant can control the appearance of the unfamiliar event. Eight- to nine-month-old infants presented with a cymbal-clapping monkey showed behavioral signs of fear if the toy's appearance was unexpected, but displayed little fear if they could control the onset of the toy's motions (Gunnar-vonGnechten, 1978). Infants, as well as older children, usually approach unfamiliar objects they can assimilate, especially if they have an appropriate response, but avoid them if they cannot be assimilated immediately, or they have no appropriate behavior. Infant monkeys given a choice of approaching a familiar family member or an unfamiliar adult monkey usually approached the former (Mayeaux, Mason, & Mendoza, 2002).

The universal display of avoidance or crying to strangers, which usually occurs in most infants between 7 and 10 months, requires an enhanced working memory. The face, body, and gait of an approaching stranger are discrepant from the 7-month-old's schemata for her familiar caretakers. The infant attends to the stranger and retrieves the schemata for the adults she knows. If the infant cannot assimilate the stranger's features to her schemata, and has no control over the situation, she will cry. This phenomenon is called *stranger anxiety* or *stranger fear* (Bronson, 1970). The cry is not always immediate. Initially, the infant studies the stranger, a few seconds later her face becomes serious, a frown appears, and several seconds later, she may cry. Two- to three-month-old monkeys, comparable to seven- to eight-month-old infants, also show behavioral avoidance or grimaces to discrepant events, including threatening postures and unfamiliar people, objects, or situations (Harlow, 1973; Mason, 1960; Sackett, 1966).

A cry to the unexpected disappearance of a caretaker, called *separation anxiety*, occurs at the same age and for the same reason. The unexpected departure of the mother, especially if it occurs in an unfamiliar place, presents a child with the discrepancy of being alone in an unfamiliar place. After the parent departs, the child retrieves a schema for her former presence and relates it to the current perception of her absence. The infant who cannot assimilate the mother's absence to the schema for her former presence may cry. Even in the familiar home environment, the mother's departure produces more crying if she leaves by an unfamiliar exit, like the basement door, than if she leaves by a familiar exit, like the front door.

Children from four different cultures (rural Botswana, a city in Guatemala, an Israeli kibbutz, a Mayan Indian village in northwest Guatemala) first showed separation fear at similar ages. Figure 4.5 shows the proportion of infants who cried following the unexpected departure of the mother when both were in an unfamiliar place. The proportion of children who cried was low before 7 months, but rose sharply between 6 and 15 months in all four settings. A similar function was observed in American children attending a day-care center (Kagan, 1976; Littenberg, Tulkin, & Kagan, 1971). This similarity is remarkable given the fact that the children on the kibbutz see their mother only a few hours a day whereas the Botswana infants are with their mothers almost continually. It cannot be a coincidence that infant Rhesus monkeys less than 3 months old do not become agitated when separated from their mothers, but those older than 3 months emit distress cries and show an increased adrenal response to separation (Kalin & Shelton, 1989; Kalin, Shelton, & Barksdale, 1989; Kalin,

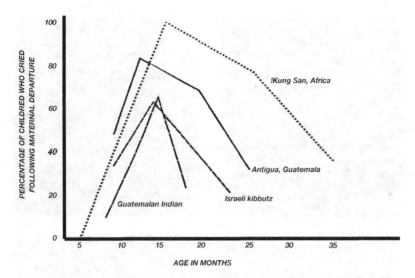

FIG. 4.5.   Age changes in the onset of separation fear in four different cultural settings.

Shelton, & Snowdon, 1992; Kalin, Shelton, & Takahashi, 1991; Sackett, 1966).

The ability to retrieve schemata for the immediate past and to hold them and a perception of the present in a working memory circuit while attempting assimilation are necessary for the avoidant or distress reactions to unfamiliar events. The growth of the prefrontal cortex, especially the rostrolateral prefrontal cortex, and its connections to temporal lobe structures, contribute to this competence (Christoff, Ream, Geddes, & Gabrieli, 2003).

Visual Cliff

The infant's avoidant behavior on an apparatus called the *visual cliff* provides a third example of a state that might be dependent on the inability to assimilate a discrepant event (see Fig. 4.6). The visual cliff consists of a clear sheet of plexiglass on which infants can crawl. A checkerboard cloth is placed just beneath the surface of one side of the plexiglass. The same cloth is put several feet below the transparent surface on the other side to produce the suggestion of depth. The infant is placed on a small platform between the "safe" and the apparently "deep" side. Although mothers call to their infants to cross over the deep side to approach them, most infants older than 7 or 8 months are unwilling to do so (Gibson & Walk, 1960). Failure to assimilate the inconsistent information coming from dif-

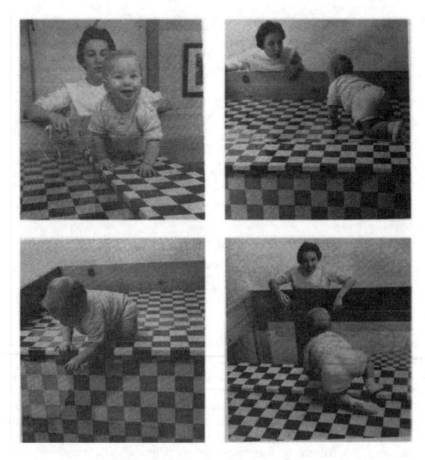

FIG. 4.6.   Illustration of the visual cliff.

ferent sensory modalities on the deep side may contribute to the avoidance. The visual, and probably vestibular, information on the deep side implies a drop-off, whereas the tactile information from the contact of hands and legs with the glass implies a solid surface. If infants cannot assimilate the discrepancy between information from the different sensory modalities, they are likely to avoid crawling onto the deep side. Infants this age, and younger, can perceive depth, for 2-month-olds show a decrease in heart rate if lowered onto the deep side. Nine-month-olds, by contrast, show an increase in heart rate when lowered onto the deep side, indicating a sympathetic, and presumably more fearful, reaction to the same perception.

However, the experiences that accompany crawling also contribute to avoidance of the deep side. Seven-month-old infants who had already begun to crawl, or were given locomotor experience, more often avoided the deep side of the cliff, and showed a larger rise in heart rate when lowered onto the deep side, than infants who had not yet begun to crawl. It is likely that the experiences that accompany crawling award salience to the information from vision, tactile, and vestibular systems (Campos, Bertenthal, & Kermoian, 1992).

The Role of the Amygdala in Reaction to Novelty

The integrity of the amygdala, and its connections to the cortex, hippocampus, parahippocampal region, hypothalamus, basal ganglia, and brainstem, probably contribute to both stranger and separation fear, and perhaps, to behavior on the visual cliff as well, because this structure is activated by unfamiliar or unexpected events.

The amygdala consists of many neuronal clusters, each characterized by a distinct pattern of connectivity and functions. Each cluster projects to at least 15 different sites, and each receives input from about the same number of regions, resulting in at least 600 known amygdalar connections (Amaral, 1992; Petrovich, Canteras, & Swanson, 2001).

Although a simplification, most anatomists conceptualize the amygdala as composed of three basic areas: the basolateral, corticomedial, and central area, with the first two sending information to the latter site. The basolateral area, which became larger with primate evolution, receives thalamic and cortical inputs from vision, audition, olfaction, and tactile modalities, and is connected primarily, but not exclusively, to the cortex, striatum, parahippocampal region, and hippocampus. The corticomedial nucleus receives primarily olfactory information. The central nucleus receives information from the basolateral and corticomedial nuclei, as well as from the viscera, and, in addition, is the origin of projections to many sites, including the bed nucleus of the stria terminalis, cortex, medial and lateral hypothalamus, brain stem, and autonomic nervous system.

The projections from the amygdala to the bed nucleus lead to the secretion of stress hormones; projections to the parabrachial nucleus lead to modulation of the parasympathetic nervous system; those to the central gray influence postural changes; projections to the hypothalamus affect the autonomic nervous system; projections to the reticularis pontis caudalis potentiate the startle reflex; and those to the cortex contribute to the conscious awareness of a change in feeling. Because activation of amygdalar neurons, directly or indirectly, can affect almost every site in the central nervous system, variation in the excitability of any one of the neural clusters has consequences for mood and behavior (see Fig. 4.7; Amaral, 2002; Knight, 1996).

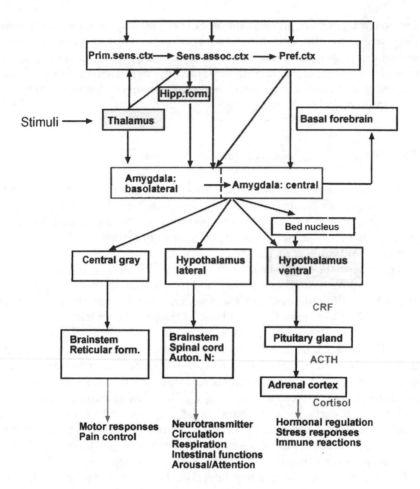

FIG. 4.7.   Cortico-limbic amygdala network.

The amygdala has a rich monoamine innervation. Dopaminergic tracts from the substantia nigra and tegmental area project to the central nucleus and modulate the amygdala's output to the brainstem, hypothalamus, and basal ganglia. The serotonergic innervation is widespread, but particularly dense in the basal nucleus, which is involved in the processing of visual and auditory information. The densest norepinephrine concentrations are in the central and basal nuclei (Amaral, 2002; Davis & Whalen, 2001).

Connections between the amygdala and the cortex are strengthened between 7 and 12 months, in part, through axons within the capsula interna that develop mature myelin (Brody et al., 1987; Chrousos & Gold, 1992).

TABLE 4.1
Targets and Functions of the Amygdala

Target	Biological Consequence	Select Reactions
Hypothalamus	Sympathetic activity	Tachycardia
		Blood pressure rise
Vagus nerve	Parasympathetic activity	Drop in heart rate
Parabrachial nucleus	Increase in respiration rate	Panting
Ventral tegmentum	Secretion of dopamine	Cortical arousal
Locus ceruleus	Secretion of norepinephrine	Vigilance
Nucleus reticularis pontis caudalis	Potentiation of reflexes	Enhanced startle
Periaqueductal grey	Immobility, Vocal tract activity	Freezing, crying
Facial nucleus, Trigeminal nucleus	Facial movement	Facial expressions
Basal ganglia	Secretion of acetylcholine	Motor tone, activity
HPA Axis	Secretion of ACTH,	Stress reactions
	Corticosteroids	

The myelination is accompanied by faster communication between the amygdala and sites that modulate the behavioral indexes of fear, especially freezing and distress cries. (A summary of the varied reactions mediated by the amygdala appears in Table 4.1; Davis, 1992.)

What Provokes the Amygdala?

The fundamental nature of the events likely to activate the amygdala, and the biological and psychological states that follow, remain a focus of debate. The central question is whether the amygdala is biologically prepared to react primarily to imminently threatening events to produce a state called *fear*, or to unexpected or unfamiliar events to produce a state called *surprise*. The popular view is that the amygdala reacts primarily to signs of danger rather than to unfamiliarity. Ohman and Mineka (2003) argued that all animals inherit a fear module, located in the amygdala, that reacts to events that pose a potential threat of bodily harm (snakes are presumed to be a classic example of a fear-evoking event). There are serious problems with this theoretical position (Davey, 1995).

First, the behavioral reaction of most primates, as well as human infants, to a snake is no different from their reaction to most discrepant events that are harmless, like a tortoise or skeins of seaweed. Further, monkeys born and reared in the laboratory, who were protected from all contact with snakes, only showed a longer period of motor restraint to a live or toy snake, compared with blue masking tape, on the first testing session but not on the second and third sessions. Only 30% of the monkeys showed a longer duration of withdrawal to a live snake than to the masking tape; a majority of animals showed equivalent withdrawal to the snake and the tape (Nelson, Shelton, & Kalin, 2003). Further, monkeys with chemical lesions that destroyed about one half of the amygdala, compared with controls, were more likely to approach unfamiliar foods, whether palatable or unpalatable, and to approach an unfamiliar puppet or leather glove as reliably as they approached a toy snake (Stefanacci, Clark, & Zola, 2003). If the amygdala were primarily responsive to threatening events, the animals should have shown a more consistent approach to the unpalatable foods and toy snake than to the palatable foods and leather glove. However, unfamiliarity is not the only factor of influence, for the lesioned animals behaved like controls to a bottle, box, tape, and block of foam rubber, although these objects were also unfamiliar. Further, the difference in degree of avoidance of the unfamiliar between the lesioned and normal animals was independent of their tendency to look longer at a novel than at a familiar stimulus in a standard paired comparison test. That is, the failure of the lesioned animals to avoid unfamiliar objects was not due to an inability to discriminate familiar from unfamiliar events. The functions compromised by the lesion were behavioral, not perceptual.

Second, discrepant or unexpected events that pose no danger can produce the same level of amygdalar activation as dangerous ones (Amaral, Capitanio, Jourdain, & Mason, 2003). Adults lying in an fMRI scanner looking at photos of faces with neutral expressions showed greater amygdalar activation to unfamiliar, compared with familiar, faces, although no face had a fearful, disgusting, or threatening expression—they were simply discrepant from the familiar ones (Schwartz et al., 2003). One group of adolescents even showed greater amygdalar activity to happy than to neutral or sad faces (Yang, Menon, Reid, Gotlib, & Reiss, 2003). Further, the amygdala showed equivalent activation to (a) a neutral face that gradually assumed a fearful expression and (b) a face with a neutral expression that gradually assumed the identity of a different person with a neutral expression (La Bar, Crupain, Voyvodic, & McCarthy, 2003). Mothers showed greater amygdalar activity to photos of their own children than to photos of their children's friends, or unfamiliar children or adults, because the former events were unexpected in this unusual context.

Rats presented many times with a light, followed by a tone, which, in turn, was followed by food, showed an orienting behavioral reaction when the light suddenly appeared without the tone because omission of the tone was discrepant from their prior experience and the central nucleus of the amygdala, alerted by the discrepancy, provoked an orienting response. Rats without an amygdala were not alerted—or aroused—by the discrepancy of the light appearing without the tone, and did not orient to the light (Holland & Gallagher, 1999).

The central nucleus of the amygdala is required for orienting to the unexpected presentation of a conditioned stimulus for food, but is not required to acquire a conditioned behavioral approach to a location where food appears (Holland, Han, & Winfield, 2002). An unexpected conditioned stimulus that signals an opportunity for sexual behavior also activates the basolateral nucleus of the rat amygdala (Kippin, Cain, & Pfaus, 2003).

Although the amygdala is necessary for the acquisition of a classically-conditioned reaction of body immobility, potentiated startle, or heart rate increase to a previously neutral stimulus that had been paired with electric shock, rats without an amygdala continue to display some behaviors that scientists regard as signs of a fear state (LeDoux, 1996). For example, lesioned rats freeze to the odor of a predator (Fendt, Endres, & Apfelbach, 2003) and defecate in the place where they had been shocked on an earlier occasion (Antoniadis & McDonald, 2000). These observations suggest that (a) freezing and defecation do not reflect a state of fear; (b) there are distinctly different fear states, each mediated by a different biology; or (c) freezing and defecation are automatic, biologically prepared reactions to unexpected or discrepant events and there is no theoretical utility to attributing a state of fear to animals who display these responses. All three statements might be true. It appears that when the conditioned stimulus in a Pavlovian conditioning paradigm is a discrete event (for example, a tone or light), the lateral nucleus is a major interface between the conditioned stimulus and the projection from the central nucleus to targets that lead to freezing and an increase in heart rate. However, if the conditioned stimulus is a context, the basal amygdalar nucleus is the more important interface and its projections to the striatum produce changes in gross motor behavior (for example, fleeing or defensive responses; Yaniv, Desmedt, Jaffard, & Richter-Levin, 2004). The brain and the psychological states created by pairing a conditioned stimulus with an electric shock involve different circuits and reactions when the conditioned stimulus is a discrete event or a location.

The decision to attribute a state of fear to a rat that has been conditioned to freeze, or to show potentiated bodily startle to an acoustic stimulus preceded by an event that had signaled electric shock, violates an earlier reluctance by psychologists to attribute any emotional state to an animal or human that was based on a classically-conditioned response. Pavlov did not attribute a state of hunger to the dogs he conditioned to salivate to the sound of a metronome. And early 20th-century psychologists did not attribute fear to an adult conditioned to display an eye blink to a tone that signaled an aversive air puff to the cornea. A critical fact is that select neurons in the amygdala, as well as in the bed nucleus, parahippocampal regions, striatum, and brainstem, respond to unexpected or unfamiliar events, whether or not they are potentially harmful. Further, this neuronal reaction habituates, often rapidly, as the event becomes familiar (Habib, McIntosh, & Wheeler, 2003; LaBar, Gatenby, & Gore, 1998; Wilson & Rolls, 1993).

Finally, an avoidant or distress reaction to unfamiliarity matures over the first year. Newborn monkeys with bilateral lesions of the amygdala were compared with controls for the next 8½ months (Prather et al., 2001). Initially, the two groups spent the same amount of time in ventral contact with the mother. Behavioral differences between the lesioned and control animals did not appear until after weaning, when the controls, but not the lesioned monkeys, hesitated before retrieving food placed next to an unfamiliar object (for example, a rubber snake). Although the lesioned animals showed less avoidance of unfamiliar, inanimate objects, they did show some behavioral signs of fear when placed with another animal: they grimaced, screamed, and failed to explore a cage containing unfamiliar objects. By contrast, lesions of the amygdala of adult animals lead to less fear and more affiliative social behavior with unfamiliar animals, compared with controls. Thus, the behavioral consequences of amygdalar lesions are different in infants than in adult animals. One possible explanation is that the amygdala is essential for display of the typical social behavior of this species. The lesioned infants did not have sufficient time to learn appropriate social habits; hence, they screamed to unfamiliar animals because of the uncertainty generated by not having a response to make in an arousing situation.

Although amygdalar activity can contribute to the human psychological states called uncertainty, fear, or anxiety, amygdalar activity alone is insufficient to create these psychological states. The English word *fear* was invented millennia ago to describe a conscious feeling in an awake human. The amygdalar neurons of totally anesthetized animals display increased activity to a conditioned stimulus that had been paired with electric shock (Rosenkranz & Grace, 2002); it is troubling to call an anesthetized rat fearful. Further, many animals increase their rate of instrumental responding if the reward is amygdalar activation through a brief infusion of cocaine or amphetamine. Humans take these drugs to feel aroused or excited, not to feel afraid.

The neuroscientists' decision to use the word fear to name the cascade that begins with a tone signaling shock and ending a second later with an immobile rat was based on the premise that the state of a rat expecting shock resembles the state of a human expecting to be attacked. However, neuroscientists could have selected terms like *alert, surprised*, or *vigilant*, rather than fear, because body immobility and a change in heart rate also occur to an unexpected or unfamiliar event, whether or not it is threatening (for example, the sound of a bus backfiring, or a bright flash of lightning outside the window). These events would cause a brief startle, period of immobility, and a change in heart rate, but most persons asked about their feeling would reply that they were surprised rather than afraid. Further, if the backfire occurred several times over the next hour, the startle and change in heart rate would cease to occur because the event had lost its surprise value and the neurons in the amygdala would have habituated to the repetitions of the unexpected event. A person held hostage by armed bandits for 6 months would feel continually fearful, but not continually surprised.

Many of the events or objects that are targets of human phobias—spiders, snakes—had not physically harmed those who claimed that they were afraid of these events. These objects became targets of a phobia because they were conditioned stimuli for a strong emotional reaction evoked by a surprising event. For example, a 5-year-old boy developed a phobia of buttons when he went to the front of his kindergarten classroom to retrieve additional buttons to finish a teacher-assigned task. The boy slipped as he reached for the bowl of buttons, and all of the buttons fell over him. This unexpected event was accompanied by an intense feeling of embarrassment in front of the teacher and his peers. The phobic avoidance of buttons began that day and lasted for 4 years (Saavedra & Silverman, 2002). The Pavlovian conditioning of an avoidant reaction to buttons (first to the perception of buttons and later to the thought of buttons) had nothing to do with physical harm to the body. The unconditioned stimulus was the combination of surprise and shame that followed the spilling of buttons in front of the classroom—this emotional state is not synonymous with fear.

In sum, the amygdala is activated not only by stimuli with a potential to cause harm (electric shock or bitter tastes) but also by unfamiliar or unexpected events without aversive properties. Activity in the parahippocampal region supplies the amygdala with information indicating that an event has discrepant features. This information, combined with the current context, determines the behavioral and biological consequences that will occur. For example, if the stimulus is a tone signaling possible electric shock and the animal is alone in a cage, immobility is the likely reaction. If the stimulus is an intruder, the animal will bite if it cannot escape, but flee if it can do so. If the stimulus is a nonthreatening discrepancy (for example, a tone is omitted following exposure to several light–tone sequences), the animal orients. The amygdala forms an association between an unexpected or discrepant event (including aversive ones) and a state of neuronal excitability, and initiates reactions appropriate to the incentive and the local context. This process is immature during the early months of life. Hence, the usual behavioral signs of fear do not emerge until the second half of the first year.

The fact that a fear reaction to unfamiliarity does not appear reliably until after 6 or 7 months illustrates a phenomenon biologists call *hetero-chrony*. Some species of birds, ducklings for example, approach moving objects during the first week after hatching. As a result they imprint on the first moving object they perceive and, thereafter, avoid other unfamiliar animals. Because many human infants are cared for by adults other than the biological mother, it is advantageous to delay the time of onset of a distressed and avoidant reaction to unfamiliar humans until the second half of the first year.

SENSORY–MOTOR STRUCTURES

The transition at 7 to 12 months is accompanied by the enhanced ability to adjust sensory–motor structures in the service of attaining a goal. Five-month-olds use both hands to reach toward an object, whether small or large, whereas 8-month-olds reach with one hand toward a small object, and with both hands toward a large object (Rochat & Senders, 1991). And 12-month-olds will look longer at the larger of two objects but will reach for the smaller one (Newman, Atkinson, & Braddick, 2001), a result that renders the concept of infant preference ambiguous. The fact that 7-month-olds are more likely to reach for a toy seen seconds earlier if the room is completely dark than if the toy is hidden under a cover in a brightly lit room also leads us to question the popular assumption that the infant reaches for an invisible object because he wants the object (Shinskey & Munakata, 2003). The reaching seems to be a biologically prepared reaction to the fading schema of the object rather than a reaction motivated by a desire to obtain the object.

The behaviors of 7-month-olds illustrate the ease with which sensori-motor representations can be acquired. Infants initially saw a small and a large ring-shaped hoop, each associated with a distinctive sound. After a number of familiarization trials, the room was darkened, and the infant heard one of the two distinctive sounds, but could not see whether the object producing the sound was the small or the large hoop. Surprisingly, the infants adjusted their arms and hands appropriately. They reached with both hands to the sound that had accompanied the large object, but with one hand to the sound that had accompanied the small object (Clifton, Rochat, Litovsky, & Perris, 1991). That is, the infants retrieved the sensory–motor schemata established when they manipulated the objects earlier in the brightly lit room. We suspect that 5-month-olds are unable to do so.

The significance of the transition at 7 to 9 months is also revealed in a study of 5- to 11-month-old infants who had begun to make stepping movements. Each infant, held by an adult, first made a few successful stepping movements. An invisible bar was then placed in the infant's path of motion causing the child to stumble. On subsequent trials, after the bar was removed, the scientists noted which infants raised their foot higher than normal, implying they had learned a sensory motor scheme to avoid striking the bar. Remarkably, over 90% of the infants who were less than 9 months old did not raise their foot, whereas 70% of those older than 9 months did, suggesting they had learned a sensory motor scheme from the earlier experience of stumbling over the bar (Pang, Lam, & Yang, 2003). Although cats without a cerebrum can learn this postural adjustment, it is possible that this form of learning in humans, who are bipedal, requires the cortex. The fact that both an enhanced working memory and new sensory motor adjustments appear after 9 months implies important maturational changes after 7 or 8 months of age.

Prototypic sensory–motor schemes are acquired as a result of frequent reaching for small objects, lifting large objects, and touching their mother's face. The neuronal representations in the motor cortex that mediate each prototypic action are comparable to words in a child's vocabulary. One neuronal ensemble is activated when a monkey prepares to grasp a small object with the thumb and forefinger; a different ensemble is activated when the whole hand is used to grasp a larger object. The profile of neuronal activity represents an intended action toward a class of objects, rather than the separate muscle fibers involved in a response (Rizzolatti, Fogassi, & Gallese, 2000).

SCHEMATIC CONCEPTS

Schematic concepts, which also emerge after 7 months, are cognitive "averages" created from multiple exposures to the same, or very similar, events (Kuhl, 1991). The infant's representations of the phonemes of its language—the vowels and consonant–vowel combinations that are the elementary sounds of every language—are schematic concepts (Saffran & Thiessen, 2003). Because different speakers pronounce each phoneme somewhat differently, infants have to construct a schematic concept for the phonemes of their language. Most are able to do this by 8 months of age.

A schematic concept of a phoneme is organized around its best exemplar, called a *prototype*. The prototype reduces the perceptual distance between it and all vowels with a similar sound. All the vowel sounds that are acoustically similar to the prototype become, over time, less discriminable than sounds that differ clearly from the prototype (for example, the phoneme "ba" in bake and baby are similar; the "ba" in ball and baby are different).

A popular method to assess the presence of a schematic concept for a phoneme relies on the infant's turning its head to a sound source when it hears a novel sound following habituation to a series of identical sounds. The experimenter first attracts the infant's attention to a small, silent toy in front of him or her while a sound is emitted from a loudspeaker to the left or right of the infant. Whenever the infant turns his head toward the loud-speaker, the examiner rewards that response by showing the infant an an-imated toy that is adjacent to the loudspeaker. After the infant has habitu-ated, and no longer turns his head toward the sound, a different sound is presented. If the infant orients to the new sound, by turning to the right or left, the investigator concludes that it discriminated the new sound from the familiar one. This technique is not used with infants less than 5 months because younger infants have poor motor control of the head.

Six-month-old infants can discriminate between many phonemic con-trasts heard regularly (for example, "ba" and "da"; Werker & Tees, 1983). However, after 8 months, they lose the ability to distinguish between simi-lar sounding phonemic contrasts that are heard regularly, but are not im-portant in the language the child is learning. For example, Japanese speech does not distinguish between the phonemes "ra" and "la," and 8-month-old Japanese infants do not attend to a change from one of these phonemes to the other, although 2-month-old Japanese infants can dis-criminate between these two phonemes. The 8-month-old Japanese in-fants lost an ability they had 6 months earlier (Kuhl, 1991, 1993).

However, if the phonemic contrast is completely unrelated to any pho-neme in the child's language, infants might not lose the ability to discrimi-nate between the sounds. For example, the Zulu language contains click sounds that do not occur in English and 1-year-old American infants can discriminate between different click sounds. Thus, infants only lose the capacity to discriminate between similar sounding phonemes that are heard regularly. They can continue to discriminate between similar dis-tinctive sounds if they do not occur in their speech environment (Best, 1995).

However, different procedures can lead to different conclusions. The evidence noted earlier is based on changes in behavioral orientation to a loudspeaker, rather than changes in brain activity. Although adults do not consciously perceive a subtle change in the acoustic envelope of a syllable like "ba," the brain generates a distinct ERP if, following a string of one variant of "ba," a slightly different "ba" is heard.

A second experiment is equally persuasive. Italian students read sen-tences, one word at a time. Some sentences were regular, without any syntactic or semantic violation; others contained a semantic violation in the verb following a noun (for example, "The new guard sprouts at the departure of the locomotive"). Other sentences contained a syntactic violation in the verb (for example, "The old waiter serve with a vacant look"). Both the semantic and the syntactic violations were followed by a significant waveform in the ERP. However, the participants who were instructed to read each sentence aloud only paused as they read the anomalous syntactic violation; they did not pause as they read the semantic violation (De Vincenzi et al., 2003). Thus, there was a difference between the brain's reaction to the semantic violation and the participant's behavior. There remains the possibility, therefore, that 1-year-olds who fail to orient to a similar sounding phoneme might, nonetheless, show a distinct cortical response to the discrepant sound, a reminder of the principle that the validity of all conclusions rests with the source of evidence.

Schematic Concepts for Visual Events

Infants acquire schematic concepts for visual stimuli as well. Six-month-olds saw repetitions of photos of eight different equally attractive female faces (Rubenstein, Kalakanis, & Langlois, 1999). If the infants created a schematic concept for these eight faces, they should look longer at a novel face never seen before than at the constructed average—or prototype—of the eight faces, although they had never seen the constructed average. As predicted, the infants did look longer at the novel than at the average face, indicating they had created a schematic concept for the eight faces.

In a second study, 9-month-olds first saw three different kinds of physically distinct birds and then saw either a horse or a new bird not seen before (Haith, 1980). The infants looked longer at the horse than at the new bird because they had created a schematic concept for the birds presented during the familiarization and the novel bird was assimilated to that schematic concept. Nine and eleven-month-olds can also create a schematic concept for "diminishing size." After familiarization with a series of squares that decreased in size, they showed increased attention when a series of squares increased in size (Brannon, 2002).

A temporal pattern of sounds can become a schematic concept. Seven-month-olds first heard a 2-min speech sample containing three instances of 16 different, three-syllable utterances having the form a-b-a. The syllables in each utterance were different; for example, the infant might hear on the first trial "ga-ti-ga," on the next trial "li-no-li," and on the third trial "bo-gu-bo." The only feature shared across all the utterances was that the first and third syllables were identical. Following familiarization on this a-b-a pattern, the infants heard either a new utterance with the same a-b-a form or a new trio of syllables with a new form, for example a-b-b, as in "wo-fe-fe." The infants showed greater attention to the unfamiliar a-b-b pattern, indicating that they had created a schematic concept for the temporal configuration of a-b-a. This ability, which surprised many developmental psychologists, requires detection of the features of identical sounds in positions 1 and 3, despite the variation in the particular sounds, and the ability to relate the novel pattern (a-b-b) to that schematic concept (Marcus, Vijayan, Rao, & Vishton, 1999). Adult Tamarin monkeys have the same ability, but 4-month-olds do not (Hauser, Dehaene, Dehaene-Lambertz, & Patalano, 2002).

The enhanced working memory, due to changes in brain organization, should make it easier to create schematic concepts. Consider the schematic concept a-b-a for the syllables in the experiment described earlier. The infant must hold in a working memory circuit the identical sounds of the first and third syllables over a series of trials in which the first and third syllables change their acoustic properties. If that representation vanished every 2 to 3 sec, as it does for the 3-month-old, the schematic concept could not be established. In addition, the infant must relate the current test stimulus (for example, "bo-gu-gu") to the representation of the a-b-a pattern created on prior trials. We believe that the growth of the prefrontal cortex, and its enhanced connectivity to the medial temporal lobe, are necessary for this cognitive advance.

The ability to create schematic concepts before the first birthday implies that these structures are easily constructed. This ability, combined with a sensitivity to discrepant events, helps explain why humans across all societies treat objects, animals, and people, whose features depart from a prototype, in special ways. Some discrepancies are evaluated benevolently; some are judged as dangerous or as tabooed objects. One classic illustration is the Hebrew prohibition on certain foods; pork is an example. Sheep, cattle, oxen, goats, and pigs were typical animals in the world of the ancient Israelites. The first four combined a cloven hoof with chewing of cud. The pig, however, deviated from this prototype because it has a cloven hoof, but does not chew cud. This discrepant feature may be one reason why the pig was judged as an inappropriate food.

Generally, schematic concepts for actions are more closely tied to a context than schematic concepts for humans or animals. A child's schematic concepts for the faces of parents and siblings were created from encounters in varied locations. However, the schematic concepts for actions, like going to sleep, were generated in a narrower range of contexts. Schemata for the behaviors involved in preparing for sleep are tied more closely to the child's bedroom. It is likely that the development of a decontextualized prototype requires exposure to a class of events across varied contexts.

IMITATION

Although some imitation of a behavior displayed by another person appears during the first 6 months, this phenomenon becomes much more reliable after the 7- to 12-month transition. A similar conclusion holds for nonhuman primate infants (Maestripieri, Ross, & Megna, 2002). It is important to distinguish between spontaneous and provoked imitation. In the former, the child retrieves a sensory motor schema for a behavior witnessed in the past, finds the appropriate objects, and implements the action. For example, 1-year-olds will treat a piece of plain cloth as if it were a blanket because the cloth possesses a feature that is a component of their schemata for blankets. If the context changes, an infant might select a different property of the same object; some 1-year-olds will treat the piece of cloth as a dress for a doll.

Provoked imitation occurs when a person displays a novel act in front of the child and the latter immediately implements a version of that behavior when the props are present as incentives. Although it is rare for children under 6 months to show spontaneous imitation, a limited form of provoked imitation can be observed a few months earlier.

The claim that newborns are capable of provoked imitation is controversial because the evidence is open to an alternative interpretation. The classic source of support for the bolder claim is that infants only a few days old protrude their tongue after seeing an adult protrude a tongue at them (Meltzoff & Moore, 1977). On the surface, the infant's behavior appears to be an example of a provoked imitation. However, very young infants also protrude their tongue to any slender object that is moved toward and away from their face. Young infants (4 to 5 weeks old) often protrude their tongue to an object that moves close to their face because they use their tongue to explore objects (Jones, 1996). Further, this "imitative" response is less likely after the transition at 3 months, implying that the newborn's response is a brainstem reflex that requires minimal cortical involvement, and therefore, should be distinguished from the imitation of the 1-year old which does involve the cortex (Nakagawa, Sukigara, & Benga, 2003). Remember, all behaviors are ambiguous in meaning. That is why we suggest that spontaneous imitation of adult actions does not emerge reliably until infants can retrieve schemata following a substantial delay between exposure to the event and its display, a state that is potentiated during the second half of the first year.

Because infants younger than 6 or 7 months have difficulty retrieving schemata from past events, imitation is less likely if there is a long delay between the time the act was first seen and the time when the imitative response is evoked (Collie & Hayne, 1999). Most 9-month-olds will imitate a single action seen 1 day earlier; a majority will imitate an act following a 3-

month delay, and less than one half imitate an action seen 6 months earlier (Bauer, 2002). If 9-month-old infants are exposed to three novel actions (involving two components) on three separate occasions, about one half (46%) will spontaneously imitate at least one of the sequences 1 month later. However, 54% of these infants did not display any imitation (Bauer, Wiebe, Carver, Waters, & Nelson, 2003). It is important that the infants who did show some imitation following the 1-month delay displayed a faster latency in the negative waveform (at 400 msec) evoked by a novel sequence witnessed 1 week after their last familiarization session. These data suggest that delayed spontaneous imitation is possible, but it is a relatively fragile competence at 9 months of age. The main point is that there is a major improvement in spontaneous imitation between 9 and 12 months of age.

Imitation might be aided by a disposition, usually observed after 9 months, to follow the direction of an adult's gaze. A 1-year-old who sees her mother move her head upward to stare at the ceiling automatically directs her gaze at the same location. The infant's tracking of the target of attention of an adult implies that caretakers, and other familiar adults, have become salient objects whose actions contain information. Chimpanzees are less likely to use the behaviors of other animals to guide their visual explorations.

Infants do not imitate every act they see and are selective in the behaviors they mimic. The most important determinants of imitation are the discrepant nature of the adult act, and the uncertainty over the ability (or inability) to perform the action. There must be some discrepancy between the schema for the act witnessed and the sensory–motor representation of the child's ability to display it. One-year-olds are most likely to imitate actions that alert them and are in the process of being mastered. These two conditions monitor the likelihood that a child will imitate an adult behavior. Infants are most likely to imitate an act when they are moderately uncertain about their ability to perform it. One-year-olds usually do not imitate acts that are beyond their motor ability, like standing on one foot, and they are not likely to imitate actions that are well within their competence, like moving a finger, but they are likely to imitate a woman who claps her hands because this act is in the process of being mastered. The great apes display the same principle. Observations of orangutans in a forest area near a research site revealed that they rarely imitated acts of other animals or humans that were difficult to implement or were displayed by unfamiliar animals or humans (Russon & Galdikas, 1995).

TEMPERAMENT

This book is concerned primarily with the development of the universal psychological properties of children, rather than with the multiple sources of individual variation that include parental treatment, identification with varied persons and social categories, and historical era. We include a discussion of temperament, however, because some psychological differences are traceable to the inheritance of specific biological profiles. It is difficult for younger scholars to appreciate that only 50 years ago most psychologists thought that biology had little relevance for understanding behavioral variation among children. Every stitch of the psychological tapestry was sewn by experience. As with all shifts in perspective, historical events are the handmaidens; in this case, four independent story lines comprise the narrative that explains why the concept of temperament has returned to scholarly discussions.

The ascendance of genetics, molecular biology, and neuroscience is the most important reason why temperament has again become popular. A second factor is the psychologists' failure to find robust preservation of the consequences of most early experiences. Siblings treated similarly by the same parents develop different personalities and cognitive skills, and identical twins are usually more similar in psychological qualities than fraternal twins raised in the same homes. Further, longitudinal studies of children, although often White and middle class, discovered relatively weak predictive relations between variation in the behavioral traits of 1- and 2-year-olds and variation in similar traits 10 years later. If some of the bizarre behaviors of infant monkeys totally isolated during the first few months of life can be eliminated by placing them with normal infant monkeys, it is difficult to argue that habits acquired early in life cannot be changed by later experience.

The third historical event is traceable to the writings of Noam Chomsky who satirized the behaviorists' tedious description of how a child learned to say, "Mama, more milk," and argued that the ability to learn a language was a biologically prepared competence. Finally, behavioral biologists had discovered that animals of different strains or related species, usually mice and rats, but occasionally dogs and monkeys, behaved in different ways to the same incentive, despite identical rearing conditions. Thus, four independent events came together to persuade developmental scientists that the child's biology was a legitimate member of the choir chanting each person's autobiography. The new Zeitgeist motivated Thomas and Chess (1977) to reintroduce the concept of temperament in the 1950s following a half century of indifference to this idea.

Infants differ on a number of behavioral characteristics; the most obvious are motor activity, irritability, ease of regulating distress, smiling, laughter, and the intensity of a fear reaction to unfamiliar events. When the variation in any of these characteristics is the partial result of biological processes (either genetic or prenatal events), rather than only experience, the disposition is called *temperamental*. The term *temperament* refers to moderately stable psycho-biological profiles that emerge during infancy or early childhood.

The power of a temperamental bias for experiencing particular emotions is revealed in a study of infants born to parents from developing countries who were adopted by middle-class Dutch families. The best predictor of dysphoric affect (e.g., guilt and anxiety) when the children were 7 years old was the child's temperament in the second year (indexed by the adoptive parents' descriptions), rather than the adoptive mother's behaviors with her child (Stams, Juffer, & IJzendoorn, 2002).

NEUROCHEMISTRY AND TEMPERAMENT

Scientists do not know the causes of most temperamental biases because this domain of study is in an early stage. Some temperamental traits could be the result of chemical events that influence the embryo or fetus. For example, 4-year-old girls with masculine interests and styles of play were born to mothers who, during gestational weeks 16 to 20, had higher blood levels of testosterone. This molecule can cross the placental barrier and affect the developing fetus (Nordenstroom, Servin, Bohlin, Larsson, & Wedell, 2002).

It is likely that most, but certainly not all, temperamental biases are the result of heritable variation in the concentration and turnover of the more than 150 molecules that affect brain function, or the density and location of their receptors. The large number of possible neurochemical patterns implies the possibility of many temperamental types. Even if a majority of these patterns have little functional relevance for mood or behavior, nonetheless, given the extraordinarily large number of possible profiles, it is likely that there are many temperaments, each defined by a neurobiology involving transmitters, modulators, receptors, enzymes, and hormones that affect psychological reactions to particular classes of events.

The genetics of blood types provides an analogy. The red blood cells differ genetically in their surface antigen. There are many different variants of the 12 major blood types, each called a polymorphism, and there are 290,304 distinct combinations of the polymorphisms of the 12 blood types. Because there are many more than 12 molecules that affect brain function, there should be a large number of temperamental types. Some, like some blood types, will be rare; others will be common. Some molecular candidates that could mediate temperamental types include norepinephrine, GABA, dopamine, serotonin, corticotropin releasing hormone (CRH), and opioids (Bradford, 1986).

To illustrate, GABA-ergic and serotonergic circuits are usually inhibitory; hence, infants born with a compromise in any one of these circuits might be less able to modulate extreme states of excitation or distress. This suggestion has empirical support. Female cynomologus monkeys with low concentrations of serotonin metabolites are likely to approach an unfamiliar intruder rapidly whereas most animals are initially restrained (Manuck, Kaplan, Rymeski, Fairbanks, & Wilson, 2003).

The promoter region for the serotonin transporter gene has many alleles and very irritable 2-month-old infants differ from relaxed, less irritable ones in one of these alleles (Auerbach et al., 1999). Japanese and European populations differ in the frequency of this allele, and Japanese infants are far less irritable than European White infants (Kumakira et al., 1999). It is reasonable to speculate that infants who inherited high levels of the serotonin transporter, which is accompanied by more rapid removal of serotonin from the synaptic cleft, should be more prone to anxiety or uncertainty (Hariri et al., 2002).

Variation in dopamine and its varied receptors are related to the intensity of sensory pleasure, reaction to novelty, and cortical excitability (Bevins et al., 2002). But dopamine, like other neurotransmitters, is modulated by other molecules. For example, estrogen potentiates dopamine function, and therefore, sex differences in a temperamental measure could be influenced by action of estrogen or testosterone and their receptors. One team of scientists reported that women with a specific polymorphism of the gene for the estrogen receptor alpha are less conforming to community standards than other women (Westberg et al., 2003).

Although controversial, several investigators posited an association between presence of the long form of the gene for the D4 receptor (DRD4) and behavioral signs of a preference for novelty and high activity level in animals and children, especially when the long form of DRD4 is present along with the long variant of 5-HTTLPR—the serotonin transporter molecule (Kluger, Siegfried, & Ebstein, 2002; Lakatos, Nemoda, Birkas, Ronai, & Kovacs, 2003). Further, high dopamine levels in the cortex suppress neuronal activity in the corpus striatum, resulting in fewer neural volleys from the striatum to the cortex and a lower level of cortical excitability that should have behavioral correlates.

Norepinephrine and its receptors are related to alertness, the capacity for sustained attention despite distraction, and the threshold for detecting subtle changes in sensory signals. The gene for MAO A, located on the X-chromosome, encodes the MAO enzyme which metabolizes norepinephrine, serotonin, and dopamine to render them less active in the synapse. A deficiency in MAO A activity, which is correlated with aggressive behavior in animals and humans, is accompanied by prolonged presence of the molecule in the synapse. A small group of participants with low MAO A activity who were abused as children were the most antisocial adults in a large sample of New Zealand individuals (Caspi, McClay, Moffitt, Mill, & Martin, 2002).

Opioid activity affects visceral afferent feedback from the body to the nucleus tractus solitarius in the medulla. Opioid receptors within these structures mute the intensity of the visceral signal; hence, less opioid activity implies that projections from the medulla to the amygdala will be more intense, and as a consequence, the orbitofrontal prefrontal cortex will be subject to greater activation. One possible consequence of this cascade is a phenomenological state characterized by worry or dysphoria. There was a significant deactivation in mu-opioid transmission when a sad mood was induced in a sample of women (Zubieta et al., 2003). By contrast, individuals with greater opioid activity in the medulla should experience more frequent moments of serenity, happiness, or imperturbability (Miyawaki, Goodchild, & Pilowsky, 2002; Wang & Wessendorf, 2002).

Corticotropin releasing hormone, secreted by the hypothalamus, influences many systems, but especially the HPA-axis, which provokes secretion of cortisol by the adrenal cortex. Capuchin monkeys with high cortisol levels are more avoidant of novelty than animals with lower levels (Byrne & Suomi, 2002), and rats reluctant to explore a novel environment secrete more corticosterone—a molecule related to cortisol—than animals who explore the unfamiliar (Cavigelli & McClintock, 2003). Ten- to twelve-year-old boys with low cortisol values were more likely than others to be impulsive and aggressive 5 years later (Shoal, Giancola, & Kirillova, 2003).

Unfortunately, the corpus of reliable relations between any of these neurochemical profiles and behavior or psychological states is so lean, scientists can imagine a large number of possible scripts, of which only a small number will prove valid.

REACTION TO UNFAMILIARITY

Two extensively-studied temperamental categories refer to young children's typical reactions to unfamiliar people, situations, or objects, whether emotional restraint, caution, and avoidance, on the one hand, or spontaneity and a tendency to approach, on the other. There are three reasons for interest in these two temperamental types. First, the behaviors that define each temperamental bias are easily quantified. Second, apparently similar variation has been observed within every vertebrate species studied. Intraspecies variation in the tendency to approach or to avoid unfamiliar objects or places has been documented in mice, rats, wolves, foxes, dogs, cats, cows, monkeys, birds, and fish. It is possible, of course, that the biological bases for this variation in one species are not the bases for the apparently similar variation in other species.

The preferred reaction to unfamiliarity can be bred, but it is surprising that this behavioral outcome can be achieved after a relatively small number of generations of selective breeding. Some quail chicks become immobile for a long time after being placed on their back and restricted by a human hand. Remaining immobile (analogous to bodily freezing in the rat) is regarded by behavioral biologists as one index of a fear state. When quail chicks that display the prolonged immobility were bred only with animals that had the same trait, it took less than 10 generations to produce a relatively homogeneous line of chicks that showed prolonged immobility when restrained (Jones, Mills, Faure, & Williams, 1994).

Children who are usually shy, timid, or subdued with unfamiliar people, objects, or situations because of a temperamental bias are called inhibited. Children who usually approach unfamiliar people and situations because of their temperament are called uninhibited. If the avoidant or approach styles are due to experience rather than a temperamental bias, which is possible, the children should be called timid or bold, rather than inhibited or uninhibited, to distinguish the different etiologies. The heritability of inhibited and uninhibited profiles, based on laboratory observations of a large sample of monozygotic and dizygotic twins observed at 14, 20, and 24 months, approached 0.5 (Robinson, Kagan, Reznick, & Corley, 1992). The heritability estimate was even higher—over .90—when the analysis was restricted to children who were extremely inhibited in a play session with four children (DiLalla, Kagan, & Reznick, 1994).

Predicting Inhibited and Uninhibited Children

Kagan (1994) and his colleagues (Kagan, Snidman, Zentner, & Peterson, 1999) have been studying early infant predictors of the inhibited and uninhibited temperamental profiles that emerge early in the second year. These two categories can be predicted from variation in motor activity and distress to unfamiliar stimuli in 4-month-old infants. This fact implicates the amygdala because, as noted earlier, this structure is activated by unfamiliar events and projects to sites that potentiate both motor activity and distress. Hence, infants born with a neurochemistry that renders the amygdala excitable to unfamiliarity should show higher levels of limb activity and crying to unfamiliar events and should be biased to become inhibited children. Infants born with a different neurochemistry that raised the threshold of the amygdala to unfamiliar events should show minimal motor activity and little distress to the same stimuli; these infants should become uninhibited children. Mice from seven different inbred strains varied in the magnitude of enhanced bodily startle to a loud noise administered after a series of electric shocks applied to the paws had activated the amygdala. The strains that showed the greatest potentiation of bodily startle had a greater density of kainate and serotonin receptors in the amygdala (Yilmazer-Hanke, Roskoden, Zilles, & Schwegler, 2003). Parental descriptions of infant twin pairs, 3 to 16 months old, reveal a genetic contribution to the variation in distress to unfamiliar events (Goldsmith, Lemery, Buss, & Campos, 1999; Miller, 2002).

The selection of the amygdala as an important foundation for the behavioral differences is not mandatory, for the parahippocampal region, which includes the rhinal cortex, is activated by unfamiliarity and is reciprocally connected to the basolateral amygdala. But the variation in infant limb activity, arching of the back, and crying is due to projections from the amygdala rather than projections from the parahippocampal region.

This hypothesis finds support in the fact that newborns who displayed an increased rate of sucking when the liquid they were receiving through a nipple unexpectedly turned sweet were most likely to become inhibited 2 years later (LaGasse, Gruber, & Lipsitt, 1989). The unexpected change in taste sensation would have provoked the cortical medial and central nuclei of the amygdala of all infants; therefore, those who showed a large increase in rate of sucking probably had a lower threshold of excitability in these structures. The display of timid, shy behavior 2 years later implies an association between threshold of excitability in the amygdala during the first week of life and a temperamental bias to avoid unfamiliar events or people in the second year.

A group of over 500 healthy White children, born at term to middle-class families, were first observed at 4 months of age (Kagan, 1994). Each infant was classified into one of four temperamental groups based on their behavior to a battery of unfamiliar visual, auditory, and olfactory stimuli (colorful mobiles, voices speaking short sentences through a speaker, and dilute butyl alcohol applied to the nostrils). Infants who showed frequent vigorous motor activity—often thrashing of limbs and arching of the back—combined with frequent crying were classified as high reactive (22% of the sample). Infants who showed the opposite profile of infrequent motor activity and infrequent distress were classified as low reactive (40% of the sample). Infants who showed low motor activity but cried a great deal were classified as distressed (25%); infants who showed frequent motor activity but did not cry were classified as aroused (10%).

The behavioral reactions of these children to unfamiliar people, situations, and procedures were evaluated on two occasions in the second year. The 14- and 21-month-olds who had been categorized as high reactive at 4 months were more likely than the low reactives to display high levels of crying and avoidance to the unfamiliar events.

These children were observed again at 4½ years in a play session with two other unfamiliar children of the same sex and age while the three mothers sat on a couch in a playroom. Each child was classified as either inhibited, uninhibited, or neither based on their behavior with the children and their reactions to unfamiliar events that occurred after the play session. Many more high than low reactives were classified as inhibited because they remained close to their mother and were reluctant to talk or play with the other children.

The presence of anxious symptoms, especially extreme shyness, worry about the future, fear of storms, animals, or loud noises, nightmares, and occasional reluctance to go to school, was evaluated when these children were 7½ years old. About one quarter of the children possessed one or more of these anxious symptoms. Forty-five percent of high reactive infants, but only fifteen percent of those who had been low reactive, showed anxious symptoms. The high reactives who developed anxious symptoms had been the most fearful in the laboratory during the second year of life (Kagan, Snidman, Zentner, & Peterson, 1999).

These children were evaluated 4 years later when they were 11 years old. Four classes of biological variables, each potentially influenced by the amygdala, were measured. These variables were: (a) hemispheric asymmetry in the magnitude of desynchronization of alpha frequencies in the EEG (the greater the desynchronization, the greater the activation in that hemisphere); (b) magnitude of the brain stem evoked potential from the inferior colliculus to a series of clicks; (c) sympathetic tone in the cardiovascular system; and (d) magnitude of the negative waveform in the ERP at 400 msec to discrepant visual scenes.

Children who had been high reactive infants should show greater EEG activation in the right, compared with the left, hemisphere because unfamiliarity and states provoked by salient visceral feedback to the brain are linked with greater activity in the right hemisphere, often including the right amygdala (see Martin et al., 1999, and Persinger & LaLonde, 2002). Ipsilateral projections from the amygdala to the cortex should lead to greater desynchronization of alpha frequencies on the right side, and therefore, greater right, rather than left, hemisphere activation.

High reactives should show a larger brain stem evoked potential from the inferior colliculus—called wave 5—to a series of clicks because the amygdala primes the inferior colliculus through the locus ceruleus and the central gray. Hence, a more excitable amygdala should be accompanied by a larger wave 5.

High reactives should show greater sympathetic tone in the cardiovascular system because amygdalar activity enhances sympathetic tone on the heart and circulatory vessels through projections to the lateral hypothalamus. Finally, high reactives should show a larger ERP at 400 msec to discrepant visual scenes because the locus ceruleus and ventral tegmentum, which receive projections from the amygdala, send axons to the cortex that enhance the synchronization of pyramidal neurons, and, as a consequence, a larger waveform in the ERP. In addition, the basolateral nucleus sends projections to the prefrontal cortex through the basal nucleus of Meynert. Cholinergic projections from this nucleus to the prefrontal cortex can enhance the magnitude of ERP waveforms to discrepant events.

All four expectations were affirmed. The high reactives were more likely than low reactives to show (a) greater right than left hemisphere activation in the EEG, (b) a larger evoked potential from the inferior colliculus, (c) greater sympathetic tone in the cardiovascular system, and (d) a larger negative waveform at 400 msec to discrepant visual scenes. In addition, twice as many high as low reactives were extremely shy and emotionally subdued as they interacted with the examiner in a laboratory setting, whereas many more low reactives were sociable and spontaneous. The most exuberant, ebullient 11-year-old was a 4-month-old who showed extremely low levels of motor and emotional arousal. This dramatic reversal from low arousal to stimulation at 4 months to an affectively spontaneous vitality 11 years later suggests that discovery of the neurochemical bases for very low or very high behavioral arousal at 4 months might provide a significant insight into the temperamental bases for extraversion compared with introversion.

About one in four children who had been high reactive infants at 4 months, and one in four who had been low reactive infants, developed a behavioral and biological profile at 11 years that was in accord with theoretical expectations for their temperament. By contrast, only 1 in 20 children developed a behavioral and biological profile that violated the pattern expected from their infant temperament, despite the varied social experiences these children encountered over the prior 11 years. The adult temperamental concepts of melancholic versus sanguine, and introvert versus extrovert, which have a long history, appear to be adult derivatives of these two infant categories.

It is not possible at present to specify the brain profile that differentiates high from low reactive infants. Even if the critical difference between the groups is differential excitability of the amygdala and its projections to events that are unfamiliar, a large number of distinct conditions could mediate these brain states. Three possibilities include (a) variation in the concentration of, or density of receptors for, GABA, opioids, CRH, or norepinephrine within the amygdala; (b) greater activity in the locus ceruleus or parahippocampal region; or (c) greater activity in the paraventricular nucleus of the hypothalamus, which secretes corticotropin-releasing hormone that, in turn, activates the locus ceruleus.

Two other biological features that are more frequent in high reactive infants who become inhibited children invite speculation regarding the possible origins of these temperamental categories. More older children who had been high versus low reactive infants possessed a narrow face (ratio of width of the face at the bizygomatic over the length of the face), and had light blue eyes. More children who had been low reactive had broader faces and dark eyes. Some derivatives of neural crest cells (discussed in chapter 2) become facial bone, some become the melanocytes of the iris and skin, and some end up in the aortic arch (Francis-West, Robson, & Evans, 2003; Hutson & Kirby, 2003). The fact that high and low reactives differ in the distribution of facial bone, iris pigmentation, and sympathetic activity in the cardiovascular system invites the speculation that perhaps these two groups inherit genes that influence the chemistry and migration of neural crest cells. It is relevant that serotonin and norepinephrine transporter molecules affect the migration of neural crest cells (Ren, Porzgen, Youn, & Sieber-Blum, 2003; Vitalis et al., 2003).

It is important to appreciate, however, that the prediction that a high reactive infant will not become a highly sociable, exuberant child with low biological arousal at age 11 can be made with greater confidence than the prediction that this infant will be extremely subdued and show high arousal in cortical and autonomic targets at adolescence. And the prediction that a low reactive infant will not be shy and show high biological arousal will be more often correct than the prediction that this infant will be highly sociable and show low biological arousal.

The suggestion that a temperamental bias constrains the development of many more outcomes than it determines applies to environmental conditions, too. If all one knows about a group of 100 children is that they were born to economically secure, well educated, nurturing parents, and must predict their likely adult psychological profile, the most accurate guesses will refer to the profiles that will not be actualized—criminality, school failure, homelessness, drug addiction, and poverty. However, prediction of the specific features that will be part of the adult personality are far less likely to be affirmed. A similar principle holds for the cells of the young embryo. The final fate of a neural crest cell in a 3-week-old embryo, for example, whether sensory ganglion or maxillary bone, is less certain than the fact that this cell will definitely not become a tendon or part of the uterus.

Some high reactives who had been fearful to unfamiliarity in the second year, and, in addition, showed several of the biological signs of amygdalar excitability, were not particularly shy as adolescents, but they described themselves as serious and desirous of a more relaxed feeling tone. This fact means that there can be a dissociation between the biological processes that are the foundation of the infant temperamental category and later social behavior, but less of a dissociation between infant temperament and private feelings as adolescents. This distinction is captured by the cliché, "You can't judge a book by its cover," and by Jung's distinction between an adult's persona and anima.

The fact that some aspects of the child's biology, presumed to be the foundation of a temperamental type, need not remain linked indefinitely to their behavioral response to unfamiliarity, implies that the biological properties of the high- and low-reactive infants changed less than their public behaviors. Experience can change a childhood behavioral profile of extreme timidity to a more normative pattern without eliminating completely the excitability of limbic structures presumed to be the bases for the infant's behavior. The genes controlling the color of feathers and the size of beaks in finches living on different islands can change in only a few generations, but the Hox genes controlling a bilaterally symmetrical body plan are not altered as easily.

Other psychologists have been studying the development of children classified as high or low reactive as infants and inhibited or uninhibited in the second year. An assessment of these children at 4 years of age revealed that those who had been inhibited earlier were reticent with unfamiliar children, displayed lower heart rate variability (a sign of sympathetic tone), and had higher levels of cortical arousal than other children (Henderson, Marshall, Fox, & Rubin, 2004).

Temperamental dispositions predict differential susceptibility to particular feeling states. Children with greater reactivity in visceral targets—heart, gut, muscles, or labyrinth—are biased to experience somatic sensations that, if detected, might be interpreted as an emotion. The central nervous system honors the difference between external events, originating in vision, hearing, and touch, and internally generated stimuli. The former information is processed preferentially by the thalamus and lateral areas of the cortex while the internal bodily information is preferentially processed by the medial prefrontal cortex. Because all languages have a richer vocabulary for external events than for feelings, it is difficult to ascertain the exact nature of the visceral experience from verbal descriptions, and similar verbal descriptions can accompany distinctly different brain states.

Equally significant, the child's temperament can modulate activity in varied visceral targets and their projections back to the brain. Some individuals have a reactive cardiovascular system; others a more reactive gastrointestinal system; others a more reactive labyrinth. As a result, some individuals will react to a challenge with a racing heart, others with cramps, still others with dizziness and the feeling they are about to faint. These sensations are so different it is likely that they evoke different interpretations, and lead to different behaviors.

The nature of the links between the temperamental bias and later emotions and moods is modulated by each person's unique history, as well as by the cultural context in which that history is actualized. For example, a high-reactive infant with overprotective parents will become a more inhibited child than one whose parents encouraged their child to cope with unfamiliar situations. However, the psychological states and adjustment of a shy, quiet adult, compared with an ebullient one, in 17th-century, colonial Massachusetts should be different from one living in contemporary Boston. Both personal experiences, as well as the normative traits defining a historical era, exert independent influences on children born with the same temperament. The implicit norm in contemporary America encourages adolescent girls to seek rather than to avoid challenge; the opposite profile was dominant 300 years ago.

On some occasions, the intrusion of somatic sensations occurs first and the person's interpretation of the sensations determines the behavioral reaction. On other occasions, a thought occurs first and provokes a somatic change that invites an interpretation. The first sequence—somatic change initially—often leads to the interpretation that one is physically ill or fatigued. The second sequence—thought first—more often leads to the judgment that one is worried, angry, sad, or guilty.

Some inhibited adolescents recognize that they are especially vulnerable to feelings of uncertainty in unfamiliar situations and try to avoid these contexts. These individuals are likely to select adult vocations that allow them to control uncertainty (for example, writer, computer programmer, librarian). Those who resist or fail to attain that insight may select a life that contains more uncertainty than they are prepared to deal with effectively. These adult decisions are not easily traced to the infant's biology, and hence, cannot be predicted from the initial temperamental profile.

It is likely that human populations that have been reproductively isolated for long periods will differ in the prevalence of particular temperaments. Current evidence suggests that infants born to Asian parents, whether in America or abroad, are less likely than White Europeans to be high reactive at 4 months of age (Kagan et al., 1994). White American, compared with Chinese-American, newborns reach a peak level of excitement to stimulation sooner, struggle more to remove a cloth placed on their face, and are more difficult to soothe when upset (Freedman, 1976). Because Chinese and European adults differ in several inherited biological features (for example, prevalence of the Rh– blood type), it is likely that these populations also differ in neurochemical profiles that are the foundations of some temperamental biases.

The puzzle surrounding the psychological variation among humans is analogous to the 19th-century debate on the reasons for species variation in survival, prevalence, and extinction among fauna and flora. It is now assumed that the reproductive success of a species is a function of its inherited features and the local ecology. We suggest that the psychological

adaptation of individuals (a property that can be independent of reproductive success) depends on their biologically based temperaments and
the environments they encounter over the first decades of life.

Temperament and Attachment

This chapter has not considered variation in behavior due to the quality of
attachment to a caretaker because of the absence of consensus on how to
measure the variation in this complex, but real, state. Infants acquire emotional reactions to the face, voice, smell, actions, and presence of those
adults who care for them on a regular basis. When a caretaker relieves an
infant's distress, or provides moments of pleasure through playing,
touching, talking, and feeding, she becomes a conditioned signal that can
evoke a variety of pleasant hedonic states as well as protect the infant
from a fear state. This collection of states does not have a consensual
name. John Bowlby (1973), and those who agree with his views, called
them a *secure attachment*. However, the name is less important than its psychological consequences and how they are measured.

The importance of the infant's quality of attachment is affirmed by the
fact that nurturant caretakers are better able to soothe a distressed infant
than other adults, distressed infants are more likely to approach a caretaker than another adult, and infants show less fear to a discrepant event if
a caretaker is present than if she is absent. These outcomes are less probable when caretakers are neglecting or indifferent. These facts suggest that
caretaker actions do affect the psychological states of infants. It is reasonable to call the schemata and sensory motor structures that are preferentially associated with a particular adult an *attachment bond*.

However, the method used most often to measure the variation in this
bond is controversial. Most scientists, European and American, have relied
on a procedure called the *Strange Situation* to assess variation in the attachment relationship. In this procedure, which takes place in an unfamiliar
room, observers note whether 1-year-olds cry when the caretaker, usually
the mother, suddenly leaves the room (either leaving the infant alone or
with a stranger), and whether the infant is, or is not, soothed easily when
the mother returns 3 min later. The 1-year-olds who cry following the maternal departure, but are soothed easily when the parent returned, are
called *securely attached*. Infants are classified as *insecurely attached* if they cry
intensely and cannot be soothed by the mother, or if they do not cry when
the mother left and ignore her when she returns. Advocates of this method
believe that these behaviors in this situation are due, primarily, to the history of interactions between the caretaker and infant.

One problem with this assumption is that 1-year-olds vary in their temperamental vulnerability to becoming distressed following the discrepant

experience of being left with a stranger or alone in an unfamiliar room. A large proportion of children who cry intensely and cannot be soothed had been high-reactive infants. Some infants who do not cry at all, or cry briefly and are easily soothed by the mother, had been low-reactive infants. Both types of infants could have experienced similar rearing regimens from their parents and their behavior was not the result of significant differences in parental care.

This conjecture finds support in the fact that children who were classified as insecurely attached, because they did not become upset when their mother left and ignored her when she returned (called Type A–Insecurely Attached), were, at age 2 years, extremely uninhibited, and at age 4, had low heart rates. Further, the 4-year-olds who were both Type A–Insecurely Attached at 14 months and uninhibited at 2 years—about 10% of the sample—were described by their mothers as frequently disobedient (Burgess, Marshall, Rubin, & Fox, 2003). These results imply that infant temperament makes a contribution to the attachment classifications. A similar phenomenon can be observed in dogs of different pedigrees tested in the Strange Situation with familiar and unfamiliar humans. The animals' temperamental susceptibility to become fearful in unfamiliar places was the main determinant of their behavior in the Strange Situation (Topal, Miklosi, Csanyi, & Doka, 1998).

An analysis of the behaviors of over 1,000 15-month-old children assessed in the Strange Situation revealed that the behaviors might be due to two continuous traits: (a) the tendency to seek contact with or to avoid the mother (presumably reflecting the degree of uncertainty), and (b) the degree of resistance to the mother's attempt to nurture the child (presumably reflecting the intensity of distress in the situation; Fraley & Spieker, 2003). Both traits could have had temperamental origins.

Human infants, like all young primates, acquire behavioral and emotional states as a result of interactions with their caretakers. Although there is important variation in the form and quality of these complex states, we suspect that a child's behavior in a single context—like the Strange Situation—is insufficient to index the variation in home experience. We note again that the meaning of behavior in one situation is often ambiguous. Hence, current conclusions about the origins and behavioral consequences of a secure or insecure attachment to a caretaker are vulnerable to criticism if based only on behavior in the Strange Situation.

SUMMARY

The newborn is transformed over the course of the first year from an agent with very poor motor coordination, a fragile working memory, and a compromised ability to detect significant features embedded within another pattern, to one who can do all three effectively across varied contexts. A central feature of the behavioral changes that occur between 7 and 12 months is the ability to retrieve schemata and to hold them and the perception of the current situation in a working memory circuit for 20 to 30 sec while comparing the two representations. The biological foundation for these advances rests, in part, on growth and differentiation of neurons in the prefrontal cortex, and perhaps, enhanced connectivity between the prefrontal cortex and the hippocampus, parahippocampal region, and association cortex. The parallels between brain and biological growth in monkeys and humans add credibility to this view.

Infants older than 7 to 8 months are able to create schematic concepts for events because brain maturation permits them to relate variation in a class of events to representations being established and to retrieve these representations following relatively long delays. These cognitive advances allow infants to become fearful to discrepant events that cannot be assimilated, and there is temperamental variation in the frequency and intensity of this state. Perhaps this is one reason why most infants reared from birth in depriving Romanian institutions, but adopted by nurturant British families before 6 to 8 months, showed minimal signs of their depriving environments when they were 6 years old, although about one third of the infants adopted after 8 months did show compromises in cognitive and emotional functioning (Rutter & O'Connor, 2004).

As the first year ends, the child can explore his environment, show coordinated reaching, retrieve schemata, and experience fear to discrepant experiences—functions present in other primates. However, as the second year begins, humans acquire a set of psychological characteristics that alters dramatically the ways in which experiences are categorized and interpreted.

5

The Second Year

The second year is distinguished by at least four psychological competences that, although dissimilar in their surface features, may depend, in part, on the same, or similar, changes in the brain. The quartet of abilities includes (a) initial comprehension and expression of meaningful speech; (b) a capacity to infer selected mental and feeling states in others; (c) representations of actions that are prohibited, as well as encouraged, by adults together with an early understanding of the semantic concepts "right," "wrong," "good," and "bad"; and (d) the conscious awareness of some of self's feelings and intentions. The close temporal correspondence in the time of emergence of these four functions, usually between 12 and 24 months, suggests that they share a set of biological features that are necessary, but not sufficient, for their actualization.

LANGUAGE COMPREHENSION AND SPEECH

It is important to distinguish between the acquisition of semantic representations mediating language comprehension and the expression of these structures in speech, for young children acquire many semantic structures long before they speak their first word. Most children, across all societies, show their first comprehension of words as the first year ends, speak meaningful words early in the second year, and display an increase in the size of their spoken vocabulary, and the length of their utterances, as the second year ends. The universality of these phenomena implies a dependence on the maturation of specific brain structures and circuits, especially neuronal ensembles in the temporal and frontal lobes, and connectivity between the two hemispheres (Brown, 1973; Caramazza & Shelton, 1998). Recall from chapter 3 that sleeping 3-month-olds showed temporal lobe activation to speech read forward or backward (Dehaene-Lambertz et al., 2002).

Although there is no consensus on the origin of human speech, scientists estimate that an important anatomical change occurred about 300,000 years ago when the human larynx descended to a position lower than the location in apes. However, there is no sound evidence for human language until about 50,000 years ago—over 250,000 years later. All experts agree that human languages, which number over 6,000 in the contemporary world, change their features and syntax as a function of the mixing of populations. The problem associated with deciding whether a particular dialect deserves to be classified as a distinct language is similar to the problem facing biologists trying to decide whether a particular group of animals should be classified as a species (Pennisi, 2004).

Students of language development disagree on the specificity of the biological foundations of language. One group, for whom Noam Chomsky and Steven Pinker are intellectual leaders, believes that the human brain possesses unique capacities devoted only to language, and, especially that children possess a biological preparedness to learn the grammar of the language to which they are exposed. A second group acknowledges the unique anatomy necessary for language, but believes that many of the biologically prepared cognitive competences exploited in language acquisition are also used for other purposes (Tomasello, 2003). These competences include the ability to (a) infer the intentions of others, especially the intention of an adult to communicate information; (b) perceive entities in dynamic states of change; (c) attend to physically salient sounds (for example, the sound "s" for plural in English); (d) detect discrepancy; (e) be aware of self's motives and actions; (f) infer low-level correlations between different classes of events (for example, transitional probabilities between words in speech); and (g) form schematic concepts. It is hard to imagine a universal human cognitive talent that relies on functions restricted to that talent alone.

The fact that there are far less than 6,000 distinct grammars across the more than 6,000 human languages implies that each language exploits a small set of basic human capacities. One capacity permits young children to segment continuous speech flow into separate words by detecting the statistical regularities in the language they hear (Saffran, 2003). The sound p-r-e in English usually occurs before a number of other syllables, as in the words "pretty," "present," "prefer," and "prepare." The probability that the sound p-r-e will be followed by the sound t-y is about .80 in adult speech directed to young infants. By contrast, the probability that the sound t-y will be followed by b-a (as in "pretty baby") is less than 1%. As a result, children find it easy to learn that p-r-e-t-t-y is a word, but t-y-b-a is not (Saffran, 2003).

Similarly, the sound "a" often follows the sound "m" as in "mama," but the sound "g" rarely follows the sound "s." Thus, infants who regularly hear their parents say, "Mama's giving you a kiss," gradually acquire a lexical structure for "mamas" that is separate from the structure for "giving" (Saffran, Aslin, & Newport, 1996). Although these cognitive functions contribute to language acquisition, they are exploited in other domains.

Working memory capacity, which is required for language, also has multiple functions. The typical 2-year-old is able to hold about two—or perhaps three—independent cognitive representations in working memory for 5 to 10 sec. Parents understand this limitation implicitly, and, as a result, speak in short, telegraphic utterances, like, "Want cookie?," rather than "Would you like some cookies?" Adolescents need a robust working memory to recognize that the word "preferred" refers to Mary in the sentence, "The new red dress that Mary's mother wanted her to wear to the party for Susan was rejected in favor of the old blue one that she preferred for school days."

The attraction to discrepancy is also exploited in language learning, for adults usually place vocal emphasis on words that have greater significance. Seven-month-olds can segment words with three syllables from fluent speech if the first syllable is given vocal emphasis or stress, as in the word "*canteloupe*," but not if the stress is put on the last syllable, as in "*cavalier*." Vocal emphasis in speech functions like contour in visual events. A parent is likely to emphasize the word "stop" when, for the second time, she says to her child, who has been playing with dirt, "I said stop."

New words are learned more easily if the child has acquired schematic concepts for the events being named. Events that are distinctive, because they are less frequent variants of a class of events, are most likely to become schematic concepts. Some less frequent variants include: (a) moving compared with static objects, (b) large compared with small objects, (c) near compared with far objects, (d) graspable compared with nongraspable objects, (e) objects that produce a sound compared with those that are silent, (f) events that are transient compared with those that are more permanent, and (g) events that evoke feelings compared with those that do not. Thus, 2-year-olds are more prepared to learn the semantic terms for "go," "big," and "cookie" than for "still," "small," and "vase."

Cooing and Babbling

The relation between infant babbling and later speech is controversial. On the one hand, babbling, like speech, appears to be under greater control of the left, rather than the right, hemisphere. We noted in chapter 3 that the differential contribution of each hemisphere to mouth movements can be inferred by noting whether the distance between the lips is larger on the right or the left side. The left side is larger when infants smile, implying right-hemisphere dominance, but the right side is larger when infants babble, implying left-hemisphere dominance (Holowka & Petitto, 2002).

However, one argument against the view that babbling is an early form of speech is that congenitally deaf infants begin to babble at the same age as hearing children, but the former fail to progress to meaningful speech (Amunts, Schleicher, Ditterich, & Zilles, 2000, 2001; Hiscock & Kinsbourne, 1998).

Semantic Structures

Children create schemata for the sound patterns of the words they hear regularly. Infants who hear the phrase, "good baby" hundreds of times in the opening months create representations of this sequence of sounds, although these representations might have a minimal link to schemata, and therefore, have no semantic meaning. Semantic meaning emerges when these representations are linked to a perceptual or visceral schema or sensory motor representation. No other species finds it as easy to associate an initially meaningless auditory stimulus with a representation of an event. Very young infants associate any salient sound, whether a bell or a spoken utterance, with an object, although they can discriminate the sound spectra of a human voice from similar sounds. However, this equivalence vanishes by the end of the first year when children preferentially link speech to an event in their perceptual space because they infer that the speaker intended to communicate some information (Balaban & Waxman, 1997; Tomasello, 2003; Woodward & Hayne, 1999). Now, on hearing the word "milk," the child activates a schematic representation of that substance or the sensory motor representation for drinking (Namy & Waxman, 1998).

Surprisingly, deaf children learning sign language display meaningful hand signs at the same age, and show the same rate of vocabulary growth, as hearing children, although the information perceived and expressed is represented by hand and finger movements. Children learning sign language make signs before they make symbolic gestures and do not confuse a meaningful sign with a gesture made by another, although both are visual signals (Petitto, 1992). These facts suggest that humans possess a set of biologically-prepared cognitive abilities that make it especially easy to discover units of meaning in the organization of the phonetic or syllabic units common to all languages, whether expressed in speech sounds or in hand movements. It appears that the syllable serves as the building block for the lexical structures that will gain semantic meaning (Eimas, 1997).

The simplest semantic representation consists of an association between the representation of an auditory event (for example, the schematic representation of the acoustic profile for "cookie") and an example of that object in the environment. Eleven-month-olds who had been taught to associate an unfamiliar word with an unfamiliar object (for example, a piece of styrofoam) showed a distinctive waveform in the ERP when an adult spoke the word in the presence of the object (Molfese, Morse, & Peters, 1990). Meaningful, compared with meaningless, words produce different waveforms in the left hemisphere of 2-year-olds within the first 200 msec following the onset of a word (Mills, Coffey-Corina, & Neville, 1997). Magnetoencephalography evidence from adults suggests that recognition of the similar semantic meaning of two words, whether seen or heard, usually occurs at about 400 msec (Marinkovic et al., 2003).

Children form semantic structures quickly, and their number expands dramatically from the first to the fourth birthday. The average American adult has about 50,000 words in their active vocabulary. Although the schematic representations of objects or actions linked to a word are its most distinctive features, the brain also represents the sound pattern, length, and syllabic emphasis of a word. That is why rhymes evoke interest, and why the word "chair" is retrieved more quickly than "table" if the person has just seen the word "bear," whereas "table" is retrieved more quickly if the person has just seen the word "label" (Rapp & Samuel, 2002).

The increasing number of semantic representations leads to the formation of semantic networks, which are patterns of associations among semantic representations that vary in their schematic contribution. The semantic network for "food," which includes apples, bread, and pizza, has a rich schematic contribution. The network for "truth," which includes terms for "science," "authority," and "experience," has a much weaker schematic contribution. The relations between schemata and semantic structures in a person's representations of experience remain a mystery. For example, the abstract semantic statement, "Force is the product of mass and acceleration," can be understood semantically without any referents to the schemata created by seeing a baseball, travelling at 15 miles per hour, strike and break a window. Apparently, the schematic or sensory motor structures associated with words that represent movements of the arm, leg, and face are represented in different circuits, for adults reading single words that named varied movements of those body parts produced three distinctive ERP profiles. Words that name actions of the arm produce greater activity in the right frontal cortex; words representing leg movements activate the vertex; and terms that name facial actions activate the inferior frontal cortex on the left side (Hauk & Pulvermuller, 2004).

The semantic network often links perceptually distinct events that are not linked as schematic concepts. Some 2-year-olds, for example, have acquired a semantic network that includes the words *"mama," "kiss," "eat," "milk," "cookie, "good," "baby,"* and *"sleep."* The events to which these semantic terms refer share no physical features, although they might share a visceral schemata. Many 2-year-olds have acquired an initial form of the semantic networks for "man" and "woman" for they look longer at a picture of a man performing a typical female action (e.g., putting on makeup) than at a woman performing the same behavior because they were surprised by the former event (Serbin, Poulin-Doubois, & Eichstedt, 2002). Scientists will have attained a profound insight into the distinctive character of the human brain-mind when they understand the brain bases for semantic networks.

Parents from different societies, and social classes within a society, emphasize different events when they communicate to children to create differences in their vocabularies. English-speaking children, 15 to 40 months old, compared with Japanese children of the same age, have more names for objects and more often use shape as a primary basis for naming animals (Yoshida & Smith, 2003).

Names for colors usually develop later than names for objects and actions because the color of an object rarely contains information implying its function or association with pleasant or unpleasant feelings. Further, color is usually represented in combination with the context in which the object appears. The names for colors in many languages combine the color with its usual context. For example, the word "chloros" in ancient Greek referred to the green hue of moist foliage, and not to the green hue of a vase. English has fewer examples; "robin's egg blue" is one illustration. Surprisingly, many 2-year-olds who know that the word "color" refers to the surface hue of an object do not know the correct referent for specific color words and will say *blue* as often as *red* when asked, "What color is this tomato?" (Sandhofer & Smith, 1999).

The first four years may represent a sensitive period in language development because the potential to acquire proficiency in a language appears to decline somewhat after this time. Adults who acquired some language in the first few years, but learned American Sign Language after they became deaf, eventually acquired an excellent sign language vocabulary. But adults who had been congenitally deaf as children, and were not exposed to any sign language until they were 6 or 7 years old, showed a less extensive sign language vocabulary (Mayberry, Lock, & Kazmi, 2002).

The variety of semantic and syntactic utterances the child hears, rather than the absolute number of words to which it is exposed, is the most important determinant of the rate of vocabulary growth. This principle is reasonable because children are alerted by discrepancy. A parent who, 90% of the time, says to her child, "time to eat," but, on occasion, says, "time for your cereal," alerts the child with the less frequent word "cereal" and provokes an attempt to infer the meaning of the less familiar word. Unfamiliar words in a familiar context are as alerting to 2-year-olds as strangers entering the home are to 8-month-olds (Samuelson & Smith, 2000).

The significance of discrepant or unexpected experience explains why the speech of 2-year-olds is penetrated with words referring to transformations; for example, the sudden appearance or disappearance of an object (move, gone), the sudden movement of an object (go, off), or a sudden change in an object's state (break, fix).

Initial Biases. Ellen Markman (1992) has proposed that young children learning a language begin with three biases called whole object, categorical, and mutual exclusivity. The first is defined by the tendency to assume that a spoken word applies to a whole, solid object, rather than to a part, although children eventually learn when to ignore this bias as they acquire terms for the parts of objects. Two-year-olds, on hearing an adult speak the unfamiliar word "spider" as the adult points to an unfamiliar dark object on a brown sand pile, assume that the word refers to the entire animal, and not to its location, legs, behavior, or the sand pile.

If there were no object present when a child heard a parent say an unfamiliar word, the former would look for other properties to associate with the word. For example, a child who sees a dollop of whipped cream on a plate and hears the parent say, "look at the cream" interprets the unfamiliar word as the name for the dollop of cream. Thus, the bias for whole objects serves as a first guess, and can be overridden (Samuelson & Smith, 2000).

Although human languages differ in the acoustic distinctiveness of nouns, verbs, adjectives, and adverbs, many linguists believe that the semantic representations of solid objects are psychologically different from those for actions or nonsolid phenomena, like water. One reason is that stroke patients with localized brain damage often lose the ability to comprehend only one of these syntactic forms more profoundly. Because the semantic representations of most nouns are richer in schemata than those for verbs, the pattern of impairment in stroke patients might mean that semantic forms that are rich, compared with lean, in schemata are represented in different brain sites.

One reason the shape of an object is more distinctive than its size, color, or surface texture is that the objects parents usually name for their children are most often distinguished by their shape (examples are cup, dog, and ball; Sandhofer & Smith, 1999). Thus, a 2-year-old who hears a new word while looking at an unfamiliar object infers that shape is probably the defining feature of the object. However, this rule, too, is occasionally violated (Yoshida & Smith, 2003). Children are most likely to extend a word just learned to objects with the same shape after they have acquired a vocabulary of about 50 different words for objects, and have about 80 words in their productive vocabulary (Samuelson & Smith, 1999). This level of mastery usually occurs by the end of the second year.

The child's mental set affects the features awarded priority. Children were shown a 2 × 2-in. blue wooden object in the shape of a ⊔ and were told, "this is a dax" (Landau, Smith, & Jones, 1988). The examiner then showed the children this object along with objects of a different shape but made of the same material, or objects of the same shape that differed in size or texture, and asked, for each one, "Is this a dax?" Most children applied the word "dax" to test objects with the same shape as the original, and refused to call objects of different shapes by that name, even if they had the same texture and size. However, if the examiner changed the verbal instruction and asked, "Which one matches this?" the children used size as a defining feature. Thus, the way an adult poses a question to the child is a critical determinant of the child's inference, and the initial bias for shape can be superseded when it is not useful (Landau et al., 1988).

A second bias in language acquisition, called the categorical bias, is the assumption that a word probably refers to a category of similar objects, and is not restricted to the specific object in the perceptual field. The assumption of generality permeates word learning, but is far less common for perceptual or visceral schemata derived from sensory experiences. Thus, the child who first hears the word *dog*, while looking at a picture book with his parent, assumes that all objects with similar features have the same name and the word "dog" does not refer only to that particular animal. Two-year-olds with a larger than average vocabulary, who are especially likely to honor this bias, will treat a caricature of a real object as if it were the object (e.g., treat a tiny cup as if it were a typical cup and drink from it in a play sequence). This is one reason why symbolic play with objects is elaborated, in a major way, during the second year (Smith, Jones, & Landau, 1996).

The child also understands that a semantic term can refer to features that are not observable. As the child acquires the semantic network for the word "dog," she appreciates that some invisible features are essential properties of the semantic category. A child who believes that a bird and a dog share the property "alive" assumes that they belong to a common semantic category (Diesendruck, 2001).

The third bias, mutual exclusivity, tempts the child to assume that if he knows a name for an object and hears an unfamiliar word in the presence of that object, the new word must apply either to some property of the object, or to another event in the environment. Put plainly, infants as young as 16 to 18 months assume initially that each object has only one name (Markman, 1992; Markman, Wasow, & Hanson, 2003; Smith, 1995). If a 2-

year-old is shown two familiar objects for which he has distinct names (for example, a cup and doll) along with an unfamiliar piece of styrofoam for which he has no name, and the adult says, "Give me the zoob," most children give the examiner the unfamiliar, styrofoam object. They infer that the adult intended to name the only object for which she had no name. A chimpanzee raised by humans and exposed to human speech would not leap to that inference.

The problem facing the young child trying to understand adult speech can be described. When an adult names an object while the child is either looking at or manipulating it, the child is likely to learn a new word. Two-year-olds will also infer the object's correct name when an adult names an object she is studying. A two-year-old listening to her mother chat with a friend hears the mother say, "Have one more roll," as she removes the baked object from a basket and places it on her neighbor's plate. The fact that the word "roll" was unfamiliar, and was articulated with vocal emphasis, leads the child to infer that the object (that is, the roll) was the referent for the word. If the child had no initial cognitive biases to focus on objects and to attend to words spoken with emphasis, the word "roll" could have referred to the basket or the act of placing the roll on the plate. And if the mother were not looking at the object, the child would be less likely to infer that the word named that object (Baldwin et al., 1996). One-year-olds, but not ten-month-olds, watching a film depicting an adult with a happy or unhappy facial and postural reaction to an object behaved in accord with the emotion simulated by the adult. There may be a transition between 10 and 12 months in the tendency to assume that a stranger's face and posture communicate relevant information (Mumme & Fernald, 2003).

In addition, the child's inference regarding the meaning of a new word is aided if he or she knows the meanings of the other words in the adult utterance. If the child knew the meaning of "eat" and the parent had said, "Eat the roll," 2-year-olds would have found it easier to guess that the word roll referred to the edible object. The probability that a new word will be added to the child's vocabulary is a function primarily of (a) the frequency with which it is used by others, and (b) the variety of contexts and grammatical forms in which it appears (Naigles & Hoff-Ginsberg, 1998).

We noted in chapter 4 that learning schematic concepts for events is easier if the event occurs in a variety of contexts. This variety is more frequent for objects than for actions. As a result, nouns that name people, animals, and objects have a less ambiguous meaning than verbs for action. For example, in the sentence, "The boy ate," the schematic reference for "boy" is less ambiguous than the schematic reference for "ate," because the act of eating varies with the food eaten, whether cereal, ice cream, or pizza, and the context is the home or a restaurant.

The failure of English verbs to specify context means that many predicates are ambiguous in meaning if no agent or target is specified. Hence, the predicate "bit" could refer to a person biting an apple, a thread, plastic wrap, or another person. The verbs in some other languages do refer to a context; for example, Mayan Indian dialects contain a verb that refers specifically to eating tortillas. English has a few such predicates (for example, to electrocute, to fax, and to e-mail, but these words are derived from the nouns "electric chair," "fax machine," and "computer").

The increasing richness of semantic structures makes it possible for children to differentiate between semantically consistent and incomprehensible sentences. Children who were 6, 12, 18, or 24 months old watched one of two films: (a) a comprehensible pictorial excerpt from Sesame Street accompanied by a coherent narration, or (b) a series of designs interspersed with incomprehensible Sesame Street verbal excerpts. The 6- and 12-month-olds, who had minimal language, looked equally long at both films. The 2-year-olds looked longer at the film with incomprehensible speech because the sentences were discrepant from their semantic knowledge. Thus, semantic meaning begins to guide attention by the first birthday and does so more clearly by age 2 (Richards & Crouse, 2000).

Some scientists do not distinguish sufficiently between the name for a class of events and the physical features of the events to which the word refers. We noted in chapter 3 that the brain is especially prepared to notice the motion of an object. Because animals and humans move spontaneously, it is relatively easy for the infant to learn the semantic concept "alive." However, the brain circuits that detect motion are not the circuits that represent the semantic concept "alive." The semantic structures that appear in the second year, and become dominant nodes of classification during late childhood, are not inherent in the events named. A Thanksgiving table can be represented semantically as "two platters of turkey, four bowls of vegetables, twelve dinner plates, or one holiday table." However, the child's schematic representation of this scene is far less arbitrary.

Syntax and Grammar

The syntax of a language consists of representations of the permissible orders of semantic forms in well-formed sentences. This competence requires 2-year-olds to be sensitive to the order of words that they hear. We noted in chapter 4 that infants under 1 year can create a schema for such patterns. Some linguists regard syntactic rules as Platonic ideals. A mother, on seeing her 6-year-old kiss a puppy, might say, "Why did you kiss the puppy?" However, if the mother had said, "You kissed the puppy, why?" the child would have understood that question to have exactly the same meaning, although the syntax was different. The term "grammar" refers not only to the rules for word order, but also to rules for forming tenses, plurals, participles, prefixes, and suffixes. Most English verbs form the past tense by adding "ed" (work- worked). However, some verbs, less than 200 in English, form the past tense idiosyncratically (sing-sang). When children are learning the grammatical rule for the past tense, usually in the second and third years, they often generalize the common rule and apply the "ed" rule to all verbs (sing-singed), especially when they cannot remember the correct, irregular form (Jackendoff, 2002; Marcus, 1996).

The two fundamental syntactic categories represent entities and their functions. The first category is called a noun phrase; the second a predicate or clause. These two linguistic classes refer to the child's most common perceptual experiences; namely, objects, animals, plants, or people, changing their state in some way. The young child's first sentences most often refer to such sequences (e.g., doggy run; ball fall; mama eat). We noted earlier that the acquisition of semantic forms is aided by the brief pauses occurring at word boundaries (Bates, Devescovi, & Wulfeck, 2001). The acquisition of the syntactic representations for nouns and verbs is aided by the fact that speakers usually pause very briefly between subject and predicate. For example, in the sentence, "The big bear is going home," most speakers insert a very brief pause between the noun phrase "the big bear" and the predicate "is going." This pause helps the child differentiate between nouns and verbs. A sensitivity to brief temporal gaps in a coherent sequence is exploited in other domains; for example, a 2-year-old reaching for a bouncing ball accommodates to slight differences in its velocity as it bounces across a rug.

Words that violate the semantic meaning of a sentence produce distinct ERP wave forms different from those evoked by words that violate a grammatical rule. For example, adults display a large negative waveform at frontal and central sites, with a peak magnitude at 400 msec, when a word at the end of a sentence is inconsistent with the semantic meaning contained in the prior terms; for example, "The girl put the bread in the computer." But a positive waveform with a peak magnitude at 600 msec at posterior sites is observed when a word violates a grammatical rule, as in, "The girl putted the bread in the toaster" (Brown, Hagoort, & Kutas, 2002), suggesting that the brain required more time to detect the grammatical violation than the semantic one. It is generally the case that the longer the latency to the peak magnitude of an ERP waveform, the more cognitive work was required.

Given the universality of the events that recruit attention in 2-year-olds, one might have expected that all human languages would have a similar syntax. The puzzle is that they do not. Although English, like three fourths of human languages, usually places the subject of a sentence before the verb and the verb before the object (for example, "The boy ate the cake"), Japanese and Turkish usually place the verb at the end of the sentence. Other languages place the verb in the initial position. About 2% of known languages are more radical, for they place the subject at the end of the sentence (for example, "ate the cake boy"). The fact that children in these cultures learn their local language as easily as children learning English means that the brain-mind is biologically prepared to detect and to learn a variety of orders of agents, actions, and targets.

The variation in grammars implies that there are fewer biological constraints on learning a language than there are on the learning of sensorimotor schemes. All children prefer to push an object away with their hands rather than with their elbows, and to signal a need for help by lifting their arms rather than waving them. The meanings of many words change over time (for example, "rap" or "fuzz"), but the meaning of an open, extended hand or clenched fist has changed less over the same historical period. Thus, despite an obvious biological foundation for language, its cognitive structures are more malleable than those involved in other psychological talents.

In sum, the biologically-prepared competences for language acquisition include selective attention to adults when they speak, the ability to infer the speaker's intention, the capacity to detect correlations between events, the sensitivity to physically distinct features, and finally, the ability to perceive the similarity and differences between classes of events to infer categories (see Tomasello, 2003, for an elaboration of these ideas).

Speech

The preceding discussion has focused on the acquisition of semantic and syntactic structures. However, most children also begin to speak during the second year. The most important motive for this behavior is to communicate information that cannot be communicated in other ways. A child who wants the parent to take a cookie from the cupboard, or give him or her a cup of milk, can communicate these desires more effectively with language than with a gesture (Bloom, 1993). The use of speech to convey a desire requires the assumption that the child infers that the adult will understand him when he speaks.

The desire to practice a new form is a second motive for speech. Children talk when they are playing alone, or while lying in bed before falling asleep. Speech in these contexts serves the urge to practice a competence that is being acquired. Young children dress and undress a doll, throw and retrieve a ball, and talk while alone because of a biologically-prepared propensity to practice skills that are incompletely mastered.

THE BRAIN AND LANGUAGE

The neural contributions to language are embedded in broad cortico-cortical networks that link the auditory and temporal cortex to the parietal, frontal, striatal, and cerebellar regions involved in representations of temporal sequences (Boatman, 2004; Lieberman, 2002).

Primary Auditory Cortex

The analysis of speech sounds requires two main classes of neurons in the primary auditory cortex. One class reacts to pure tones; the other detects patterns in human speech. Peak synaptic density in the primary auditory cortex, usually reached by 3 months, remains high until about 3 years at about 140% of adult values. The extraction of the phonetic features of speech is mediated primarily, but not exclusively, by the superior temporal lobes. Lexical representations are represented more fully in the left posterior region; semantic representations are more fully represented in the left and middle inferior temporal gyri (Martin, 2003).

The synaptic density in the primary auditory cortex (Brodmann, 41, 42), Wernicke's area (Brodmann, 40), Broca's area (Brodmann, 44, 45), and prefrontal cortex, differ during the first 4 years of life. However, by the fourth birthday, synaptic density has become roughly equivalent in these four sites, twice the value found in adults (Huttenlocher & Dabholkar, 1997), and does not reach adult levels in the primary auditory cortex until 12 to 13 years of age. It is also relevant that cortical lamination is established in Broca's area by age 4 (Judas, 1987), and predominant blood flow shifts from the right to the left hemisphere between 3 and 4 years of age (Chiron et al., 1997).

Cortical Areas in Language

Wernicke's and Broca's areas are two of the many cortical regions that play major roles in the language network. The results of scanning studies have revealed a broad distribution of cortical sites that participate in language functions (Poeppel & Hickok, 2004). Although Wernicke's area plays a greater role in the comprehension of speech, and Broca's area a greater role in the motor components, and perhaps, grammatical competence, both sites participate in other psychological functions. Wernicke's area, named for the German psychiatrist and neurologist Karl Wernicke

(1848–1905), and located in the left temporo-parietal cortex (the posterior third of the superior temporal gyri), receives information from the auditory cortex, and participates in the phonological analysis of information. This cortical area is the site of the convergence of cortico-cortical interactions that map sounds onto words and mediate meaning by activating relevant representations in other brain regions (Damasio, 1992). A spurt in the elongation of the dendrites on pyramidal neurons in layer 3 of Wernicke's area, is accompanied by the emergence of language comprehension and speech, although this process does not plateau until about 10 years of age.

Wernicke's area is linked through the arcuate fasciculus to Broca's area located in the left prefrontal cortex adjacent to the orofacial area of the primary motor cortex, which contains neurons that activate the muscles of articulation. Broca's area, named for Pierre Paul Broca (1824–1880), the anthropologist and surgeon who discovered the connection between language deficits and abnormalities in this particular region, participates in the programming of word articulation by storing representations of motor patterns for particular words. These two areas work together. Elegant studies of marmosets reveal that, about 200 msec before an animal vocalizes, a select set of neurons in the auditory cortex is suppressed, presumably in the service of permitting the animal to monitor its own sounds (Eliades & Wang, 2003). Once the animal has vocalized, another set of neurons in the auditory cortex is activated.

Intensive dendritic growth in layer 5 of the orofacial area of the right primary motor cortex is observed at 3 months of age when infant cooing appears (Amunts et al., 2000, 2001; Hiscock & Kinsbourne, 1998; Locke, 1990). The shift in rate of dendritic growth to the left orofacial motor area by 12 to 15 months is correlated with more precisely synchronized movements of the mouth and tongue and the appearance of words (Simonds & Scheibel, 1989). It is believed that projections from the motor cortex to the larynx, which are more substantial in humans than in apes, permit more voluntary control of vocalizations (Ploog, 2002). Rapid growth occurs in both left and right Broca areas from two to three years, a period of accelerated speech development. From four to six years dendritic length increases more in the Broca region on the right than the left, suggesting the importance of speech intonation in conveying meaning and emotional tone.

Although Wernicke's area plays a greater role in the comprehension of speech, and Broca's area a greater role in the motor components, and perhaps, grammatical competence, both sites participate in other psychological functions. Although the comprehension and production of speech are mediated in most children by the middle and inferior temporal lobes in the left hemisphere, the right hemisphere can assume some competence for both comprehension and production if the left hemisphere is damaged. However, this competence is better for concrete words (for example, "dog," "tree," and "pizza") that are associated with schemata than for abstract words like "justice" and "theory."

Inferior frontal regions of the right hemisphere participate more than the left in the detection and production of prosody (inflection of speech). Hence, when adults discriminate words based on their phonemic structure, the left prefrontal region is activated. However, when they discriminate words based on the emotional tone contained in prosody, the right frontal region is more active (Buchanan, Lutz, Mirzazode, Specht, & Shah, 2000). However, the important distinction between left and right hemisphere capacities involves the rate of change in information. The left temporal lobe participates more in processing auditory input with rapid change, as is true of speech, whereas the right temporal lobe participates more in processing events characterized by a slower rate of change, as is true of music and most environmental sounds (Tervaniemi & Hugdahl, 2003).

Neuronal activity (recorded by PET) in the monkey brain to species specific calls, as well as other sounds (the sound of breaking glass or water dripping), revealed that the former evoked greater activity in the dorsal temporal pole of the left hemisphere than in other parts of the superior temporal gyrus. However, when the connections between the left and right forebrain were cut, there was no asymmetry of activity to the two classes of sounds. This fact suggests that the left hemisphere suppresses activity in the right when familiar, species specific calls are heard (Poremba et al., 2004).

Many scholars have wondered whether Wernicke's and Broca's areas in the left hemisphere evolved primarily to serve language, or whether these areas mediate a general capacity to process all rapidly-occurring sequential information, speech being only one example. This latter hypothesis is reasonable because many cognitive skills require the processing of rapidly-occurring sequential information. Sign languages, for example, require the processing of rapid changes in hand motions. The fact that the development of both forms of language follows a similar timetable implies that speech may be a member of a more general set of cognitive processes (Neville & Bavelier, 1998). Bates, Devescovi, and Wulfeck (2001) proposed that language areas evolved from brain structures optimally suited for language functions. Although children who suffered early damage to the left perisylvian area (where the temporal and frontal lobe meet) usually develop normal language abilities, some lesions are linked to specific delays in language acquisition (Bates & Dick, 2000; Vicari, Albertoni,

& Chilosi, 2000). Thus, the brain is not equipotential at birth, and some regions are specialized for particular functions.

Cerebellum

The speaking of single words is accompanied by cerebellar activation, and impairment in word articulation is more common following damage to the left, compared with the right, cerebellum (Fiez & Raichle, 1997). There is also an increase in cerebellar volume during the second year (Courchesne, 1997; Fiez & Raichle, 1997; Schmahmann & Pandy, 1997). Dendrites on neurons of the dentate nucleus of the cerebellum show intensive lengthening and extension after the first birthday, and mature forms are attained by the second birthday (Hayakawa, Konishi, Matsuda, Masanori, & Konishi, 1989; Mihajlovic & Zecevic, 1986; Yamaguchi, Goto, & Yamamoto, 1989).

The contribution of the cerebellum to language ability is revealed in a study of Chinese-speaking adults who saw a single probe word placed above a pair of target words. The subject had to decide which target word was semantically closer to the probe word. On some trials, only one target word was related to the probe (for example, the targets might be "rose" and "ball" and the probe word "flower"). On other trials, both targets were semantically related to the probe (for example, the targets might be "chair" and "desk" and the probe word "bench"). These more difficult semantic discriminations were accompanied by activity in the right cerebellum, although participants did not speak any words during the experiment (Xiang et al., 2000).

Basal Ganglia

The basal ganglia, which undergo intense development during the second year, might also participate in language. Dopamine-1 and dopamine-2 receptors in the caudate nucleus reach peak density around 18 months, and plateau until about 10 years, after which their density decreases (Schultz, 2000; Seeman et al., 1987).

The study of a three-generation family, in which half the members had severe articulation difficulties, implicates the basal ganglia in language ability. MRI measurements of these individuals revealed a significantly smaller caudate area in the basal ganglia of both hemispheres (Vargha-Khadem, Watkins, Alcook, Fletcher, & Passingham, 1995). The gene responsible for this phenomenon (SPCH1) has been localized on chromosome 7 (Fisher, Vargha-Khadem, Watkins, Monaco, & Pembrey, 1998; Vargha-Khadem et al., 1998).

A PAIR OF HYPOTHESES

Two hypotheses, admittedly speculative, may contribute to the fact that speech emerges in most children after the first birthday. The first assumption is that 12-month-olds have created a schematic concept for humans that includes the self and other persons, but excludes other objects (animals, plants, natural objects, artifacts). This schematic concept is perceptually salient because it is based on shared physical and behavioral features that no other object possesses and the fact that adults provide children with pleasure and relief from pain. As a result, children are especially attentive to adult facial expressions, gestures, and verbal communications.

The second assumption is that schemata are more fully represented in the right hemisphere, whereas lexical and semantic structures are more fully represented in the left (Lauder, 1983; Thierry & Giraud, 2003; Warrington & McCarthy, 1994). Thus, when the neurons in layer 3 of the prefrontal cortex elongate and grow spines, and the axons of one hemisphere make contact with neurons in the opposite hemisphere through the corpus callosum—which occurs during the second year—the speed of integrating the information in both hemispheres is accelerated (Mrzljak et al., 1990). Neural activity is greater in specific sites in the right than in the left hemisphere when a person is trying to generate schemata for the color or duration of an event (Coull, Vidal, Nazarian, & Macar, 2004).

Adults deciding whether two pictures did or did not belong to the same semantic category were faster if one picture was presented in the left visual field and the other in the right than if both pictures were processed by one hemisphere (Koivisto & Revonsuo, 2003). Further, the left hemisphere is more active than the right when the adult must decide whether a word on a screen contains the letter "A" (a semantic task). However, the right hemisphere is more active when the participant must decide if a letter, printed in red ink, is to the left or the right of the word's center (a nonlinguistic task; Stephan et al., 2003; see also Hoptman & Davidson, 1994). Finally, familiar, but not unfamiliar, objects produce a coherence of alpha frequencies between left and right occipital regions in adults, suggesting that the schema and the appropriate semantic form were activated simultaneously (Oluwatimilehin, Hiraoka, & Halle, 2001).

Hence, when a child sees a cup on a table, it is possible that the activated schema for cup is integrated rapidly with the semantic representation, and the child says "cup." It is of interest that the compromised ability to retrieve the name of a familiar person, which is common in older adults, is accompanied by callosal thinning, suggesting the waning of a process in the elderly that is waxing in the second year (Sullivan, Pfefferbaum, Adalsteinsson, Swan, & Carmelli, 2002).

Support for this argument comes from the pattern of coherence of alpha frequencies in the EEG across different brain sites while adults were memorizing lists of either concrete or abstract nouns. Only the abstract nouns were associated with transfer from the left to the right hemisphere; the transfer was reciprocal for concrete nouns. The authors suggested that more rapid comprehension of abstract nouns is attained by gaining access to right hemispheric resources (Schack, Weiss, & Rappelsberger, 2003).

Another study is also supportive. Adults saw a large number of pictures of objects from four different semantic categories with rich schematic content (forest animals, flowers, clothing, and furniture) while magnetoencephalogram recordings were made. The participants had to indicate whether each object was a human artifact or a natural object. The peak neuromagnetic activity at 150 to 200 msec was in posterior areas of the right hemisphere, presumably reflecting activation of schemata relevant to the pictures. However, about 150 msec later, between 210 to 450 msec, peak activity was in the temporal area in the left hemisphere, presumably reflecting the subsequent activation of semantic structures (Low, Bentin, Rockstroh, Silberman, & Gomolla, 2003).

Clinical Evidence

Studies of children with brain lesions have implications for the differential hemispheric contributions to language. Children who suffer lesions in either the left or right hemisphere before speech emerges, as confirmed by MRI or CT scan, show delayed onset of babbling and communicative gestures, as well as impaired comprehension and production of speech in the second year, although many recover adequate language function. However, the severity of the delay is similar whether the lesion is on the left or right side (Rapin, 1995). However, if the lesion occurs in adolescence or adulthood, speech production is delayed more severely if the damage occurred to the left rather than the right hemisphere.

Children who suffered a focal brain lesion early in development and a second group of children with a specific language impairment were compared with normal children. The lesioned group had lower scores than the normal children on grammatical judgments, but higher scores than those with a specific language impairment. Further, the children with lesions showed evidence of plasticity, although their compensatory growth resulted in profiles different from those seen in adult aphasic patients with comparable lesions (Bates et al., 2001). These findings suggest that the brain sites compromised in children with specific language impairments are less plastic than those produced by early focal lesions (Wulfeck, Bates, & Krupa-Kwiatkowski, 2004).

The corpus of evidence supports the speculation that enhancement in the efficiency of communication between the left and right hemispheres, which occurs in the second year, contributes to the emergence of speech in most children (see Cook, 2002, for support of this view).

INFERENCES OF OTHERS' MENTAL STATES

The ability to infer selected intentions, thoughts, and feelings in others is a second psychological competence of this era, and as we noted, necessary for language. This new talent can be seen when an adult hides a toy under one of three covers behind a barrier so the child cannot see where the toy is hidden. If, after removing the barrier, the adult directs her gaze toward the toy's location, 2-year-olds, but not 1-year-olds, look in the direction of the adult's orientation and reach toward that place, suggesting that they inferred that the adult was looking at the correct location. Eighteen- and nineteen-month-olds, but not younger children, used the direction of an adult's gaze to guide the direction of their orientation to a target (Moore & Corkum, 1998; Tomasello, 1999; Tomasello & Haber, 2003). This behavior is present, but is considerably less reliable, in apes (Call & Tomasello, 1998). A subordinate chimpanzee infers whether a dominant animal can or cannot see the location of an attractive piece of food. But there is no evidence that chimpanzees regularly infer the intentions or feelings of another animal.

The inferential capacity is also seen in a more difficult version of the test for object permanence. We noted in chapter 4 that 8- to 10-month-olds, as well as rhesus monkeys, will search for an object they saw hidden under one of two covers. Although infants this young will not look for the toy if the experimenter surreptitiously removed it from the place where it was hidden, children older than 18 months search for the object if they do not find it under the cover because they infer that the object must be somewhere. Monkeys seem incapable of that inference, for they do not search if they find no object after lifting the cover (de Blois, Novak, & Bond, 1998).

The ability to infer select mental and feeling states in others renders children capable of empathy. A group of 14- and 21-month-olds, observed both at home and in the laboratory, saw an examiner pretend to hurt herself by closing her fingers in the suitcase that held some testing materials and saw the mother pretend to hurt her knee. The 20-month-olds showed more signs of empathy in face, voice, and gesture than the 14-month-olds, suggesting that the capacity to infer an adult state of pain matured over this 6-month interval (Zahn-Waxler, Robinson, & Emde, 1992).

The ability to infer the thoughts of others makes a contribution to the growth of language because children infer that an adult who is speaking is referring to events in the world, and when directed at the child, intends to communicate a fact or a request. Children would be less likely to link the words they hear to events in their perceptual space and relevant schemata if they did not make that assumption. An example of this cognitive advance is seen in a study in which an examiner picked up a toy pig and said, "See what I am doing to the pig." The examiner then pretended to pick up an imaginary milk carton and pour imaginary milk on the neck of the toy. The adult then showed the child three pictures, only one of which illustrated a pig with milk spilled on its neck, and asked the child to point to the picture illustrating what happened. Children younger than 2 years old did not point to the correct picture, but children older than 2 years did, implying that by age 2, children understand the symbolic relation between speech, on the one hand, and an adult's pretend actions and a picture, on the other (Harris, Kavanaugh, & Dowson, 1997). The capacity to imagine events never experienced is a defining feature of our species. Some Etruscan drawings dating from 800 B.C. were of animal forms no artist could have seen.

Although chimpanzees occasionally track the gaze of another animal, they show no behaviors implying that they understand that another animal or human intends to share information. Chimpanzees watching an adult human perform simple acts with a tool and objects focus their attention on the objects, rather than on the adult movements, because they do not infer that the adult has a private intention guiding his behavior. Humans feel uncertain when they infer that another person might harbor undesirable thoughts about them. Chimpanzees become uncertain when they anticipate actions another animal might direct at them. Doubt over whether another person will regard self as dumb, disloyal, or deviant is very different from doubt over whether another animal is about to attack, dominate, or seize the food one is eating. Anxiety is the name we apply to the former state; fear to the latter. A major event in the evolution of humans from apes was the replacement of a vigilant set to the potentially threatening actions of another with a state of worry over the private opinions of another (Povinelli & Bering, 2002).

The suggestion that 2-year-olds infer the thoughts and feelings of others does not mean that this process is as acutely conscious as it is when an adult infers that a friend is ill from the quality of her voice. The adult inference involves conscious selection of one possible cause from a set of alternatives. The 2-year-old's inference is more automatic and depends, in part, on acquired associations between the schematic representations of her own prior feeling states and perception of another's state.

Once the child regularly infers the intentions and thoughts of others, she begins to treat purposeful and accidental actions in different ways. A group of 14- and 18-month-olds watched an adult perform a series of two-step actions on objects. As the adult implemented one class of actions, she said a word indicating that her behavior was intentional. But the adult said "Whoops!" for the other class of acts to indicate that her behavior was accidental. The child was then allowed to imitate the adults' actions. Both 14- and 18-month-olds imitated more intentional than accidental behaviors, implying that they inferred the motivational state of the adult (Carpenter, Akhtar, & Tomasello, 1998).

To infer another's intention or state, the brain-mind must detect in the reactions of another the features shared with schemata the child had created from her prior behaviors, and relate the product of that cognitive work to stored representations of intentions or states. That is, the 2-year-old, on seeing a parent scream as she catches her hand in a closing door, detects the similarity between the scream and the schemata of his own past cries, and relates the latter to the visceral schemata of past feelings of distress. The joint occurrence of these two processes is followed by the recognition that the parent must be in a state of distress. This hypothetical sequence is the definition of empathic inference.

The capacity for empathy helps children restrain aggressive behavior toward others. Once children have experienced the distress that accompanies being teased, struck by another, or losing a desired object, they infer that others will feel the same unpleasant state when those events occur to others. Hence, the initial tendency to inhibit acts that harm another is universal, although this restraint is not always honored. The belief that aggression should be controlled may be one of the few moral standards children acquire that does not require direct instruction or punishment.

The enhanced connectivity between left and right hemispheres could contribute to the ability to infer the state of another. The visceral schemata of the child's past feelings, stored primarily, but perhaps not exclusively, in the right hemisphere, are integrated with semantic representations of the state of another, represented primarily in the left hemisphere. As a result, the structures in each hemisphere activated by the sight of another in pain are integrated more rapidly. This suggestion finds support in a comparison of adults who had lesions of either the frontal lobe or the posterior cortex with healthy controls. The patients with right-hemisphere lesions had the lowest scores on self-report measures of empathic feelings, implying that the right hemisphere contributed more than the left to the activation of the visceral schemata that are essential for empathy (Shamay-Tsoory, Tomer, Berger, & Aharon-Peretz, 2003). We do not suggest that maturation of the neurons of the corpus callosum is the sole basis for this advance; only that this growth might be a necessary, although not a sufficient, component. The capacity for inferring the thoughts and feelings of others has implications for a third competence; namely, an appreciation of right and wrong actions and good and bad events.

THE INITIAL CONCEPT OF GOOD AND BAD

Most 20th-century American scholars writing on the acquisition of morality, unlike earlier ones, assumed that all moral standards were learned
through parental praise and punishment. The typical account stated that a
child learned that hitting another was wrong because adults punished
such acts and praised their restraint. Therefore, learning to inhibit aggression to another was no different in principle from learning to use a fork or
to remain quiet at the dinner table.

However, 2-year-olds from varied cultures show signs of uncertainty
when they see a broken object, or fail a self-assigned task or one assigned
to them. Because it is unlikely that parents across the world socialize inhibition of property destruction and avoidance of failure at the same time,
the temporal concordance implies a biologically-based preparedness to
create categories of punishable versus praiseworthy actions and good and
bad events, where "preparedness" has the same meaning linguists intend
when they write that 1-year-olds are biologically prepared to learn language.

This first stage of moral development takes advantage of the alerting
power of discrepant experience. A mother who has just seen her 14-
month-old spill milk on a table says in a voice louder, and a face sterner,
than usual, "Don't do that." The unexpected chastisement is a discrepant
event that alerts the child and creates a state of uncertainty that is assimilated to the schematic category for hedonically unpleasant experiences,
like pain, hunger, and cold. The child quickly learns that spilling food is
usually followed by a chastisement and a feeling of uncertainty and, as a
result, inhibits such acts. Thus, the first phase of moral development rests
on a feeling of uncertainty provoked by the discrepant features inherent in
a parent's disciplinary response to a child's actions. Because a parent's actions following the violation of a standard, whether a frown, raising of the
voice, or a slap on the wrist, is unexpected, it activates the amygdala and
its projections, causing a rise in heart rate, muscle tension, and perhaps
crying.

The schematic representations of the action, the context, the parental
disciplinary reaction, and the subsequent feeling of uncertainty become
associated. Repetitions of these experiences create a conditioned reaction
of uncertainty when the child is in a situation that has provoked parental
discipline. As a result, suppression of a potentially punishable action becomes more probable. Even if a parent never chastised her child, it is probably impossible to raise a child without interrupting some action that was
potentially harmful or violated a family standard, most often destruction
of property, aggression, or soiling one's clothes. The parents' reaction is
the conditioned stimulus for a response of uncertainty in the child. All the

acts that provoke the uncertainty become exemplars of a concept of prohibited actions. This learning is implicit and resembles the learning of prototypic phonemes.

The behaviors that imply acquisition of a concept of prohibited actions, and therefore, the first elements of a conscience, often appear by the middle of the second year, and almost certainly by the second birthday. One such behavioral sign is refusal to perform an action that violates a family norm, although the child is told to do so by a parent. Most 2- to 3-year-olds will hesitate, or not perform at all, if a parent asks them to pour cranberry juice on a clean tablecloth, or scribble on a clean page of a new book, although these acts had never been chastised in the past. The refusal implies that the child possesses a concept of "prohibited actions" (Kagan, 1981).

Children also refuse to perform behaviors that are too difficult to execute. If an examiner models three coherent actions with toys and then says, "It is your turn to play," many 2-year-olds, but no 1-year-old, cry because they infer that the adult wanted them to imitate those actions and they sensed their inability to do so. The distress implies that the child inferred that failure to perform would provoke adult disapproval. Such an inference requires some comprehension of the meaning of "ought" and a category of improper actions. On the other hand, if the child sensed that she could meet the standard implied by the request, she would make some attempt and might be successful (see Fig. 5.1). For example, 21-month-olds showed some ability to combine three small toys to construct an object with a meaningful function (for example, a rattle or an object that allows horses to spin; Bauer, Schwade, Wewerka, & Delaney, 1999). It is likely that children less than 1 year old would not perform this task because of an inability to understand that there was a goal the adult wanted them to attain.

The category of improper actions is extended to objects whose integrity is flawed because the child infers that someone produced the flaw. Two-year-olds will point to a small hole in a shirt, a missing button, or an ink spot on a chair, and, with a serious tone of voice, say, "boo-boo" or "uh oh," indicating that they regard the flaw as discrepant from an ideal state and, therefore, improper. One of the authors observed a 2-year-old girl who became visibly upset in a playroom because she held a small doll and saw a large toy bed, but could not find a small bed that was more appropriate for the doll. This girl possessed a schema for the ideal bed for the doll.

The ability to imagine the best object or action for a situation, which is a seminal component of morality, requires the ability to generate a category one might call the *ideal,* as well as the complementary category *flawed.* Both categories contribute to a moral sense. Parents living on isolated atolls in the Fijian chain recognize this advance for they tell informants

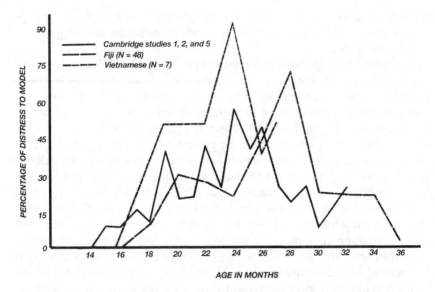

FIG. 5.1. Proportion of children from three different cultures displaying distress when an adult models three actions and tells the child the resume play. The display of distress after 18 months suggests that children assumed an obligation to imitate the adult but sensed their inability to do so.

that children acquire *vakayala,* meaning good sense, soon after the second birthday (Kagan, 1981).

The next phase of moral development, which usually occurs early in the third year, involves the acquisition and application of the semantic concepts "good" and "bad" to objects, events, actions, and people. The word "good" is applied to sweet tastes, embraces, praise, sleeping babies, and a gentle touch. The word "bad" is applied to bitter tastes, crying babies, loud noises, foul odors, criticism, and storms. The essential feature of the semantic representation for "good" is a visceral schematic concept experienced as hedonically pleasant. The critical feature of "bad" is a visceral schema experienced as unpleasant.

It is not known whether the brain patterns evoked by the very different events called good or bad share any feature that could be the basis for two visceral schematic concepts, one underlying the semantic concept "good" and one for "bad." Although it is theoretically possible that a particular circuit is activated whenever the semantic network for good (or bad) is provoked, it is equally likely that there is no unitary brain state for each concept. The shared feature is simply a semantic term, as is true for the concept *game.*

Once children possess the semantic categories "good" and "bad," they assume that some acts that have never been punished are potential targets of criticism, and therefore, bad. For example, 2-year-olds regard a man putting on make-up as discrepant from their expectations, and presumably, bad. Children evaluate their intentions as good or bad, depending, in part, on anticipations of how they will feel should their intention be implemented in behavior; for example, whether they will feel anxiety or shame if an action were displayed. The resulting suppression of such behaviors is not a conditioned reaction. If 2-year-olds were never punished for harming another they would, nonetheless, create the category "bad" because they have experienced the unpleasant state that follows criticism, aggression, or teasing, and can infer these states in others. Hence, most children believe that harming another, physically or psychologically, is a bad act.

There are differences, as well as similarities, across cultures in the acts judged good or bad. Brahmans regard the ritual avoidance of menstruating women as morally proper; Americans do not. Americans regard praising a child's autonomy as proper; Brahmans do not. But members of both cultures agree that ignoring the victim of an accident and kicking a helpless animal are morally wrong because of the universal capacity for empathy (Shweder, Mahapatra, & Miller, 1987).

The emergence of a moral sense by the end of the second year has a distinct advantage for younger siblings. Before humans had access to contraceptive devices, most mothers gave birth to an infant when the next oldest sibling was between 2 and 3 years old. The older child is usually jealous of the attention given the infant, and has both the strength and opportunity to harm the latter. However, almost all older children inhibit such behavior because they are capable of empathy and appreciate that harming the younger sibling is a bad action.

In sum, the initial development of a moral sense involves the following sequence:

1. A feeling of uncertainty provoked by unexpected parental reactions to particular acts, present by the end of the first year.
2. Creation of schematic concepts for prohibited acts and ideal states, and, therefore, a readiness to feel uncertain when the ideal is violated or compromised, and a motive to suppress prohibited acts; usually seen by the middle of the second year.
3. The ability to infer the thoughts and feelings of others, to feel empathy for the distressed state of another, and to anticipate adult disapproval for certain behaviors; usually seen during the second year.
4. Acquisition of the semantic concepts "good" and "bad" and their application to actions, events, people, and self; usually seen during the third year.

These processes are so universal that observations of 5-year-olds in most places in the world reveal that the number of sociable and cooperative behaviors toward others is larger than the number of aggressive or destructive acts (Whiting & Whiting, 1975).

Two-year-old children feel an obligation to act in ways that match their acquired standards on behavior and to inhibit acts that violate those standards; that is, they experience a feeling that is a feature of the concept "ought." This psychological state requires the anticipation of unpleasant adult sanctions for violations of a standard, (because of the ability to infer the thoughts of others), an awareness of the self's ability to control certain behaviors, and the capacity for an emotion that follows matching the self's behavior to a standard. There is no evidence that apes are capable of these states. Apes can detect discrepant responses in others and acquire schematic representations of other's behaviors, but it is unlikely that they track the relation between their schematic concepts and their actions, and experience a feeling when they do, or do not, match their behavior to their schematic knowledge. Chimps do not feel that they "ought" to behave in a particular way. Hence, evolution awarded humans a unique motive that is not present in apes.

We suggest that the emergence of these phenomena, like language and inference, could be aided by the more efficient coordination of information between the two hemispheres. The visceral schemata that represent the unpleasant feelings of uncertainty following parental criticism are more fully represented in the right hemisphere; the semantic representations of good and bad acts and intentions are mediated more fully by the left hemisphere. Thus, creation of the moral categories "good" and "bad," and the restraint imposed on actions evaluated as bad, could be a function, in part, of the growth of neurons in cortical layer 3 during the second year.

SELF-AWARENESS

The initial components of self-awareness represent a fourth competence of this developmental phase. Two-year-olds, but not one-year-olds, act as if they are aware of their intentions, feelings, and abilities. For example, they display a smile following completion of a difficult task (called a mastery smile), direct adults to act in particular ways, show signs of distress-crying, retreating, or an embarrassed lowering of the head when they cannot imitate the behavior of another, and describe what they are doing as they are doing it.

A classic sign of self-awareness can be seen when a mother surreptitiously puts rouge on her child's nose and tells him to stand in front of a full-length mirror. Most children older than 18 months, but fewer younger children, automatically touch their nose (Lewis & Brooks-Gunn, 1979). This behavior suggests that the older children recognized that the reflection in the mirror represented themselves. Three-year-olds can even pick out a photo of their face in an array of several faces of unfamiliar children (Nolan & Kagan, 1980).

The longer duration of a play episode, a striking characteristic of the second year, becomes possible because the child is now conscious of an action plan directed at a goal, and therefore, sustains a longer play bout. The "stage" on which knowledge of a goal guides actions does not collapse every 30 sec or so, as it did during the first year. As a result, the child does not forget the goal he decided to pursue several minutes earlier.

A third sign of self-awareness is distress over actual or potential task failure. If an examiner models some acts with toys in front of the child and then says, "Now it is your turn to play," many 18- to 19-month-olds, from different cultural settings, are likely to cry (see Fig. 5.1). The distress is due to at least two processes. The first, noted in the discussion of a moral sense, is that the child assumes an obligation to implement the adult's acts. However, we must also posit some awareness of the inability to imitate the adult acts.

The occurrence of a smile after the child has attained a goal through effort, for example, placing a seventh block on a tower of six blocks, is a fourth sign of self-awareness. Smiling following such acts of mastery, which are not social smiles, is rare before the second year. The mastery smiles occur because the child recognizes that she has attained a goal following the investment of effort. The smile requires an awareness that self has reached a previously imagined goal. Lowering of the head when an effort has failed requires an awareness that others might be evaluating the child in undesirable terms.

A fifth sign of self-awareness is the emergence of behaviors that reflect the expectation that the self is an agent who can influence the behaviors of others. Some examples include attempts to change the behavior of a parent, or a request for help with a problem. For example, children will put a toy telephone to the mother's ear and gesture or vocalize to indicate they want the mother to talk on the telephone. Children would not direct adults if they did not have an expectation that the adult would comply. Thus, the increased frequency of this behavior implies that the child believes he can influence the actions of others.

The appearance of self-descriptive utterances is a sixth sign of self-awareness. These verbal descriptions of behavior usually occur when the child is engaged in an action. For example, the child will say "climb" as she climbs up on a chair, or "up" as she tries to get up on a box. These statements occur because the child has an awareness of her capacity to initiate certain behaviors. This awareness is a novel experience, and therefore, an incentive for a verbal description. The child's speech also contains the words "I," "my," "mine," or the child's name, as in "I sit" or "Mary eat." The child does not begin to talk about herself and her actions because she has a larger vocabulary, but because she has experienced the discrepant state of conscious awareness of what she is doing. When the state of surprise, due to the novelty of being aware of what one is doing, wears off, the child stops describing her behavior.

Finally, the child will substitute a toy for the self in pretend play sequences. For example, as the second year ends, the child will put a telephone to the head of a doll rather than to her own ear, or put a bottle in an animal's mouth rather than in her own mouth, implying that the child is playing the role of director in a script. These behaviors are generally regarded as play. The word "play" does not refer to any particular class of behavior. Learning to ride a bicycle is usually called play, although the child may have a serious facial expression and will cry if she is not mastering the skill easily. By contrast, some scientists and musicians regard their daily work as play. Play, therefore, refers to a state of mind that occurs when a behavior is initiated voluntarily, without coercion. This definition implies that a playful state is as common in adults as it is in children.

As with our explanation of language, inference, and a moral sense, we turn again to the enhanced connectivity between the two hemispheres as enabling self-awareness. Changes within the body vary, often subtly, from moment to moment and day to day. During the second year, the child becomes consciously aware of changes in feeling tone. The coordination of visceral schemata for the self's usual feeling tone, represented primarily in the orbitofrontal prefrontal cortex of the right hemisphere, with the semantic categories for the self's properties, represented primarily in the association of areas in the left hemisphere, could contribute to the phenomena of self-awareness. If a child did not experience changes in internal feelings, doubts about the self would emerge. One 18-year-old reported to a therapist that she felt "like a stick" because she experienced no change in feeling tone. The claim, "I feel, therefore I am," should probably be added to Descartes's "I think, therefore I am" (Damasio, 1994).

Children can impose different interpretations on a perceived change in feeling tone. When the change is interpreted as apprehension, fear, shame, or guilt, the child is more likely to inhibit asocial behavior. One of the most reliable differences between boys and girls, across cultures, is the greater female restraint on physically aggressive behavior. It is of interest, therefore, that the ratio of the volume of the orbitofrontal prefrontal cortex to the amygdala is larger in women than in men, suggesting that women may experience a more acute awareness of subtle changes in feeling tone (Gur, Gunning-Dixon, Bilker, & Gur, 2002).

Many research reports and theoretical essays on the neural foundations of consciousness assume that this word refers to one phenomenon, rather than to a family of processes mediated by different neural profiles. The perception of a soaring hawk against the blue sky is experienced as a unity, but scientists have learned that the detection of the motion, shape, and color in the scene is mediated by different brain areas. The same principle probably applies to consciousness. It is likely that the awareness of (a) sensations (for example, heat, sound, taste, balance, pain, or a change within these sensory inputs); (b) intentions to act; (c) thoughts involved in solving a problem; and (d) semantic networks representing the self and others, are mediated by distinct brain circuits. The first stage of consciousness, which appears in the second year, involves the awareness of sensations and intentions to act, but not the other two properties. We noted that the brain can react to a change in sensory input without an accompanying consciousness of that change. Adults attending to repeated 500 msec exposures of a complex scene showed a positive waveform at 350 to 600 msec at frontal and central sites when the scene contained a subtle alteration, although the participants who were instructed to report whenever they became aware of a change in the scene, failed to indicate any awareness of a change in input (Fernandez-Duque, Grossi, Thornton, & Neville, 2003). When the participants finally became aware of the change, the magnitude of the waveform was only increased by a small amount.

The suggestion that the self-consciousness of the second year requires maturation of the central nervous system is inconsistent with traditional descriptions of self-awareness. Psychoanalytic theorists had assumed that the self was initially merged with another person, and the child had to differentiate the self from the parent. We suggest that there is no self prior to the middle of the second year, as there is no frog in the tadpole, and no blossom in the seed.

A second view holds that a sense of self develops gradually as a result of the child acting in the world. Guillaume (1971) argued that the first phase of self-awareness was a derivative of imitating others. George Herbert Mead (1934) believed that social interaction was mandatory for the first stage of self-awareness. Although Charles Cooley (1902) was closer to 19th-century suppositions when he awarded more influence to perceptual and emotional components than to actions in creating a sense of self, he insisted that acts informing the young child of her effectiveness were prerequisites for self-awareness. Piaget (1950), too, insisted that the child only learns about self when he acts on objects. Lewis and Brooks-Gunn (1979) agreed that a child's awareness of self had its source in interactions with others. Although a child isolated from all people and objects might not develop self-awareness, we are less certain that the first form of this human property requires social feedback.

An awareness of the self's feelings, intentions, actions, and their consequences contributes to the universal assumption that events have a cause, and motivates children to search for causal relations between events that may have none. The ancients assumed that a pattern of stars during a particular month, or a bit of amnion tissue on a newborn's face, had prophetic significance. The reluctance to assume randomness or arbitrary meaning to experience might be due, in part, to the fact that after the second year, humans are aware of their voluntary actions. When they act, they have the certain intuition that their behaviors have an intention and a purpose. Human adults resist the conclusion that life has no particular purpose; they wish to believe that some actions and events are more useful, more moral, or more beautiful than others.

BRAIN MATURATION DURING THE SECOND YEAR

In addition to the callosal connectivity between the hemispheres, other biological changes are important bases for the talents of the second year. First, maturation of the prefrontal cortex, which is elaborated more extensively in humans than in other primates, probably makes a contribution to language, inference, morality, and self-awareness.

The prefrontal cortex has reciprocal links to all associational cortices, as well as the amygdala, hypothalamus, hippocampus, basal ganglia, and cerebellum. In addition, the amygdala, as well as the diffuse nuclei in the mediodorsal nucleus of the thalamus, send information from bodily targets to the orbitofrontal prefrontal cortex. Rakic (1995a) has suggested that prenatal migration of neurons from the telencephalon to the diencephalon only occurs in humans. This anatomical arrangement, combined with the extensive dendritic arborization of pyramidal cells in the prefrontal cortex, might be critical for the competences of the second year.

The long-term sequellae of prefrontal lesions acquired early in childhood also implicate the prefrontal cortex (Anderson, Damasio, Tranel, & Damasio, 2000; Eslinger, Grattan, Damasio, & Damasio, 1992; Tranel & Eslinger, 2000). Patients with prefrontal lesions acquired between 7 days and 7 years show a loss in the ability to maintain representations of a goal, regardless of the location of the lesion or the patient's gender or age at the time of the lesion (Grattan & Eslinger, 1991; Marlowe, 1992; Miller & Cohen, 2001; Price, Daffner, Stowe, & Mesulam, 1990).

Finally, changes in neurochemistry might contribute to the actualization of the four competences (Johnston & Singer, 1982; Kalaria, Fiedler, Hunsaker, & Sparks, 1993). Peak levels of glutamate-binding activity of glutamate decarboxylase (a molecule required for the synthesis of GABA), as well as a spurt in GABA activity in inhibitory interneurons of layer 3, occur between 1 and 2 years of age (Huttenlocher & Dabholkar, 1997; Kornhuber, Mack-Burkhardt, Konradi, Fritze, & Riederer, 1989; McDonald & Johnston, 1990; Reichelt et al., 1991; Slater, McConnell, D'Souza, Barson, & Simpson, 1992).

The maturation of GABA-ergic inhibitory functions is revealed in the fact that the period of greatest improvement in the delayed nonmatch to sample procedure occurs at maturationally comparable times in monkeys and human infants. Monkeys show their greatest improvement on this task between 3 and 6 months; human infants between 10 and 18 months. Success on this task requires inhibition of the strong tendency to reach for an object that was rewarded on the immediately prior trial, and instead, to reach toward the unfamiliar object (Diamond, 1990a). All observers recognize the increased ability of 2-year-olds to regulate their behavior, and GABA mediates inhibitory functions. In plainer language, the first signs of what 19th-century citizens called the human "will" emerge in the second year.

The second year is also marked by increased turnover of acetylcholine. Activity of choline acetyltransferase, an enzyme involved in the synthesis of acetylcholine, increases sharply during the second year when pyramidal neurons begin to express acetylcholinesterase in cell bodies and fibrillary networks (Black, 1991; Blokland, 1996; Court, Johnson, Piggot, Kerwin, & Perry, 1993; Decker & McGaugh, 1991; Kostovic, 1987). The innervation of layer 3 pyramidal neurons by acetylcholinesterase, which may be unique in apes and humans, might contribute to the psychological functions of this period (Kostovic, 1987, 1990; Kostovic et al., 1988; Mesulam & Geula, 1988, 1991).

AUTISTIC DISORDER

The symptoms of autism, characterized by profound disturbances in cognitive, emotional, and social behavior, are usually seen at the end of the second year. The primary symptoms are serious disturbances in interacting with others, impaired verbal communication, and stereotyped or ritual actions. Although 60% of children diagnosed with autism are cognitively compromised, the atypical social behavior is more distinctive and more prevalent than the delays in cognitive development. That is, the variation in language ability is greater than the variation in social behavior (Tager-Flusberg & Joseph, 2002). Although the diagnosis of autism might represent a spectrum of symptoms with a single biological etiology, most scientists believe that the symptoms can be the result of different causes. The diagnoses most often used by physicians and psychiatrists include the following: (a) autism, (b) Asperger Syndrome, (c) pervasive developmental disorder, and (d) autistic spectrum disorder, which com-

TABLE 5.1
Current Criteria for the Diagnosis of Autism

---

1. A severe abnormality of reciprocal social relatedness.
2. A severe abnormality of communication development (including language).
3. Restricted, repetitive behavior and patterns of behavior. Restricted interests, activities and imagination.
4. Onset before the age of 3 years.

---

bines the classic symptoms of autism with mental retardation (see Table 5.1; Gillberg & Coleman, 2000; Sparks et al., 2002).

Prevalence of the Autistic Syndrome

The prevalence of any one of the autistic diagnoses is estimated to be between 0.1% and 0.2% of the population. However, if all four categories of autism are included, the prevalence can rise to 1%. The fact that estimates of prevalence have risen over the last 20 years could be due to a real increase in this disease or an increase in the professional diagnosis of autism due to alterations in the diagnostic criteria. For example, the apparent increase in the diagnosis was found in a population-based study of eight successive California birth cohorts born between 1987 and 1994. A total of 5,038 children with the full syndrome of autism were identified from 4,590,333 California births, a prevalence of 11 children per 10,000. During these 7 years, the prevalence of an autistic diagnosis increased from 5.8 per 10,000 to 14.9 per 10,000, an absolute change of 9.1 per 10,000. During this same period, the prevalence of a diagnosis of mental retardation without autism decreased from 28.8 per 10,000 to 19.5 per 10,000, an absolute change of 9.3 per 10,000. These data suggest that changes in diagnostic decisions might account in part for the apparent increase in autism (Croen, Grether, Hoogstrate, & Selvin, 2002).

Possible Causes of Autism

Autism has a genetic component, although the pathological mechanisms are not known (Trottier, Srivastava, & Walker, 1999). Twin studies revealed a concordance rate for a broad definition of autism of 70% to 90% in monozygotic, but less than 10% in dizygotic twins (Zoghbi, 2003). Second, the frequency of autism in siblings of autistic patients is 2% to 5%, compared with 0.1% to 0.2% in the general population (Lotspeich & Ciaranello, 1993). One study of 153 families found a locus for autism on Chromosome 7. One region on this chromosome is a putative locus for language (Stokstad, 2001); another region is the site of the reelin gene, which is crucial for neuronal migration. A mutation in this gene leads to disturbances in the formation of the neuronal layers of both the cerebral and the cerebellar cortices. Inheritance of this variant of the reelin gene increases the risk for autism by a factor of 3.5.

Early Symptoms of Autism

Although the diagnosis of autism is usually made by the third birthday, a small number of cases display symptoms during the first year. The mothers of such children report that their infants seem different, either because they do not appear to need their affection, or because they become limp or rigid when held. Social smiling and babbling are either absent or develop late, and these infants react to normal sounds with extreme irritability (Ornitz, 1983).

One team of scientists examined home movies made during the first 6 months of life of 15 children who later developed symptoms characteristic of the autistic spectrum. The films of these autistic children were compared with films of normal children. The former were less likely to look at adults, as well as less likely to smile and vocalize, but they were as attentive as normals to inanimate objects (Maestro, Muratori, Cavallaro, Pei, & Stern, 2002).

Baron-Cohen, Allen, and Gillberg (1992) proposed three behaviors that appear in almost all normal children by 18 months. The three behaviors are as follows:

1. Pointing—The infant points to an object to direct another person's attention to it.
2. Gaze monitoring—The child looks in the same direction of an adult.
3. Pretend play—An object serves as a symbol for another object, or the child makes use of imaginary objects (e.g., the child puts three dolls in a row and pretends they are riding in a bus).

Absence of these three behaviors implies that the child might have autism (Baron-Cohen, Allen, & Gillberg, 1992; Baron-Cohen et al., 1996). Unfortunately, many 2-year-olds who display the behaviors that imply normal growth develop autistic symptoms a year or two later (Baird et al., 2001). These facts suggest either that one or more genes that become active after the second birthday create a brain state that disrupts or prevents normal development, or the behaviors that define normal development in 3-

year-olds require a circuitry that is not required for a normative profile during the first 2 years of life.

Structural Anomalies

Autistic children have structural anomalies in many parts of the nervous system; but no scientist has been able to find a single focal defect as a defining sign of autism. Autopsies reveal both primary lesions, as well as compensatory structural changes that developed later. Modern imaging methods, as well as microscopic examination of the brains of deceased autistic patients, reveal structural abnormalities in the hippocampus, entorhinal cortex, amygdala, septal nuclei, mammillary bodies, and anterior cingulate cortex (Bauman & Kemper, 1985, 1994; Courchesne et al., 2001; Raymond, Bauman, & Kemper, 1996; Stokstad, 2001). An MRI analysis of sulcal patterns in preadolescent autistics and controls revealed that the patients had abnormal patterns in the superior frontal sulcus, an area believed to participate in working memory, affect, language, and eye gaze (Levitt et al., 2003). Studies using MRI have revealed a significant reduction of the cross-sectional area of the dentate gyrus and the CA4 area of Ammon's horn in adult patients (Saitoh, Karns, & Courchesne, 2001). Further, preadolescent autistic patients, compared with controls, had a larger white matter volume for the axons that radiate to the prefrontal cortex, (including the corona radiata that myelinate in the first or the second year), and in cortico-cortical connections. But they did not have larger volumes for sagittal or bridging compartments (for example, the internal capsule and the corpus callosum) that connect the two hemispheres or the cortex with subcortical structures (Herbert et al., in press).

The brains of some autistic patients, but not all, have smaller neurons with shorter dendritic extensions, and structural abnormalities in the columns of the prefrontal and temporal cortex (Casanova, Buxhoeveden, Switala, & Roy, 2002). Although the brains of autistic patients had more columns than those of normal children, each column was narrower, and the neuronal configuration was less compact. The greater dispersion of neurons within a column might be accompanied by a reduction in inhibitory potential, and perhaps, by an inability to discriminate between competing sources of sensory information (Casanova et al., 2002).

Hisaoka and colleagues, using magnetic resonance spectroscopy, measured the amount of N-acetyl-aspartate (NAA), an index of the neuropil, in the frontal and temporal lobes of autistic patients and age-matched controls ranging from 2 to 20 years of age (Hisaoka, Harada, Nishitani, & Mori, 2001). The patients showed a significant reduction in NAA in the right temporal cortex, corresponding to Wernicke's area, implying either fewer neurons or a less dense dendritic tree. Disturbances in the right temporal lobe should impair the ability to discriminate linguistic from non-linguistic sounds and could contribute to the language difficulties of autistic patients.

Autistic symptoms are also associated with anomalies in the occipito-temporal cortex, particularly in regions mediating the perception of facial expressions. The ability to interpret facial expressions correctly is central to harmonious social interaction. Autistic patients usually avoid social interaction, as well as eye-to-eye contact (Pierce, Müller, Ambrose, Allen, & Courchesne, 2001). Autistic patients presented with faces show aberrant activity in the frontal or primary visual cortex, but not in the fusiform gyrus of the occipito-temporal cortex. Normals show maximal activation in the fusiform gyrus.

Unlike normal children, 3- to 4-year-old autistic children do not show a larger ERP waveform (P400) to a photo of an unfamiliar person than to a photo of the mother, but do show a larger waveform to an unfamiliar, compared with a familiar, object (Dawson, Carver, & Meltzoff, 2002), and they show a large N400 waveform to semantically incongruent words (Valdizan et al., 2003). One possible interpretation of these results is that the autistic children did not analyze the internal stimulus elements within a bounded event (that is, the eyes, nose, and mouth, of the face), and therefore, failed to detect the difference between the face of the mother and that of a stranger. Kevin Pelphrey (2003, unpublished), who recorded the visual scan patterns of autistic and normal adults, found that the autistic patients focused their gaze on the forehead or outline of the cheek whereas the "normals" focused their gaze on the eyes, nose, and mouth. This compromise in perceptual function should be accompanied by anomalous social behavior.

Finally, unlike "normal" adults, autistic adults failed to show amygdalar activation when asked to guess the expressions implied by a person's eyes (Baron-Cohen et al., 2000; Baron-Cohen et al., 1999). If autistic patients had abnormal amygdalar function, we would expect a compromise in social-perceptual skills (Pierce et al., 2001). This hypothesis finds support in the fact that 4-year-old autistic patients, compared with 4-year-olds who have developmental delay and normal children of the same mental age, are least likely to orient to both unexpected social and nonsocial events. The social events included the examiner humming, calling the child's name, or snapping her fingers. The nonsocial events included the sound of a timer, the ring of a telephone, and a whistle. However, the difference between autistics and other children was greater for the social than for the nonsocial stimuli (Dawson et al., 2004). Because the amygdala mediates the orienting reaction to an unexpected event, this finding implies a compromise in amygdalar functioning in autistic children. One pair of scientists have reported abnormally small, tightly packed neurons in the medial nucleus of the amygdala (Bauman & Kemper, 2003). Because the amygdala primes the inferior colliculus, the fifth wave in the brainstem evoked potential might be abnormal. It is of interest, therefore, that one team of scientists reported a prolongation of this waveform in autistic compared with normal children (Rosenhall, Nordin, Brantberg, & Gillberg, 2003).

Biochemical Abnormalities

The biochemistry of the neurons' outer membranes, which mediates cell-to-cell interactions, can be assessed indirectly through estimates of the concentration of membrane markers in the cerebrospinal fluid (CSF), or directly through biochemical measurements. Gangliosides, a complex lipid molecule necessary for cell interaction and dendritic formation, are sensitive markers of synaptic membrane activity (Minshew, Goldstein, Dombrowski, Panchalingam, & Pettegrew, 1993).

Gangliosides are released into the intercellular space in membrane turnover and communicate with the CSF. Thus, the concentration of gangliosides in the CSF is an indirect index of ganglioside turnover. Some autistic children show significantly higher concentrations of gangliosides in the CSF, implying a greater than normal turnover in this molecule (Nordin, Lekman, Johansson, & Fredman, 1998). One scientist has suggested that some cases of autism could be a disorder of synaptic modulation or maintenance (Zoghbi, 2003). Magnetic resonance spectroscopy (MRS) provides a noninvasive estimate of phospholipid turnover in the brain (Minshew et al., 1993) and membrane phospholipids are another marker of membrane metabolism. Autistic patients show greater phospholipid turnover than controls, supporting the inference drawn from studies of the gangliosides.

A group of 4- to 11-year-old autistic boys displayed alterations in serotonin synthesis (based on PET methodology) in the cerebello-thalamo-cortical pathway (Chugani et al., 1997). The assumption that autistic patients have anomalous serotonin metabolism led scientists to treat a group of 68 children diagnosed with primary autism (ages 3 to 8) with a selective inhibitor of serotonin uptake (fluoxetine). Assessments of the patients before and after drug treatment revealed that 22% of the patients responded well to the drug and showed improvements in language, cognition, emotional, and social behavior. Forty-nine percent were good responders, but continued to show some autistic symptoms; twenty-nine percent were poor responders to the drug. Most of the children who were excellent or good responders had a family history of major affective disorder; this was less true of the poor responders. This suggests that patients diagnosed with autism belong to different etiological groups (Delong, Teague, & Kamran, 1998).

Fortunately, the work of many investigators over the past 50 years has disconfirmed an earlier, popular hypothesis that autism was created by a cold, unresponsive mother. Although contemporary scientists are only beginning to understand all the factors that lead to autism and related syndromes, it is likely that the symptoms are due to disruption in the normal physiology of neurons and their synapses.

SUMMARY

The four universal psychological properties that emerge in the second year are accompanied by a set of maturational changes that are necessary, but not sufficient, for their actualization. When schemata for events are integrated with semantic structures, speech can emerge. When visceral schemata for the child's feelings are integrated with semantic representations of the state of another, inference and empathy can occur. When visceral schemata for the uncertainty that follows chastisement are linked with semantic representations of prohibited acts, the first phase of a moral sense can appear. Finally, when visceral schemata for moment-to-moment changes in feeling tone are linked to semantic representations of the child's qualities, self-awareness can appear. In addition, the increased brain connectivity and enhanced GABAergic functions should contribute to the above competences.

We recognize the substantial explanatory gap between the biological and the psychological changes. Neuroscientists who knew only the biological features of this era would be unable to predict the psychological properties. And psychologists who knew only the behavioral events would be unable to imagine the underlying biology. However, knowledge of both the biology and the psychology permits the invention of possible interpretations of the correlations between the two domains. If biologists knew only the structure of the base pairs of DNA, and had no knowledge of amino acids, they could imagine a very large number of possible molecular products. However, knowing both sources of information permits theorists to speculate on the reasons for the relation between the two sets of phenomena and their products.

The behaviors and cognitive abilities of 1-year-olds resemble those of infant chimpanzees. Both species show enhanced working memory, fear to unassimilable discrepancy, and imitation. But by the end of the second year, the differences between the two species have become distinct. No observer would confuse a 2-year-old child with a chimp of any age, even one raised by humans in a home. Most 2-year-olds, but no chimpanzee, will engage another in a collaborative game in which they both shake a piece of cloth to make a small ball on a cloth roll back and forth. Chimpanzees seem unable to represent the coordinated actions of two agents in contexts unrelated to obtaining food or safety.

The unique anatomical and biochemical events that occur during the second year permit language, inference of another's thoughts and feelings, a concept of prohibited acts, and self-awareness to emerge in their first forms, as long as children live with people and objects. These experiences are required, but these competences cannot appear until the brain has attained a certain level of growth.

This discussion resurrects the ancient problem of historical sequence: what propositions could describe how a new function uses and subsumes earlier ones, but is not an inevitable derivative of them? The biologist who wishes to explain morphological changes in phylogeny faces the same problem. The convolutions of the cerebral cortex depend on the prior existence of a forebrain. But without the mutations that were a part of the evolution from frog to primate, no convolutions would have occurred. Retrieval of schemata for past events, inferring causality, semantic terms for human qualities, and consciousness of feelings and intentions are necessary for self awareness, but they are not sufficient. The developmental interval that begins with the first smile following completion of a block tower and ends with the embarrassed confession, "I can't do that," contains a set of characteristics that distinguishes our species from every other.

2 to 8 Years

PSYCHOLOGICAL CHANGES

The belief that a set of universal abilities emerges after the second birthday and accelerates between 5 and 8 years is an old idea that can be found in essays written centuries earlier (White, 1996). Medieval Europeans regarded the seventh birthday as the end of the stage of infancy, and parents who are uncertain of their children's exact ages first assign them chores at this age because children display behaviors signifying they are ready for new assignments (Orme, 2001). Parents now expect children to be able to care for young infants, tend animals, work in the field, inhibit inappropriate behavior, and conform to the mores of the community (Rogoff, 1996). Children growing up in a village in the Orinoco delta in Venezuela, for example, are first assigned the task of cooking, using a machete, harvesting coconuts, feeding large animals, or hunting, when they are between 6 and 8 years of age and rarely before that time (Ruddle, 1993). Both families and communities assume that 6- and 7-year-olds are now teachable, responsible, capable of inferring the minds of others, and understanding rational explanations. Hence most societies, ancient and modern, begin pedagogical training at this time.

Five cognitive abilities that appear during this prolonged era include: (a) the reliable integration of past with present, (b) anticipation of the future, (c) appreciation of causality, (d) enhanced reliance on semantic categories, and (e) detection of shared relations between events and categories. Changes in social behavior and emotions which Freud and Piaget conceptualized in different ways accompany these cognitive advances.

INTEGRATION OF PAST WITH PRESENT

An early sign of this new phase, usually observed by the fourth birthday, is the more regular activation of past representations to interpret the present moment. This does not mean that 3-year-olds never relate past to present; they do, but far less reliably. To illustrate, the 4-year-old, but not the 3-year-old, will, on seeing the mother enter the door with a package, retrieve the schema of the parent leaving an hour earlier to buy ice cream. The 3-year-old, who knew the mother's purpose when she left, is less likely to retrieve that knowledge on seeing the mother enter the front door.

An experimental study affirms this claim. An examiner presented parts of a coherent narrative on three separate days to 3- and 4-year-old children. On the first day, the experimenter showed the child a puppet in the shape of a clam named Clem. The experimenter told the child that Clem liked to eat frogs, showed the child a bright orange frog, and asked her to feed the frog to the puppet.

On the second day, the examiner led the child to a corner of the room where there was a small toy house with three brightly colored locked doors, and showed the child how to use a red key to open one of the doors to find an orange frog seen the previous day. The frog was then placed back into the house and the door locked.

On the third day, the examiner led the child to a different part of the room where they found a set of three keys, one of which was the red key used the day before to unlock the door, but the examiner did not mention that fact.

Five days later, the examiner returned, produced the puppet, and said to the child, "Clem is hungry. Can you give Clem something to eat?" and waited to see whether the children remembered that they had to find the red key, open the door, retrieve the frog, and feed it to the puppet. If the child did nothing after the examiner's question, he provided some prompts, such as "What does Clem want?" or "Clem wants a frog. Can you get him a frog?" Two thirds of the 4-year olds retrieved their memory of the events of the second day, integrated it with the present situation, and went immediately to the house that contained the frog, compared with only one fourth of the 3-year-olds. However, 3-year-olds performed as well as 4-year-olds when the three parts of the narrative were presented in one continuous 5-min session (Loken, Leichtman, & Kagan, 2002; see also Povinelli, Landry, Thall, Clark, & Castille, 1999, for a similar result).

The fragile capacity to integrate past with present helps to explain why 3-year-olds do not appreciate the difference between how an object appears in perception and their knowledge of its true properties. After showing a child a red object, the examiner placed a filter on it to alter its color, and then asked the child to name the color of the object. Three-year-olds named the color perceived with the filter present; 6-year-olds named the object's original color as it was perceived before the filter was placed on it. One possible explanation is that the 3-year-olds did not integrate their schema for the original unfiltered color with their current perception; they treated the question as if it had no relation to the immediate past (Flavell, Green, & Flavell, 1986).

The fragility of integrating past with present in children under 4 years of age is paralleled by the interesting fact that 4-year-olds are less susceptible than adults to the effects of the stimulus context when estimating the size of an object. Four-year-olds and adults were shown a pair of stimuli simultaneously. Each stimulus contained a circle of equal area, but one was surrounded by eight smaller circles and the other was surrounded by five much larger circles. This is the Ebbinghaus illusion. The participants had to say which of the two target circles was bigger. Adults were influenced by the surrounding context and judged the circle surrounded by the smaller circles as larger. However, the 4-year-olds were far less susceptible to this illusion (Kaldy & Kovacs, 2003). The authors suggested that the illusion depends on the integration of cortical areas. Immature connectivity between the primary visual area (V1) on the one hand, and the ventral path to the medial temporal lobe, on the other, might contribute to the age differences in the susceptibility to the illusion. However, independent of this biological interpretation, the fact that preschool children often fail to integrate past with present, or events surrounding a stimulus, implies that integration of events, although present, is immature at this stage of development.

Surprisingly, some 2- and 4-year-old children will, on occasion, fail the "A not B" procedure described in chapter 4. Each child watched an examiner bury a toy in the sand at location A on each of six trials, and after waiting for 3 sec, the adult retrieved the hidden toy. After repeating this sequence six times, on the next trial the examiner buried the toy at location B and imposed a delay of 10 sec before allowing the child to retrieve the toy. Some children reached toward location A (Spencer & Schutte, 2004). This unexpected result implies that even in very simple situations, some 4-year-olds will, on occasion, fail to integrate an event that happened 10 sec earlier with the present moment. That is one reason why children younger than 4 years occasionally fail what are called "false belief problems" (Saxe, Carey, & Kanwisher, 2004). In a popular version of this problem, the young participant is told a story about a child, called Max, who knows the correct location of an object; for example, he knows that a piece of chocolate is in a green box. When Max is playing outside, his mother moves the chocolate from the green box to a blue one. The participant is then asked, "Where does Max think the chocolate is?" or "Why did Max look for the chocolate in the green box?" To generate an answer, the child must integrate the initial information he heard with the later information.

The automatic integration of past with present probably affects the phenomena Jean Piaget (1950) called "conservation." Piaget claimed that between 5 and 7 years, children acquire a set of intellectual abilities called "concrete operational thought." One of these abilities, called "conservation of mass," represents the knowledge that the mass of an object does not change (that is, it is conserved) when its shape is modified. In a classic demonstration of this competence, an examiner shows a child two identical balls of clay and asks whether the two balls have the same amount of clay, or whether one ball has more clay than the other. All children acknowledge that the two balls have equivalent amounts of clay. The examiner then rolls one of the two balls into the shape of a sausage and asks the child again, "Which one has more clay?" The 4-year-olds treat this question as if it were independent of the first, and, because the longer sausage appears to have more substance, say that the sausage has more clay than the ball.

By contrast, 7-year-olds regard the sausage as part of a temporal sequence that began when the examiner showed the child the two identical balls and asked the first question. After the examiner transformed one ball of clay into the sausage and asked the question again, the older children understood that the examiner intended to ask, "Given the sequence you have seen over the last minute or two, which ball has more clay?" The older child retrieves the schema of the two identical balls of clay, recalls his prior answer, and answers correctly. Piaget argued that the older child answered correctly because he knew that the sausage could be transformed into the ball—a process called reversibility. We suggest that, in addition to the ability to mentally transform the sausage back into the original ball, it is useful to acknowledge that the older child treats the second question as part of a coherent sequence. The automatic retrieval of information relevant to a present moment increases the possible range of behaviors children display because of their different life histories. The approach of a stranger evokes a vigilant posture in a majority of 8-month-olds; the same event elicits a more varied set of reactions in 4-year-olds.

ANTICIPATING THE FUTURE

The ability to relate the present to representations of the future also matures over this era. Four- and seven-year-old children were shown a timeline marked by familiar events and asked to indicate how long it would be before each event would occur (for example, their next birthday, Christmas, or Thanksgiving). Most 4-year-olds did not differentiate events close in time from those that were distant, but 7-year-olds did (Friedman, 2000).

Relevance to Memory.   Anticipating the difficulty of a future task—for example, remembering a long series of numbers—motivates older children to activate strategies that might aid performance. Seven-year-olds trying to remember a long series of numbers rehearsed each number silently as it was being read, because, recalling prior occasions when they had to remember a great deal of information, they appreciated the difficulty of the task. Younger children usually fail to rehearse the numbers.

Rehearsal and other strategies that aid memory are called metamemory functions. A second metamemory strategy is to study an event to be remembered for a longer time. Four-, six-, and eight-year-olds were told they had to remember a set of 40 pictures for either a few minutes, 1 day, or 7 days. Any child who did not understand the difference between a few minutes and 7 days was excluded. The 4- and 6-year-olds who had to remember the picture for 7 days failed to spend more time studying each picture than those who believed they had to remember it for only 1 day. By contrast, the 8-year-olds, who knew the delay would be as long as 7 days, studied the pictures for a longer period because they realized that accurate recall following a long delay required study of each picture for an additional few seconds (Rogoff, Newcombe, & Kagan, 1974).

The cultural setting and the information to be remembered influence the age when specific metamemory strategies emerge. Children 6 to 13 years old from three different communities were administered a variety of difficult memory tasks. One group consisted of middle-class Boston children; the other two were Mayan Indian children from two different communities located on the shores of Lake Atitlan in northwest Guatemala. One community—San Pedro—was large and had both a school and electricity; the other—San Marcos—was small and had neither a school nor electricity. A group of 17- to 20-year-olds from the small village was also tested.

The children had to remember the order of 12 different items belonging to three classes of stimuli: (a) pictures of familiar objects, (b) lists of familiar words, or (c) the orientations of a number of identical dolls (either upside down or right side up). The examiner always began the task with two items, and then added one additional item on each succeeding trial, until the child had to remember the order of all 12 items. The child placed the pictures and dolls on a table and spoke the words. Figure 6.1 shows the memory performance scores, by age, for the children in each community.

Although the memory scores of children from all three communities improved with age, the level of performance of the 7-year-old Boston children was not attained by the Mayans until 11 to 13 years. The children from the

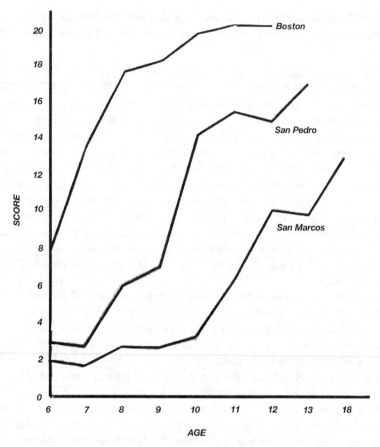

FIG. 6.1.   The increase in memory scores across age for American children and Mayan children from two different communities.

larger Mayan town showed their greatest memory improvement between 8 and 11 years; the children from the smaller village of San Marcos showed their greatest improvement between 11 and 13 years. However, despite the lack of schooling, the 17- to 20-year-olds in the small village performed better than the 8- to 9-year-olds living in the same isolated community. Although schooling and the variety present in the larger town influenced the age when children activated metamemory strategies, nonetheless, the memory scores improved each year in both Mayan settings, implying the influence of maturation (Kagan, Klein, et al., 1979). A recent study of recall memory in middle-class children from 4 to 15 years of age also revealed a linear increase in performance, but the more interesting fact is that the degree of improvement was greatest between 4 and 5 years of age (Gathercole, Pickering, Ambridge, & Wearing, 2004).

APPRECIATION OF CAUSALITY

The regular tendency to relate the present to the past and the future motivates children to wonder about causal connections between events. The
belief that the occurrence of an event requires a prior one appears early in
human thought, before complete mastery of the grammar of one's language and reproductive maturity. Adults from many cultures, ancient
and contemporary, assume that sudden illness, death of a loved one, or
loss of property were caused by their disregard for an ethical norm. Their
moral lapse provoked a dead ancestor, sorcerer, or god to punish them, as
their parents had done years earlier. Not all catastrophe is interpreted as
retribution. Medieval Europeans were not frightened by an infant born
with four fingers if they thought the cause was natural; they only became
frightened if they believed that the deformation was a sign of God's wrath
for commission of a sin (Daston & Park, 1998). The implicit question,
"Why did this event occur?" motivates children to retrieve structures that
might represent the possible antecedents of a current situation.

Although 3-year-olds occasionally wonder about the conditions that
precede a familiar event, they are less likely to do so for unfamiliar events.
Seven-year-olds search more regularly for causal connections between
unfamiliar events that capture their attention because they understand
that events from the recent past can causally determine the present
(Povinelli et al., 1999). We are not suggesting that 3-year-olds never think
causally. Three-year-olds will express cause–effect ideas in their spontaneous speech; for example, "My shoe fell off because the ties are loose" or
"I got medicine because it makes my fever go away" (Hickling &
Wellman, 2001). However, causal interpretations are far less frequent in
children under 4 years of age.

Although the tendency to assume causality is a biologically-prepared
competence, it requires experience to be actualized. One critical class of
experience is the child's reflective evaluations of his actions. The child
bangs a spoon on the table and a sound occurs, kicks a ball and it rolls,
throws a cookie and it breaks into pieces. It is easy for children to conclude
that each outcome required a prior causal action.

When parents chastise children for violating family rules, they often re-
mind them that it was their actions that provoked the punishment. When
5- and 6-year-olds harm a person or damage property, they relate that outcome to a prior intention, or a clumsy or impulsive act. As a result, they
are vulnerable to feelings of remorse. A 5- or 6-year-old child who makes
an error reflects on the possible reasons for the mistake, and, on occasion,
corrects herself. For example, if a child has to find the one picture in a set
of four very similar ones that is exactly like a standard, 6- and 7-year-olds
are usually reflective following a mistake; that is, they take more time

studying the next item. Younger children are less reflective because they do not appreciate that the reason for their error was a failure to consider all the alternatives carefully—this is an example of the competence called executive control (Kagan, 1984).

A failure to be reflective is also observed when children must inhibit a highly practiced response. For example, children were told to say "day" to a dark picture illustrating the moon and stars, and to say "night" to a white picture illustrating the sun. Children under 6 years found this task very difficult, although they had no difficulty when the stimuli for night and day did not have strong competing associations (Diamond, Kirkhan, & Amso, 2002).

The reflective posture of 6- and 7-year-olds is one of the clues parents use to decide that their child is ready for responsibilities. The more reflective attitude implies that the child understands that if he is not careful, or fails to weigh all the alternatives, he may make a mistake. The community now holds 6- and 7-year-olds responsible for violating its norms; that is one reason why the Catholic Church does not require confession until children are at least 7 years old.

THE DOMINANCE OF SEMANTIC CATEGORIES

A third significant feature of this era is an expanded reliance on semantic networks in categorizing experience. The addition of semantic structures to the schemata for an event creates a qualitatively new representation. The evolution of wings permitting bird flight is an apt analogy. The bird soaring in the sky has a unique perception of its ecology that land and sea animals do not possess. One important advantage of semantic forms is that they facilitate the ability to tell others their memories for events that occurred in the past.

Most adults can remember many events that occurred after their fifth or sixth birthday, but few can remember many events that occurred before their fourth birthday—a phenomenon called "infantile amnesia" (White & Pillemer, 1979). One reason for the amnesia is that young children do not regularly use semantic structures to code their experiences; therefore, they cannot describe them verbally. An examiner, who visited children, 27, 33, or 39 months old at home on two successive days, brought a large box with a handle that, when moved, made sounds and appeared to swallow toys thrown into its opening. In addition, the examiner evaluated each child's vocabulary.

The children's memory for this experience was assessed either 6 or 12 months later at home, but without the presence of the distinctive box. The examiner first asked the child if she remembered anything about the occasions they had played together 6 or 12 months earlier. A verbal answer required the retrieval of semantic structures. The examiner then showed each child a photo of the box and asked whether she remembered how to manipulate the handle. She also showed the child photographs of four toys, only one of which had been put in the box on the earlier visits, and asked if she could remember which toy (of the four) was thrown into the box. These two questions relied on the child's schematic representations for the original event, rather than semantic ones.

The children who had been less than 3 years old on the original visits reported very little information about the earlier visit because they had sparse vocabularies and failed to represent the original experience semantically. The children older than 3 years, who had richer vocabularies, had represented the event with semantic structures and were able to describe it a year later. However, all children, young and old, had created schematic representations for the toys and the box. They recognized the correct toy from the photographs and reenacted the correct action with the handle (Simock & Hayne, 2002, 2003). This finding affirms the distinction between schematic and semantic representations which become integrated as the child develops. The general principle is that the improvement in retrieval memory over the years 2 through 8 is due, in part, to the use of language to structure experience (Nelson, 1996). That is why there is a qualitative improvement in an adult's recall of a younger sibling's birth at about 2½ years of age, following the burst in vocabulary size (Eacott & Crawley, 2002).

The application of semantic categories to experience influences the way retrieved knowledge is structured. If 4- and 7-year-olds listen to a list of 12 words containing two semantic categories (for example, animals and foods), only the older children cluster in their recall words belonging to the same semantic category. That is, they remember several animal or food words together, although these words were not next to each other in the original list. This phenomenon could only occur if the children automatically grouped words that were members of the same semantic category.

A child's decision to use schematic or semantic structures, or both, to categorize an event, depends on the child's mental set at the moment. Four-year-olds were shown simultaneously two line drawings of familiar objects belonging to the same category (for example, an apple and a pear). The examiner labeled both objects with the same nonsense word (for example, she said, "These are blix."). The examiner then showed the child a second pair of pictures, each belonging to a distinct category (for example, a pineapple and a bowl), and asked, "Which one is the blix?" Not surprisingly, most children selected the pineapple from the second pair because it belonged to the category "fruit," which was the appropriate category for the first pair of objects.

However, when the original pair of pictures did not belong to the same semantic category (for example, a pear and a cat), the child selected a picture on the second trial that shared perceptual, rather than semantic, features with a picture in the first pair. Children under 5 years must be primed to use semantic categories; older children use semantic categories more automatically (Namy & Gentner, 2002). The brain honors this principle. Adults show a negative waveform in the ERP (at about 300 msec) when, having first read the word "duck," they see a picture of a collie. They do not show this waveform if the picture is of a bird other than a duck (Hamm, Johnson, & Kirk, 2002) because the brain is especially sensitive to events that violate an expected semantic category.

The essential features of the semantic and schematic representations of a particular object are different; for example, the essential features of the child's semantic network for "food" include terms like *dinner, vegetable, breakfast,* and *table.* The most essential features of a schematic concept for food include a loaf of bread, an ice-cream cone, a glass of milk, a hot dog, and a piece of pizza. The right and left hemispheres make differential contributions to the processing of semantic and schematic representations. We noted earlier that the right hemisphere processes words with a rich schematic contribution, for example, rose and giraffe, more efficiently than it processes abstract words like "honest" or "fair."

Only semantic structures imply both the essential features of an event, as well as the features that the event does not possess. That is, most "is" statements are also "is not" statements. The sentence, "The leaf is on the grass," implies that there was a time in the past when it was not on the grass. This logic does not apply to schematic representations because the schema of a leaf on a lawn need not contain representations of its prior presence on a tree. The statement, "Mary will see new things on her trip," is understandable without any schematic referents for the word "new" or "things." The same argument holds for semantic terms like *unforgettable, unmanageable, unbelievable,* and *unrelenting.*

A second distinction between the two forms is that schemata can be transformed without any accompanying cognitive dissonance. Daydreams and cartoons on television provide examples. The image of a smiling face can turn into a pumpkin without the cognitive dissonance that would occur if a person read, "A smiling face is a pumpkin." Einstein's image of riding a light wave supposedly contributed to his ideas on relativity. However, the printed sentence, "Humans can move at the speed of light," would evoke an immediate sense of impossibility in all readers.

Perhaps the most important difference between perceptually-based schemata and semantic structures involves their relations to other representations. The relations of similarity, part-whole, and if-then contingency can apply to both schematic and semantic representations. However, only semantic networks possess the quasi-logical relations in the form of hierarchically nested categories for objects and events (hyponyms) or opposites for qualities (antonyms). These two relations become prominent after 6 years of age.

If 5-year-olds are asked to say the first word that comes to mind when presented with a noun that names an object, they usually offer a verb (for example, sun-shine, dog-bark). Seven-year-olds typically reply with a noun that belongs to the same semantic category (for example, sun–moon, dog–cat), implying that representations of objects with schematic features have become incorporated into semantic categories (Case & Okomoto, 1996). Seven-year-olds and adults display very similar profiles of cortical activation (measured by fMRI) when they silently generate words associated with a particular semantic category (for example, animals or food), and activity is greatest in the left anterior and left middle frontal gyrus (Gaillard et al., 2003).

Consider the semantic knowledge one must ascribe to a school-age child who knows that the sentence, "The ball is round and red," could be true, but "The ball is round and square" is impossible, and "The ball is round and eleven" is silly, although the child has never heard any of these three sentences before. The child must appreciate that (a) each concept (for example, ball) has a limited set of possible features; (b) some legitimate features cannot be present simultaneously; and (c) some features are always illegitimate. This semantic knowledge is not totally dependent on experience with balls, but represents the unconscious construction of semantic rules inferred from exposure to language. These rules, which are unique to human languages, probably require activation of a distinctive brain circuitry whenever a feature of one concept is illegitimately ascribed to another. The current unrest in America over the meaning of the concept of "marriage" is an example of the emotion that can be generated when some citizens propose to change what has been a central feature of this term.

Although the semantic representations of some objects belong to conceptual hierarchies (this is especially true for the concept "animals"), these hierarchies are absent for the schemata representing the same objects. The 6-year-old child appreciates that dogs are pets, pets are animals, and animals are living things, but the schema of a pet dog does not have these categorical implications. When words are combined to form sentences and sentences combined into a narrative, a degree of coherence emerges that was not present in the events described. Biographies and historical essays render a sequence of events more coherent than they were when they occurred. Experience is a sequence of continually changing relations among events; semantic networks freeze those dynamic relations into static essences. Wittgenstein's profound insight, in the early decades of the 20th century, was that words have no essential, or fixed, meaning. The meaning of a word is contained in the ways it is used. Consider the new meaning of the term *cool* that developed over the last 25 years. No 2-year-old understands this idea; 8-year-olds have an initial awareness of this truth.

Because emotions have a rich semantic component for older, but not for younger, children, 7-year-olds might say, "I was happy that I got a present, but mad that it is wasn't exactly what I wanted." Younger children do not believe in that possibility because the sensory components of feelings are the primary defining features of an emotion and one can experience only one feeling at any one moment. Because semantic structures participate in the older child's understanding of the meaning of an emotional term, a word like *anger* includes semantic representations of its origins and usual behavioral consequences. As a result, 7-year-olds might say they are "mad" without any change in feeling, simply because their semantic network links a frustrated wish with the terms *angry* or *mad*. Older children will say, and even believe, they are mad at a parent, although they do not experience any of the physiological changes that are inherent features of this emotion. Hence, they do not feel angry; they are simply using the word "mad" to describe a situation that could evoke an emotion.

This difference between younger and older children has interesting consequences. After a 3-year-old's feeling of frustration has vanished, often within minutes, the emotion vanishes, too. The older child, however, might remember the fact that he was mad at a parent a week earlier and display a rebellious act without any feeling of anger. Once emotions become part of a semantic network, children can retrieve past occasions when they felt angry without experiencing a change in feeling. That is why some patients with a lesioned amygdala report feeling anger, joy, or guilt, although they cannot experience the biological events that accompany these feelings in normal adults. National, ethnic, and religious groups often preserve the semantic components of anger toward other groups for generations (Yuill & Pearson, 1998). Demagogues take advantage of this trait by reminding their citizens of those they should hate.

Adults who have been relying on semantic networks for years find it difficult to appreciate this shift from schematic to semantic functioning. The semantic structures activated while gazing at a spring meadow include trees and flowers, rather than tall, dark objects with small green features and small green objects with very small red features. Compare the experience of viewing a Monet painting while standing one or 20 feet away from the wall where it hangs. This change in the vehicle of representing and understanding experience is a profound alteration in the way humans know the world.

SEMANTIC CATEGORIES FOR SELF

The increased reliance on semantic categories has implications for the concept of identification. We noted in chapter 5 that 2-year-olds have a schematic concept for humans that includes the self. By the third or fourth birthday, children have elaborated this concept to include semantic concepts for "girl," "boy," "adult," and "child." Children are acutely aware of the obvious differences between their psychological and physical features and those of adults—parents and relatives—as well as older siblings. These discrepancies, which recruit attention, generate a desire to command some of the attractive characteristics that others, but not the child, possess. Size, strength, skills, freedom from coercion, apparent self-confidence, and the ability to control fear, are six attractive qualities 6-year-olds would like to have as part of their character. The human mind is biased to assume that if two objects share a small number of obvious features, it is likely they share some nonobvious ones. Hence, most 6-year-olds unconsciously assume, incorrectly, that they possess some of the attractive features of their parents and close relatives, simply because they and these adults are members of the semantic category "family," although they cannot articulate the reasons why this category is meaningful. Children affirm Plato's intuition that each living form possesses an invisible set of features that is the basis for its category name. Most children insist, for example, that even if a dog lost its legs, tail, fur, and bark, what remained would still be a dog. Six- and seven-year-olds believe that they and their parents belong to a unique semantic category whose essential feature is a shared biology. When this belief is combined with the experience of vicarious affect appropriate to one or both parents, psychologists say that the child is identified with the target person.

Of course, a child can believe she is a member of a social category, like "family," but not feel any vicarious affect with members of that category. Vicarious affect refers to an agent's feeling of pride, joy, sadness, or shame when an event that should produce one of these emotions occurs to another person. Thus, a child might feel vicarious shame if a parent who drank too many cocktails fell down, or, in a clumsy movement, spilled ice cream on her clothes. A 2-year-old in these situations would feel empathy toward a parent, but is not mature enough to experience vicarious shame. Octavio Paz, a Nobel Laureate in literature, recalled feeling ashamed of his Mexican ethnicity when, as a recent immigrant to California, he was ridiculed by peers in the school cafeteria because he did not know how to ask for a spoon in English (Paz, 1999). Some Americans and Europeans who are aware of the human destruction of the natural environment occasionally feel a brief bout of shame over their species category when a film or book reminds them of this less than desirable trait. Eighteenth-century

Europeans, by contrast, were more likely to feel a moment of pride over their humanness when they heard about an important discovery by an Enlightenment scholar.

A 7-year-old feels proud when her mother wins a community prize for leadership, but shame if her alcoholic father is jeered by a neighbor because children assume that others regard self and self's family as belonging to a common category. Thus, if a parent does something praiseworthy, the child infers that others will regard the self as praiseworthy, too, and will experience a moment of pride. The more distinct the category, the stronger the identification and the more likely a vicarious emotion will occur. Each child's family has unique features; therefore, identifications with family members are usually strong. A Hispanic boy living in rural Quebec is rare, and identification with his ethnic category will be stronger than if he lived in a village in Mexico.

A 7-year-old can believe that she belongs to a variety of social categories. The most common are: developmental stage, gender, ethnicity, religion, nationality, and social class. A child who experienced vicarious affect when a member of any of these categories had an experience that should provoke an appropriate emotion would be regarded as identified with that category.

The features defining a social category include particular actions, beliefs, standards, and emotions. Obviously, the behavioral features for gender are different from those for ethnicity. Once a child learns the features of a social category to which he belongs, he feels an obligation to be loyal to those features. Each child can evaluate her actions and knows whether a behavior is, or is not, consistent with the features of the category.

The relative salience of a social category depends, in part, on the context, for each setting can prime a particular social category. Gender is an ascendant category on the school playground; religion is ascendant at a church service. Most 2-year-olds have not learned most of the social categories to which they belong; hence, their behavior is not motivated by that knowledge. By 6 years, however, their actions are linked to these symbolic structures.

Relevance for Morality

Six-year-olds have acquired semantic categories for gender, family, and developmental stage, know some of the moral standards appropriate for these categories, and feel obligated to maintain semantic consistency between self's features, on the one hand, and their behavior, on the other. This motive is unique to humans. Six-year-old boys understand that they should not wear girl's clothes or cry from a minor bruise, although they have never done either, and therefore, have never been punished for these behaviors. A 7-year-old boy who puts on a dress detects the semantic inconsistency between his behavior and his gender category and is likely to feel uncertain, embarrassed, or guilty. As a result, he experiences a temporary challenge to his virtue, where virtue is defined as the judgment of how close the self's features are to meeting the standards the child has acquired. These standards differ in salience, and the hierarchy of salience changes with development. Obedience to parental requests has salience for 3-year-olds; academic accomplishment, acceptability to peers, and physical attractiveness have greater salience for 8-year-olds in contemporary Western communities.

The moral power of these social categories derives, in part, from the fact that the young child's initial words are for observable objects and events with fixed features. Objects called dogs should bark and have fur; if not, they are less than ideal dogs. Thus, when children learn the names for social categories, like boy, girl, Catholic, or Hispanic, they are prepared to believe that these words, too, name a set of unchanging psychological characteristics appropriate to members of the category. Children believe they ought to be loyal to the psychological features that define the categories to which they belong, and will experience as much dissonance if they stray from these obligations as they would if they saw an animal without fur who never barked that was called a dog.

Older adolescents, and of course, adults, can experience a feeling of tension if their education, vocation, dress, or habits differ seriously from others with whom they are in regular contact. For example, some adolescents from economically-disadvantaged families who are matriculating at elite colleges, where many classmates came from upper-middle-class families, feel uneasy if they wonder whether the category "graduate of an elite college" is appropriate for them. Membership in a religious category can protect some adolescents from a bout of depression because it contributes to a feeling of virtue (Horowitz & Garber, 2003). It is important to appreciate that although loyalty to a religion enhances a child's sense of virtue, failure to do so need not compromise that evaluation. Many adolescents who are not religious report that, although they feel good when they attend a religious service, they do not feel guilty or self-abasing when they do not. This fact should not be surprising. Receipt of the best grade on a test is accompanied by a feeling of pride, but failure to get the best grade does not always evoke shame or guilt. The state that accompanies meeting a moral standard is not the psychological opposite of the state that occurs when self violates that standard.

Children who believe they possess a compromised sense of virtue, because of consistently harsh parental criticism, poverty, minority status, deviant physical features, violation of moral standards, or failure at academic or peer valued skills, usually react in one of two ways. Some accept the flaw in their character and assume a passive or deferential posture with others. Members of a second group, more often those with a talent or property that they or others recognize as desirable, expend extraordinary energy and perseverance to achieve excellence in some domain to silence the gnawing doubt that was created during childhood. The extraordinary accomplishments of many eminent adults in science, politics, art, law, and medicine were attempts to transcend an earlier history that the child interpreted as morally tainted. The large number of Nobel Laureates who belonged to a minority group that experienced prejudice as children—for example, Einstein, Luria, Rabi, Yalow, Jacob, and Levi-Montalcini—are examples of this dynamic. The latter two scientists described in memoirs their feelings of difference and tension because they were Jews in Catholic European countries that had anti-Semitic attitudes. Members of minority categories, who are a little more likely to feel uncertain about their virtue, are motivated to correct the undesirable categorization they believe others hold toward them.

Restraint on actions that define a community's moral standards rests on two different feelings. One state is defined by worry over possible punishment, criticism, or rejection from others for violating a standard. The second is the feeling that accompanies recognition of a semantic inconsistency between the features that define the child's primary social categories and the self's evaluation of the degree to which he possesses these features.

Two Classes of Social Categories.   There are two types of social categories. Nominal categories, like gender, with relatively fixed features and functions within a society, appear first in development. Children older than 4 or 5 years add the nominal categories of ethnicity, religion, place of residence, and nationality. The ethical obligations of these social categories are not tied to a specific other person and apply across varied contexts.

The second class, acquired later, is defined by a social relationship between self and others, and includes the categories "friend," "son," "daughter," "brother," and "sister." The ethical obligations linked to these categories, which usually call for loyalty, affection, honesty, and nurture, are tied to a specific person or persons.

The distinction between nominal and relational social categories is an instance of a more general principle in cognitive development. The child's first categorizations are based on observable features and functions shared by a set of objects. Children must be older than 5 or 6 years to understand that the meanings of relational categories, like left–right or bigger–smaller, vary with the context. The social category "friend" applies to a specific person and the ethical obligations to one friend may differ from those that apply to a different peer. For example, if one friend is anxious and passive, self will feel an obligation to be gentle. If a second friend is popular and dominating, self may feel obliged to display deference. This specificity explains why individuals are selective with respect to the persons or groups they will cooperate with to attain a benevolent goal. Most individuals cooperate with those who share their moral values, whether the others are genetically related or unrelated. Scholars loyal to a Darwinian interpretation of cooperative behavior have difficulty explaining why people join the Peace Corps, send checks to the Red Cross, walk for hunger, or roll bandages in a local hospital, because these acts have little relevance for a person's inclusive fitness. Humans behave this way because they wish to assure the self of its virtue, and people select different actions to gain this psychological prize.

The elaboration of semantic categories has particular importance for the semantic network that defines authority. The differences between children and adults in strength, intellectual competence, power, and control of fear generate a psychological state in the former who belong to the less potent category. The English language has no good word for this feeling that blends intimidation with envy in some, shame with anger in others. A critical feature of the child's network for adult authority is an ethical imperative to show deference and a readiness to conform to requests made by those in a position of authority and to accept, at least initially, their declarations as to which ideas are true and which false.

This readiness is not based solely on what authority figures can do to the child, characteristic of 4- and 5-year-olds, but on a desire to maintain semantic consistency among the semantic concepts for authority, power, and deference. That is why adult participants in a psychological laboratory administered high levels of electric shock to a person they did not know, although the stranger screamed in pain, simply because the experimenter told them to do so. (No shock was administered because the victim was a collaborator of the experimenter; Milgram, 1974.)

Children who accept the standards of their family and community, because of effective earlier socialization, regard self as conforming to the norms of legitimate authority. Children who do not comply regard self as opposing family and community norms. Members of the latter group are at a slightly higher risk for developing a psychiatric illness because their traits are less well adapted to the daily demands of modern society (Hofstra, Van Der Ende, & Verhulst, 2002). Thus, an extremely anxious child who conforms to family and social demands is at less risk for a serious adult mental illness in contemporary American society than a disobedient child who refuses to conform to the school's requirements.

Humans are extremely sensitive to similarities and differences among people. When variation in the physical and psychological features of most members of a community is minimal, those with a deviant feature are salient and likely to be either admired or targets of prejudice, depending on the feature. On the other hand, when the physical, behavioral, or ideological variation in a society is extensive, individual deviations are less salient. The extraordinary increase in the diversity of physical features, behaviors, and values among Americans and Europeans over the past 50 years has made it more difficult to construct a clearly defined prototypic concept for the category "American" or "European." There are few actions that a majority will regard as inconsistent with these categories. As a result, ethnic and religious categories have become more salient than national ones.

Some physical features present a century ago have become rare. For example, before amniocentesis, genetic counseling, and the medical termination of a pregnancy carrying an impaired embryo, it was not uncommon to see children with Down's syndrome or cerebral palsy on city streets. These defects were regarded as beyond anyone's control and therefore not a reason for a parent to feel the guilt of self-blame. However, many contemporary mothers believe they have some control over their pregnancies and assume they should give birth to a perfect infant. Hence they worry more than 19th-century mothers about the possibility of a physically impaired child and feel more responsible should such a child be born.

The technical advances that made worldwide access to radio, television, and the Internet possible are creating a change in the referent groups that youth select for comparisons with self. Two hundred years ago, most adolescents and adults had little knowledge of the circumstances or characteristics of those living in geographically distant places. Each person evaluated his skills, privileges, and material possessions by comparing self with those he knew in his region, town, or neighborhood. Fifteen-year-olds in Bangor, Maine, or a village in rural Indonesia, compared self with fewer than a hundred other adolescents. Because the range of talents and privileges was small, it was easier to conclude that self was not seriously deprived or incompetent. Contemporary 15-year-olds are aware of the talents and privileges of adolescents in distant places, and therefore, are more vulnerable to feeling less talented or privileged. This knowledge can create both doubt over self's virtue, and envy and anger toward those with greater advantage. Chimpanzees are protected from this source of uncertainty.

DETECTING THE RELATIONS BETWEEN CONCEPTS

Detection of semantic relations between, or among, concepts is a fourth competence of this era. Children under 6 years can detect a physical feature shared by two or more events (color, shape, presence of eyes), a shared function (moves, makes noise, produces light), or a shared name (animal, alive). But young children are unlikely to detect a shared semantic relation between events that belong to different categories (for example, the gentlest of six dogs shares the semantic relation of "best" with the smartest of six children). This cognitive ability does not emerge reliably until after 6 or 7 years.

The reason for the delay is that the shared relation is not given in perception, as is true for color or motion, but must be inferred with a semantic form. The gentlest of six dogs and the smartest of six children do not announce that each set of events shares the quality "most desirable." The child must compare the six dogs and six children and extract the abstract semantic feature. This cognitive task is inherently more difficult than detecting a shared perceptual feature like size or shape.

The sensitivity to shared semantic relations is revealed in experiments on the relative size of objects. Both 4- and 7-year-olds answer correctly if shown a large and small object (for example, a toy dog) and asked "Which dog is smaller?" However, if shown the same small dog from the prior trial alongside a new dog that is even smaller and asked again, "Which dog is smaller?" 4-year-olds have difficulty. Seven-year-olds understand that the semantic concepts "smaller" and "bigger" refer to a relation between objects, and are not absolute properties of any object (Kuenne, 1946). Similarly, young children do not understand that "right" and "left" refer to the relation between two objects, or between an object and a location, and are not fixed properties of any object.

The ability to appreciate the relations between and among concepts for events is exploited in a social context when the child compares herself with friends on desirable traits like reading ability, popularity, strength, bravery, or attractiveness. The addictive habit of comparing self with others on motivationally salient properties is revealed in children's descriptions of themselves. Four- to five-year-olds usually state their name, possessions, desires, and actions they normally perform. Seven-year-olds, by contrast, often compare their attributes with those of peers, especially with respect to moral virtues and shortcomings. A typical 4-year-old will say, "My name is Jason and I live in a big house with my mother, father, and sister Lisa. I have a key that is orange and a television in my own room." The younger child emphasizes observable behavioral characteristics and possessions (Harter, 1996).

Compare the above terse reply with the typical response of an 8-year-old: "I'm in third grade and pretty popular at least with the girls. I control my temper, I'd be ashamed of myself if I didn't. At school I'm feeling pretty smart in certain subjects but I'm feeling pretty dumb in arithmetic and science, especially when I see how well the other kids are doing." The older child's descriptions more often involve comparisons with others on traits with ethical connotations.

Each 7-year-old compares the ethical standards he believes others hold for him with his own standards. That is, the older child regularly evaluates the relation between the ethical evaluation of his behavior and his understanding of the adult standard for that action. As a result, children are concerned over what a teacher might think of them and are reluctant to expose themselves to criticism. The ability to infer selected thoughts and feelings in others, which appeared in the second year, is combined by age 7 with the appreciation that their private evaluation of self's features might be different from the evaluations of another. The ability to take the perspective of another, and to appreciate that it is different from one's own, are qualitatively different from the 2-year-old's ability to infer the thoughts of another. The former requires an appreciation that self and other can have different understandings of the same event. That is why 12- to 14-year-olds will incorporate conflicting themes in their written narratives (McKeough & Genereux, 2003).

The relative frequency of an event is a feature of many categories. Among North Americans, apples are frequent members of the category *fruit;* whereas persimmons are infrequent. Seven-year-old children are sensitive to the relative frequency of each social category and the behaviors of those in those categories. In addition, children, like adults, are tempted to categorize others by their most distinctive features. Because most children are not chronically aggressive, most regard a bully's aggression as a salient trait, although the bully may read or play baseball well, because the latter two properties are more frequent than chronic aggression.

A discrepancy in the relative frequency of the features of a social category can create cognitive dissonance and the intuition that a standard on fairness has been violated. At the end of the 19th century, only 10% of the Viennese population was Jewish; but 50% of Viennese lawyers and physicians were Jews. The discrepancy between the two frequencies helped to fuel the virulent anti-Semitism that Hitler exploited. One basis for the political pressure in America to establish affirmative action programs in education and the workplace was the dissonance created by the fact that too few citizens of color were being admitted to elite colleges or given jobs with challenge and a good salary. The ability to detect the relative frequency of features in different domains does not emerge until 6 or 7 years; hence, strong prejudicial attitudes toward minority groups usually do not appear until this developmental phase has been attained.

For reasons that are not clear, some youth are unusually sensitive to the fairness of desirable events and ask, implicitly, "Do I deserve this prize?" or "Am I worthy of this reward?" If the answer is negative, they might act in ways that result in losing the prize or denigrating its source. Claude Steele (1997), a psychologist at Stanford University, has suggested that some African American students who believe that admission to an elite college or attaining a good grade record is a result of faculty charity, rather than their talent and effort, may denigrate their educational attainment or the academic institution. George Orwell's impoverished hero in the novel *Keep the Aspidistra Flying* had convinced himself that money was the source of all evil. Hence, after receiving a small check for a poem submitted to a literary magazine, he immediately spent the money in a night of debauched drunkenness, and, soon after, sank into a deep depression.

MANIPULATING MULTIPLE DIMENSIONS AND FEATURES

The ability to detect shared relations is accompanied by the ability to assign an object to a category based on more than one dimension or feature. For example, 7-year-olds will, but 5-year-olds will not, sort a pile of toys that vary in size (small or large) and hue (pink or deep red) into four groups that share both size and hue.

Although a 4-year-old knows that she is both a girl and a child, and her mother is both a woman and a wife, appreciating that a particular person can belong simultaneously to more than one category is limited to familiar objects and events, and is extended less often to unfamiliar ones. We noted in chapter 5 that 2- and 3-year-olds are prone to assume that, most of the time, an object has only one name. By contrast, 7-year-olds can assign an unfamiliar object to different semantic categories depending on the features emphasized (Piaget, 1950). This talent is one of the competences of concrete operational thought.

Most 4-year-olds answered correctly when asked to pick out the one object most different from the others in an array of three blue circles and one red circle. But when faced with a large blue circle, a large red square, a small red triangle, and a large red triangle, 4-year-olds were puzzled by the same question because they had difficulty recognizing that the large blue circle differed from each of the other three objects on either two or three features, rather than one. Seven-year-olds had no difficulty solving this problem (Chalmers & Halford, 2003).

Siegler (1996) demonstrated the older child's ability to manipulate multiple features by using a "balance scale" that had a fulcrum and an arm that could rotate around it (see Fig. 6.2). The arm could tip left, right, or remain level, depending on how many weights of different sizes were arranged on the pegs located on each side of the fulcrum. The child's task was to examine a particular arrangement of weights and to predict which, if any, side would tip down if the arm were allowed to move freely. Two variables determined how the scale would tip: the number of weights on each side of the fulcrum, and the distance of each weight from the fulcrum. Five- and six-year-olds usually focus on only one dimension. If the

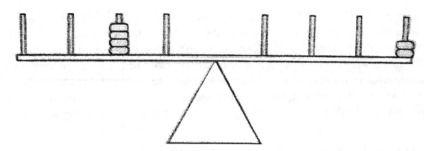

FIG. 6.2.   Illustration of the balance beam used by Siegler, 1996.

number, or sizes, of the weights are exactly the same on both sides, the child predicts the scale will balance. But young children do not simultaneously evaluate both the weight of each peg and its distance from the fulcrum. If the weights on each side differ, the young child predicts that the side with the greater weight will tip down, but he fails to take into account the distance of each weight from the fulcrum. Older children, by contrast, accommodate to both the number of weights on each side and the distance of each from the fulcrum. Nine- and ten-year-olds accommodate to the two independent factors and understand that if the weights on two sides are equal, the side with the weight furthest from the fulcrum will be the one to tip down (Siegler, 1996).

GROWTH OF THE BRAIN

The psychological competences that appear during this era require the coordination of many maturing brain sites, rather than one localized circuit (for example, cortical inhibition of brainstem reflexes described in chapter 3). Mesulam (1990) has suggested that complex cognitive functions are mapped at the level of neural systems, rather than localized in a specific site. We now describe some changes in structure, metabolism, and neurochemistry that might be related to the emerging psychological abilities of this era. Obviously, both the psychological and biological transformations are the result of profound interactions between experience and maturation, and it is more difficult to map the cognitive functions of this era onto changes in brain than it was for the earlier years.

Structural and Metabolic Changes

The rate of increase in total cortical surface accelerates between the second and the sixth birthday, and the human brain attains 90% of its adult weight by eight years (Giedd et al., 1996). This growth is accompanied by increased glucose uptake, which remains high until 8 or 9 years, followed by a decrease that reaches adult values by 18 to 20 years (Chugani, 1991; Chugani et al., 1987). This developmental pattern, which is less pronounced for subcortical structures, is due to the fact that the balance between the number of new synapses formed and the number eliminated (pruning) shifts after age 6 or 7 years to a ratio that favors the latter process. The reduction of superfluous synapses through pruning reflects a consolidation of the active synaptic networks representing what the child has learned and the elimination of synapses used less often. The pruning process lasts longer in humans than in nonhuman primates.

We suggested that a more robust working memory is essential for the integration of past with present. Hippocampal integrity may contribute to this competence, for excrescences on the proximal dendrites of hippocampal neurons reach adult size and form by 5 years of age (Seress & Mrzljak, 1992).

Neurotransmitters

Changes in neurotransmitters and in the morphology and density of their receptors also occur during this era. Receptor densities for glutamate and GABA, which complement each other, reach a maximum within the first 10 years (Huttenlocher, 1994; Reichelt et al., 1991). Norepinephrine levels in the dorsolateral and orbitofrontal prefrontal cortex of the rhesus monkeys are highest between 8 months and 3 years (corresponding to 3 to 10 years in children; Brown & Goldman, 1977).

Dopamine concentrations in the monkey prefrontal cortex approach adult values between 2 and 3 years (corresponding to 6 to 9 years in children) and dopaminergic fibers attain their maximal extension in layer 3 of the monkey prefrontal cortex at about 3 years (comparable to age 9 in children; Rosenberg & Lewis, 1994). Dopamine-1 receptors (D1R) attain peak density in the human putamen and caudate nuclei between 3 and 8 years; dopamine-2 receptors (D2R) attain peak density a little earlier, between 1 and 2 years of age (Seeman et al., 1987). Maximal activity of the dopamine transporter molecule, which removes dopamine from the synapse and affects synaptic activity, occurs between 9 and 16 years (Meng, Obonai, & Takashima, 1998; Meng, Ozawa, Itoh, & Takashima, 1999; Seeman et al., 1987). It may not be a coincidence that most children do not set long-range goals, or implement behaviors to attain them, until they are 6 or 7 years old. The anticipation of a desired goal is accompanied by the release of dopamine from the brain stem. The projection of dopaminergic fibers to varied sites, including the nucleus accumbens and the frontal cortex, probably contributes to this motivational state.

Although the rate of serotonin synthesis in many brain sites peaks at 3 years, serotonin receptors do not reach maximal density in the basal ganglia, hippocampus, and cerebellum until 5 or 6 years. Children under 6 years are more impulsive than older children; the latter find it easier to suppress inappropriate behavior. The increased serotonergic activity in the basal ganglia, hippocampus, and cerebellum at 5 to 6 years could contribute to the more reflective behavioral style.

Acetylcholine may also be central to the cognitive advances of this era because this transmitter influences frontal lobe functions. Acetylcholine-sterase-positive pyramidal neurons, believed to be restricted to humans and apes, first appear in layer 3 in the frontal, motor, and associational cortex, as well as the hippocampus after the fourth birthday (Kostovic et al., 1988; Mesulam & Geula, 1988, 1991). GABA receptor density reaches a maximum within the first decade (Reichelt et al., 1991) and it is possible that this increase in receptor density for GABA compensates for the decrease in GABA synthesis during early childhood.

Connectivity

The increased connectivity of the brain, a seminal characteristic of this period, is reflected in changes in myelination and EEG coherence.

Myelination

Myelination of the brain is enhanced in three dimensions—between hemispheres, across hemispheres, and from cortical to subcortical structures resulting, by 7 or 8 years of age, in a massively interconnected brain. The axons projecting from cortical layer 5 to the brainstem and spinal cord undergo a spurt of myelination before the third birthday (Curnes, Burger, Djang, & Boyko, 2000). Myelination of the axons of the anterior corpus callosum, which links the frontal lobes of the two hemispheres, is accelerated between 3 and 6 years (Young, Fox, & Zahn-Waxler, 1999). Myelination of the posterior corpus callosum, which links temporal and parietal sites, accelerates a bit later, between 6 and 15 years. In addition, the anterior commissure, a small, compact bundle of fibers linking the middle and inferior temporal gyri of the hemispheres, and anatomically separate from the larger corpus callosum, myelinates after the third birthday.

Longer tracts that link noncontiguous sites within a hemisphere also display a spurt of myelination after the third birthday (Curnes et al., 2000; Yakovlev & Lecours, 1967). These longer tracts include the inferior occipital-frontal fasiculus, linking the frontal and occipital cortices; the uncinatus, linking orbito-prefrontal and temporal cortices; the superior longitudinal tract, linking parietal and occipital regions; and the arcuate, linking prefrontal and temporal cortices, and part of the cingulum that connects frontal, parietal, temporal, and parahippocampal regions. This growth enhances the ability to utilize information from varied sites and may contribute to the hierarchical nature of semantic networks.

In sum, myelination is enhanced in three dimensions during the period of 2 to 8 years: axons connecting the two hemispheres, axons connecting various areas within each hemisphere, and axons linking cortical to subcortical structures. These processes result in a massively interconnected brain by the age of 8 years. As a result of the increased myelination, the ratio of white to gray matter in layers 1 and 2, which favored gray matter during the first 3 years, is reversed and white matter now exceeds gray for the first time.

EEG Coherence

The coherence of EEG frequency bands, defined as the degree to which different brain regions show synchronized neuronal activity, is a second sign of enhanced connectivity. The magnitude of coherence between frontal sites, on the one hand, and occipital and temporal areas, on the other, increases between 3 and 6 years (Ornitz, 2002; Thatcher, 1992). There is a substantial correlation between the changes in coherence between 4 and 6 years and the degree of improvement in the ability to remember, after a short delay, how many squares in a 16-cell matrix had been colored blue (Case, 1992).

Faster latencies to the peaks of the standard ERP waveforms accompany the enhanced coherence. The latency to the peak value of a waveform that occurs to faces—called the N170—decreases by more than 10% between 5 and 7 years of age (Taylor, McCarthy, Saliba, & Degiovanni, 1999), and the latency to the mismatch negativity waveform (MMN) to a deviant tone decreases linearly from 4 to 10 years of age (Shafer, Moor, Kreuzer, & Kurtzberg, 2000).

The enhanced coherence should aid the brain's ability to integrate past with present. When there is a brief 1-sec delay between the last member of a series of identical tones and the onset of a discrepant tone that differs in frequency or loudness, a negative waveform in the ERP of children and adults appears at about 200 msec—called MMN. However, if there is a 6-sec delay between the last member of the identical series of tones and the discrepant tone, many children who are less than 7 or 8 years old fail to show the negative waveform. This interesting fact implies that the brains of younger children do not automatically relate the delayed discrepant tone to the prior series (Gomes et al., 1999).

INTEGRATIVE FUNCTIONS

The abilities to integrate past with present, construct semantic networks, and to detect relations between categories, require the integration of many brain areas, but especially, those that contribute to language function.

Language-Related Areas

The increased reliance on semantic networks is accompanied by a change in the direction of predominant blood flow to sites in the parietal-temporal cortex involved in the processing of visuospatial and auditory information. Blood flow to this area during the first 3 years is greater in the right than in the left hemisphere, but by age 5 is greater to the left hemisphere (Chiron, 1992; Chiron et al., 1997; Chugani, 1996, 1998; Takahashi, Shirane, Sato, & Yoshimoto, 1999). It may not be a coincidence that this shift is accompanied by the ascendance of semantic categories.

The connections between Wernicke's and Broca's areas myelinate and display increased synaptic density by the third birthday (Curnes et al., 2000). Dendritic growth in Broca's area in the left hemisphere exceeds growth in the orofacial area between 4 and 6 years. However, after age 6, growth in Broca's area is greater in the right hemisphere, implying that the neuronal ensembles of Broca's area in the right hemisphere contribute to the emotional and prosodic components of language (Jacobs, Schall, & Scheibel, 1993; Jacobs & Scheibel, 1993; Simonds & Scheibel, 1989). The comprehension and expression of irony, sarcasm, and humor are enhanced after the sixth birthday.

The acquisition of a second language, whether acquired simultaneously with the native language or learned later in life, has attracted considerable scientific attention in recent years. Adults who acquired a second language while they were learning their native language (early learners) were compared to adults who learned their second language as adults (adult learners). The participants silently read a passage of text while lying in an fMRI scanner. The early learners showed patterns of neuronal activity to both languages within the same sites in Broca's area. However, in the adult learners, the two languages evoked activity in different Broca sites. This evidence suggests that the age when a second language is learned can affect the organization of Broca's area, and may explain why it is easier to learn a second language in childhood than later in life (Kim, Relkin, Lee, & Hirsch, 1997).

Moderately fluent French–English bilinguals were scanned while they listened to stories spoken either in their original language (French) or their second language (English) acquired after they were 7 years old. All the participants showed activity in the same sites in the left temporal lobe while listening to French, but the English sentences activated more variable sites in both the left and right temporal and frontal lobes. The authors suggested that the representations of French, the first language, had exploited a dedicated part of the left hemisphere, whereas the representations of the second language had not done so (Dehaene, Dupoux, Mehler, Cohen, & Paulescu, 1997). Adults who acquire a second language before 7 years can gain complete mastery without any compromise in either language as long as they have no serious cognitive impairments (Gordon, 2000).

Although deaf and hearing children exposed to language during infancy are equally proficient when they try to learn a second language later in life, deaf adults who failed to acquire any language during the early years are less proficient, whether the language was spoken or signed (Neville & Bavelier, 1998; Woodward & Hayne, 1999).

It is difficult, perhaps impossible, to prove that an adult has lost semantic representations acquired during early childhood. However, a recent study of 27-year-olds born in Korea to Korean parents, and adopted by French families when they were between 3 and 8 years of age, suggested that some early semantic representations might be lost. The adopted adults, who had been exposed only to the French language for over 20 years, along with controls who spent their entire lives in France, heard sentences in four different languages (including French and Korean). The recognition of Korean words by the adopted adults was not seriously different from the controls. Neither group could recognize words or sentences spoken in Korean and the fMRI patterns of activation to Korean words were similar in the adopted and control adults (Pallier et al., 2003). If such loss is possible for language, it is possible for other cognitive structures as well.

Prefrontal Cortex

The volume of the prefrontal cortex increases slowly from infancy to about 8 years of age and then undergoes an accelerated growth from 8 to 14 years of age (Kanemura, Aihara, Aoki, Araki, & Nakazawa, 2003). The integrative functions of the prefrontal cortex, which participate in working memory, planning, control of inappropriate actions, and conscious awareness of feeling tone, are inferred from the dense set of anatomical connections to subcortical and other cortical regions. The mediodorsal nucleus of the thalamus, a prominent source of afferents to the prefrontal cortex, projects to three main structures: the orbital and medial prefrontal cortex (involved in feelings), the dorsolateral prefrontal cortex (involved in cognitive processes), and the cingulate cortex (involved in modulating motor and cognitive functions; Fan et al., 2001; Paus, 2001). The prefrontal cortex is also connected to cortical sites that mediate somatic, auditory, visual, olfactory, and gustatory information—a sign of its importance in multimodal associations.

A salient feature of the prefrontal cortex between 2 and 8 years is the appearance of dendritic trees covered with short spines resembling adult morphology on large-layer 3 pyramidal neurons (Mrzljak et al., 1990). The number of spines on the dendritic arbor of the pyramidal cells is greater in the prefrontal cortex than in other cortical sites. The difference in dendritic arbors between the prefrontal and the visual cortex approaches a factor of 7—a fact that is also true of monkeys (Elston, 2003).

Further, prefrontal cortex neurons are tonically more active than those in other cortical sites. It may not be a coincidence that the most anterior area of the prefrontal cortex, called the frontal pole, is enlarged in humans compared with monkeys, and, in addition, humans are distinguished by their extraordinary ability to detect the relations between two or more semantic representations (Ramnani & Owen, 2004).

ATTENTION DEFICIT HYPERACTIVITY DISORDER

Attention Deficit Hyperactivity Disorder, or ADHD, is the most common psychiatric, pediatric, or psychological diagnosis given to American and European children during this era. The estimated prevalence is 2% to 5% of the school-age population, with three or four boys to every girl given this classification (Dehaene, Changeux, & Nadal, 1987; Swanson et al., 1998). The three defining symptoms of ADHD are: (a) difficulty maintaining attention, accompanied by excessive distractibility; (b) difficulty controlling motor activity, especially restless fidgeting; and (c) impulsive decisions that lead to inappropriate behaviors (Castellanos & Tannock, 2002).

Two thirds of the ADHD diagnoses occur during the early school years when the demands for attention and control of motor activity become more severe. Children diagnosed with ADHD before the third birthday, who are only one third of all cases, are more likely than others to preserve their symptoms into adulthood.

However, these symptoms do not define a unitary syndrome with a single etiology because the correlations among the three defining symptoms of compromised attention, hyperactivity, and impulsivity can be low. Some children show compromised attention without hyperactivity; others show the reverse profile. The prevalence of the ADHD diagnosis in American children has increased to almost 15% of the school population over the past quarter century. This alarming fact suggests that some children given this diagnosis would have been given a different diagnosis 25 years ago: probably minimal brain damage, learning disabled, or conduct disorder.

Despite some problems with the validity of current diagnoses, most experts believe that a small group of children, probably between 2% and 5%, were born with a compromise in brain function that interferes with sustained attention and control of impulsive decisions and restlessness. The following sections summarize some initial insights into this special category of children.

A genetic contribution to ADHD is likely because studies of twins, adopted children, and first-degree relatives of ADHD patients, imply a heritability coefficient for ADHD between .50 and .70 (Biederman et al., 1992; Castellanos & Tannock, 2002; Rapoport, 2002; State, Lombroso, Pauls, & Leckman, 2000). Over 30% of the siblings of ADHD patients, compared to only 5% of the general population, are at risk for the same diagnosis (Biederman et al., 1992; Castellanos & Tannock, 2002).

Children and adolescents diagnosed with ADHD, compared to controls, have smaller volumes in the right prefrontal cortex, right anterior white matter, right caudate nucleus, and the anterior portion of the corpus callosum, implying, but not proving, a genetic contribution to aberrations in brain growth (Giedd, Blumenthal, Molloy, & Castellanos, 2001; Giedd et al., 1996; Paule et al., 2000; Rubia et al., 1999). Among a sample of identical twin pairs, the sibling with ADHD had a smaller caudate volume than his unaffected sibling (Castellanos et al., 2003).

The genes that control dopamine metabolism probably contribute to ADHD. One relevant allele is at the locus for the Dopamine-4 receptor; another is at the locus for the dopamine transporter (DAT) protein that monitors the reuptake of dopamine from the synapse (Dougherty et al., 1999; Madras, Miller, & Fischman, 2002; Miller, De La Garza, Novak, & Madras, 2001; Miller & Madras, 2002).

The alleles of the COMP gene (catechol-o-methyltransferase), which codes for an enzyme that degrades dopamine in the synapse, might also be relevant. Methianine is substituted for valine in about 40% to 50% of Whites with a mutation in the COMP gene. These individuals show a slower turnover of dopamine, and therefore, this molecule remains in the synapse for a longer period of time. Nine-year-old, otherwise healthy, children with the methianine substitution in both alleles were better able to inhibit inappropriate responses in a simple cognitive task (Diamond, Lee, & Hayden, in press). One sample of ADHD children with attention problems showed EEG profiles characterized by less alpha and more theta frequencies, implying a lower level of cortical arousal (Clarke, Barry, McCarthy, & Selikowitz, 2003).

Environmental Influences

A variety of environmental events, including severe head injuries, early malnutrition, social deprivation, prematurity, and maternal smoking during pregnancy, acting alone or in combination with genetic influences, contribute to the risk of ADHD (Castellanos & Tannock, 2002; Kates et al., 1998; Minshew, Pettegrew, Payton, & Panchalingam, 1989; Weinstock, 1997). Maternal smoking is a likely risk factor because a possible pathophysiology has been described.

Nicotinic acetylcholine receptors (NAR), to which nicotine binds, are expressed in the spinal cord, medulla oblongata, pons, subcortical forebrain, and cortex, as early as 4 to 5 weeks after fertilization. Human fetal neurons in cell cultures exposed to nicotine for 3 days show an increase in nicotinic receptor mRNA and a subsequent increase in nicotine binding to these cells (Hellstrom-Lindahl, Seiger, Kjaeldgaard, & Nordberg, 2001). The presence of nicotinic receptors so early in development implies a contribution to brain growth (Hellstrom-Lindahl, Gorbounova, Seiger, Mousavi, & Nordberg, 1998). It has been suggested that maternal smoking, which exposes the embryo and fetus to nicotine, facilitates abnormal differentiation of neurons in the hippocampus and somatosensory cortex (Oliff & Gallardo, 1999; Roy, Seidler, & Slotkin, 2002).

Treatment

The physiological consequences of two drugs with clear therapeutic effects on ADHD provide a clue to the compromised biochemistry that contributes to the symptoms of ADHD. One drug, methylphenidate (Mph, trademark Ritalin), slows the reuptake of dopamine in the synaptic cleft by blocking the dopamine transporter molecule (Roman et al., 2002; Volkow, Fowler, Wang, Ding, & Gatley, 2002).

Rats become hyperactive when their dopaminergic neurons are destroyed, but recover following treatment with Mph (Johnston & Singer, 1982; Shaywitz, Fletcher, & Shaywitz, 1995; Shaywitz, Yager, & Klopper, 1976). The variation among children in the therapeutic efficacy of Mph could be mediated by an allelic mutation (10 repeat allele) of the dopamine transporter gene. Seventy-five percent of a sample of 50 patients without the 10 repeat allele improved during drug treatment, compared with forty-seven percent who had the 10 repeat allele (Roman et al., 2002).

Atomoxetine, another drug used to treat ADHD, inhibits the reuptake of norepinephrine, rather than dopamine, by selectively blocking the norepinephrine transporter. Atomoxetine does not increase dopamine levels in either the striatum or the nucleus accumbens, suggesting it is not vulnerable to abuse, but, at the moment, the relative superiority of atomoxetine over Mph is unclear (Bymaster et al., 2002; Spencer, Biederman, Wilens, & Faraone, 2002).

SUMMARY

Two fundamental features of the psychological advances of this era are the rapid, almost automatic, evocation of semantic representations relevant to an incentive, and the ability to inhibit inappropriate behavior. Children retrieve the past, integrate it with the present, and detect semantic relations between categories. As a result, the separate cognitive representations of experience that were linked to one or two contexts become associated and create more abstract representations. The concept of number provides an example. Most 2-year-olds have separate schematic representations for the number of eyes on a face, the number of hands on a person, the number of horns on a bull, and the number of pictures on a bedroom wall. At some point during this developmental era, the semantic representation "two" emerges as a category for these and all other pairs of events.

The enhanced abilities of this era are facilitated by a massive interconnectedness that involves both hemispheres, anterior and posterior cortical sites, and cortical and subcortical structures. Myelination of axonal tracts, synaptic densities, concentrations of neurotransmitters, and degree of glucose uptake show significant changes during this era. We regard two facts as especially important. One is the shift in predominant blood flow from the temporal and parietal areas in the right hemisphere to homologous areas in the left hemisphere. Second, the number of synapses eliminated exceeds that of new synapses formed, first in sensory, and later in frontal areas, reflecting the strengthening of circuits that experience has rendered adaptive.

The ascending control of the prefrontal cortex over other parts of the brain, attained by the end of this era, prepares children in all societies, ancient and modern, for pedagogical training and responsibilities. English common law and the Catholic Church appreciated centuries ago what Sigmund Freud and Jean Piaget recognized later; namely, qualitatively distinct psychological profiles emerge between 4 and 8 years of age. We believe that specific aspects of brain growth allow children to use their rich corpus of past experience to generate new talents, while acknowledging that, without these experiences, the maturing brain would be unable to display its new potencies.

7

Reflections

The times of emergence of select psychological features during the first 8 years, summarized in Table 7.1, are partially dependent on specific changes in brain anatomy, physiology, and biochemistry. The disappearance of the newborn's reflexes is due, in part, to increased synaptic contact between the supplementary motor cortex and the brainstem; the improved recognition memory at 12 weeks requires hippocampal growth; the enhanced working memory at 7 to 12 months profits from maturation of the prefrontal cortex; the appearance of speech is enabled by the dendritic growth in Wernicke's, Broca's, and the orofacial motor areas; and the appearance of inference, a moral sense, and self-awareness, should be aided by the enhanced connectivity of the two hemispheres. The psychological properties that appear after age 3, especially the increased reliance on semantic categories and integration of present with past, should be facilitated by the attainment of maximum synaptic density in the prefrontal cortex, refinement of circuitry, changes in neurotransmitter function, increased coherence, and the shift in predominant blood flow from the right to the left hemisphere.

However, despite all that has been learned, we remain unable to answer a significant question: how do psychological phenomena—schemata, semantic representations, motor acts, or the private judgment that one feels "happy"—emerge from neural activity? These psychological constructs—like the concept "four" representing the number of opening chords in Beethoven's Fifth Symphony, or "consistency" representing an arrangement of the meaningless symbols of a mathematical proof—are to be distinguished from the brain processes that are the foundation of these

TABLE 7.1
Summary of Psychological and Biological
Changes Over the First 8 Years

Age	Psychological Advances	Biological Changes
8–12 weeks	Inhibition of brainstem reflexes; decrease in crying and endogenous smiles	• Synaptic contact between supplementary motor area and brainstem and between cingulate cortex and brainstem
		• Myelination of pyramidal tracts
	Establish circadian rhythm	• Increased number of neurons in suprachiasmatic nucleus of the hypothalamus
		• Increase in melatonin synthesis
	Enhanced recognition memory	• Growth of the hippocampus
7–12 months	Enhanced working memory; stranger and separation fear; schematic concepts	• Enhanced growth of pyramidal neurons and interneurons in the prefrontal cortex
		• Increased number of spines in CA-3 region of the hippocampus
		• Myelination of connections between the amygdala and cortex
		• Establishment of 6 to 9 Hz alpha rhythm and 40-Hz gamma rhythm
12–24 months	Language, inference, moral sense, self-awareness	• Growth of pyramidal neurons and dendrites in layer 3 of prefrontal cortex
		• Enhanced linking of the two hemispheres
		• Elongation of dendrites in Wernicke's area
		• Increased GABA-ergic and acetylcholine activity in layer 3
2–8 years	Integration of past with present; increased reliance on semantic categories; detecting the relations between different categories	• Brain attains 90% of its weight
		• Peak synaptic density in prefrontal cortex
		• Peak glucose uptake
		• Pruning
		• Peak density of GABA and glutamate receptors
		• Peak dopamine and norepinephrine receptors
		• Myelination of long cortical tracts
		• Increased coherence
		• Shift in blood flow from right to left hemisphere
		• Appearance of AchE+ neurons
		• Maximum dendritic differentiation in hippocampus

concepts. This distinction should not be a source of discouragement. The ancient Greeks knew that an amber rod rubbed with fur attracted small particles of hair and a lodestone attracted metal, but it took more than 2,000 years for scientists to understand that both phenomena were emergent derivatives of the properties of electrons under specific conditions. We now consider some implications of the facts and hypotheses presented in the prior six chapters.

COINCIDENCE OR CONTINGENT

Historians are distinguished by the conceptual frame they impose on their evidence. Some prefer the journalist's sequential narration of events; others favor a skeptical, sardonic, or optimistic construction of the facts; still others celebrate an aesthetically pleasing coherence of cause–effect relations among events that were independent. We place ourselves to the right of the skeptic and to the left of the Platonist whose ideas shimmer with the gleam of perfect understanding. A wrinkled guru who knows how brains and minds grow might shake his head after reading our arguments and mutter that all we have done is to describe a few approximately temporal correspondences between changes in brain and psychological functions and suggested, with insufficient caution, that the appearance of the latter required the former, although they would not appear unless the proper experiences had intervened.

The history of science is littered with examples of this easy error. Many were certain that foul air was the villainous culprit when Europe was struck with the plague over 6 centuries ago; others were equally sure that a Jewish curse caused the epidemic. Sixteenth-century naturalists believed that a burned log lost its original weight because it released its store of phlogiston. And only 50 years ago, child psychiatrists were convinced that a mother's rejecting, aloof attitude could cause her child to show the compromised social and language functions characteristic of autism.

We have reminded readers repeatedly that brain maturation only constrains the earliest age of appearance of select psychological functions; it does not guarantee the actualization of those functions. Most 1-year-olds, regardless of geographical setting, can retrieve representations of the past and hold them and their perception of the current context in a working memory circuit for intervals as long as 30 sec. The fact that pyramidal neurons in frontal sites display accelerated growth during the second half of the first year bolsters the argument that the behavioral phenomena require the biological changes. No set of experiences would allow 2-month-olds to retrieve a representation of an event that occurred 30 sec earlier and to hold that retrieved representation, along with aspects of the current situation, in a working memory circuit for half a minute. That is why 2-month-olds do not show any surprise when, after a parent lifts a cover, the infants do not see the toy the parent hid there only seconds earlier.

The developing brain also modulates the emotions that require new cognitive abilities. Most infants do not cry to temporary separation from the mother before 6 months, show shame following failure before 16 months, experience dissonance to inconsistent semantic categories before 3 years, or feel guilt over lying to a parent before they are 4 or 5 years old.

The correspondences between brain and psychological development during the first 2 years are less ambiguous than they are for the next 6. Nonetheless, it is reasonable to assume that the attainment of maximal brain size, increased connectivity, and shift of blood flow to the left hemisphere allow 8-year-olds to integrate past with present, create semantic networks, and detect shared relations between disparate phenomena. The maturation of the brain does not guarantee any of these psychological advances—experience must cooperate—but maturation sets a lower limit on the age when these characteristics emerge.

Mark Johnson (Johnson, 2003) places greater emphasis than we on the role of the child's activities in facilitating connectivity between cortical regions—a principle that Johnson calls "interactive specialization." This position argues that the functional properties of a brain region are determined partly by genetic factors that lay down particular circuits, and partly by the child's activity. The difference between Johnson's view and our own, which is slight and subtle, is that Johnson awards to the infant's experiences and actions more power to create major brain structures than we do. Future research will determine which perspective is closer to nature's plan.

It is relevant that both 19th-century evolutionists and early 20th-century psychologists placed greater emphasis on the contributions of the environment, in the form of natural selection of species or conditioning of habits in children. Following the evolutionary synthesis a half century ago, biologists corrected the imbalance and acknowledged the role of changes in the genome. Some contemporary developmental psychologists continue to resist the influence of genetic instructions on brain and behavioral development in the early years.

The psychological sequence during the first decade proceeds from (a) establishing initial connectivity among sensory, limbic, and medial temporal structures; to (b) connecting the frontal lobe to the above sites; to (c) improved integration of the two hemispheres; and finally, to (d) massive connectivity among all brain sites as the child prepares for school, or, in villages without schools, for assumption of family responsibilities. Nature's plan is, first, to grow the separate parts of the brain, and then to link the components in sets of reciprocal relations.

A PLEA FOR SPECIFICITY

The stark contrast between the extraordinary specificity of brain function and the generality of psychological constructs is a rarely discussed paradox. Most neurotransmitters have several receptors; pyramidal and interneurons have different origins and functions; novel events produce a brief surge of dopamine in the shell of the nucleus accumbens, but not in the core; GABA is usually an inhibitory transmitter in adults, but can be excitatory in the newborn (Stein & Nicoll, 2003); the ventral gray mediates an animal's immobility to a threat, but the dorsal gray mediates the defensive biting of an intruder; and pair bonding is facilitated in male voles by vasopressin, but in female voles by oxytocin. (Curtis & Wang, 2003) Almost every time a biologist posits a relation between different aspects of brain function, or between brain activity and a psychological outcome, other scientists soon discover that the claim was too general.

The specificity can be excruciatingly frustrating. Related strains of knockout mice were tested on two similar procedures presumed to index a fear state. One is avoidance of the brightly lit areas in a black circular platform with open and closed quadrants. A mouse is placed initially in a closed, dark quadrant and investigators measure the total time the animal spends in any of the open, lit quadrants. Mice prefer the closed quadrants; therefore, a mouse who spends very little time in the open quadrants is presumed to be more fearful. A second index of fear is failure to explore an unfamiliar area; animals who explore less are presumed to be more fearful. Despite the apparent similarity in the behaviors coded, there was no relation between these two measures of fear (Cook et al., 2002). Further, repeated immobilization of male rats for an hour a day for 13 days resulted in decreasing concentrations of ACTH and corticosterone, implying habituation of the stress response, but increasing levels of corticotropin-releasing hormone in the paraventricular nucleus of the hypothalamus, which implies an increase in stress (Marquez, Nadal, & Armario, 2004).

These facts, and many others, force neurobiologists to be "splitters" when they deal with biological data but not always when they borrow psychological concepts to explain the biological evidence. The need to restrict the meaning and validity of a conclusion to its empirical source is a principle in all the sciences. The genetic distance between two species depends on whether fossils or proteins are used to index degree of relatedness. Lord Kelvin's 19th-century estimate of the relatively young age of the earth, which intimidated Darwin, differs from the current value based on new evidence for the velocity of receding galaxies and the uniform temperature of the cosmos. Astrophysicists had a brief moment of embarrassment when they realized that one source of evidence implied that a particular star was older than the universe; fortunately, the inconsistency was resolved.

Contemporary psychologists and psychiatrists, by contrast, tend to be "lumpers," preferring abstract constructs to constrained ones. For example, psychologists are fond of the word "stress" although the biological reactions following a threat to the body are different from those evoked by worry over a critical evaluation (Kemeny, 2003). And the reaction to a critical evaluation differs from the reaction evoked by a moment of shame (Dickerson, Kemeny, Aziz, Kim, & Fahey, 2004). The cardiovascular reaction to the challenge of a cognitive task, as well as the pain that accompanies immersion of the hand into ice cold water, are muted if the person is tested with a pet dog or cat present in the room, but not if alone (Blascovich & Mendes, 2002). Although restraint, forced swimming, and inescapable foot shock are all regarded as "stressors" for rats, each is accompanied by different reactions (Mercier, Canini, Cespuglio, Martin, & Bourdon, 2003).

Two distinguished neuroscientists, following a review of the anatomy and physiology of the hypothalamus, wrote: "In other words, challenges or stressors do not activate individual components of the visceromotor system in isolation, and the profile of particular integrated responses depends specifically on the nature of the initiating stimulus pattern, so that each challenge results in a characteristic set of responses" (Thompson & Swanson, 2002, p. 35).

Many scientists regard "intelligence" as a theoretically useful concept, although duration of short-term memory for pictures, inferring the meanings of fragmented words, failure to inhibit an inappropriate response, and learning the spatial location of a target are statistically independent abilities that rely on different brain circuits. Patients with lesions in different sites, often due to stroke, show selective loss of a particular intellectual competence, rather than equivalent compromise in all cognitive abilities. Kurt Gödel displayed exceptional cognitive talent when he proved that some true statements about numbers could not be proven. But he showed severely compromised rational abilities when he insisted that people were poisoning his food and refused to eat unless his wife sampled the food first.

The psychological term *reward* is a third overly abstract word. This concept originated almost a century ago in studies of animal behavior where it referred to any event that increased the probability of a response that produced it, or any event an animal approached spontaneously. The rewards in the laboratory were usually food, water, copulation, novelty, activity, and recently, cocaine. But these events do not share a common brain state. Although rats prefer sweet-tasting foods, different qualities of sweetness evoke distinct profiles of dopamine change in the rat brain. Sucrose produces an increase in dopamine in the prefrontal cortex, but not in the nucleus accumbens, whereas a combination of sucrose and chocolate, which is an unfamiliar taste for rats, provokes a dopamine increase in both sites. Although both sweet substances are rewards, each elicits a distinct brain state (Bassareo, DeLuca, & DiChiara, 2002).

Further, a reward assumes a state of motivation; an event that is rewarding under conditions of desire may not be a reward when motivation is absent (Salamone & Correa, 2002). That is why the activity of the amygdala and the OBPFC of hungry adults exposed to a stimulus that signaled the odor of a particular food decreased dramatically after the participants were sated on that food (Gottfried, O'Doherty, & Dolan, 2003).

The names of popular emotional concepts, borrowed from an ancient vocabulary, also fail to specify the evocative situation. A 10-year-old criticized by her mother for talking too loudly at a dinner table is likely to become angry. The same child criticized by an adult stranger for talking too loudly in the town library is likely to feel ashamed. The concepts of positive and negative affect have similar problems. Advocates of these constructs let readers decide which emotions should be called positive or negative. Some individuals enjoy bullying; others feel guilty over the same behavior. Some find pleasure in reading alone; whereas others are anxious when alone. Because the activities that create a positive emotion vary, in a serious way, across individuals and cultures, it is unlikely that there is a specific brain state that defines "feeling good."

THE SIGNIFICANCE OF PROCEDURE

The splitter's attraction to specificity is supported by the fact that subtle details in a laboratory procedure can affect biological and behavioral phenomena. For example, the age when young children are able to infer the correct rule in the delayed nonmatch to sample procedure is a function of small details in the testing procedure. If the reward (for example, a toy) is physically separate from the object the child must lift to obtain the reward, 9- and 12-month-olds are unable to learn that they should pick up a novel, rather than a familiar, object. However, if the reward is attached to the object to be lifted, the infants perform well because the reward and the object are perceived as a unity (Diamond, Lee, & Hayden, 2003).

Preschool children tested in a small room (4 by 6 feet) without windows usually fail to use a landmark (in this case, a single blue wall) to find an object they saw an adult hide in one corner of the room. But the same children will use the blue wall as a landmark if they are tested in a larger room (8 by 12 feet). Simply changing the size of the room leads to a different conclusion about the child's ability to use a landmark (Learmonth, Nadel, & Newcombe, 2002).

Five-year-old Canadian children who see a card with the printed word "dog" and hear an adult say "dog" while placing the card under a picture of a dog will say "dog" if the examiner asks, "What does the card say?" But if the examiner says "dog" while placing the card with the printed word "dog" under a picture of a kangaroo, the child assumes that the printed word changed its meaning (Bialystok & Martin, 2003).

A rat's behavior following stimulation of the hypothalamus depends on the objects in the present environment. The stimulation is followed by eating if food is available, drinking if water is present, and by gathering of wood chips if these materials are present in the cage (Valenstein, Cox, & Kakolewski, 1970). Theoretical progress, therefore, requires scientists to specify the species, relevant incentive, context, and the agent's expectations when they use psychological predicates.

Context Again

A deeper understanding of the relation between brain activity and psychological outcomes will follow when we acknowledge that the latter is always dependent on the context in which the animal or person is acting. Every event presented to an animal or human, as part of an experimental protocol, occurs in a particular context. Nonetheless, many neuroscientists and psychologists describe the effect of an incentive on brain or behavior as if it were independent of the situation in which the outcome appeared. Physicists have accommodated to the fact that the product of a beam of electrons aimed at a pair of slits depends on whether the experimenter does or does not measure the event. Patterns of interconnected neural ensembles, and their associated mental representations, should not be conceptualized as if they were colors that could be painted on any surface, for the context affects the agent's expectations, which are a product, in part, of past history. A person reading alone in a quiet room at midnight is primed for one set of representations if she hears the sound of a crashing object, but quite another if she hears exactly the same sound in a city street at high noon. If neuroscientists could measure every possible representation that could be evoked by the sound of a crashing object, they would discover that semantic representations for "danger," "animals," "burglars," "construction," "bulldozers," and "cranes," were all potential candidates. The context of the room at midnight primes the first three, the street setting primes the others. Each trio of representations has a distinct neural foundation.

Male and female college students attending a midwestern American university activated different semantic networks when the psychologist asked them to reflect on their mortality (control students thought about feeling pain in a dentist's office). After a short delay, the students were given a word fragment task in which they had to guess the complete word from a few letters. The word fragments were constructed so that a patriotic-nationalistic word, a word with romantic connotations, or a neutral word, were possible (for example, f — g could be flag or frog; - ate could be date or late). The men who had been thinking about death tended to choose patriotic words, the women chose words with connotations for romantic relationships (Arndt, Greenberg, & Cook, 2002).

The importance of a person's mental expectations was also revealed in a study in which adults were told to read groups of three numbers, or three letters, as fast as possible. One of the stimuli was ambiguous and could be read either as the letter "B" or the number "13." This ambiguous stimulus elicited a different pattern of neuronal activity in the frontal lobe, depending on whether the participant's set was to read letters or numbers, although the neuronal profile in the primary visual cortex was almost identical under the two different mental sets (Johnston & Chesney, 1974). A third example of the importance of mental set was revealed when the MMN waveform was recorded in adults under two conditions. In the first, the interstimulus interval between the string of identical tones was 0.5 sec, but the delay between the last standard tone and the deviant one was 7 sec. In the second condition, the interstimulus intervals were always 7 sec—both between each of the standard tones and between the last standard tone and the deviant one. The participants showed no MMN under the first condition, but did show a clear MMN under the second condition (Winkler, Schroger, & Cowan, 2001). Only when the participants expected the interstimulus interval to be long did the brain react to the deviant tone with the longer delay. One could not ask for a clearer example of the principle that the brain's response is a function of higher order expectations. That is why adults lying in an fMRI scanner watching the same 30-min film segment taken from the movie, "The Good, the Bad, and the Ugly," did not show similar patterns of activation in the prefrontal cortex, and only modestly similar activity in sensory and association areas (Hasson, Nir, Levy, Fuhrmann, & Malach, 2004). Even when the context and the perceptual input are identical, humans fail to display even close to identical brain reactions because each individual reacts in a distinct way to the information.

The brain, and its heir the mind, are always in a particular state of expectation for a probable class of events. Although the brain-mind can never be absolutely certain which particular member of the class might occur, both react immediately to any event that falls outside that category. The profile of ERPs to sentence endings supports this claim. In the following four sentences, each with a familiar noun for a subject, the final word elicits a larger negative waveform (at 400 msec) in sentences 3 and 4, than in sentences 1 and 2.

1. The number is zero.
2. The book is brown.
3. The number is brown.
4. The book is zero.

The word "zero" falls outside the envelope of words that might follow the phrase, "The book is," and "brown" falls outside the envelope of possibilities for the phrase, "The number is." Although the number of words that could occur after "The book is . . ." is very large, the brain-mind is aroused automatically by any word that falls outside the expectations it has acquired. However, if the individual expects to read a metaphor, for example, "Old age is a sunset," the magnitude of the waveform is small, although "sunset" violates the acquired transitional probabilities for the noun phrase "old age . . ." if the person was prepared to interpret the sentence literally. Once again, the person's "frame of mind" is critical.

When an unexpected event evokes an acquired representation immediately and renders it understandable, the state of surprise is muted. An unexpected clap of thunder arouses children more than adults because the latter have acquired representations that render the sound assimilable, although it fell outside the envelope of expected sensory events. The important developmental principle is that the probability of a state of cortical arousal to unexpected events decreases with age because the acquisition of knowledge renders many unexpected events immediately understandable.

Each person's network of possible schemata and semantic representations for an event is analogous to the physicist's notion of a phase space. A collection of gas molecules in a vessel can assume a very large number of states, only one of which can be measured at a given time. The sound of a crashing object can activate a large number of representations, and no member of that family is knowable until an investigator intervenes with a probe to measure it. No member is more essential than any other and none is active while the person is sipping coffee on a sunny morning. This suggestion means that the pattern of brain activation in a person lying in an MRI scanner looking at pictures of poisonous snakes is not the only or most valid profile these stimuli could provoke. The same pictures would create a different brain state if the person were seeing them on a television screen at home while sipping wine. There is no master clock for the universe, and no God's eye view of the brain's response to an incentive. Because each person's current frame of mind and prior history affect the neuronal ensembles and psychological representations that will be activated, every inference from a neural profile to a psychological event is only valid for the context in which the measurement occurred. If the magnitude of a P300 waveform is the measurement of interest, participants show their greatest magnitude to the infrequent appearance of novel pictures (presented 7% of the time) they were instructed to ignore. But if the variable of interest in the same participants is the amount of neural activity, as measured by fMRI, the greatest neural activity occurs to the letter "X" (which also occurred 7% of the time) which they were instructed to respond to when it appeared (Foucher, Otzenberger, & Gounot, 2003). Thus, conclusions about the relation of brain activity to an incentive depend on the particular measurement. That is why Bohr suggested that scientists can never know what nature is; they can only know what they are able to measure.

The attraction to "unconstrained" psychological processes is due, in part, to the fact that most languages contain predicates that can be used with different classes of agents in varied contexts. The predicate "running," for example, can apply to a boy fleeing a bear, a girl racing toward a friend, or a stream of water flowing down a hill. The easy availability of the word running, and the absence of other verbs with a similar meaning, tempts readers to assume a core meaning, or essence, to this word although its referential meaning depends on the agent and the situation.

There is always more ambiguity surrounding the meaning of a predicate than the meaning of a noun specifying an agent or object. A listener is always more certain of the correct referent for the nouns "cat," "tornado," and "cup" than for the predicates "ran," "struck," and "fell." Because most predicates serve a large number of nouns, each can assume a distinct meaning. That is why, "the cat ran" and "the water ran" have different meanings. Too many terms for human psychological processes resemble the predicate "run," for they contain no information about the agent or goal and could refer to a mouse, dog, or monkey, fleeing a predator, approaching food, or chasing a mate.

Adults in a scanner reading single verbs on a screen and deciding whether the action was possible for a dog, a human, or neither, showed greater activity in the right prefrontal cortex when making the judgment for humans, but greater activity in the occipito-temporal area when making the judgment for dogs (Mason, Banfield, & Macrae, 2004).

Most psychological concepts are ambiguous in meaning if they fail to specify the class of agent, the provocative event, and its context, and, where appropriate, the target of the behavior. By contrast, most concepts in biology contain an explicit or implicit specification of the agent (e.g., species and gender) and context; for example, a substance is only an antigen for a select class of hosts. Many behavioral and biological measurements gathered in children (or adults) are ambiguous in meaning if the gender or temperament of the individual is unspecified. Recall from chapter 4 the adolescents who had been classified as high or low reactive as infants. When they were 15 years old they were asked to describe the frequency of conscious somatic reactions to 9 different situations. The somatic reactions included a rise in heart rate, sweating, muscle tension, or difficulty breathing. The incentives included speaking in front of a class, criticism from a teacher or parent, meeting a stranger, insects, and the sight of blood. The biological correlates of frequency of somatic reactions varied with the temperament and gender of the adolescent. Boys who had been low reactive infants who reported many somatic reactions were characterized by high vagal tone in the cardiovascular system. But girls who had been high reactive infants who reported many reactions were characterized by high sympathetic tone. Most studies of humans are indifferent to the temperaments of the participants and assume that a well defined variable—behavioral or biological—has the same theoretical meaning across all participants.

The psychologist's attraction to Platonic essences is understandable. Isaac Newton posited an absolute time, originating eons earlier, implying that the time at a particular moment was identical in Shanghai, Paris, and Chicago. Einstein substituted simultaneity of events for Newton's definition and grounded this concept in the observable phenomena of lights going on and off in front of moving or stationary observers. This conception permitted the revolutionary insight that simultaneity is always relative to the frame of the observer. We suggest, with more modesty, that many psychological concepts must be grounded in the types of agents and the situations in which they (humans or animals) perceive, feel, remember, and act.

Insistence on one state of fear, consciousness, or attention, rather than a family of related states, is more aesthetic, makes experimentation easier, and allows scientists to be indifferent to the species and method used to evaluate a process. It is not a coincidence that beauty and convenience are the primary criteria mathematicians use to decide which equations deserve celebration. Dirac believed that the beauty of a mathematical solution should always take precedence over correspondence with evidence when the two are inconsistent. However, the natural phenomena existed long before humans evolved with an appreciation of beauty and a desire for convenience. A pyramidal neuron and an infant's cry to separation from a parent are neither beautiful nor easy to study. Many popular concepts proposed to explain human behavior, belief, and emotion are too pretty to be true. These ideas remain appealing because they satisfy a desire for simple, parsimonious explanations that generalize broadly. Behaviorism and psychoanalysis owe their initial popularity to the belief that a small number of psychological concepts might explain a great deal of human behavior. Both theories lost their favored status when the evidence revealed their failure to predict or to explain important phenomena.

The Influence of Technology

The introduction of a new technology in physics, chemistry, and biology usually produces novel evidence that requires the invention of new concepts. For example, the capacity to measure radio energy from the cosmos led to the positing of "dark matter," the linear accelerator led to the hypothesis of quarks, and the electron microscope revealed the novel forms called viruses. This sequence has not occurred among scientists who study the correlation between brain evidence and psychological phenomena. The availability of fMRI scanners and amplifiers to record ERPs has made it possible to measure variation in neuronal activity in brain sites. However, some scientists who exploit these technical advances continue to use the psychological concepts that had been used to name the behavioral observations recorded before the machines were invented (for example, fear, memory, and reward), rather than invent new concepts to explain the novel sources of evidence. The human brain produces a positive waveform in the ERP between 350 and 600 msec to a subtle change in a complex scene presented repeatedly in half-second exposures, although the subjects are unaware of any change in the scene (Fernandez-Duque, Grassi, Thornton, & Neville, 2003). Hence, scientists should invent a new concept to explain this biological fact and should not use words like *surprise* or *vigilant* to describe the brain's reaction because these terms imply conscious awareness.

A half century ago, when it was not possible to measure dynamic profiles of activity in different brain sites, the primary psychological constructs were defined by observed behaviors. For example, the concept "learning" referred to an animal's correct turn in a maze or an adult's verbal recall of a list of words. Contemporary neuroscientists use changes in synaptic activity or cortical activation as indexes of "learning." The concept of "emotionality" in an animal used to be measured by the number of fecal boli dropped in a novel area. Today, activity in the amygdala is treated as an index of the same construct. The older psychological concepts were treated as broad, essential processes with similar features. The new biological data suggest that these psychological terms are too broad, too static, and too indifferent to local context.

The second edition of Edward L. Thorndike's popular 1907 text, *The Elements of Psychology,* nominated capacities, habits, feelings, emotions, and memories as fundamental ideas. Each was free of contextual constraints.

The new physiological evidence, which requires more contextualized concepts, will lead to radically new conceptualizations of psychological processes. The fact that adults reading sentences one word at a time fail to pause when a semantic violation occurs (e.g., "The cow ate the race"), although a clear negative waveform appears in the ERP to the word *race*, implies that scientists must invent two different concepts for the process called "recognition of meaning" (De Vincenzi et al., 2003). One concept is appropriate when behavior is the referent; a second is appropriate when a brain reaction is the referent.

We believe theoretical progress will follow the invention of new neurobiological constructs to account for the relations between an experimental manipulation and a subsequent brain profile; for example, we need a term to capture the relation between the presence of a novel event and increased activity in the parahippocampal region and the amygdala. One possibility is to call the brain reaction "the medial temporal response to novelty." The terms *surprise* or *fear* are inappropriate names for this neural profile. Similarly, parts of the fusiform cortex are activated by human faces, as well as by other bounded stimuli with internal elements. This reaction might be called the "fusiform profile," but not the "face perception profile." New sources of evidence are supposed to generate new concepts rather than sustain old ones invented to describe behavioral and self-report evidence.

Alfred North Whitehead, reflecting on the recent discoveries in quantum mechanics, noted, over 70 years ago, that 20th-century physicists were not smarter than their 19th-century colleagues; they just had better machines which, like travel to a new country, uncovered evidence that allowed a new perspective on a familiar idea.

The concepts that will dominate psychology a half century from now will combine five features: (a) a class of agent, (b) an agent's expectations, (c) the incentive event and the context in which it occurred, (d) the cascade of brain activity and psychological structures provoked by the brain activity, and finally, (e) subsequent behavioral or phenomenological reactions. No concept in contemporary psychology combines these features. The term fear (or anxiety), for example, will be replaced with a family of concepts that specifies the above features and scientists will not use the same term to describe: (a) the psychological state of a rat who, having just heard a tone that signals electric shock, freezes; (b) a person in a dark alley who, having encountered a man wielding a knife, feels his heart racing; and (c) a parent of three children who, having been fired from his job, wonders how he will pay his bills. Fear (and anxiety) will be conceptualized as dynamic states rather than permanent features of the brain-mind of a person or animal. As a result, a therapeutic regimen for an anxious adolescent might include aerobic exercise instead of Prozac; the former effectively mutes worry over the possibility of a racing heart and tense muscles when meeting a stranger.

The suggestion to parse the abstract constructs that dominate current psychological theory into a number of more restricted ones that are in closer accord with what is known about the brain is not a defense of reductionism, but a plea for consistency in the level of specificity contained in the different descriptions of brain and mind. The resistance to such an analysis is due to pragmatic demands, an understandable loyalty to parsimony, and a desire for theoretical elegance.

The number of basic forms in physics, chemistry, and biology is much smaller than the number of phenomena that emerge from these fundamental entities. The number of chemical elements is smaller than the number of molecules, the number of base pairs in DNA strands is smaller than the number of genes, and the number of amino acids is smaller than the number of proteins. A stark exception to this generalization is the current asymmetry between the number of possible brain states and the small number of psychological concepts that dominate empirical inquiry. This anomaly invites psychologists, psychiatrists, and neuroscientists who theorize about psychological states to reflect on the utility of their current conceptualizations.

It would be aesthetically pleasing if every perception, retrieval of a past experience, motor act, and pleasant or unpleasant feeling originated in five distinct and coherent brain systems. But this assumption is so wildly incorrect it does not even warrant the judgment "wrong."

LOCALIZATION

The notion that each psychological process emerges from activity in a particular site remains attractive, despite the repeated failure to affirm this idea, because most psychological processes recruit interconnected structures across diverse sites. The headline of a report in the respected journal *Nature* read, "The part of the brain that can induce out-of-body experiences has been located" (Blanke, Ortigue, Landis, & Seeck, 2002). Although the ability to inhibit an inappropriate response, or to hold information in working memory for 30 sec, requires the integrity of the frontal lobe, neither function is localized in this site. Even the simple task of detecting a 1500 Hz tone that occurred only 12.5% of the time, is accompanied by activity in the frontal, temporal, parietal, and cingulate cortex, as well as in the thalamus, putamen, and amygdala (Kiehl & Liddle, 2003).

Consider a 2-year-old playing happily with toys who suddenly sees a door open and a person dressed as a clown step into the room. The im-

mediate scream and retreat to the parent shown by some children require activation of the thalamus, visual, auditory, entorhinal, perirhinal,
parahippocampal, motor, and prefrontal cortex, hippocampus, amygdala, and subcortical structures mediating the flight and cry of distress.
The retreat and the distress cry to the clown are not located in any of
these structures; they were created by the interconnections among all of
them.

The current enthusiasm for finding the places in the central nervous
system where particular psychological phenomena are mediated is due, in
part, to a reluctance, especially among Western scientists, to believe in the
lawfulness of any phenomenon that cannot be instantiated in a material
form that the scientist can imagine. Readers will recall that Ernst Mach re-
sisted the positing of atoms because there was no observable evidence for
their existence. Many 19th-century scientists rejected Pasteur's hypothesis
of microbes for the same reason. Although the structures and functions of
proteins emerge from DNA, and the contractions of the left ventricle
emerge from the proteins comprising the heart muscle, neither of these
emergent phenomena is localizable in its origins. The lungs are necessary
for the distribution of oxygen to the body, but the lungs are not the place
where the distribution occurs. Similarly, select sites in the brain are "necessary for" a particular psychological function, but none is the "place
where" that function is actualized.

Claims for localization of a cognitive or emotional process, usually
based on scanning data, are vulnerable to a critique because scientists
usually subtract the baseline activity in one or more brain areas from activity in the same areas to an event presumed to mediate a discrete psychological process. Detection of a difference invites the suggestion that
the psychological activity is localized in the sites where the difference
scores were large. However, the nature of the inference depends on the
baseline condition selected. Investigators interested in the place, or
places, where "a fear of snakes" resided, who subtracted the profile of
cerebral blood flow displayed when the child was looking at pictures of
unfamiliar scenes from the profile to a snake might conclude that the
amygdala was not involved in the reaction to the snake because unfamiliar scenes also activate this structure.

More important, the logic in most scanning studies requires the two unreasonable assumptions that psychological functions are linearly additive
(a necessary premise if one subtracts one value from another) and mental
activity is modular (Peterson, 2003). Further, some cortical areas serve a
general, rather than a specific, function. Several years ago, a group of scientists suggested that the fusiform gyrus in the inferior temporal cortex
was specialized for the recognition of faces. However, later work revealed
that this area was activated whenever an individual had to analyze the in-

ternal features of any object, faces as well as automobiles, and especially, when the contoured elements of the object were in the upper part of the visual field (Gauthier, Behrmann, & Tarr, 1999).

Adolescents and adults often use different cognitive strategies to solve what the scientists assumed was a narrowly defined problem; for example, a semantic versus a schematic representation of a stimulus in a memory task. As a result, there can be unique patterns of activation associated with each strategy, and the average profile of activation will not be a faithful representation of the evidence (Glabus et al., 2003).

Another problem with evidence from fMRI or PET imaging data is that changes in cerebral blood flow or glucose utilization are correlated with task difficulty. For example, fMRI activity was greater in the temporal area to grammatically correct pseudosentences without semantic meaning than to ordinary sentences as participants judged whether each sentence was in the active or passive voice (Meyer, Alter, Friederici, Lohmann, & von Cramon, 2002). These facts imply that a brain that processes an event quickly and with ease may display little activation in the neuronal area participating in the cognitive work. Minimal activation of a particular site need not mean that it was not involved in the psychological processing or manipulation of an event.

Moreover, the site of greatest activity can be inconsistent with a person's subjective perceptual experience (Whitney et al., 2003). One neuroscientist concluded that there is no simple answer to the question of whether an fMRI index of brain activity in the sensory cortex represents a truthful mirror of the physical input or the participant's perception: "In many cases the image of the world within the brain is congruent with neither the real nor the perceived world" (Eysel, 2003, p. 791).

Finally, there is the possibility that the profile of brain activity to a stimulus while a person is lying supine (which is necessary in today's scanners) is different from the profile evoked by the same event when one is sitting in a quiet forest or standing in a queue.

There is no single place in the brain where the brief shiver produced by a memory of a past automobile accident, the inference that another is in pain, or a feeling of vitality is located, just as there is no place where the fatigue caused by influenza is located, although some sites make a greater, and some a lesser, contribution to the psychological phenomenon.

A critical review of 275 studies that used PET or fMRI revealed that several brain regions are engaged by most cognitive challenges. Simple mapping of a cognitive process on neural ensembles in prefrontal cortex may not be possible. The prefrontal cortex should be regarded as a general computational resource activated by different cognitive challenges (Cabeza & Nyberg, 2000; Duncan & Miller, 2002).

WHAT DEVELOPS?

Although behaviors, emotions, and cognitive processes change dramatically over the first decade of development, each theorist's unstated premises influence the phenomenon selected as primary. Twentieth-century behaviorists celebrated conditioned responses. Freud made cognition a handmaiden to the affective processes of libido and cathexes. We have emphasized cognitive functions and their close links to emotions. John Watson would have explained the 9-month-old's cry following separation from the mother as a conditioned response established through past experiences of distress when the caretaker was absent. Freud regarded the cry following separation from the mother as due to the child's feelings of loss. We argued that the cry to separation is due to advances in cognitive function. The 9-month-old is capable of retrieving the caretaker's former presence and relating it to the present, but is unable to assimilate the two schemata. The data on the growth of the hippocampus and prefrontal cortex are in closer consonance with this view than with the explanations proposed by Watson or Freud. The 2-year-old's display of empathy to a parent in pain requires the ability to infer the thoughts and feelings of others; the guilt of the 6-year-old requires the ability to rerun mentally a behavioral sequence and to assume causal responsibility for a behavior.

A second reason for our emphasis on interrelated cognitive and affective processes is the seminal assumption that unfamiliar events create a state of uncertainty which is an important catalyst for attention and a subsequent change in psychological structures. Unfamiliarity refers to the relation between an event and an individual's cognitive representations. Events that are totally familiar or totally unfamiliar provoke less attention, and less secretion of brainstem dopamine, than events with intermediate probabilities. The inverted "U" relation between the behavioral and biological responsivity to an event, on the one hand, and the familiarity of an event, on the other, penetrates diverse domains of psychological function. The unfamiliarity of an event can be as important as its hedonic quality. The magnitude of increase in corticotropin releasing hormone in the central nucleus of the amygdala is equally large when rats are unexpectedly restrained, which they do not like, and when they unexpectedly encounter food, which they do like.

When 2-year-olds first appreciate the meanings of "right" and "wrong," they are uncertain as to which behaviors belong to each category. To gain this knowledge, they provoke their parents by disobeying or having a tantrum in order to learn whether that action is or is not permitted. A second source of uncertainty occurs at the transition at 5 to 7 years when children are able to compare self with peers on culturally desirable features. The large number of children who are in the middle of the distribution for a particular trait are maximally uncertain of their rank and adopt either a competitive attitude to attain a higher rank or an avoidant strategy because they believe they cannot improve their position.

PREFRONTAL CORTEX AND PSYCHOLOGICAL PROPERTIES

The most significant maturational events of the first 8 years are the increasing connectivity within the prefrontal cortex and between it and other cortical and subcortical structures. The cognitive and emotional changes that require maturation of the prefrontal cortex are the buoys around which the development of beliefs, standards, skills, emotions, and social behavior turn as they sail toward their mature forms. The evolutionary expansion of the human prefrontal cortex to about one third of the total cortical surface, compared with only one tenth in the gorilla, appears to be a seminal basis for the properties that differentiate humans from all other primates. These properties are required for the functions shared by all human societies.

An object, whether animal, plant, mineral, or artifact, can be defined in terms of its properties. A lemon is a yellow, smooth-skinned, edible plant with an oval shape and a sour taste. However, this listing of the lemon's attributes fails to award special weighting to any one feature or features. A hierarchy of feature salience emerges, however, if one compares lemons with a related fruit, like oranges or grapefruits.

This principle applies to a definition of humans. A list of human features—two eyes, four limbs, long gracile legs, hairless body, bipedal posture, language, guilt—does not award differential salience to any property. But a hierarchy of relative salience emerges if we compare humans with chimpanzees. We suggest that nine properties distinguish humans from other primates. The first four appear to be unique to humans; the remaining five are quantitative enhancements of competences apes display.

Unique Properties

1. The ability to infer thoughts, intentions, and feelings in others permits language, empathy, cooperation, and a defensive posture toward those the self believes harbor hostile attitudes. This ability probably enabled the first humans to live in groups much larger than the typical size of chimpanzee groups.

2. A symbolic language consisting of hierarchically organized sets of semantic networks that classify experience allows invention of relations of

similarity and difference among varied representations. E. O. Wilson (1999) suggested that the basic unit of culture is the symbolic node in a semantic network. Two- and ten-year-old children can detect the crescent shape shared by a slice of lemon and a new moon, but the former cannot detect the relation between a smiling face and a set of arcs, or between the kindest of three acts and the most competent of three soccer players. This competence is hard to understand. At the least, it requires a brain-mind that can rapidly scan a large number of schematic and semantic features possessed by different events in search of a shared feature or relation. That is why we emphasized the increasing interconnectedness of the human brain during the first decade. This talent requires inferring a feature defined by a relation among events in different domains and creating a representation of the shared, but abstract, relational property. This ability, which is the foundation of metaphor, makes it possible for 8-year-olds to understand, "Anger is a jagged dark boulder; but joy is a smooth pink pebble." It also permits 12-year-olds, completely blind from birth, to learn to draw recognizable pictures of objects (D'Anguilly & Maggi, 2003).

3. The creation of categories of prohibited acts, semantic concepts "good" and "bad," capacities for "anxiety," "shame," or "guilt" when an action, attribute, or thought violates an ethical standard, or pride when they match an ideal, comprise a *moral sense*. Early forms of these capacities emerge by the third birthday. The anthropologist George Murdock (1945) listed 67 features present in all societies studied, and therefore, presumed to be universal. Ethical rules comprised the largest number of universals, for almost one half of the features referred to activities that ought or ought not to be displayed.

The extensive semantic network for the complementary concepts "improper" and "proper" has three different branches. One refers to the actions that violate community standards, are subject to punishment, and comprise the network "bad," as well as those that are praised because they meet those standards and are categorized as "good." A second branch involves the obligations linked to the self's social categories (for example, most girls believe they should not cut their hair very short). The third branch, which emerges by 7 years of age, involves imagining ideal or perfect forms. It is easy to explain how a child might learn that lying, stealing, and property destruction are bad and will be punished. It is harder to explain how children construct the ideal form of a motor skill, oral presentation, or act of courage, because most children do not attain the ideal, and therefore, could not be praised for its display. The construction of these ideals shares features with the acquisition of grammar. Parents criticize children for statements that are factually incorrect, but rarely comment on a grammatically incorrect utterance. Children acquire the grammar of their language by inferring the correct form from the speech that they hear. The child's ability to imagine the perfect parent, soccer player, or friend, despite the lack of direct encounters with such persons, requires a prefrontal cortex that can generate thoughts of what is possible and semantic networks whose central node refers to an ideal event.

Although a moral sense emerges by the second birthday, humans require an additional dozen years before they will feel morally obligated to hold a consistent set of ethical premises. Adolescents, but not 6-year-olds, wonder about their place in society, make serious plans for the distant future, and integrate memories of childhood with their current experience to understand their life circumstances. That is one reason why medieval Europeans did not permit any child younger than 13 or 14 to take monastic vows. The recent discovery of an enhancement of gray matter at puberty probably makes a contribution to these psychological characteristics (Giedd et al., 1999).

4. A conscious awareness of self's varied properties is a fourth unique human characteristic. The OBPFC contributes to the awareness of moment-to-moment changes in feeling tone originating in bodily changes. A second component of consciousness involves semantic or schematic representations of more permanent physical features, as well as beliefs and skills. These representations are based, in part, on identifications with role models and comparisons with peers.

A person can experience two forms of uncertainty regarding the representations of self. The first is created by unexpected or discrepant visceral feelings (for example, a normally relaxed, happy child suddenly feels tense). A second follows detection of a semantic inconsistency in the networks that describe self (for example, a child who regards herself as a good student has several academic failures). After puberty, youths possess coherent representations of desired goal states, each linked to beliefs, emotions, and actions. These hierarchically-organized networks differ in their emotional significance. Although most American children want to be accepted by peers, praised by parents, and allowed to make autonomous choices that please neither audience, each goal varies in emotional salience among children. Peer acceptance is primary for some children; parental praise is more important for others. Children, like adults, find it difficult to tolerate semantic inconsistency within the network that refers to a particular class of desired goals, but are better able to tolerate inconsistency between networks representing different motivational domains. For example, a boy for whom peer acceptance is primary would experience uncertainty if he violated an ethical standard held by his peer group (for example, he failed to control outward signs of fear). This same boy might feel less uncertainty if he showed fear to a lightening storm at home, although his parents urged control of fear, because gaining parental praise was less important than winning peer acceptance. This contextual independence of standards makes it possible for a child to regard a behavior that is unacceptable in one context to be perfectly acceptable in another. Hence, some children who would never steal from a friend find it easy to steal from a stranger, or even a parent.

Enhanced Properties

5. Humans have a more robust working memory than chimpanzees for they can hold up to seven unrelated, but familiar, semantic representations in a working memory circuit for intervals as long as 30 sec. This ability permits comparison of various representations, detection of similarities and differences among them, and reorganization of the representations into a new structure. This competence, which emerges in an early form between 7 and 12 months, depends, in part, on the prefrontal cortex and its connectivity to temporal lobe sites.

6. The ability to retrieve representations of past experiences that include temporal and spatial properties—called episodic memory—emerges in early form during the fourth year.

7. The ability to generate representations of future states permits children to generate goals they may pursue for years, but leads to anxiety if the imagined representations are unwanted. Most children possess an initial form of this capacity by 3 to 4 years of age. The brain is biologically prepared to facilitate actions directed at goal states. Humans are the only animals that can persuade self that an imagined goal is unattainable or that no goal is worth the effort. Hence, humans find it easier than apes to sink into a state of apathy that is in direct opposition to the biologically prepared propensity to engage the world.

8. Humans have an extraordinary ability to inhibit distracting thoughts and responses irrelevant to a goal being pursued, and the capacity to alter a response or train of thought to accommodate a change in the demands of a situation. This talent, present by 6 or 7 years of age, and called flexibility or the ability to shift sets, might be aided by the enhanced connectivity of the anterior cingulate to frontal brain sites.

9. Humans are attracted to unfamiliar events that can be understood and coped with effectively. This feature, which appears in an early form before the first birthday, depends, in part, on the integrity of the frontal lobe (Daffner et al., 2000). Although macaque monkeys prefer an unfamiliar video clip over receipt of a tasty liquid (Andrews & Rosenblum, 2002), humans spend more time than any other animal looking for new sensations, places to explore, ideas to brood on, and acts to master. This fact implies that unfamiliar events that can be assimilated and unfamiliar tasks that can be mastered create a hedonically pleasant state. No other primate would

risk survival and a compromised reproductive fitness by engaging in behaviors that had the level of risk associated with climbing Mt. Everest, para-
chuting from a plane, or swimming the English Channel. The amount of
media coverage devoted to new movies, television shows, and athletic
events, which is far greater today than it was a generation ago, implies that
the lives of many Americans have become so predictable entertainment has
become a major source of novelty. However, unfamiliar events that cannot
be understood, or dealt with effectively, generate uncertainty, anxiety, or
fear. Humans spend their days in a narrow psychological corridor, bor-
dered on the left by boredom with the familiar and on the right by fear of in-
explicable novelties that cannot be comprehended or controlled.

Each of these nine competences, embedded in appropriate contexts, requires participation of the prefrontal cortex and its multiple connections
to other brain sites. It is surely significant that the prefrontal cortex has a
greater density of spines, is tonically more active, and maintains synaptic
pruning for a longer time than other brain sites. These biological facts and
their psychological consequences were made possible by mutations, or
recombinations, that permitted the progenitor cells in the embryo's ventricular zone to continue to divide for about 72 hr longer than they do in
chimpanzees—a dramatic example of the butterfly effect—to produce 100
billion neurons compared to the 10 billion in apes.

GENES, EXPERIENCE, AND INCLUSIVE FITNESS

Heritability of Human Traits

Disagreements over the differential magnitudes of the contributions of
biology and experience to human psychological properties, often acri-
monious, have subsided a bit as scientists realized, and should have earlier, that the question was phrased incorrectly. The traditional form of
the question implied that two painters had worked simultaneously on
the same canvas and a visitor to the gallery where the painting hung
wanted to know how many square inches each artist had contributed to
the canvas.

   A more fruitful conception recognizes the distinct, but joint, contributions of biology and experience to specific outcomes over the course of development. Nature makes the more substantial contribution to the initial
developmental stages and then works collaboratively with nurture to
complete the mural. After the basic brain architecture, determined in large
measure by genetic programs, is in place, the biological products of genes
join with experience to sculpt synapses into microcircuits and circuits into

networks of connections, that eventually render each person unique. Of course, a strict division between early and late contributions is a caricature, for experience makes some strokes on the canvas of brain-mind during gestation, and, after birth, paints more feverishly.

A similar argument applies to psychological properties. The genome of the finch determines the basic form of its song, but the young bird must hear the songs of others, as well as its own sounds, to produce the melody that birdwatchers hear each spring. As with the final synaptic network, experience fine-tunes the inherent competences nature intended. Although pairs of monozygotic twins had very similar volumes of each brain lobe, the level of complexity of the shapes and surfaces of the sulci and gyri were far less similar (White & Andreasen, 2002).

A nice demonstration of the interaction of genetic vulnerability and experience involves alleles in the promoter region of the gene for the serotonin transporter molecule which affects the amount of serotonin in the synaptic cleft. Individuals who inherit the two short forms of this allele in the promoter region will have less transcriptive efficiency of the gene for the promoter, and therefore, less effective activity of the transporter molecule. Seventeen percent of the adults in a longitudinal sample of New Zealand participants studied from childhood had the two short forms, whereas 31% had the two long forms of this allele. The occurrence of a bout of depression was more frequent in the adults who had the two short forms, and, in addition, reported experiencing several stressful events. Adults with the short forms of the allele who reported minimal stress, as well as adults with the long forms who experienced frequent stress, were not especially susceptible to depression. The onset of a depression required both the genetic feature and the experience of frequent stress (Caspi et al., 2003). The explanation favored by the authors is that those with the short allele who developed depression actually experienced more stressful experiences than others. An alternative interpretation holds that those with the short form of the allele experienced loss of a job or a relationship as more distressing than those with the long form, although the frequency of stressful events, if it had been witnessed by an impartial observer, would have been roughly equal for the two groups.

The exciting advances in genetics over the last few decades have emboldened some scientists to argue that genetic mechanisms account for most of the variation in common human characteristics. There are two reasons why this claim is too strong. First, the mathematical equation usually used to estimate the heritability of a human trait assumes that genetic and environmental forces are additive, interactions between genes and between genes and the environment are small, and finally, the relation between variation in a gene (or genes) and variation in a trait is linear. All four assumptions are vulnerable to a critique (Nijhout, 2003). Most biological phenotypes are not a function of additive factors, and most psychological traits are products of nonlinear interactions between genetic propensities and experience. For example, fighting in two inbred strains of mice varied as a function of rearing conditions and the relation between genotype and experience was nonadditive (Levine, Grossfield, & Rockwell, 1979).

Current heritability estimates for human traits are probably exaggerated because they fail to evaluate the environmental component of the interaction term with direct measurements, and assign its potentially large amount of variance to genes. That is one reason why the heritability of IQ scores in 7-year-olds is close to zero for children growing up in poverty but high for those growing up in middle-class homes (Turkheimer et al., 2003). The authors wrote, ". . . the developmental forces that work in poor environments are qualitatively different from those that work in adequate ones . . . additive models of linear and independent contributions of genes and environment to variation in intelligence can not do justice to the complexity of the development of intelligence in children" (Turkheimer et al., 2003, p. 628). Further, only one half of the members of a sample of identical twin pairs with an XYY karyotype developed psychological problems by school entrance (Geerts, Steyaert, & Fryns, 2003).

There is another reason to doubt the currently high heritability estimates for IQ and some personality traits. When scientists selectively bred two distinct strains of rats raised under controlled laboratory conditions for high versus low avoidance to a signal for shock, the heritability was less than 0.2 (Brush, 2003). If the heritability for these two specific behavioral traits, which have biological correlates, is only 0.16, it is unlikely that the genetic contribution to more complex human properties, monitored by many more genes, is as high as 0.5 or 0.6.

The reports of behavioral geneticists minimize the influence of the environment on human traits because the most important environmental influences on a child's beliefs about self are idiosyncratic, symbolic constructions of experience that cannot be measured because of the absence of sensitive methods. A 10-year-old who knows that her family is poor, her father is unemployed, and her parents are minimally educated broods on the possible causes of these conditions and constructs beliefs about the properties of self and family. A 12-year-old sibling in the same home, who did not reflect on these facts, would develop a different personality. African-American men with minimal education who described themselves as always trying to cope with stress showed a large rise in blood pressure and heart rate when stressed in a laboratory. But those who were well educated did not. This fact implies that being a member of a less-advantaged social-class category can have a profound effect on the physiological reactions to a stressor (Merritt, Bennett, Williams, Sollers, &

Thayer, 2004). Private interpretations, which affect mood and behavior in a profound way, are not measured in current research on the heritability of human traits. These personal constructions render each person's psychological environment unique and imply that there is no shared environment for some human psychological traits. All of the variance for these traits now assigned to the environment in heritability equations is unshared.

Inclusive Fitness

Some scientists have suggested that the biological urge to maximize inclusive fitness, which presumably explains the anatomy and physiology that humans share, can explain behaviors, motives, social rituals, and structures observed in many societies. Inclusive fitness refers not only to a particular animal's lifetime fecundity, which is measurable, but also his contribution to the health, longevity, and reproductive success of his offspring and all genetic relatives. This construct is difficult to quantify, and its predictions impossible to refute if the trait in question is controlled by more than one gene, which is a property of most human psychological traits. There is no rational way to decide whether wealthy American couples with one healthy child are more or less fit than impoverished couples with three less healthy children.

A more serious problem, which advocates of sociobiology understand, is that an inherited trait that enhances fitness in one ecology, or under some social conditions, can impair fitness in another. Inheritance of the sickled shape of the red blood cell among some indigenous Africans protects these individuals from malaria, although it exacts the price of fatigue and vulnerability to other diseases. The evolution of a large prefrontal cortex has adaptive consequences for human cognition, but because the genes that determine the female pelvic girdle did not change appropriately, human infants had to be born prematurely. The balance between advantage and disadvantage can even occur at the level of the cell. Some spermatogonia, preferentially selected to become mature sperm because of their chemical properties, give rise to a defective embryo if they fertilize an egg.

Homo sapiens emerged between 100,000 and 150,000 years ago in a warm savannah setting with a social organization consisting of foraging bands of 30 to 50 individuals, many of whom were genetically related. The fact that this initial social structure lasted in some places for over 3,000 generations implies that it contributed to inclusive fitness. Although scholars assume these early humans were capable of competition and unbridled self-interest, cooperation and the suppression of excessive self-aggrandizement were habits required for survival.

Evolutionary biologists are puzzled by the fact that each day there are more acts of helping, kindness, and cooperation with genetically unrelated strangers than acts of stealing, rape, or murder. Because this imbalance is inconsistent with the criteria for inclusive fitness, some scientists engage in tortuous arguments that try to render the cooperative, nurturant actions rational choices. Because these scholars resist an explanation that does not apply to all animals, they suppress the fact that only humans possess a motive to regard self as a "good" person. This desire explains why the ratio of altruistic over asocial responses is positive everyday in every community in the world.

Moreover, the concept of inclusive fitness, and the mechanism of natural selection, are intended to explain the differential survival of species over the long period that began with the first living forms. These concepts cannot explain why the beliefs and institutions of ancient Rome were replaced with the ideology and structures of Christianity. Nor can they explain why Muslims, Christians, Buddhists, and Jews hold different beliefs and practice different customs.

If, as biologists believe, the genomes of the first humans and contemporary populations are essentially similar, the replacement of early cooperation with an increasingly individualistic, self-aggrandizing posture, especially over the last 2,000 years, required a sequence of unpredictable historical events. Consider some differences between the social ecology of the first humans, on the one hand, and the social environments of contemporary Europeans and North Americans, on the other. The latter groups are characterized by: (a) frequent geographical separation of the adult from parents and siblings, (b) awareness of the beliefs and life circumstances of strangers living in distant places, (c) greater worry over symbols of relative status than the availability of food and presence of predators, (d) status awarded for wealth and education rather than strength and endurance, (e) large status differentials between the top and bottom 20% of the population, (f) a belief in chance rather than determinism in everyday events, (g) minimal punishment for a lack of loyalty to the group, (h) the ability to control fertility and to separate reproduction from pleasure in sexual activity, (i) an egalitarian relationship between men and women, (j) protection of infants and the elderly with serious physical compromise, and (k) a stronger desire to be happy and free than to maintain group acceptance by conforming to local mores.

These changes between foragers and contemporary American and Europeans required many historical events, including:

1. The receding of glaciers, which made the establishment of agriculture in Europe, Asia, and the Middle East more probable about 10,000 years ago.

2. The replacement of foraging bands with smaller households in hamlets and villages which led to increased competition among families for signs of relative status. Uncertainty over relative status vis-à-vis others is always a significant human concern, but the shift from foraging bands to agricultural hamlets probably potentiated this uncertainty.

3. A more stable food supply led to improved health and increased population size, and, as a result, greater pressure on the available food, which motivated the invention of technologies to enhance the supply.

4. The invention of writing, and, much later, the printing press, radio, television, and the Internet, enabled many persons to learn about the psychological states of strangers living thousands of miles away. This knowledge gradually enlarged the size of the reference group used to compare self with others from the local hamlet, village, or city to everyone in the world in the same age cohort. It is much easier to feel competent, rich, or virtuous when an agent compares self with 100 others than with millions of others. The recognition that self, or self's reference group, is less privileged, provokes the human sensitivity to fairness and, in some, a demand to be treated with greater dignity.

5. Efficient, inexpensive means of transportation made it possible for adults to separate from their family and to live with strangers thousands of miles from their natal group; the invention of inexpensive contraceptives permitted couples to limit their family size.

6. Finally, the expansion of natural science, from Galileo's discoveries to the establishment of graduate schools in America in the late 19th century, was accompanied by novel assumptions for at least one third of the world's peoples. The philosophical foundations of science include five premises: (a) nature has no ethical values; therefore, no particular moral position has an a priori validity that can be defended on scientific grounds; (b) there are no nonmaterial causal forces; those who believe in such metaphysical processes are superstitious; (c) there is no determinism in the natural world; every outcome has a probability distribution; (d) there are no permanently true facts; every current belief about nature is subject to revision or replacement should new evidence be discovered; and (e) humans are genetically related to other animals, especially primates, and are motivated primarily by the desire to maximize self-interest, survival, and inclusive fitness.

The belief in natural laws as explanations of regular events and acceptance of inherently unpredictable events that are the result of a set of low probability phenomena were combined with an egalitarian ethos in Western societies to create an ideology that would be foreign to the first humans. This set of ideas, which affects each person's emotions and actions, is the product of relatively recent historical events that could not be predicted from knowledge of the human genome.

This sequence of historical events, which was not inevitable, altered the social and physical ecology in which humans acted and required radically new behaviors and institutions. A conscious awareness of self, an evaluation of self and others on a good–bad dimension, and the belief that maximizing self's pleasure and status should take precedence over loyalty to others motivated humans to behave in ways that enhanced their feeling of virtue, while minimizing signs that compromised that judgment. The important bases for an evaluation of virtue among the first humans probably included fixed characteristics, like gender, size, strength, endurance, and perhaps, physical attractiveness. The significant bases for this judgment in contemporary Western societies are personal accomplishments, especially the attainment of enhanced status, education, wealth, and socially-valued skills.

It is also important that the historical changes described earlier created conditions in which the desire to regard self as virtuous required some actions inconsistent with the demand for inclusive fitness. Specifically, the wish for enhanced status through personal achievement, combined with the ability to control fecundity, motivated many couples in industrialized societies to marry later and to limit the size of their families, or, in some cases, to have no children at all. Although these decisions do not serve inclusive fitness, the values of Western society, whose members comprise a small proportion of the world's population, are replacing the values of a more fecund majority because of machines, medicine, contraceptives, weapons, chlorination of water, books, radio, television, and the Internet. This split between psychological dominance and fitness could not have occurred in any species but our own.

Young rhesus monkeys interact with conspecifics in both natural and laboratory environments. However, these monkeys are capable of sitting crouched in the corner of a cage away from their peers if they are taken from their mother early in life and placed with an inanimate object that supplied them with food. The potential to crouch in a corner distant from others, which does not enhance the monkey's inclusive fitness, is an inherent capacity in the rhesus monkey genome, but its actualization requires very special conditions. Although lions are genetically programmed to roam over large ranges, those who live in zoos show stereotyped pacing and a high rate of infant mortality (Clubb & Mason, 2003). We suggest that the prevalence of unconflicted self-interest and extreme levels of individual competitiveness among contemporary Europeans and North Americans is analogous to a monkey's crouched posture or a lion's pacing in a zoo, for these traits must overcome a biologically based resistance to their expression and probably reduce inclusive fitness.

Celebrated novelists, poets, and playwrights usually detect the prevalent mood of a society. Contemporary writers dwell on the loneliness, sadness, cynicism, and lack of loyalty among contemporary Europeans and North Americans. These states breed suicide, depression, anxiety, violence, divorce, and neglect of children, even as they provide for a longevity twice the life span enjoyed by the foragers. However, survival to age 80 is only one component of inclusive fitness; fecundity is the more important component. History, not mutation or natural catastrophe, exploited the human capacities for self-awareness and a moral sense to permit some humans to separate survival from inclusive fitness.

Adam Smith (1776) thought that society would prosper if each individual pursued his own interests first, but he was equally certain that the human propensity to worry about the opinions of neighbors would act as an effective constraint against unconflicted self-interest. Smith could not have imagined, 200 years after he wrote *The Wealth of Nations,* that large numbers of Americans and Europeans would live in high-rise apartment buildings, work in large bureaucratic organizations, and be less concerned with the opinions of neighbors and colleagues than with the enhancement of self's virtue through attainment of talent, status, power, wealth, and frequent sensory delight.

The first humans lived in small groups in which no one was a stranger, most held similar beliefs, and there was little or no appreciation of the fact that most events had probabilistic functions independent of the person's actions or thoughts. Many contemporary adults living in dense, urban areas know fewer than 1 in 10,000 others, continually meet individuals holding different beliefs, and understand that impersonal forces following probabilistic functions affect their lives. These changes have been accompanied by a degree of variation among human groups that is substantially greater than the difference between contemporary chimpanzees and those living 10,000 years ago. The extraordinary range of human behaviors across cultures is due in large measure to the social conditions within a society. Historical events have selected the current social arrangements in the West from a larger number of possibilities. The immune system works on a similar principle. The genes responsible for initiating the sequence that culminates in antibodies against foreign viruses and bacteria are capable of generating many different antibodies. Each antigen selects the ones that are produced.

We suspect that one important reason for the popularity of evolutionary psychology and sociobiology is that their ideas rationalized the increase in unconflicted self-interest endemic in modern society and alleviated a feeling of compromised virtue created by being forced to assume a self-interested posture for many hours of every day. No one need feel excessive guilt over these intentions if respected scientists declare that they are perfectly natural. A century earlier, Francis Galton suggested that eminence ran in families because intellectual capacity, zeal, and vigor were inherited. This idea was greeted with applause by an upper-middle-class English society eager to be told that their privilege was inevitable, rather than a historical accident. Because the poor were more fecund, it seemed rational to suppress their reproductive capacity for the good of society. Humans are capable of being both lamb and lion. Historical events potentiated the lion component in our nature, and our lamb-like circuits feel better when biologists, functioning as therapists, tell the larger community that their relentless self-interest is perfectly reasonable.

It is a fruitful exercise to ask how autonomous from human biology are current social structures and institutions. Which social arrangements for work, marriage, childrearing, leisure, and governance are so incompatible with human biology they could not occur, or, if they did, would not survive for very long? Consider some possible candidates: (a) marriages are 10-year contracts between two adults of any gender or all marriages must be between a man and a woman with no divorce permitted, (b) family size is legislated or there is no restriction on family size, (c) adults work alone or in large groups, (d) every individual belongs to the same religion or no one has any religion, (e) every person must end their life by euthanasia when they reach age 75 or everyone can live as long as they wish, (f) all seriously deformed infants are killed in a humane way or all are cared for by the state, (g) primary loyalty is to the state or the family, (h) each adult must change his vocation and residence every 10 years or no one is permitted to change residence or vocation after age 21, (i) every person has a vote or no person has a vote, (j) no city can be larger than 5,000 or cities can be of any size, (k) there are no public educational institutions or everyone must have 16 years of formal education, and (l) everyone is self-employed or everyone works in a bureaucratic organization.

Any of the above outcomes is possible; indeed, Chinese society under Mao Tse-Tung survived for a quarter of a century with some of these features. The autonomy of many social arrangements from human biology resembles the variation in the semantic networks of individuals living in different societies. The semantic networks for the words *ancestor, loyalty, love,* and *beauty* in varied cultures cannot be predicted from the biological bases for human language.

However, humans are not infinitely malleable. They cannot refrain from: (a) classifying experience semantically; (b) evaluating people, events, and objects on a good–bad dimension; (c) anticipating the future or brooding on the past; (d) ascribing causality to events; (e) a continuing awareness of self as an object with intentions, feelings, and features; and (f) treating the family as a primary target of loyalty.

The hardiness of the family as the primary social structure across cultures is due to some of the psychological competences described in this book. The human moral sense guarantees that most parents will feel responsible for the welfare of the children they have produced. The reliance on semantic categories renders the family name a significant, perhaps the most significant, category to which a person belongs. Third, the wife and husband in most societies had complementary, rather than competitive, roles, and therefore, the uncertainty generated by competition with a same-sex peer was minimized. Fourth, interactions among spouses and between parents and children generate strong emotions that enhance the strength of these social relationships. Ducks imprint on the first moving object that they see; humans become attached to those who generate intense feelings. Finally, the typical family has the proper size. The human mind is able to hold six or seven independent representations in working memory and a majority of nuclear families consist of five to seven individuals. Thus, the preservation of the family for over 100,000 years may be traceable, in part, to the psychology of our species.

Contemporary citizens are presented with two extreme descriptions of the human brain-mind. The favored metaphor during the first half of the last century was a stretch of moist sand that recorded every footprint impressed on its soft surface. The stone slopes of Mt. Everest became more popular during the past 50 years. We suggest that a better metaphor is a loom with threads of 30,000 different hues. The size of the loom and the colors of the threads are fixed, but a weaver can create a staggeringly large number of patterns within these constraints. Each gene has a chemical structure that codes for a particular protein; however, neural activity provoked by experience affects how, when, and how much of the protein is expressed, or whether it will be expressed at all. The human genome guarantees that members of our species will acquire, to varying degrees, the competences described earlier. But each is only a potentiality; an unfinished vessel to be filled with meanings, and that responsibility belongs to experience. Recall from chapter 1 that American children unconsciously acquire associations between maleness and single-syllable names ending in stop consonants (Mark) and between femaleness and multisyllable names ending in vowels (Rebecca). Children in other cultures might learn different associations between names and gender (Cassidy et al., 1999)

All humans hold beliefs about the origin and nature of their surroundings and the behaviors of self and others, but the content of those beliefs is the product of particular times and places and lies far beyond the reach of the 30,000 human genes. Most Bostonians in 1820 believed in the validity of an orderly world, laissez-faire economics, the superiority of Whites, rigid loyalty to one's beliefs, marital fidelity, and their city as the hub of America.

Only a century later, the historical interventions of the Civil War, Darwin's theories, industrialization, the rise of science, urban sprawl, European emigration, and World War I mocked these truths and forced citizens to create a different set to accommodate history's mischievousness, although the new premises will appear as silly when history sends the surprises it has been wrapping for delivery later in this new century.

Although the content of Bostonians' beliefs was altered seriously over the past 180 years, every person holds beliefs because their biology demands it. They have no choice. All adolescents develop beliefs regarding the reasons for their social position, but the content of the causal network varies with culture and history. Commentators on Western society changed their explanation of poverty over the last 200 years. Nineteenth-century scholars attributed a family's poverty to deficiencies in intellectual ability, skill, and motivation. Contemporary analysts, more conscious of ethnic prejudices and reluctant to blame victims, assume the cause is government practices and the reluctance of the privileged few to help the large number of poor. Consider, as a final example, the abhorrence Americans feel toward inflicting physical harm on others. Union soldiers who deserted during the Civil War often had a capital "D" branded on their cheek with a hot poker. This level of cruelty would not be tolerated in the contemporary American Army, although some punishment of deserters has been preserved because a desire for retribution is common when a member of the community fails to adhere to its ethical standards.

Per Lagerqvist (1971), who understood that humans had to believe in some ethical standard, wrote a short story describing an infinitely large number of dead who went on a search to find God. When at last they saw Him chopping wood, the leader of the group stepped forward and asked, "What was your purpose when you created humans?" The author had God answer, "I only intended humans would never be satisfied with nothing." Lagerqvist understood that humans must hold ethical standards, but the networks that represent these structures are not preserved indefinitely. As societies change, most humans alter their ideas and actions to avoid the terrible feeling of tension (psychologists call it *cognitive dissonance*) created when a detected inconsistency between a belief and an action demands the replacing of a worn belief with a new one that is semantically consistent with the action the community requires. The small proportion who remain loyal to beliefs their society has outgrown, or finds repugnant, are categorized either as psychotic or heroic, depending on the logical defense of their position and the content of their beliefs. Thus, the content of human beliefs has considerable, but not infinite, autonomy from biology. Because, at some times in some places humans believed there were witches, angels, gods, ghosts, heaven, hell, migrating uteruses, a cosmic ether, and inherently evil infants, it is reasonable to suppose that the human genome is relatively permissive with respect to the ideas humans are capable of believing as true.

TWO VOCABULARIES

We end by asking whether it will ever be possible to translate sentences describing psychological phenomena into sentences that contain only biological words. The answer is uncertain at present, but there are reasons to be skeptical of the possibility of a faithful translation. The terms in Newton's inverse square law refer to forces, masses, and distances. It is unlikely that this law, and its constituent terms, will be replaced with the equations of quantum mechanics, although these equations are believed to be the foundation of the moon's movement around the earth and the earth's movement around the sun. The chemist Roald Hoffman (2001) reminds us that it is not even possible to translate the chemical description of the oxidation of iron into the vocabulary of physics without losing the central meaning of the "oxidative state of a molecule."

The problem is captured by a frustrating 19th-century discussion between Heinrich von Helmholtz, who had written on the physics of tone as a basis for music, and the composer, Johannes Brahms. The two men were unable to understand each other because Brahms spoke of form and counterpoint, whereas the physicist talked about sine waves and spectra. Although sine waves and spectra are the physical foundations of musical form and counterpoint, Brahms understood that the vocabulary used to describe a symphony cannot be replaced with von Helmholtz's concepts.

The psychological terms *pleasure* and *displeasure* cannot be replaced with biological words that describe only brain activity because each is a human psychological judgment, rather than a property of a neuronal circuit. Pleasure is as inappropriate a descriptor for neuronal ensembles as yellow is for electrons. Rats will lick a drinking tube delivering sucrose, but not one delivering quinine. However, if select neurons in the nucleus tractus solitarius in the medulla receive a sequence of electrical pulses that simulate the sequence recorded when quinine activates sensory receptors on the tongue, rats turn away from the drinking tube, although their taste receptors have not been stimulated. This fact implies that the following two statements are not synonymous (Di Lorenzo, Hallock, & Kennedy, 2003):

1. Rats avoid licking a tube that delivers quinine.
2. Rats avoid licking a tube delivering water when select neurons in the medulla are stimulated with a sequence of pulses simulating the sequence recorded when rats taste quinine.

The meanings of psychological concepts like "anger," "anxiety," "empathy," and "consciousness" include references to phenomena lying outside the brain; in this case, the targets of anger, anxiety, empathy, or consciousness. Future scientists might be able to discriminate among the profiles of brain activity that accompany each of these states, but they could not know whether a participant was angry at his brother for taking his sweater or angry at a stranger who scratched his new car. A description of the neuronal excitations that occurs when a rat enters a cage containing a novel object cannot replace the following psychological statement: "Rats prefer to enter places where they had encountered unfamiliar objects in the past," although we want to know what circuits were activated and what chemicals released when a rat placed his paws in a cage that contained a novel object and ignored the empty cage nearby.

The need for distinct vocabularies is also revealed in a study that used ERPs. We noted that when adults hear a sentence that ends with a word that is semantically inconsistent with the preceding words, a larger negative waveform appears in the EEG (the N400) than occurs to a consistent word. For example, a large N400 is evoked by the word *cabbage* when a participant reads or hears, "The museum walls were lined with cabbage." Because most experiments with the N400 are conducted with awake adults, scientists assumed that the large N400 was the brain's index of a psychological state of surprise created by the semantic inconsistency. However, the N400 occurs to a semantically inconsistent word in adults who are in stage 2 or REM sleep (Bastuji, Perrin, & Garcia-Larrea, 2002). This fact suggests that the brain's reaction was automatic, and did not reflect a psychological state of surprise, for surprise requires an awake state. Thus, we must invent a new term to describe the brain state that created the N400 in sleeping adults.

The statement, "Presentation of a 1 sec, 1000 Hz tone at 70 dB that signals electric shock evokes synchronous 4 to 8 Hz activity in the basal ganglia and area CA1 of the rat's hippocampus," is coherent. However, scientists who wish to describe the psychological state of the animal must use different words. The statement, "Presentation of a tone that had signaled electric shock evokes fear in a rat" is not equivalent to the earlier statement about synchronous 4 to 8 Hz activity. A description of the area (in square miles), velocity (in miles per hour), and direction (northwest) of a hurricane cannot be replaced with statements describing the molecules of air and water that are the constituents of the storm.

Put differently, the different nouns that name biological and psychological structures are preferentially linked to classes of predicates that name biological and psychological phenomena, respectively. The rods of the retina respond to photons, not to faces; neurons in the visual cortex respond to motion, not to a raised eyebrow. But the person's schemata and semantic networks respond to faces and eyebrows. The problems that arise when scientists use psychological predicates to describe nouns naming biological structures are apparent if one reflects on the sentence, "The oligodendrocytes (which produce myelin on axonal shafts) are the causes of rapid typing," without referring to the psychological states that permit the skilled motor response. The phenomena we wish to understand, which were present long before any humans had language, are hidden from us. Scientists use evidence to obtain increasingly more accurate representations of those phenomena, but they should not violate this linguistic rule in their descriptions. Lovers are permitted to say, "Your eyes are brilliant sapphires," but scientists are denied this permissive use of language.

The need for distinct vocabularies for biological and psychological events has an analog in Bohr's insistence that physicists must use the concepts of classical physics, not those of quantum theory, to describe an experiment, although the quantum concepts are the foundation of the experimental procedures. When Edward Teller challenged this apparently dualist position, Bohr replied that if the investigations were summarized in the language of quantum mechanics, the two of them would be imagining their conversation rather than sitting together drinking tea. Bohr would probably agree with the claim that the sentence, "The rat froze and remained fearful for six seconds when placed in the compartment where it had received one electric shock a day earlier" cannot be translated into sentences containing words referring only to events in the brain. Scientists who acknowledge that thought, feeling, and action depend on brain events, but insist that these events must be described with a language different from the one that describes the underlying processes, are not metaphysical dualists. All natural phenomena cannot be described with one vocabulary.

The semantic network for a neurobiological term often differs from the network of what seems to be the same word in a psychological text. Thomas Kuhn (2000) used the example of the French word *douce* and the English word *sweet* to make this point. Although sugar would be called douce by French and sweet by Americans, only the French would use the word douce to describe a bland tasting soup, and only Americans would apply the word sweet to young, ingenuous, pretty girls. Thus, douce and sweet have related, but not synonymous, meanings. The neurobiological network in which the word fear is a salient node has *amygdala, conditioned freezing,* and *electric shock* as central terms, but *separation, panic attack, spiders,* and *speaking in public* are salient nodes in the psychological network for fear in humans. The neuroscientist might reply that the meaning of a word is a function of how it is used by a language community, as Wittgenstein argued. But psychologists, as well as ordinary citizens, assume a different meaning when they use the word fear. Neuroscientists can call an immobile rat fearful, but they should permit others to hold a different, equally legitimate, understanding of the meaning of the same term.

The heart of the problem is that words describing physiological or biochemical events in the brain do not satisfy the need to know the psychological consequences of those changes. A botanist's description of the changes that occur in the leaves of Vermont maple trees as the autumn equinox approaches contains chemical terms that make no reference to the colors that humans, but not all animals, perceive. Thus, the sentence, "Changes in temperature and light cause chemical changes in the leaves of maple trees that make it possible for humans to see a gradual replacement of the color green with the colors red and yellow," cannot be inferred from the chemical descriptions without extra information. The botanists' sentences make no reference to the emergent properties that permit humans to see the reds and yellows in fall foliage.

A molecule of dopamine has a stable structure that has not changed since it first appeared in living forms. But the actions, feelings, or thoughts provoked by a rise in dopamine are not fixed. They have changed over historical time and over a life span. Hence, the psychological consequences of dopaminergic activity are not knowable without information about the agent.

The statement by an eminent neuroscientist that a particular brain state "possesses the inherent physical property of consciousness" tries to solve this problem with brute force by declaring that consciousness is a physical property of the neuronal ensembles, rather than acknowledging that it is an emergent psychological phenomenon (John, 2003). No chemist claims that the chemical structure of arsenic possesses the inherent property of "able to cause death," because the latter is an emergent property that requires a specific host. Molecules of DNA do not contain proteins, proteins do not contain muscle strands, and muscle strands do not contain motor habits. The second member of each of these pairs emerges as a qualitatively distinct phenomenon from a confluence of conditions in specific host organisms.

Let us return to a 9-month-old infant in the object permanence procedure who has reached toward location A on three successive occasions to retrieve a toy. After the infant watches the examiner hide the toy at location B on the fourth trial, the child first looks at B, but reaches toward A. The saccade to location B is due, in part, to reciprocal circuits between the mediotemporal and prefrontal lobes; the reaching response to location A is due, in part, to a failure of the still immature inhibitory functions of the anterior cingulate, dorsolateral prefrontal cortex, and supplementary motor cortex. It is not obvious that the psychological description of this behavior can be replaced with sentences containing only biological words, although that knowledge adds to our understanding (Schall, 2004). When an adult says that he did not hear the difference between a "ba" sound physically different from eight prior "ba" sounds, but his EEG reveals a negative wave form at about 250 msec, it is not clear how investigators would describe this event without using a psychological word for lack of conscious awareness. The fact that an ERP index of brain activity and conscious report can, on occasion, lead to different conclusions diminishes neither the power of the brain nor celebrates consciousness. It suggests only that each source of evidence tells us something different about the natural phenomenon we are trying to understand. There is, at present, an incommensurability between the large body of research on humans that comes from questionnaires and interviews and the corpus of evidence that quantifies biological events in the brain and body.

Physicists grapple with a similar conceptual problem. Although they prefer a world in which symmetry is the major principle, they acknowledge that symmetry can be broken. For example, the molecules of water in a vessel full of steam have symmetry. However, should the temperature change and the steam convert to drops of water, the symmetry would be broken. The vocabulary used to describe the steam in the vessel (temperature and pressure) must be replaced with terms that describe the water drops (number and size). This duality of description does not mean that one is superior to another, only that they are different. Knowledge of the temperature and pressure of the steam in the vessel is insufficient to predict the exact number and size of each water drop. That is why Max Planck urged scientists to display caution whenever they used the word *real*.

This position is not a rejection of attempts to understand the biological contributions to psychological processes, for the products of the biological research deepen our understanding of the behavioral events. The discovery that the connections between medial, temporal, and frontal structures mature during the last half of the first year implies a major improvement in working memory, and that inference leads to a new conceptualization of the phenomena of "object permanence" and "stranger anxiety."

A second advantage of studying the brain's contribution to behavior is that a failure to find an expected correspondence often provides fruitful seeds for a new hypothesis that can be tested with contemporary methods in psychology and the neurosciences. The fact that lesions of the dorsolateral prefrontal cortex impair working memory but do not impair the retrieval of motor habits invites a distinction among different types of memory. Thus, knowledge of the relation of brain activity to psychological events enhances comprehension, although a complete translation of the latter into the former may not be possible.

A behavior, thought, or feeling is the product of a series of cascades that began with an external provocation or spontaneous biological event.

The number of cascades varies with the psychological outcome of interest. Adults presented with single words on a screen that described either desirable or undesirable human traits had to judge whether the trait did or did not apply to self (during one block of trials) or did or did not apply to a friend (during another block of trials). The EEG patterns revealed three results. First, there was no effect of the desirability of the trait word on the ERP waveform during the first 300 msec. Second, at about 300 msec, the desirable trait words produced a positive waveform, while the undesirable traits produced a negative waveform, but the waveforms for self and friend were similar. Finally, at about 475 msec, the waveforms for self and friend became differentiated. The participants showed larger positive waveforms when they affirmed a desirable trait for self, but a larger negative waveform when they denied possessing an undesirable trait (Tucker et al., 2003). Similarly, adults showed larger waveforms at 170 msec to pictures of their face and the face of a famous person (both familiar) than to unfamiliar faces, but at 250 msec, the waveforms were larger to the unfamiliar face (Caharel, 2002). Thus, different brain and psychological states appear in rapid succession during the first half-second following the appearance of a stimulus.

The phenomena that comprise each cascade have to be described with a distinct vocabulary. Genes, chromosomes, neurons, animals, and species require unique predicates because each has unique functions. Genes mutate, chromosomes separate, neurons synapse, animals mate, and species evolve. Although biologists might write, "Chromosomes separate at meiosis," and psychologists might write, "Adolescents separate from their families when they go to college," the predicate "separate" has different meanings in the two sentences. Distinct forms of control characterize the progression from genotype to phenotype and each forms a dynamic system whose products are governed by laws we do not yet understand (Strohman, 2002).

The way a phenomenon and its prior causal conditions are conceptualized can help or hinder understanding. If the conceptual unit selected is too far removed from the phenomena of interest, the most fruitful explanation will be delayed. For instance, the phoneme is the proper unit if the interest is in the acquisition of lexical structures; but the morpheme is the better choice if one wishes to explain the growth of vocabulary between 1 and 3 years. The same principle applies to biology. The most useful conceptual unit for understanding a Mendelian symptom, for example, Huntington's disease, is a gene. A phosphate molecule, a constituent of a gene, is too small and a chromosome too large. However, a phosphate molecule is the proper unit when cell metabolism is the target of inquiry, and the chromosome is proper when Down's syndrome is the focus of the research.

The apparently correct choices in these examples were the hard-won products of extensive research by many scientists who recognized the necessity of inventing new words. Morpheme, working memory, exon, protein, and synapse were not in anyone's vocabulary 200 years ago; each had to be invented to explain unexpected observations.

There is an increase in order as we move from the forms and functions comprising one cascade to those of the next; for example, from neuronal excitation in the motor cortex to an infant reaching toward a rattle because there are fewer possible ways an infant can reach for a rattle than possible neuronal ensembles. But the increase in order in the psychological outcome is accompanied by some loss of determinism at the junction between brain activity and the psychological reaction. It is not possible to predict the exact direction and velocity of a child's reaching for a rattle on a table from complete knowledge of the immediately preceding and accompanying neuronal profile. That is why there is only a modest positive relation between the time when an adult felt the urge to move his finger and neural activity in the dorsal prefrontal cortex or the supplementary motor area (Lau, Roger, Haggard, & Passingham, 2004). Scientists monitoring brain activity to predict when a person experienced the urge to move his finger would be incorrect on many occasions. As the brain matures, the predictability of the psychological properties of the next developmental stage is attenuated a bit, permitting the mind, like a child in a rising balloon, to realize that there is more than one way to view the world below.

References

Addie, W. J., & Critchley, M. (1927). Forced grasping and groping. *Brain, 50,* 142–170.

Ahmed, A., & Ruffino, T. (1998). Why do infants make A not B errors in a search task, yet show memory for the location of hidden objects in a non-search task? *Developmental Psychology, 34,* 441–453.

Akbarian, S., Viñuela, A., Kim, J. J., Potkin, S. G., Bunney, W. E., Jr., & Jones, G. (1993). Distorted distribution of nicotinamine-adenine dinucleotide phosphate-diaphorase neurons in temporal lobe of schizophrenics implies anomalous cortical development. *Archives of General Psychiatry, 50,* 178–187.

Akert, K. (1994). Limbisches System. In D. Drenckhahn & W. Zenker (Eds.), *Benninghoff Anatomie* (15th ed., p. 493). München: Urban und Schwarzenberg.

Alexander, G. M., & Hines, M. (2002). Sex differences in response to children's toys in nonhuman primates (cercopithecus aethiops sabaeus). *Evolution and Human Behavior, 23,* 467–479.

Alvarez-Buylla, A., & Garcia-Verdugo, J. M. (2001). A unified hypothesis on the lineage of neural stem cells. *Nature Reviews Neuroscience, 2,* 287–293.

Amaral, D. G. (1992). Anatomical organization of the primate amygdaloid complex. In J. P. Aggleton (Ed.), *The amygdala* (pp. 1–66). New York: Wiley–Liss.

Amaral, D. G. (2002). The primate amygdala and the neurobiology of social behavior: Implications for understanding social anxiety. *Biological Psychiatry, 51,* 11–17.

Amaral, D. G., Capitanio, J. P., Jourdain, M., & Mason, W. A. (2003). The amygdala: Is it an essential component of the neural network for social cognition? *Neuropsychologia, 41,* 235–240.

Amunts, K., Schlaug, G., Schleicher, A., Steinmetz, H., & Dabringhaus, A. (1996). Asymmetry in the human motor cortex and handedness. *NeuroImage, 4,* 216–222.

Amunts, K., Schleicher, A., Ditterich, A., & Zilles, K. (2000). Postnatal changes in cytoarchitectonic asymmetry of Broca's region. *NeuroImage, 11,* S259.

Amunts, K., Schleicher, A., Ditterich, A., & Zilles, K. (2001). *Broca's region: Cytoarchitectonic asymmetry and developmental changes.* Unpublished manuscript.

Anderson, D. J., Gage, F. H., & Weissman, I. L. (2001). Can stem cells cross lineage boundaries? *Nature Medicine, 7,* 393–395.

Anderson, S., Damasio, H., Tranel, D., & Damasio, A. (2000). Long-term sequelae of prefrontal cortex damage acquired in early childhood. *Developmental Neuropsychology, 18,* 281–296.

Andrews, M. W., & Rosenblum, L. A. (2002). Response patterns of bonnet macaques following up to 75 weeks of continuous access to social video and food rewards. *American Journal of Primatology, 57,* 213–218.

Ansari, T., Sibbons, P. D., & Howard, C. V. (2001). Estimation of mean nuclear volume of neocortical neurons in sudden infant death syndrome cases using the nucleator estimator technique. *Biology of the Neonate, 80,* 48–52.

Antoniadis, E. A., & McDonald, R. J. (2000). Amygdala, hippocampus, and discriminative conditioning to context. *Behavioural Brain Research, 108,* 1–9.

Arndt, J., Greenberg, J., & Cook, A. (2002). Mortality salience and the spreading activation of worldview-relevant constructs explaining the cognitive architecture of terror management. *Journal of Experimental Psychology: General, 131,* 307–324.

Arnsten, A. F. T., Cai, J. X., Murphy, B. L., & Goldman-Rakic, P. S. (1994). Dopamine D1 receptor mechanisms in the cognitive performance of young adult and aged monkeys. *Psychopharmacology, 116,* 143–151.

Arriaga, R. (2001). *Behavioral and electrophysiological correlates of numerosity discrimination in 8-month-old infants.* Unpublished doctoral dissertation, Harvard University, Cambridge, MA.

Attanasio, A., Rager, K., & Gupta, D. (1986). Ontogeny of circadian rhythmicity for melatonin, serotonin, and N-acetylserotonin in humans. *Journal of Pineal Research, 3,* 251–256.

Auerbach, J., Geller, V., Lezer, S., Shinwell, E., Belmaker, R. H., Levine, J., et al. (1999). Dopamine D4 receptor (D4DR) and serotonin transporter promoter (5–HTTLPR) polymorphisms in the determination of temperament in two-month infants. *Molecular Psychiatry, 4,* 369–373.

Bachevalier, J. (1990). Ontogenetic development of habit and memory formation in primates. *Annals of the New York Academy of Science, 608,* 457–477.

Bachevalier, J., Brickson, M., & Hagger, C. (1993). Limbic-dependent recognition memory in monkeys develops early in infancy. *Neuroreport, 4,* 77–80.

Bahrick, L. E., Flowm, R., & Lickliter, R. (2002). Intersensory redundancy facilitates discrimination of tempo in 3 month old infants. *Developmental Psychobiology, 41,* 352–363.

Bahrick, L. E., Gogate, L. J., & Ruize, I. (2002). Attention and memory for faces and actions in infancy. *Child Development, 73,* 1629–1643.

Baird, A. (2001). *A study of frontal lobe function using optical scanning.* Unpublished doctoral dissertation, Harvard University, Cambridge, MA.

Baird, G., Cox, A., Baron-Cohen, S., Swettenham, J., Wheelwright, S., & Drew, A. (2001). Screening and surveillance for autism and pervasive developmental disorders. *Archives of Diseases in Childhood, 84,* 468–475.

Balaban, M. T., & Waxman, S. R. (1997). Do words facilitate object categorization in 9-month old infants? *Journal of Experimental Child Psychology, 64,* 3–26.

Baldwin, B. A., Markman, E. M., Bill, B., Desjardins, R. N., Irwin, J. M., & Tidball, G. (1996). Infants' reliance on a social criterion for establishing word-object relations. *Child Development, 67,* 3135–3153.

Baron-Cohen, S., Allen, J., & Gillberg, C. (1992). Can autism be detected at 18 months? The needle, the haystack, and the CHAT. *British Journal of Psychiatry, 161,* 839–843.

Baron-Cohen, S., Cox, A., Baird, G., Swettenham, J., Nightingale, N., Morgan, K., et al. (1996). Psychological markers in the detection of autism in infancy in a large population. *British Journal of Psychiatry, 168,* 158–163.

Baron-Cohen, S., Ring, H. A., Bullmore, E. T., Wheelwright, S., Ashwin, C., & Williams, S. C. (2000). The amygdala theory of autism. *Neuroscience and Biobehavioral Reviews, 24,* 355–364.

Baron-Cohen, S., Ring, H. A., Wheelwright, S., Bullmore, E. T., Brammer, M. J., Simmons, A., et al. (1999). Social intelligence in the normal and autistic brain: An fMRI study. *European Journal of Neuroscience, 11,* 1891–1898.

Barrett, D., Schumake, J., Jones, D., & Gonzalez-Lima, F. (2003). Metabolic mapping of mouse-brain activity after extinction of a conditioned emotional response. *Journal of Neuroscience, 23,* 5740–5749.

Bassareo, V., DeLuca, M. A., & DiChiara, G. (2002). Differential expression of motivational stimulus properties by dopamine in nucleus accumbens shell versus core and prefrontal cortex. *Journal of Neuroscience, 22,* 4709–4719.

Bastuji, H., Perrin, F., & Garcia-Larrea, L. (2002). Semantic analysis of auditory input during sleep. *Journal of Psychophysiology, 46,* 243–255.

Bates, E., Devescovi, A., & Wulfeck, B. B. (2001). Psycholinguistics. *Annual Review of Psychology, 52,* 369–396.

Bates, E., & Dick, F. (2000). Beyond phrenology: Brain and language in the next millennium. *Brain and Language, 71,* 18–21.

Bates, J. F., & Goldman-Rakic, P. S. (1993). Prefrontal connections of medial motor areas in the rhesus monkey. *Journal of Comparative Neurology, 336,* 211–228.

Bauer, P. J. (2002). Long-term recall memory. *Current Directions in Psychological Science, 11,* 137–141.

Bauer, P. J., Schwade, J. A., Wewerka, S. S., & Delaney, K. (1999). Planning ahead: Goal-directed problem solving by 2-year-olds. *Developmental Psychology, 35,* 1321–1337.

Bauer, P. J., Wiebe, S. A., Carver, L. J., Waters, J. M., & Nelson, C. A. (2003). Developments in long-term explicit memory late in the first year of life. *Psychological Science, 14,* 629–635.

Bauman, M. L., & Kemper, T. L. (1985). Histoanatomic observations of the brain in early infantile autism. *Neurology, 35,* 866–874.

Bauman, M. L., & Kemper, T. L. (1994). Neuroanatomical observations of the brain in autism. In M. L. Bauman & T. L. Kemper (Eds.), *The neurobiology of autism* (pp. 119–145). Baltimore: Johns Hopkins University Press.

Bauman, M. L., & Kemper, T. L. (2003). *The neuropathology of the autism spectrum disorders: What have we learned?* Paper presented at the Novartis Foundation Symposium.

Bell, M. A. (1998). Search for valid infant EEG rhythms. *Psychophysiology, 35,* S19.

Bell, M. A. (2002). Power changes in infant EEG frequency bands during a spatial working memory task. *Psychophysiology, 39,* 450–458.

Berger, A. J., Mitchell, R. A., & Severinghaus, J. W. (1977). Regulation of respiration. *New England Journal of Medicine, 297,* 138–143.

Berridge, K. C. (2003). Pleasures of the brain. *Brain and Cognition, 52,* 106–121.

Best, C. T. (1995). Learning to perceive the sound patterns of English. In C. Rovee-Collier & L. P. Lipsitt (Eds.), *Advances in infancy research* (Vol. 9, p. 1995). Norwood, NJ: Ablex.

Bevins, R. A., Besheer, J., Palmatier, M. I., Jensen, N. C., Pickett, S., & Eurek, S. (2002). Novel object place conditioning. *Behavioural Brain Research, 129,* 41–50.

Bialystok, E., & Martin, M. M. (2003). Notation to symbol. *Journal of Experimental Child Psychology, 86,* 223–243.

Biederman, J., Faraone, S. V., Keenan, K., Benjamin, J., Krifcher, B., Moore, C. M., et al. (1992). Further evidence for family-genetic risk factors in attention deficit hyperactivity disorder. Patterns of comorbidity in probands and relatives psychiatrically and pediatrically referred samples. *Archives of General Psychiatry, 49,* 728–738.

Black, I. B. (1991). *Information and the brain.* Cambridge, MA: MIT Press.

Blanke, O., Ortigue, S., Landis, T., & Seeck, M. (2002). Stimulating illusory own-body perceptions. *Nature, 419,* 269–270.

Blascovich, A. K., & Mendes, W. B. (2002). Cardiovascular reactivity in the presence of pets, friends, and spouses. *Psychosomatic Medicine, 64,* 727–739.

Blass, E. M., & Camp, C. A. (2001). The ontogeny of face recognition. *Developmental Psychology, 37*, 762–774.

Blokland, A. (1996). Acetylcholine: A neurotransmitter for learning and memory? *Brain Research Reviews, 21*, 285–300.

Bloom, L. (1993). *The transition from infancy to language: Acquiring the power of expression.* Cambridge, England: Cambridge University Press.

Bloomfield, F. H., Oliver, M. H., Hawkins, P., Campbell, M., Phillips, D. J., Gluckman, P. D., et al. (2003). A periconceptional nutritional origin for non-infectious preterm birth. *Science, 300*, 606.

Boatman, D. (2004). Cortical bases of speech perception: Evidence from functional lesion studies. *Cognition, 92*, 47–65.

Boller, K., Rovee-Collier, C., Gulya, M., & Prete, K. (1996). Infants' memory for context: Timing effects of postevent information. *Journal of Experimental Child Psychology, 63*, 583–602.

Boothe, R. G., Dobson, V., & Teller, D. Y. (1985). Postnatal development of vision in human and nonhuman primates. *Annual Review of Neuroscience, 8*, 495–545.

Bornstein, M. H. (1981). Psychological studies of color perception in human infants. In L. P. Lipsitt & C. Rovee-Collier (Eds.), *Advances in infancy research* (Vol. 1, pp. 2–40). Norwood, NJ: Ablex.

Bornstein, M. H., & Krinsky, S. J. (1985). Perception of symmetry in infancy. *Journal of Experimental Child Psychology, 39*, 1–19.

Bos, R., Meijer, M. K., Van Renselaar, J. P., van der Harst, J. E., & Spruijt, B. M. (2003). Anticipation is differentially expressed in rats and domestic cats in the same Pavlovian conditioning paradigm. *Behavioural Brain Research, 141*, 83–89.

Bourgeois, J.-P., Goldman-Rakic, P. S., & Rakic, P. (1994). Synaptogenesis in the prefrontal cortex of rhesus monkey. *Cerebral Cortex, 4*, 78–96.

Bourgeois, J.-P., & Rakic, P. (1993). Changes of synaptic density in the primary visual cortex of the macaque monkey from fetal to adult stage. *Journal of Neuroscience, 13*, 2801–2820.

Bowlby, J. (1973). *Attachment and loss: Separation* (Vol. 2). New York: Basic Books.

Boysen, S. T., Berntson, G. G., & Mukobi, K. L. (2001). Size matters. *Journal of Comparative Psychology, 115*, 106–110.

Bradford, H. F. (1986). *Chemical neurobiology.* New York: Freeman.

Brannon, E. M. (2002). The development of ordinal numerical knowledge in infancy. *Cognition, 83*, 223–240.

Brodal, A. (1981). *Neurological anatomy in relation to clinical medicine.* New York: Oxford University Press.

Brody, B. A., Kinney, H., Kloman, A., & Gilles, F. H. (1987). Sequence of central nervous system myelination in human infancy. 1. An autopsy study of myelination. *Journal of Neuropathology and Experimental Neurology, 46*, 283–301.

Bronson, G. W. (1970). Fear of visual novelty. *Developmental Psychology, 2*, 33–40.

Bronson, G. W. (1994). Infant's transition toward adult-like scanning. *Child Development, 65*, 1243–1261.

Brosnan, S. F., & de Waal, F. B. M. (2003). Monkeys reject unequal pay. *Nature, 425*, 297–299.

Brown, C. M., Hagoort, P., & Kutas, M. (2002). Post lexical integrative processes in language comprehension. In M. S. Gazzaniga (Ed.), *The new cognitive neurosciences* (pp. 881–899). Cambridge, MA: MIT Press.

Brown, R. (1973). *A first language: The early stage.* Cambridge, MA: Harvard University Press.

Brown, R. M., & Goldman, P. S. (1977). Catecholamines in neocortex of rhesus monkeys: Regional distribution and ontogenetic development. *Brain Research, 124*, 576–580.

Brozoski, T. J., & Brown, R. M. (1979). Cognitive deficit caused by regional depletion of dopamine in prefrontal cortex of rhesus monkeys. *Science, 205*, 929–931.

Brush, F. R. (2003). Selection for differences in avoidance learning. *Behavior Genetics, 33*, 677–696.

Buchanan, T. W., Lutz, K., Mirzazode, S., Specht, K., & Shah, N. J. (2000). Recognition of emotional prosody and verbal components of spoken language. *Cognitive Brain Research, 9,* 227–238.

Burgess, K. B., Marshall, P. J., Rubin, K. H., & Fox, N. A. (2003). Infant attachment and temperament as predictors of subsequent externalizing problems and cardiac physiology. *Journal of Child Psychology and Psychiatry, 44,* 819–831.

Burkhalter, A., Bernardo, K. L., & Charles, V. (1993). Development of local circuits in human visual cortex. *Journal of Neuroscience, 13,* 1916–1931.

Bymaster, F. P., Katner, J. S., Nelson, D. L., Hemrick-Luecke, S. K., Threlkeld, P. G., Heiligenstein, J. H., et al. (2002). Atomoxetine increases extracellular levels of norepinephrine and dopamine in prefrontal cortex of rat: A potential mechanism for efficacy in attention deficit/hyperactivity disorder. *Neuropsychopharmacology, 17,* 699–711.

Byrne, G., & Suomi, S. J. (2002). Cortisol reactivity and its relation to home cage behavior and personality ratings in Tufted Capuchin (Cebus apella) juveniles from birth to six years of age. *Psychoneuroendocrinology, 27,* 139–154.

Cabeza, R., & Nyberg, L. (2000). Imaging cognition II. *Journal of Cognitive Neuroscience, 12,* 1–47.

Caharel, S., Toiroux, S., Bernard, C., Thibaut, F., LaLonde, R., & Rebai, M. (2002). ERPs associated with familiarity and degree of familiarity during face recognition. *International Journal of Neuroscience, 112,* 1499–1512.

Call, J., & Tomasello, M. (1998). Distinguishing intentional from accidental actions in orangutans (pongo pigmaeus), chimpanzees (pan troglodytes), and human children (homo sapiens). *Journal of Comparative Psychology, 112,* 192–206.

Campos, J. J., Bertenthal, B. I., & Kermoian, R. (1992). Early experience and emotional development. *Psychological Science, 3,* 61–64.

Caramazza, A., & Shelton, J. R. (1998). Domain-specific knowledge systems in the brain. *Journal of Cognitive Neuroscience, 10,* 1–34.

Carpenter, M., Akhtar, N., & Tomasello, M. (1998). Fourteen through 18-month-old infants differentially imitate intentional and accidental actions. *Infant Behavior and Development, 21,* 315–330.

Casanova, M. F., Buxhoeveden, P., Switala, A. E., & Roy, E. (2002). Minicolumnar pathology in autism. *Neurology, 58,* 428–432.

Case, R. (1992). The role of the frontal lobes in the regulation of cognitive development. *Brain and Cognition, 20,* 51–73.

Case, R., & Okomoto, Y. (1996). The role of central conceptual structures in the development of children's thought. *Monographs of the Society for Research in Child Development, 61.*

Caspi, A., McClay, J., Moffitt, T. E., Mill, J., & Martin, J. (2002). Role of genotype in the cycle of violence in maltreated children. *Science, 297,* 851–853.

Caspi, A., Sugden, K., Moffitt, T. E., Taylor, M., Craig, I. W., Harrington, H., et al. (2003). Influences of life stress on depression. *Science, 301,* 386–389.

Cassia, V. M., Simion, F., Milani, I., & Ulmilta, C. (2002). Dominance of global visual perception at birth. *Journal of Experimental Psychology: General, 131,* 398–411.

Cassidy, K. W., Kelly, M. H., & Sharoni, L. J. (1999). Inferring gender from name phonology. *Journal of Experimental Psychology: General, 128,* 362–381.

Castellanos, F. X., Sharp, W. S., Gottesman, R. F., Greenstein, D. K., Giedd, J. N., & Rapoport, J. L. (2003). Anatomic brain abnormalities in monozygotic twins discordant for attention deficit hyperactivity disorder. *American Journal of Psychiatry, 160,* 1693–1696.

Castellanos, F. X., & Tannock, R. (2002). Neuroscience of attention-deficit/hyperactivity disorder: The search for endophenotypes. *Nature Reviews Neuroscience, 3,* 617–628.

Cavigelli, S. A., & McClintock, M. K. (2003). Fear of novelty in infant rats predicts adult corticosterone dynamics and early death. *Proceedings of the National Academy of Sciences, USA, 100,* 16131–16136.

Ceponiene, R., Kushnerenko, E., Fellman, V., Rendlung, M., Suominen, K., & Naatanen, R. (2002). Event related potential features indexing central auditory discrimination by newborns. *Cognitive Brain Research, 13,* 101–113.

Chalmers, K. A., & Halford, G. S. (2003). Young childrens' understanding of oddity. *Cognitive Development, 18,* 1–22.

Chang, E. F., & Merzenich, M. M. (2003). Environmental noise retards auditory cortical development. *Science, 300,* 498–502.

Chenn, A., Braisted, J. E., McConell, S. K., & O'Leary, D. D. M. (1997). Development of the cerebral cortex. In W. M. Cowan, T. M. Jessel, & S. L. Zipurski (Eds.), *Molecular and cellular approaches to neural development* (pp. 440–474). New York: Oxford University Press.

Chenn, A., & McConnell, S. K. (1995). Cleavage orientation and the asymmetric inheritance of Notch1 immunoreactivity in mammalian neurogenesis. *Cell, 82,* 631–641.

Cheour, M., Ceponiene, R., Leppanen, P., Alho, K., Kujala, T., Renlund, M., et al. (2002). The auditory sensory memory trace decays rapidly in newborns. *Scandinavian Journal of Psychology, 43,* 33–39.

Chien, S. H., Teller, D. Y., & Palmer, J. (2000). The transition from scotopic to photopic vision in 3-month-old infants and adults. *Vision Research, 40,* 3853–3871.

Chiron, C. (1992). Changes in regional cerebral blood flow during brain maturation in children and adolescents. *Journal of Nuclear Medicine, 33,* 696–703.

Chiron, C., Jambaque, I., Nabbout, R., Lounes, R., Syrota, A., & Dulac, O. (1997). The right brain hemisphere is dominant in human infants. *Brain, 120,* 1057–1065.

Chisholm, J. S. (1996). Learning respect for everything. In C. P. Huang, M. E. Lamb, & I. E. Siegel (Eds.), *Images of childhood* (pp. 167–183). Mahwah, NJ: Lawrence Erlbaum Associates, Inc.

Christoff, K., Ream, J. M., Geddes, L. P. T., & Gabrieli, J. D. E. (2003). Evaluating self-generated information. *Behavioral Neuroscience, 117,* 1161–1168.

Chrousos, G. P., & Gold, P. W. (1992). The concepts of stress and stress system disorders: Overview of physical and behavioral homeostasis. *Journal of the American Medical Association, 267,* 1244–1252.

Chugani, D. C., Muzik, O., Rothermel, R., Behen, M., Chakraborty, P., Mangner, T., et al. (1997). Altered serotonin synthesis in the dentatothalamocortical pathway in autistic boys. *Annals of Neurology, 42,* 666–669.

Chugani, H. (1996). Neuroimaging of developmental non-linearity and developmental pathologies. In R. W. Thatcher, G. R. Lyon, J. Rumsey, & N. Krasnegor (Eds.), *Developmental neuroimaging: Mapping the development of brain and behavior* (pp. 187–193). San Diego, CA: Academic.

Chugani, H. T. (1991). Imaging human brain development with PET. *Journal of Nuclear Medicine, 32,* 23–26.

Chugani, H. T. (1994). Development of regional brain glucose metabolism. In G. Dawson & K. Fischer (Eds.), *Human behavior and the developing brain* (pp. 153–175). New York: Guilford.

Chugani, H. T. (1998). A critical period of brain development: Studies of cerebral glucose utilization with PET. *Preventive Medicine, 27,* 184–188.

Chugani, H. T., Phelps, M. E., & Mazziotta, J. C. (1987). Positron emission tomography study of human brain functional development. *Annals of Neurology, 22,* 487–497.

Churchland, P. S. (1986). *Neurophilosophy.* Cambridge, MA: MIT Press.

Clarke, A. R., Barry, R. J., McCarthy, R. A., & Selikowitz, M. (2003). Effects of stimulant medication on the EEG of children with attention deficit-hyperactivity disorder predominately inattentive type. *International Journal of Psychophysiology, 47,* 129–137.

Clifton, R. K., Rochat, P., Litovsky, R. Y., & Perris, E. E. (1991). Object representation guides infants' reaching in the dark. *Journal of Experimental Psychology: Human Perception and Performance, 17,* 323–329.

Clubb, R., & Mason, G. (2003). Captivity effects on wide-ranging carnivores. *Nature, 425,* 473.

Collie, R., & Hayne, H. (1999). Deferred imitation by 6- and 9-month-old infants: More evidence for declarative memory. *Developmental Psychobiology, 35,* 83–90.

Cook, M. N., Bolivar, V. J., McFayden, M. P., & Flaherty, L. (2002). Behavioral differences among 129 substrains. *Behavioral Neuroscience, 116,* 600–611.

Cook, N. D. (2002). Bihemispheric language. In T. J. Crow (Ed.), *The speciation of modern homo sapiens* (pp. 169–194). Oxford, England: Oxford University Press.

Cooley, C. H. (1902). *Human nature and the social order.* New York: Scribner's.

Coull, J. T., Vidal, F., Nazarian, B., & Macar, F. (2004). Functional anatomy of the attentional modulation of time estimation. *Science, 303,* 1506–1508.

Courage, M. L., & Howe, M. L. (2001). Long-term retention in three-and-a-half-month-olds. *Journal of Experimental Child Psychology, 79,* 271–293.

Courage, M. L., & Howe, M. L. (2002). From infant to child. *Psychological Bulletin, 128,* 250–277.

Courchesne, E. (1997). Brainstem, cerebellar and limbic neuroanatomical abnormalities in autism. *Current Opinion in Neurobiology, 7,* 269–278.

Courchesne, E., Karns, C. M., Davis, H. R., Ziccardi, R., Carper, R. A., Tigue, Z. D., Chisum, H. J., et al. (2001). Unusual brain growth patterns in early life in patients with autistic disorder. An MRI study. *Neurology, 57,* 245–254.

Court, J. A., Johnson, M., Piggot, M., Kerwin, J. A., & Perry, R. H. (1993). Regional patterns of cholinergic and glutamate activity in the developing and aging human brain. *Developmental Brain Research, 74,* 73–82.

Croen, L. A., Grether, J. K., Curry, C., & Nelson, K. B. (2001). Congenital abnormalities among children with cerebral palsy: More evidence for prenatal antecedents. *Journal of Pediatrics, 138,* 804–810.

Croen, L. A., Grether, J. K., Hoogstrate, J., & Selvin, S. (2002). The changing prevalence of autism in California. *Journal of Autism and Developmental Disorders, 32,* 207–215.

Cruz, A., & Green, B. G. (2000). Thermal stimulation of taste. *Nature, 403,* 889–892.

Csatho, A., Osvath, A., Bicksak, E., Karadi, K., Manning, J. T., & Kallai, J. (2003). Sexual identity related to the ratio of second to fourth digit length in women. *Biological Psychiatry, 62,* 147–156.

Csibra, G., Davis, G., Spratling, M. W., & Johnson, M. H. (2000). Gamma oscillations and object processing in the infant brain. *Science, 290,* 1582–1585.

Curnes, J. T., Burger, P. C., Djang, W. T., & Boyko, O. B. (2000). MR imaging of compact white matter pathways. *American Journal of Radiology, 9,* 1061–1068.

Curran, T., & Dien, J. (2003). Differentiaating amodal familiarity from modality-specific memory processes. *Psychophysiology, 40,* 979–988.

Curtis, J. T., & Wang, Z. (2003). The neurochemistry of pair bonding. *Current Directions in Psychological Science, 12,* 49–53.

Daffner, K. R., Mesulam, M. M., Scinto, L. F. M., Acar, D., Calvo, V., Faust, R., et al. (2000). The central role of the prefrontal cortex in directing attention to novel events. *Brain, 123,* 927–939.

Damasio, A. R. (1992). Aphasia. *New England Journal of Medicine, 326,* 531–539.

Damasio, A. R. (1994). *Descartes' error.* New York: Avon Books.

D'Anguilly, A., & Maggi, S. (2003). Development of drawing abilities in a distinct population. *International Journal of Behavioral Development, 27,* 193–200.

Daston, L., & Park, K. (1998). *Wonders and the order of nature.* New York: Zone Books.

Davenport, M. D., Novak, M. A., Meyer, J. S., Tiefenbacher, S., Higley, J. D., Lindell, S. C., et al. (2003). Constancy and change in emotional reactivity in rhesus monkeys throughout the prepubertal period. *Motivation and Emotion, 27,* 57–76.

Davey, G. C. L. (1995). Preparedness and phobias. *Behavioral and Brain Sciences, 18,* 289–297.

Davis, F. C. (1997). Melatonin: Role in development. *Journal of Biological Rhythms, 12,* 498–508.

Davis, H. R., & McLeod, S. L. (2003). Why humans value sensational news. *Evolution and Human Behavior, 24,* 208–216.

Davis, M. (1992). The role of the amygdala in fear and anxiety. *Annual Review of Neuroscience, 15,* 353–375.

Davis, M., & Whalen, P. J. (2001). The amygdala. *Molecular Psychiatry, 6,* 13–34.

Dawson, G., Carver, L. J., & Meltzoff, A. N. (2002). Neural correlates of face and object recognition in young children with autism spectrum disorder, developmental delay and typical development. *Child Development, 73,* 700–717.

Dawson, G., Toth, K., Abbott, R., Osterling, J., Munson, J., Ester, A., et al. (2004). Early social attention impairments in autism. *Developmental Psychology, 40,* 271–283.

Dayan, P., & Balleine, B. W. (2002). Reward motivation and reinforcement learning. *Neuron, 36,* 285–298.

de Blois, S. T., Novak, M. A., & Bond, M. (1998). Object permanence in orangutans (pongo pygmaeus) and squirrel monkeys (saimiri sciureus). *Journal of Comparative Psychology, 112,* 137–152.

de Velis, J., & Carpenter, E. (1999). Development. In G. J. Siegel, B. W. Agranoff, R. W. Albers, S. K. Fischer, & M. D. Uhler (Eds.), *Basic neurochemistry* (pp. 537–563). Philadelphia: Lippincott-Raven.

De Vincenzi, M., Job, R., Di Matteo, R., Angrilli, A., Penolazzi, B., Ciccarelli, L., et al. (2003). Differences in the perception and time course of syntactic and semantic violations. *Brain and Language, 85,* 280–296.

De Vries, J. I. P. (1991). The first trimester. In J. G. Nijhuis (Ed.), *Fetal behaviour: Developmental and perinatal aspects* (pp. 13–15). Oxford, England: Oxford University Press.

De Vries, J. I. P., Visser, G. H. A., & Prechtl, H. F. R. (1982). The emergence of fetal behaviour. I. Qualitative aspects. *Early Human Development, 7,* 301–322.

de Weerth, C., & van Geert, V. (2002). Changing patterns of infant behavior and mother–infant interaction: Intra- and interindividual variability. *Infant Behavior & Development, 24,* 347–371.

DeCasper, A. J., & Fifer, W. P. (1980). Of human bonding. *Science, 208,* 1174–1176.

Decker, M. W., & McGaugh, J. (1991). The role of interactions between the cholinergic system and other neuromodulatory systems in learning and memory. *Synapse, 7,* 151–168.

DeHaan, M., & Nelson, C. A. (1997). Recognition of the mother's face by six-month-old infants: A neurobehavioral study. *Child Development, 68,* 187–210.

DeHaan, M., Pascalis, O., & Johnson, M. H. (2002). Specialization of neural mechanisms. Face recognition in human infants. *Journal of Cognitive Neuroscience, 14,* 199–209.

Dehaene, S., Changeux, J. P., & Nadal, J. P. (1987). Neural networks that learn temporal sequences. *Proceedings of the National Academy of Sciences, USA, 84,* 2727–2731.

Dehaene, S., Dupoux, E., Mehler, J., Cohen, L., & Paulescu, E. (1997). Anatomical variability in the cortical representation of first and second language. *Neuroreport, 8,* 3809–3815.

Dehaene-Lambertz, G. (2000). Cerebral specialization for speech and non-speech stimuli in infants. *Journal of Cognitive Neuroscience, 12,* 449–460.

Dehaene-Lambertz, G., Dehaene, S., & Hertz-Pannier, L. (2002). Functional neuroimaging of speech perception in infants. *Science, 298,* 2013–2015.

Del Fiacco, M., Diana, A., Floris, A., & Quartu, M. (1990). Substance P-like immunoreactivity in human prenatal hippocampal formation. *International Journal of Developmental Neuroscience, 8,* 289–297.

Delalle, I., Evers, P., Kostovic, I., & Uylings, H. B. M. (1997). Laminar distribution of neuropeptide Y-immunoreactive neurons in human prefrontal cortex during development. *Journal of Comparative Neurology, 379,* 515–522.

Delong, G. R., Teague, L. A., & Kamran, M. M. (1998). Effects of fluoxetine treatment in young children with idiopathic autism. *Developmental Medicine and Child Neurology, 40,* 551–562.

Demany, L., McKenzie, B., & Vurpillot, E. (1977). Rhythm perception in early infancy. *Nature, 266,* 718–719.

Demerens, C., Stankoff, B., Logak, M., Anglade, P., Allinquant, B., Couraude, F., et al. (1996). Induction of myelination in the central nervous system by electrical activity. *Proceedings of the National Academy of Sciences, USA, 93,* 9887–9892.

Di Lorenzo, P. M., Hallock, R. M., & Kennedy, D. P. (2003). Temporal coding of sensation. *Behavioral Neuroscience, 117,* 1423–1433.

Diamond, A. (1985). Development of the ability to use recall to guide action, as indicated by infants' performance on A not B. *Child Development, 56,* 868–883.

Diamond, A. (1990a). Rate of maturation of the hippocampus and the developmental progression of children's performance on the delayed non-matching to sample and visual paired comparison tasks. *Annals of the New York Academy of Science, 608,* 394–426.

Diamond, A. (1990b). The development and neural bases of memory functions as indexed by the AB and delayed response tasks in human infants and infant monkeys. *Annals of the New York Academy of Science, 608,* 267–309.

Diamond, A. (1991). Neuropsychological insights into the meaning of object concept development. In S. Carey & R. Gelman (Eds.), *The epigenesis of mind* (pp. 67–110). Hillsdale, NJ: Lawrence Erlbaum Associates, Inc.

Diamond, A., & Goldman-Rakic, P. S. (1989). Comparison of human infants and rhesus monkeys on Piaget's AB task: Evidence for dependence on dorsolateral prefrontal cortex. *Experimental Brain Research, 74,* 24–40.

Diamond, A., Kirkhan, N., & Amso, D. (2002). Conditions under which young children can hold two rules in mind and inhibit a prepotent response. *Developmental Psychology, 38,* 352–362.

Diamond, A., Lee, E. Y., & Hayden, M. (2003). Early success in using the relation between stimulus and rewards to deduce an abstract rule. *Developmental Psychology, 39,* 825–847.

Diamond, A., Lee, E. Y., & Hayden, M. (in press). *Early success on the delayed nonmatching to sample task when stimulus and reward appear to be part of a single apparatus but not when they are clearly two separate objects.*

Diamond, A., Zola-Morgan, S., & Squire, L. R. (1989). Successful performance by monkeys with lesions of the hippocampal formation on A not B and object retrieval, two tasks that mark developmental changes in human infants. *Behavioral Neuroscience, 108,* 526–537.

Dickerson, S. S., Kemeny, M. E., Aziz, N., Kim, K. H. S., & Fahey, J. L. (2004). Immunological effects of induced shame and guilt. *Psychosomatic Medicine, 66,* 124–131.

Diesendruck, G. (2001). Essentialism in Brazilian children's extensions of animal names. *Developmental Psychology, 37,* 49–60.

DiLalla, L. F., Kagan, J., & Reznick, J. S. (1994). Genetic etiology of behavioral inhibition among 2-year-old children. *Infant Behavior and Development, 17,* 401–408.

Dillon, N. (2003). Positions, please. *Nature, 425,* 457.

Dondi, M., Simion, F., & Caltran, G. (1999). Can newborns discriminate between their own cry and the cry of another newborn infant? *Developmental Psychology, 35,* 418–426.

Dorn, A., Schmidt, K., Schmidt, W., Bernstein, H.-G., & Rinne, A. (1985). Localization of cholecystokinin immunoreactivity in the human brain with special reference to ontogeny. *Journal für Hirnforschung, 26,* 167–171.

Dougherty, D. D., Bonab, A. A., Spencer, T. J., Rauch, S. L., Madras, B. K., & Fischman, A. J. (1999). Dopamine transporter density in patients with attention deficit hyperactivity disorder. *Lancet, 354,* 2132–2133.

Draganski, B., Gaser, C., Busch, V., Schuierer, G., Bogdahn, U., & May, A. (2003). Changes in grey matter induced by training. *Nature, 427,* 311–312.

Drife, J. O. (1985). Can the fetus listen and learn? *British Journal of Obstetrics and Gynecology, 92,* 777–779.

Duncan, J., & Miller, E. K. (2002). Cognitive focus through adaptive neural coding in the primate prefrontal cortex. In D. T. Stuss & R. T. Knight (Eds.), *Principles of frontal lobe function* (pp. 278–291). New York: Oxford University Press.

Eacott, M. J., & Crawley, R. A. (2002). The offset of childhood amnesia. *Journal of Experimental Psychology: General, 127,* 22–23.

Easterbrook, M. A., Kisilevsky, B. S., Muir, D. W., & Laplante, D. P. (1999). Newborns discriminate schematic faces from scrambled faces. *Canadian Journal of Experimental Psychology, 53,* 231–241.

Eimas, P. D. (1997). Infant speech perception. In R. L. Goldstone, D. L. Medin, & P. G. Schyng (Eds.), *Perceptual learning, Vol. 36. The psychology of learning and motivation* (pp. 127–169). New York: Academic.

Eliades, S. J., & Wang, X. (2003). Sensory motor integration in the primate auditory cortex during self-initiated vocalization. *Journal of Neurophysiology, 89,* 2194–2207.

Elston, G. N. (2003). Cortex, cognition, and the cell. *Cerebral Cortex, 13,* 1124–1138.

Emde, R. N., & Harmon, R. J. (1972). Endogenous and exogenous smiling systems in early infancy. *Journal of American Academy of Child Psychiatry, 11,* 177–199.

Esch, H. E., Zhang, S., Srinivasan, M. V., & Tautz, J. (2001). Honeybee dances communicate distances measured by optic flow. *Nature, 411,* 581–583.

Eslinger, P. J., Grattan, L. M., Damasio, H., & Damasio, A. R. (1992). Developmental consequences of childhood frontal lobe damage. *Archives of Neurology, 49,* 764–769.

Eswaran, H., Lowery, C. L., Robinson, S. E., Wilson, J. D., & Cheyne, D. (2000). Challenges of recording human fetal auditory-evoked response using magnetoencephalography. *Journal of Maternal and Fetal Medicine, 9,* 303–307.

Eyre, J. A., Miller, S., Clowry, G. J., Conway, E. A., & Watts, C. (2000). Functional corticospinal projections are established prenatally in the human foetus permitting involvement in the development of spinal motor centres. *Brain, 123,* 51–64.

Eysel, U. T. (2003). Illusions and perceived images in the primate brain. *Science, 302,* 789–790.

Fagen, J. W., Morrongiello, B. A., Rovee-Collier, C., & Gekoski, M. J. (1984). Expectancies and memory retrieval in three-month-old infants. *Child Development, 55,* 936–943.

Fan, J., Rueda, M. R., McCandliss, B. D., Halparin, J. D., Gruber, D. B., Lercari, L. P., et al. (2001). *Attentional networks in six to ten year old children.* Unpublished manuscript.

Fantz, R. L., & Nevis, S. (1967). Pattern preferences and perceptual cognitive development in early infancy. *Merrill-Palmer Quarterly of Behavior and Development, 13,* 88–108.

Feigenson, L., Carey, S., & Spelke, E. (2002). Infants' discrimination of number vs continuous extent. *Cognitive Psychology, 44,* 33–66.

Fendt, M., Endres, T., & Apfelbach, R. (2003). Temporary inactivation of the bed nucleus of the stria terminalis but not of the amygdala blocks freezing induced by trimethyl-thiazoline, a component of fox feces. *Journal of Neuroscience, 23,* 23–28.

Fernandez-Duque, D., Grossi, G., Thornton, I. M., & Neville, H. J. (2003). Representation of change. *Journal of Cognitive Neuroscience, 15,* 491–507.

Fiez, J. A., & Raichle, M. E. (1997). Linguistic processing. In J. D. Schmahmann (Ed.), *The cerebellum and cognition* (pp. 233–254). New York: Academic.

Finlay, B. L., & Darlington, R. B. (1995). Linked regularities in the development and evolution of mammalian brains. *Science, 268,* 1578–1584.

Finley, G. E., Kagan, J., & Layne, O. (1972). Development of young children's attention to normal and distorted stimuli. *Developmental Psychology, 6,* 288–292.

Finney, E. M., Fine, I., & Dobkins, K. R. (2001). Visual stimuli activate auditory cortex in the deaf. *Nature Neuroscience, 4,* 1171–1173.

Fiorillo, C. D., Tobler, P. N., & Schultz, W. (2003). Discrete coding of reward probability and uncertainty by dopamine neurons. *Science, 299,* 1898–1902.

Firkowska, A., Ostrowska, A., Sokolowska, M., Stein, Z., & Susser, M. (1978). Cognitive development and social policy. *Science, 200,* 1357–1362.

Fisher, S. E., Vargha-Khadem, F., Watkins, K. E., Monaco, A. P., & Pembrey, M. E. (1998). Localisation of a gene implicated in a severe speech and language disorder. *Nature Genetics, 18,* 168–170.

Fitzgerald, M. (1991). *The development of descending brain stem control of spinal cord sensory processing.* Cambridge, England: Cambridge University Press.

Flavell, J. H., Green, F. L., & Flavell, E. R. (1986). Development of knowledge about the appearance-reality distinction. *Monograph of the Society for Research in Child Development, 51.*

Fogel, A., & Melson, G. F. (1988). *Child development.* New York: West.

Foucher, J. R., Otzenberger, H., & Gounot, D. (2003). The bold response and the gamma oscillations respond differently than evoked potentials. *BMC Neuroscience, 4,* 22.

Fox, N., Kagan, J., & Weiskopf, S. (1979). The growth of memory during infancy. *Genetic Psychology Monographs, 99,* 91–130.

Fraley, K. C., & Spieker, S. J. (2003). Are infant attachment patterns continuously or categorically distributed? *Developmental Psychology, 39,* 387–404.

Francis-West, P. H., Robson, L., & Evans, D. J. (2003). Craniofacial development. *Advances in Anatomy, Embryology & Cell Biology, 169,* 1–138.

Freedman, D. G. (1976). Infancy, biology, and culture. In L. P. Lipsitt (Ed.), *Developmental psychobiology* (pp. 35–58). Hillsdale, NJ: Lawrence Erlbaum Associates, Inc.

Friedman, W. J. (2000). The development of children's knowledge of the times of future events. *Child Development, 71,* 913–932.

Friston, K. (2002). Beyond phrenology. *Annual Review of Neuroscience, 25,* 221–250.

Funahashi, S., Bruce, C. J., & Goldman-Rakic, P. S. (1989). Mnemonic coding of visual space in the monkey's dorsolateral prefrontal cortex. *Journal of Neurophysiology, 61,* 331–349.

Fuster, J. M., & Alexander, G. (1971). Neuron activity related to short-term memory. *Science, 173,* 652–654.

Gage, F. H. (2000). Mammalian neural stem cells. *Science, 287,* 1433–1438.

Gaillard, W. D., Sachs, B. C., Whitnah, J. R., Ahmed, Z., Barsamo, L. M., Petrella, J. R., et al. (2003). Developmental aspects of language processing. *Human Brain Mapping, 18,* 176–185.

Galea, M. P., & Darian-Smith, I. (1995). Postnatal maturation of the direct corticospinal projections in the macaque monkey. *Cerebral Cortex, 5,* 518–540.

Galli, L., & Maffei, L. (1988). Spontaneous impulse activity of rat retinal ganglion cells in prenatal life. *Science, 242,* 90–91.

Gathercole, S. E., Pickering, S. T., Ambridge, B., & Wearing, H. (2004). The structure of working memory from four to fifteen years of age. *Child Development, 40,* 177–190.

Gauthier, I., Behrmann, M., & Tarr, M. J. (1999). Can face recognition really be dissociated from object recognition? *Journal of Cognitive Neuroscience, 11,* 349–370.

Geerts, M., Steyaert, J., & Fryns, J. P. (2003). The XYY syndrome: A follow-up study on 38 boys. *Genetic Counseling, 14,* 267–279.

Geldart, S., Maurer, D., & Carney, K. (1999). Effects of eye size on adults' aesthetic ratings of faces and 5-month-olds' looking times. *Perception, 28,* 361–374.

Geva, R., Gardner, J. M., & Karmel, B. Z. (1999). Feeding-based arousal effects on visual recognition memory in early infancy. *Developmental Psychology, 35,* 640–650.

Ghazanfar, A. A., & Logothetis, N. K. (2003). Facial expressions linked to monkey calls. *Nature, 423,* 937.

Ghosch, A., & Greenberg, M. E. (1995). Distinct roles for bFGF and NT-3 in the regulation of cortical neurogenesis. *Neuron, 15,* 89–103.

Ghosch, A., & Shatz, C. J. (1992). Pathfinding and target selection by developing geniculo-cortical axons. *Journal of Neuroscience, 19,* 4889–4898.

Gibson, E. J., & Walk, R. D. (1960). The visual cliff. *Scientific American, 202,* 64–71.

Giedd, J. N., Blumenthal, J., Jeffries, N. O., Rajapakse, J. C., Vaituzis, A. C., Liu, H., et al. (1999). Development of the human corpus callosum during childhood and adolescence:

A longitudinal MRI study. *Progress in Neuropsychopharmacology and Biological Psychiatry, 23,* 571–588.

Giedd, J. N., Blumenthal, J., Molloy, E., & Castellanos, F. X. (2001). Brain imaging of attention deficit/hyperactivity disorder. *Annals of the New York Academy of Science, 931,* 33–49.

Giedd, J. N., Rumsey, J. M., Castellanos, F. X., Rajapakse, J. C., Kaysen, D., Vaituzis, A. C., et al. (1996). A quantitative MRI study of the corpus callosum in children and adolescents. *Brain Research Developmental Brain Research, 91,* 274–280.

Giedd, J. N., Snell, J. W., Lange, N., Rajapakse, J. C., Casey, B. J., Kozuch, P., et al. (1996). Quantitative magnetic resonance imaging of human brain development: Ages 4–18Y. *Cerebral Cortex, 6,* 551–560.

Gillberg, C., & Coleman, M. (2000). *Biology of the autism syndromes (Clinics in Developmental Medicine No. 153)* (3rd ed.). Cambridge, England: Cambridge University Press.

Girard, N. J., & Ryaybaud, C. A. (1992). In vivo MRI of fetal brain cellular migration. *Journal of Computer Assisted Tomography, 16,* 265–267.

Gitau, R., Cameron, A., Fisk, N. M., & Glover, V. (1998). Fetal exposure to maternal cortisol. *Lancet, 352,* 707–708.

Gitau, R., Fisk, N. M., Teixeira, J. M., Cameron, A., & Glover, V. (2001). Fetal hypothalamic-pituitary-adrenal stress responses to invasive procedures are independent of maternal responses. *Journal of Clinical Endocrinology and Metabolism, 86,* 104–109.

Glabus, M. F., Horwitz, B., Holt, J. L., Kohn, A. D., Gerton, D. K., Callicott, J. H., et al. (2003). Interindividual differences in functional interactions among prefrontal, parietal, and parahippocampal regions during working memory. *Cerebral Cortex, 13,* 1382–1361.

Glotzbach, S. F., & Edgar, D. M. (1994). Biological rhythmicity in normal infants during the first 3 months of life. *Pediatrics, 94,* 482–488.

Glover, V., & Fisk, N. M. (1999). Fetal pain: Implications for research and practice. *British Journal of Obstetrics and Gynaecology, 106,* 881–886.

Goldberg, G. (1985). Supplementary motor area structure and function. Review and hypotheses. *The Behavioral and Brain Sciences, 8,* 567–616.

Goldman-Rakic, P. S. (1990). Cellular and circuit basis of working memory in prefrontal cortex of nonhuman primates. *Progress in Brain Research, 85,* 325–335.

Goldman-Rakic, P. S. (1994). The issue of memory in the study of prefrontal function. In P. Thierry (Ed.), *Motor and Cognitive Function* (pp. 112–121). Berlin: Springer.

Goldman-Rakic, P. S. (1995). Cellular basis of working memory. *Neuron, 14,* 477–485.

Goldsmith, H. H., Lemery, K. S., Buss, K. A., & Campos, J. J. (1999). Genetic analyses of focal aspects of infant temperament. *Developmental Psychology, 35,* 972–985.

Gomes, H., Sussman, E., Ritter, W., Kurtzberg, D., Cowan, N., & Vaughan, H. G. Jr. (1999). Electrophysiological evidence of developmental changes in the duration of auditory sensory memory. *Developmental Psychology, 35,* 294–302.

Goos, L. M., & Silverman, I. (2001). The influence of genomic imprinting on brain development and behavior. *Evolution and Human Behavior, 22,* 385–407.

Gordon, N. (2000). The acquisition of a second language. *European Journal of Paedriatric Neurology, 4,* 3–7.

Gottfried, J. A., O'Doherty, J. O., & Dolan, R. J. (2003). Encoding predictive reward value in human amygdala and orbitofrontal cortex. *Science, 301,* 1104–1108.

Gould, S. J., & Eldredge, N. (1977). Punctuated equilibria. *Paleobiology, 3,* 115–151.

Grattan, L. M., & Eslinger, P. J. (1991). Frontal lobe damage in children and adults. *Developmental Neuropsychology, 7,* 283–326.

Greenough, W. T., Black, J. E., & Wallace, C. S. (1987). Experience and brain development. *Child Development, 58,* 539–559.

Grinvald, A., Slovin, H., & Vanzetta, I. (2000). Non-invasive visualization of cortical columns by fMRI. *Nature Neuroscience, 3,* 105–107.

Grodd, W. (1993). Normal and abnormal patterns of myelin development of the fetal and infantile human brain using magnetic resonance imaging. *Current Opinion in Neurology and Neurosurgery, 6,* 393–397.

Guillaume, P. (1971). *Imitation in children.* Chicago: University of Chicago Press.

Gunnar, M. R. (1992). Reactivity of the hypothalamic-pituitary-adrenocortical system to stressors in normal infants and children. *Pediatrics, 90,* 491–497.

Gunnar, M. R. (1998). Quality of early care and buffering of neuroendocrine stress reactions: Potential effects on the developing human brain. *Preventive Medicine, 27,* 208–211.

Gunnar-vonGnechten, M. (1978). Changing a frightening toy into a pleasant toy by allowing the infant to control its actions. *Developmental Psychology, 14,* 157–162.

Gunturkun, O. (2003). Adult persistence of head turning asymmetry. *Nature, 421,* 711.

Gur, R. C., Gunning-Dixon, F., Bilker, W. B., & Gur, R. E. (2002). Sex differences in temporolimbic and frontal brain volumes of healthy adults. *Cerebral Cortex, 12,* 998–1003.

Haaf, R. A., & Brown, C. J. (1976). Infants' response to face-like patterns. *Journal of Experimental Child Psychology, 22,* 155–160.

Habib, R., McIntosh, A. R., & Wheeler, M. A. (2003). Memory encoding and hippocampally based novelty/familiarity distinctive networks. *Neuropsychologia, 41,* 271–279.

Haith, M. M. (1980). *Rules that babies look by: The organization of newborn visual activity.* Hillsdale, NJ: Lawrence Erlbaum Associates, Inc.

Haith, M. M., Benson, J. B., Roberts, R. J., & Pennington, B. F. (1994). *The development of future oriented processes.* Chicago: University of Chicago Press.

Hala, S., & Russell, J. (2001). Executive control within strategic deception: A window on early cognitive development? *Journal of Experimental Child Psychology, 80,* 112–141.

Hamer, R. D. (1994). The development of motion sensitivity during the first year of life. *Vision Research, 34,* 2387–2402.

Hamm, J. P., Johnson, B. W., & Kirk, I. J. (2002). Comparison of the N300 and N400 ERPs to picture stimuli in congruent and incongruent contexts. *Clinical Neurophysiology, 113,* 1339–1350.

Hammarrenger, B., Lepore, F., Lippe, S., Labrosse, M., Guillemot, J. P., & Roy, M. S. (2003). Magnocellular and parvocellular developmental course in infants during the first year of life. *Documenta Ophthalmologica, 107,* 225–233.

Hanashima, C., Li, S. C., Shen, L., Lai, E., & Fishell, G. (2004). Foxg1 suppresses early cortical cell fate. *Science, 303,* 56–59.

Hariri, A. R., Mattay, V. S., Tessitore, A., Kolachana, B., Fera, F., Goldman, D., et al. (2002). Serotonin transporter genetic variation and the response of the human amygdala. *Science, 297,* 400–403.

Harley, H. E., Putman, E. A., & Roitblat, H. L. (2003). Bottle-nose dolphins perceive object features through echo location. *Nature, 424,* 667–668.

Harlow, H. F. (1973). *Learning to love.* New York: Ballantine.

Harmon, R. J., & Emde, R. N. (1972). Spontaneous REM behaviors in a microcephalic infant. *Perceptual and Motor Skills, 34,* 827–833.

Harper, R. M. (2001). Autonomic control during sleep and risk for sudden death in infancy. *Arch Ital Biol, 139,* 185–194.

Harris, P. L., Kavanaugh, R. D., & Dowson, L. (1997). The depiction of imaginary transformations: Early comprehension of a symbolic function. *Cognitive Development, 12,* 1–19.

Harter, S. (1996). Developmental changes in self transitions. In A. G. Sameroff & M. M. Haith (Eds.), *The five to seven year shift* (pp. 207–236). Chicago: University of Chicago Press.

Hasson, U., Nir, Y., Levy, I., Fuhrmann, G., & Malach, R. (2004). Intersubject synchronization of cortical activity during natural vision. *Science, 303,* 1634–1640.

Hatten, M. E. (2002). New directions in neuronal migration. *Science, 297,* 1660–1663.

Hatten, M. E., & Maron, C. A. (1990). Mechanisms of glial-guided neuronal migration in vivo and in vitro. *Experientia, 46,* 906–916.

Hauk, O., & Pulvermuller, F. (2004). Neurophysiological distinction of action words in the fronto-central cortex. *Human Brain Mapping, 21,* 191–201.

Hauser, M. D., Dehaene, S., Dehaene-Lambertz, G., & Patalano, A. L. (2002). Spontaneous number discrimination of multiformat auditory stimuli in cotton top tamarins. *Cognition, 86,* B23–B32.

Hayakawa, K., Konishi, Y., Matsuda, T., Masanori, K., & Konishi, K. (1989). Development and aging of midline structures: Assessment with MR imaging. *Radiology, 172,* 171–177.

Hekkert, P., Snelders, D., & van Wieringen, P. C. (2003). Most advanced yet acceptable. *British Journal of Psychology, 94,* 111–124.

Hellstrom-Lindahl, E., Gorbounova, O., Seiger, A., Mousavi, M., & Nordberg, A. (1998). Regional distribution of nicotinic receptors during prenatal development of human brain and spinal cord. *Brain Research Developmental Brain Research, 108,* 147–160.

Hellstrom-Lindahl, E., Seiger, A., Kjaeldgaard, A., & Nordberg, A. (2001). Nicotine-induced alterations in the expression of nicotinic receptors in primary cultures from human prenatal brain. *Neuroscience, 105,* 527–534.

Henderson, H. A., Marshall, P. J., Fox, N. A., & Rubin, K. H. (2004). Psychophysiological and behavioral evidence for varying forms and functions of non-social behavior in preschoolers. *Child Development, 75,* 251–263.

Hendrickson, A., & Drucker, D. (1992). The development of parafoveal and mid-peripheral human retina. *Behavioural Brain Research, 49,* 21–31.

Hepper, P. G. (1989). Foetal learning: Implications for psychiatry? *British Journal of Psychiatry, 155,* 289–293.

Hepper, P. G. (1992). Fetal psychology: An embryonic science. In J. G. Nijhuis (Ed.), *Fetal behaviour: Developmental and perinatal aspects* (pp. 129–155). Oxford, England: Oxford University Press.

Hepper, P. G. (1997a). Fetal habituation: Another Pandora's box? *Developmental Medicine and Child Neurology, 39,* 274–278.

Hepper, P. G. (1997b). Memory in utero. *Developmental Medicine and Child Neurology, 39,* 343–346.

Hepper, P. G., McCartney, G. R., & Shannon, E. A. (1998). Lateralised behaviour in first trimester human foetuses. *Neuropsychologia, 36,* 532–534.

Hepper, P. G., & Shahidullah, B. S. (1994). Development of fetal hearing. *Archives of Diseases in Childhood, 71,* F81–87.

Hepper, P. G., Shahidullah, S., & White, R. (1991). Handedness in the human fetus. *Neuropsychologia, 29,* 1107–1111.

Hepper, P. G., Shannon, E. A., & Dornan, J. C. (1997). Sex differences in fetal mouth movements. *Lancet, 350,* 1820.

Hepper, P. G., White, R., & Shahidulla, S. (1991). The development of fetal responsiveness to external auditory stimulation. *British Psychological Society Abstract,* p. 30.

Herbert, M. R., Ziegler, D. A., Makris, N., Filipek, P. A., Kemper, T. L., Normandin, J. J., et al. (in press). *Annals of Neurology.*

Herschkowitz, N., Kagan, J., & Zilles, K. (1997). Neurobiological bases of behavioral development in the first year. *Neuropediatrics, 28,* 296–306.

Herschkowitz, N., Kagan, J., & Zilles, K. (1999). Neurobiological bases of behavior in the second year. *Neuropediatrics, 30,* 221–230.

Hickling, A. K., & Wellman, H. M. (2001). The emergence of children's causal explanations and theories. *Developmental Psychology, 37,* 668–683.

Hildreth, K., & Rovee-Collier, C. (2002). Forgetting functions of reactivated memories over the first year of life. *Developmental Psychology, 41,* 277–288.

Hines, M. (1943). Control of movements by the cerebral cortex in primates. *Biological Reviews, 18,* 18–31.

Hisaoka, S., Harada, M., Nishitani, H., & Mori, K. (2001). Regional magnetic resonance spectroscopy of the brain in autistic individuals. *Neuroradiology, 43,* 496–498.

Hiscock, M., & Kinsbourne, M. (1998). Phylogeny and ontogeny of cerebral lateralization. In R. J. Davidson & K. Hugdahl (Eds.), *Brain asymmetry* (pp. 535–578). Cambridge, MA: MIT Press.

Hoffman, R. (2001). H. O. Silver. *American Scientist, 89*(4), 311.

Hofstra, M., Van Der Ende, J., & Verhulst, F. C. (2002). Child and adolescent problems predict DSM–IV disorders in adulthood. *Journal of the American Academy of Child and Adolescent Psychiatry, 41*, 182–289.

Holland, B., & Gallagher, M. (1999). Amygdala circuitry in attentional and representational processes. *Trends in Cognitive Sciences, 3*, 65–73.

Holland, P. C., Han, J. S., & Winfield, H. M. (2002). Operant and Pavlovian control of visual stimulus orienting and food-related behaviors in rats with lesions of the amygdala central nucleus. *Behavioral Neuroscience, 116*, 577–587.

Holowka, S., & Petitto, L. A. (2002). Left hemisphere cerebral specialization for babies while babbling. *Science, 297*, 1515.

Hood, B., Cole-Davies, V., & Dias, M. (2003). Looking and search measures of object knowledge in preschool children. *Developmental Psychology, 38*, 61–70.

Hopkins, J. R., Kagan, J., Brachfeld, S., Hans, S., & Linn, S. (1976). Infant responsivity to curvature. *Child Development, 47*, 1166–1171.

Hopkins, J. R., Zelazo, P. R., Jacobson, S. W., & Kagan, J. (1976). Infant reactivity to stimulus schema discrepancy. *Genetic Psychology Monographs, 93*, 17–62.

Hoptman, M. J., & Davidson, R. J. (1994). How and why do the two cerebral hemispheres interact? *Psychological Bulletin, 116*, 195–219.

Horowitz, J. L., & Garber, J. (2003). Relation of intelligence and religiosity to depressive disorders in offspring of depressed and nondepressed mothers. *Journal of the American Academy of Child and Adolescent Psychiatry, 42*, 578–586.

Houston, D. M., & Jusczyk, P. W. (2003). Infants' long term memory for the sound patterns of words and voices. *Journal of Experimental Psychology, 19*, 1143–1154.

Hubel, D. H. (1982). Exploration of the primary visual cortex, 1955–1978. *Nature, 299*, 515–524.

Hubel, D. H., & Wiesel, T. N. (1970). The period of susceptibility to the physiological effects of unilateral eye closure in kittens. *Journal of Physiology, 206*, 419–436.

Hudson, R., & Distel, H. (1999). The flavor of life: Perinatal development of odor and taste preferences. *Schweizerische Medizinische Wochenschrift, 129*, 176–181.

Hunot, S., & Flavell, R. A. (2001). Death of a monopoly. *Science, 292*, 865–866.

Hutson, M. R., & Kirby, M. L. (2003). Neural crest and cardiovascular development. *Birth Defects Research, 69*, 2–13.

Huttenlocher, P. R. (1974). Dendritic development in neocortex of children with mental defect and infantile spasms. *Neurology, 24*, 203–210.

Huttenlocher, P. R. (1979). Synaptic density in human frontal cortex: Developmental changes and effects of aging. *Brain Research, 163*, 195–205.

Huttenlocher, P. R. (1990). Morphometric study of human cerebral cortex development. *Neuropsychologia, 28*, 517–527.

Huttenlocher, P. R. (1994). Synaptogenesis, synapse elimination and neural plasticity in human cerebral cortex. In C. A. Nelson (Ed.), *Threats to optimal development* (pp. 35–54). Hillsdale, NJ: Lawrence Erlbaum Associates, Inc.

Huttenlocher, P. R., & Dabholkar, A. S. (1997). Regional differences in synaptogenesis in human cerebral cortex. *Journal of Comparative Neurology, 387*, 167–178.

Huttenlocher, P. R., deCourten, C., Garey, L. J., & van der Loos, H. (1982). Synaptogenesis in human visual cortex—Evidence for synapse elimination during normal development. *Neuroscience Letters, 33*, 247–252.

Iannetti, P., Spalice, A., Atzei, G., Boemi, S., & Trasimeni, G. (1996). Neuronal migrational disorders in children with epilepsy: MRI, interictal SPECT and EEG comparisons. *Brain and Development, 18,* 269–279.

Ishigaki, H., & Miyao, M. (1994). Implications for dynamic visual acuity with changes in age and sex. *Perceptual and Motor Skills, 78,* 363–369.

Ivry, R. B., & Robertson, L. C. (1998). *The two sides of perception.* Cambridge, MA: MIT Press.

Jackendoff, R. (2002). *Foundations of language.* New York: Oxford University Press.

Jacobs, B., Schall, M., & Scheibel, A. B. (1993). A quantitative dendritic analysis of Wernicke's area in humans. II. Gender, hemispheric, and environmental factors. *Journal of Comparative Neurology, 327,* 97–111.

Jacobs, B., & Scheibel, A. B. (1993). A quantitative dendritic analysis of Wernicke's area in humans. I. Life span changes. *Journal of Comparative Neurology, 327,* 83–96.

Jessell, T. M., & Sanes, J. R. (2000). Development: The decade of the developing brain. *Current Opinion in Neurobiology, 10,* 599–611.

John, E. R. (2003). A theory of consciousness. *Current Directions in Psychological Science, 12,* 244–250.

Johnson, M. H. (1996). The development of temporal dynamics of spatial orienting in infants. *Journal of Experimental Child Psychology, 63,* 171–188.

Johnson, M. H. (2000a). Functional brain development in infants: Elements of an interactive specialization framework. *Child Development, 71,* 75–81.

Johnson, M. H. (2000b). Cortical specialization for higher cognitive functions: Beyond the maturational model. *Brain and Cognition, 42,* 124–127.

Johnson, M. H. (2003). Development of human brain functions. *Biological Psychiatry, 54,* 1312–1316.

Johnston, M. V., & Singer, H. S. (1982). Brain neurotransmitters and neuromodulators in pediatrics. *Pediatrics, 70,* 57–68.

Johnston, V. S., & Chesney, G. L. (1974). Electrophysiological correlates of meaning. *Science, 186,* 944–946.

Jones, R. B., Mills, A. D., Faure, J. M., & Williams, J. B. (1994). Restraint, fear and distress in Japanese quail genetically selected for long or short tonic immobility reactions. *Physiology and Behavior, 56,* 529–534.

Jones, S. S. (1996). Imitation or exploration? *Child Development, 62,* 1952–1969.

Judas, M. (1987). *Perinatal cytoarchitectonical development in the prospective motor speech area.* Unpublished manuscript, Zagreb, University of Zagreb.

Jürgens, U. (1986). The squirrel monkey as an experimental model in the study of cerebral organization of emotional vocal utterances. *European Archives of Psychiatry and Neurological Sciences, 236,* 40–43.

Kadosh, C., Henik, A., Rubinstein, O., Dori, D. Y. B., Mohr, H., van de Ven, V., et al. (2003, March). Are numbers special? Paper presented at the tenth meeting of the Cognitive Neuroscience Society, March 30–April 1.

Kagan, J. (1976). Emergent themes in human development. *American Scientist, 64,* 186–196.

Kagan, J. (1981). *The second year.* Cambridge, MA: Harvard University Press.

Kagan, J. (1984). *The nature of the child.* New York: Basic Books.

Kagan, J. (1994). *Galen's prophecy.* New York: Basic Books.

Kagan, J., Arcus, D., Snidman, N., Yufeng, W., Hendler, J., & Green, S. (1994). Reactivity in infants: A cross-national comparison. *Developmental Psychology, 30,* 342–345.

Kagan, J., & Hamburg, M. (1981). The enhancement of memory in the first year. *Journal of Genetic Psychology, 138,* 3–14.

Kagan, J., Henker, B. A., Hen-tov, A., Levine, J., & Lewis, M. (1966). Infants' differential reactions to familiar and distorted faces. *Child Development, 37,* 519–532.

Kagan, J., Klein, R. E., Finley, C. E., Rogoff, B., & Nolan, E. (1979). A cross-cultural study of cognitive development. *Monographs of the Society for Research in Child Development, 44,* 1–66.

Kagan, J., Linn, S., Mount, R., & Reznick, J. S. (1979). Asymmetry of inference and the dishabituation paradigm. *Canadian Journal of Psychology, 33,* 288–304.

Kagan, J., & Snidman, N. (2004). *The long shadow of temperament.* Cambridge, MA: Harvard University Press.

Kagan, J., Snidman, N., Zentner, M., & Peterson, E. (1999). Infant temperament and anxious symptoms in school age children. *Development and Psychopathology, 11,* 209–224.

Kahana-Kalman, R., & Walker-Andrews, A. S. (2001). The role of person familiarity in young infants' perception of emotional expressions. *Child Development, 72,* 352–369.

Kalaria, R. N., Fiedler, C., Hunsaker, J. C. I., & Sparks, D. L. (1993). Synaptic neurochemistry of human striatum during development: Changes in SIDS. *Journal of Neurochemistry, 60,* 2098–2105.

Kaldy, Z., & Kovacs, I. (2003). Visual context integration is not fully developed in 4-year-old children. *Perception, 32,* 657–666.

Kalin, N. H., & Shelton, S. E. (1989). Defensive behavior in infant rhesus monkeys: Environmental cues and neurochemical regulation. *Science, 243,* 1718–1721.

Kalin, N. H., Shelton, S. E., & Barksdale, C. M. (1989). Behavioral and physiologic effects of CRH administered to infant primates undergoing maternal separation. *Neuropsychopharmacology, 2,* 97–104.

Kalin, N. H., Shelton, S. E., & Snowdon, C. T. (1992). Affiliative vocalizations in infant rhesus macaques. *Journal of Comparative Psychology, 106,* 254–261.

Kalin, N. H., Shelton, S. E., & Takahashi, L. K. (1991). Defensive behaviors in infant rhesus monkeys: Ontogeny and context-dependent selective expression. *Child Development, 62,* 1175–1183.

Kandel, E. R. (1995). *Essentials of neural science and behavior.* Norwalk, CT: Appleton & Lange.

Kandel, E. R. (2001). The molecular biology of memory storage: A dialogue between genes and synapses. *Science, 294,* 1030–1038.

Kanemura, H., Aihara, M., Aoki, S., Araki, T., & Nakazawa, S. (2003). Development of the prefrontal lobe in infants and young children. *Brain and Development, 25,* 195–199.

Kanold, P. O., Kara, P., Reid, R. C., & Shatz, C. J. (2003). Role of subplate neurons in functional maturation of visual cortical columns. *Science, 301,* 521–525.

Kates, W. R., Mostofsky, S., Zimmerman, A. W., Mazzocco, M. M., Landa, R., Warsofsky, I. S., et al. (1998). Neuroanatomical and neurocognitive differences in a pair of monozygous twins discordant for strictly defined autism. *Annals of Neurology, 43,* 782–791.

Katz, L. C., & Shatz, C. J. (1996). Synaptic activity and the construction of cortical circuits. *Science, 274,* 1133–1138.

Kawabata, H., Gyoba, J., Inoue, H., & Ohtsubo, H. (2001). Connectivity perception of partly occluded gratings in 4-month-old infants. *Perception, 30,* 867–874.

Kawai, N., Morokuma, S., Tomonaga, M., Horimoto, N., & Tanaka, M. (2004). Associative learning and memory in a chimpanzee fetus. *Developmental Psychobiology, 44,* 116–122.

Kearsley, R. B. (1970). Unpublished manuscript.

Keating, C., & Keating, E. G. (1993). Monkeys and mug shots. *Journal of Comparative Psychology, 107,* 131–139.

Kellman, P. J., & Spelke, E. S. (1983). Perception of partially occluded objects in infants. *Cognitive Psychology, 15,* 483–524.

Kemeny, M. E. (2003). The psychobiology of stress. *Current Directions in Psychological Science, 12,* 124–129.

Kenet, T., Bibtchkov, D., Tsodyks, M., Grinvald, A., & Arieli, A. (2003). Spontaneously emerging cortical representations of visual attributes. *Nature, 425,* 954–956.

Kennard, M. A., Viets, H. R., & Fulton, J. F. (1934). The syndrome of premotor cortex in man. Impairment of skilled movements, forced grasping, spasticity and vasomotor disturbance. *Brain, 57,* 69–84.

Kennaway, D. J., Goble, F. C., & Stamp, G. E. (1996). Factors influencing the development of melatonin rhythmicity in humans. *Journal of Clinical Endocrinology and Metabolism, 81,* 1525–1532.

Kiehl, K. A., & Liddle, P. F. (2003). Reproducibility of the hemodynamic response to auditory oddball stimuli. *Human Brain Mapping, 18,* 42–52.

Kim, K. H. S., Relkin, N. R., Lee, K. M., & Hirsch, J. (1997). Distinct cortical areas associated with native and second languages. *Nature, 388,* 171–174.

Kinney, H. C., Brody, B. A., Kloman, A. S., & Gilles, F. (1988). Sequence of central nervous system myelination in human infancy. *Journal of Neuropathology and Experimental Neurology, 47,* 217–234.

Kinney, H. C., McHugh, T., Miller, K., Belliveau, R. A., & Assmann, S. F. (2002). Subtle developmental abnormalities in the inferior olive: An indicator of prenatal brainstem injury in the sudden infant death syndrome. *Journal of Neuropathology and Experimental Neurology, 61,* 427–441.

Kippin, T. E., Cain, S. W., & Pfaus, J. G. (2003). Estrous odors and sexually conditioned novel odors activate separate neural pathways in the male rat. *Neuroscience, 117,* 971–979.

Kluger, A. N., Siegfried, Z., & Ebstein, R. P. (2002). A meta-analysis of the association between DRD4 polymorphism and novelty seeking. *Molecular Psychiatry, 7,* 712–717.

Knight, R. T. (1996). Contribution of the human hippocampal region to novelty detection. *Nature, 383,* 256–259.

Koening, M. A., & Echols, C. H. (2003). Infants' understanding of false labelling of events. *Cognition, 87,* 179–201.

Koivisto, M., & Revonsuo, A. (2003). Interhemispheric categorization of pictures and words. *Brain and Cognition, 52,* 181–191.

Kornhuber, J., Mack-Burkhardt, F., Konradi, C., Fritze, J., & Riederer, P. (1989). Effect of antemortem and postmortem factors in (3H) MK-801 binding in the human brain: Transient elevation during early childhood. *Life Sciences, 45,* 745–749.

Kostovic, I. (1987). Late postnatal development of acetylcholinesterase-reactive innervation of layer III pyramidal neurons in human prefrontal cortex. *Neuroscience, 22,* S228.

Kostovic, I. (1990). Structural and histochemical reorganization of the human prefrontal cortex during perinatal and postnatal life. *Progress in Brain Research, 85,* 223–240.

Kostovic, I., Skavic, J., & Strinovic, D. (1988). Acetylcholinesterase in the human frontal associative cortex during the period of cognitive development: Early laminar shifts and late innervation of pyramidal neurons. *Neuroscience Letters, 90,* 107–112.

Kotsoni, E., de Haan, M., & Johnson, M. H. (2001). Categorical perception of facial expressions by 7-month-old infants. *Perception, 30,* 1115–1123.

Kretschman, H. J., Kammradt, G., Krauthausen, I., & Sauer, B. (1986). Growth of the hippocampal formation in man. *Bibliotheca Anatomica, 28,* 27–52.

Kringelbach, M. L., O'Doherty, J. O., Rolls, E. T., & Andrews, C. (2003). Activation of the human orbitofrontal cortex to a liquid food stimulus is correlated with its subjective pleasantness. *Cerebral Cortex, 113,* 1064–1071.

Kubota, K., & Niki, H. (1971). Prefrontal cortical activity and delayed alternation performance in monkeys. *Journal of Neurophysiology, 34,* 337–347.

Kuenne, M. (1946). Experimental investigation of the relation of language to transposition behavior in young children. *Journal of Experimental Psychology, 36,* 471–490.

Kuhl, P. K. (1991). Human adults and human infants show a perceptual magnet effect for the prototypes of speech categories; monkeys do not. *Perception and Psychophysics, 50,* 93–107.

Kuhl, P. K. (1993). Innate predispositions and the effects of experience in speech perception. In B. D. Boysson-Bardies, S. D. Schoen, P. W. Jusczyk, P. McNeilage, & J. Norton (Eds.), *Developmental neurocognition* (pp. 259–274). Dordrecht, The Netherlands: Kluwer.

Kuhn, T. S. (2000). *The road since structure.* Chicago: University of Chicago Press.

Kumakira, C., Kodama, K., Shimizu, E., Yamanouchi, N., Okada, S., Noda, S., et al. (1999). Study of the association between the serotonin transporter gene regulating region polymorphism and personality traits in the Japanese population. *Neuroscience Letters, 263,* 205–207.

Kushnerenko, E., Ceponiene, R., Balan, P., Fellman, V., & Naatanen, R. (2002). Maturation of the auditory change detection response in infants. *Neuroreport, 13,* 1843–1848.

Kushnerenko, E., Ceponiene, R., Fellman, V., Huotilainen, M., & Winkler, I. (2001). Event related potential correlates of sound duration. *Neuroreport, 12,* 3777–3781.

Kushnerenko, E., Cheour, M., Ceponiene, R., Fellman, V., Renlund, M., Soininen, K., et al. (2001). Central auditory processing of duration changes in complex speech patterns by newborns. *Developmental Neuropsychology, 19,* 83–97.

Kuypers, H. G. J. M., & Lawrence, D. G. (1967). Cortical projections to the red nucleus and the brain stem in the rhesus monkey. *Brain Research, 4,* 151–188.

La Bar, K. S., Crupain, M. J., Voyvodic, J. T., & McCarthy, G. (2003). Dynamic perception of facial affect and identity in the human brain. *Cerebral Cortex, 13,* 1023–1033.

LaBar, K. S., Gatenby, C., & Gore, J. C. (1998). Human amygdala activation during conditioned fear acquisition and extinction. *Neuron, 29,* 937–945.

LaGasse, L., Gruber, C., & Lipsitt, L. P. (1989). The infantile expression of avidity in relation to later assessments. In J. S. Reznick (Ed.), *Perspectives on behavioral inhibition* (pp. 159–176). Chicago: University of Chicago Press.

Lagercrantz, H., & Ringstedt, T. (2001). Organization of the neuronal circuits in the central nervous system during development. *Acta Paediatrica, 90,* 707–715.

Lagerqvist, P. (1971). *The eternal smile* (E. Mesterton, Trans.). New York: Hill & Wang.

Lakatos, K., Nemoda, Z., Birkas, E., Ronai, Z., & Kovacs, E. (2003). Association of D4 dopamine receptor gene and serotonin transporter promoter polymorphisms with infants' response to novelty. *Molecular Psychiatry, 8,* 90–97.

Landau, B., Smith, L. B., & Jones, S. S. (1988). The importance of shape in early lexical learning. *Cognitive Development, 3,* 299–321.

Larson, M. C., White, B. P., Cochran, A., Donzella, B., & Gunnar, M. R. (1998). Dampening of the cortisol response to handling at 3 months in human infants and its relation to sleep, circadian cortisol activity, and behavioral distress. *Developmental Psychobiology, 33,* 327–337.

Lau, H. C., Roger, R. D., Haggard, P., & Passingham, R. E. (2004). Attention to intention. *Science, 303,* 1208–1210.

Lauder, J. M. (1983). Hormonal and humoral influences on brain development. *Psychoneuroendocrinology, 8,* 121–155.

Lavdas, A. A., Grigoriou, M., Pachnis, V., & Parnavelas, J. G. (1999). The medial ganglionic eminence gives rise to a population of early neurons in the developing cerebral cortex. *Journal of Neuroscience, 99,* 7881–7888.

Lavelli, M., & Fogel, A. (2002). Developmental changes in mother–infant face-to-face communication: Birth to 3 months. *Developmental Psychology, 38,* 288–305.

Lavigne-Rebillard, M., & Pujol, R. (1990). Auditory hair cells in human fetuses: Synaptogenesis and ciliogenesis. *Journal of Electron Microscopy Technique, 15,* 115–122.

Lawrence, D. G., & Hopkins, D. A. (1976). The development of motor control in the rhesus monkey: Evidence concerning the role of corticomotoneuronal connections. *Brain, 99,* 235–524.

Learmonth, A. E., Nadel, L., & Newcombe, N. S. (2002). Children's use of landmarks. *Psychological Science, 13,* 337–341.

Lecanuet, J.-P., & Schaal, B. (1996). Fetal sensory competencies. *European Journal of Obstetrics & Gynecology and Reproductive Biology, 68,* 1–23.

LeDoux, J. C. (1996). *The emotional brain.* New York: Simon & Schuster.

Lemelson, R. (2003). Obsessive–compulsive disorder in Bali. *Transcultural Psychiatry, 40,* 377–408.

Letinic, K., Zoncu, R., & Rakic, P. (2002). Origin of GABAergic neurons in the human neocortex. *Nature, 417,* 645–649.

LeVay, S., Wiesel, T. N., & Hubel, D. H. (1980). The development of ocular dominance columns in normal and visually deprived monkeys. *Journal of Comparative Neurology, 191,* 1–51.

Levine, L., Grossfield, J., & Rockwell, R. F. (1979). Functional relationships between genotypes and environments in behavior. *Journal of Heredity, 70,* 317–320.

Levine, R. V. (2003). The kindness of strangers. *The American Scientist, 91,* 226–233.

Levitt, J. G., Blanton, R. E., Smalley, S., Thompson, P. M., Guthrie, D., McCracken, J. T., et al. (2003). Cortical sulcal maps in autism. *Cerebral Cortex, 13,* 728–735.

Lewis, M. (1992). Individual differences in response to stress. *Pediatrics, 90,* 487–490.

Lewis, M., & Brooks-Gunn, J. (1979). *Social cognition and the acquisition of self.* New York: Plenum.

Li, X., & Borjigin, J. (1998). Molecular rhythms in the pineal gland. *Current Opinion in Neurobiology, 8,* 648–651.

Lieberman, H. R. (1986). Behavior, sleep and melatonin. *Journal of Neural Transmission, 21,* 233–241.

Lieberman, P. (2002). On the nature and evolution of the neural bases of human language. *Yearbook of Physical Anthropology, 45,* 36–62.

Littenberg, R., Tulkin, S. R., & Kagan, J. (1971). Cognitive components of separation anxiety. *Developmental Psychology, 4,* 387–388.

Locke, J. L. (1990). Structure and stimulation in the ontogeny of spoken language. *Developmental Psychobiology, 23,* 621–643.

Lohaus, A., Keller, H., & Voelker, S. (2001). Relationships between eye contact, maternal sensitivity, and infant crying. *International Journal of Behavioral Development, 25,* 542–548.

Loken, E., Leichtman, M., D., & Kagan, J. (2002). *Integration of past and present.* Unpublished manuscript.

Lotspeich, L. J., & Ciaranello, R. D. (1993). The neurobiology and genetics of infantile autism. *International Review of Neurobiology, 35,* 87–129.

Low, A., Bentin, S., Rockstroh, B., Silberman, Y., & Gomolla, A. (2003). Semantic categories in the human brain. *Psychological Science, 14,* 367–372.

Luppino, G., Matelli, M., Camarda, R., & Rizzolatti, G. (1993). Corticocortical connections of area F3 (SMA-proper) and area F6 (pre-SMA) in the macaque monkey. *Journal of Comparative Neurology, 338,* 114–140.

Luyendijk, W., & Treffers, P. D. A. (1992). The smile in anencephalic infants. *Clinical Neurology and Neurosurgery, 94,* 113–117.

Macchi, V., Snenghi, R., De Caro, R., & Parenti, A. (2002). Monolateral hypoplasia of the motor vagal nuclei in a case of sudden infant death syndrome. *Journal of Anatomy, 200,* 195–198.

Madras, B. K., Miller, G. M., & Fischman, A. J. (2002). The dopamine transporter: Relevance to attention deficit hyperactivity disorder (ADHD). *Behavioural Brain Research, 130,* 57–63.

Maestripieri, D., Ross, S. K., & Megna, N. L. (2002). Mother–infant interactions in western Lowland Gorillas (gorilla gorilla gorilla): Spatial relationships, communication, and opportunities for social learning. *Journal of Comparative Psychology, 116,* 219–227.

Maestro, S., Muratori, F., Cavallaro, M., Pei, F., & Stern, D. (2002). Attentional skills during the first 6 months of age in autistic spectrum disorder. *Journal of the American Academy of Child and Adolescent Psychiatry, 41,* 1239–1245.

Manning, J. T. (2002). The ratio of the second to the fourth digit length and performance in skiing. *Journal of Sports Medicine and Physical Fitness, 42,* 446–450.

Manuck, S. B., Kaplan, J. R., Rymeski, B. A., Fairbanks, L. A., & Wilson, M. E. (2003). Approach to a social stranger is associated with low central nervous system serotonergic responsivity in female cynomolgus monkeys (macaca fasicularis). *American Journal of Primatology, 61,* 187–194.

Marchleska-koj, A., Kruczek, M., Kaposta, J., & Pochron, E. (2003). Prenatal stress affects rate of sexual maturation and attractiveness in bank voles. *Physiology and Behavior, 79,* 305–316.

Marcus, G. F. (1996). Why do children say "breaked"? *Current Directions in Psychological Science, 5,* 81–85.

Marcus, G. F., Vijayan, S., Rao, S. B., & Vishton, P. M. (1999). Rule learning by seven-month-old infants. *Science, 283,* 77–80.

Mareschal, D., Powell, D., & Valein, A. (2003). Basic level category discriminations by 7- and 9-month old infants in an object exploration test. *Journal of Experimental Child Psychology, 86,* 87–107.

Marinkovic, K., Dhond, R. P., Dale, A. M., Glessner, M., Carr, V., & Halgren, E. (2003). Spatiotemporal dynamics of modality-specific and supramodal word processing. *Neuron, 38,* 487–497.

Marin-Padilla, M. (1970a). Prenatal and early postnatal ontogenesis of the human motor cortex II. The basket-pyramidal system. *Brain Research, 23,* 185–191.

Marin-Padilla, M. (1970b). Prenatal and early postnatal ontogenesis of the human motor cortex 1. The sequential development of cortical layers. *Brain Research, 23,* 167–183.

Marin-Padilla, M. (1990). Three-dimensional structural organization of layer I of the human cerebral cortex: A Golgi study. *Journal of Comparative Neurology, 299,* 89–105.

Marin-Teva, J. L., Dusart, I., Colin, C., Gervais, A., van Rooijen, N., & Mallat, M. (2004). Microglia promote the death of developing Purkinje cells. *Neuron, 41,* 535–547.

Markman, E. M. (1992). Constraints on word learning: Speculations about their nature, origins, and domain specificity. In M. R. Gunnar & M. Maratsos (Eds.), *Modularity and constraints in language and cognition* (Vol. 25, pp. 59–102). Hillsdale, NJ: Lawrence Erlbaum Associates, Inc.

Markman, E. M., Wasow, J. L., & Hanson, M. B. (2003). Use of the mutual exclusivity assumption by young word learners. *Journal of Experimental Child Psychology, 47,* 241–275.

Marlowe, W. B. (1992). The impact of a right prefrontal lesion on the developing brain. *Brain and Cognition, 20,* 205–213.

Marquez, C., Nadal, R., & Armario, A. (2004). The hypothalamic-pituitary-adrenal and glucose responses to daily repeated immobilisation stress in rats. *Neuroscience, 123,* 601–612.

Marrocco, R. T. (1994). Arousal systems. *Current Opinion in Neurobiology, 4,* 166–170.

Martin, E., Joeri, P., Loenneker, T., Ekatodramis, D., Vitacco, D., Hennig, J., et al. (1999). Visual processing in infants and children studied using functional MRI. *Pediatric Research, 46,* 135–140.

Martin, K. C., & Kosik, K. S. (2002). Synaptic tagging—Who's it? *Nature Reviews Neuroscience, 3,* 813–820.

Martin, R. C. (2003). Language processing. In S. T. Fiske, D. L. Schacter, & C. Zahn-Waxler (Eds.), *Annual review of psychology, vol. 54* (pp. 55–89). Palo Alto, CA: Annual Reviews.

Mason, M. F., Banfield, J. F., & Macrae, C. N. (2004). Thinking about actions. *Cerebral Cortex, 14,* 209–214.

Mason, W. A. (1960). The effects of social restriction on the behavior of rhesus monkeys: I. Free social behavior. *Journal of Comparative Physiology and Psychology, 53,* 582–589.

Matelli, M., Luppino, G., & Rizzolatti, G. (1991). Architecture of superior and mesial area 6 and the adjacent cingulate cortex in the macaque monkey. *Journal of Comparative Neurology, 311,* 445–462.

Matturri, L., Biondo, B., Suarez-Mier, M. P., & Rossi, L. (2002). Brain stem lesions in the sudden infant death syndrome: Variability in the hypoplasia of the arcuate nucleus. *Acta Neuropatholologica (Berlin), 104,* 12–20.

Maurer, D., & Barrera, M. (1981). Infants' perception of natural and distorted arrangements of a schematic face. *Child Development, 52,* 197.

Mayberry, R. I., Lock, E., & Kazmi, H. (2002). Linguistic ability and early language exposure. *Nature, 417,* 38.

Mayeaux, D. J., Mason, W. A., & Mendoza, S. P. (2002). Developmental changes in responsiveness to parents and unfamiliar adults in a monogamous monkey (callicebus moloch). *American Journal of Primatology, 58,* 71–89.

McCartney, G., & Hepper, P. (1999). Development of lateralized behavior in the human fetus from 12 to 27 weeks' gestation. *Developmental Medicine and Child Neurology, 41,* 83–86.

McConnell, S. (1992). Perspectives on early brain development and the epilepsies. In J. Engel, Jr., C. Wasterlain, E. A. Cavalheiro, U. Heinemann, & G. Avanzini (Eds.), *Molecular neurobiology of epilepsy* (Supp. 9, pp. 183–191). Amsterdam: Elsevier Science.

McDonald, J. W., & Johnston, M. V. (1990). Physiological and pathophysiological roles of excitatory amino acids during central nervous system development. *Brain Research: Brain Research Reviews, 15,* 41–70.

McEwen, B. S. (1987). External factors influencing brain development. *NIDA Research Monograph Series, 78,* 1–14.

McKee, R. D., & Squire, L. R. (1993). On the development of declarative memory. *Journal of Experimental Psychology: Learning, Memory, and Cognition, 19,* 397–404.

McKeough, A., & Genereux, R. (2003). Transformation in narrative thought during adolescence: The structure and content of story compositions. *Journal of Educational Psychology, 95,* 537–552.

Mead, G. H. (1934). *Mind, self, and society.* Chicago: University of Chicago Press.

Meister, M., Wong, R. O., Baylor, D. A., & Shatz, C. J. (1991). Synchronous bursts of action potentials in ganglion cells of the developing mammalian retina. *Science, 252,* 939–943.

Meltzoff, A. N., & Moore, M. K. (1977). Imitation of facial and manual gestures by the human neonate. *Science, 198,* 75–78.

Melzer, D., Fryers, T., Jenkins, R., Brugha, T., & McWilliams, B. (2003). Social position and the common mental disorders with disability. *Social Psychiatry and Psychiatric Epidemiology, 38,* 238–243.

Meng, S. Z., Obonai, T., & Takashima, S. (1998). A developmental study of the dopamine D2R receptors in the human ganglia and thalamus. *Early Human Development, 51,* 23–30.

Meng, S. Z., Ozawa, Y., Itoh, M., & Takashima, S. (1999). Developmental and age-related changes of dopamine transporter, and dopamine D1 and D2 receptors in human basal ganglia. *Brain Research, 843,* 136–144.

Mercier, S. F., Canini, B. A., Cespuglio, R., Martin, S., & Bourdon, L. (2003). Behavioral changes after an acute stress. *Behavioural Brain Research, 139,* 167–175.

Meredith, M. A., & Stein, B. E. (1986). Visual, auditory, and somatosensory convergence on cells in superior colliculus results in multisensory integration. *Journal of Neurophysiology, 56,* 640–662.

Merritt, M. M., Bennett, G. G., Williams, R. B., Sollers, J. J., & Thayer, J. F. (2004). Low educational attainment, John Henryism, and cardiovascular reactivity to and recovery from personally relevant stress. *Psychosomatic Medicine, 66,* 49–55.

Mesulam, M. M. (1990). Large-scale neurocognitive networks and distributed processing for attention, language, and memory. *Annals of Neurology, 28,* 597–613.

Mesulam, M. M., & Geula, C. (1988). Acetylcholinesterase-rich pyramidal neurons in the human neocortex and hippocampus: Absence at birth, development during the life span, and dissolution in Alzheimer's disease. *Annals of Neurology, 24,* 765–773.

Mesulam, M. M., & Geula, C. (1991). Acetylcholinesterase-rich neurons of the human cerebral cortex: Cytoarchitectonic and ontogenetic patterns. *Journal of Comparative Neurology, 306,* 193–220.

Meyer, M., Alter, K., Friederici, A. D., Lohmann, B., & von Cramon, D. Y. (2002). fMRI reveals brain regions mediating slow prosodic modulations in spoken sentences. *Human Brain Mapping, 17,* 73–88.

Michel, A. E., & Garey, L. J. (1984). The development of dendritic spines in the human visual cortex. *Human Neurobiology, 3,* 223–227.

Mihajlovic, P., & Zecevic, N. (1986). Development of the human dentate nucleus. *Human Neurobiology, 5,* 189–197.

Milgram, S. (1974). *Obedience to authority.* New York: Harper & Row.

Miller, E. K., & Cohen, J. D. (2001). An integrative theory of prefrontal cortex function. *Annual Review of Neuroscience, 24,* 167–202.

Miller, G. (2002). Gene's effect seen in brain's fear response. *Science, 297,* 319.

Miller, G. M., De La Garza, R. D., Novak, M. A., & Madras, B. K. (2001). Single nucleotide polymorphisms distinguish multiple dopamine transporter alleles in primates: Implications for association with attention deficit hyperactivity disorder and other neuropsychiatric disorders. *Molecular Psychiatry, 6,* 50–58.

Miller, G. M., & Madras, B. K. (2002). Polymorphisms in the 3'-untranslated region of human and monkey dopamine transporter genes affect reporter gene expression. *Molecular Psychiatry, 7,* 44–55.

Mills, D. L., Coffey-Corina, S., & Neville, H. J. (1997). Language comprehension and cerebral localization from 13 to 20 months. *Developmental Neuropsychology, 13,* 397–446.

Minshew, N. J., Goldstein, G., Dombrowski, S. M., Panchalingam, K., & Pettegrew, J. W. (1993). A preliminary 31P MRS study of autism: Evidence for undersynthesis and increased degradation of brain membranes. *Biological Psychiatry, 33,* 762–773.

Minshew, N. J., Pettegrew, J. W., Payton, J. B., & Panchalingam, K. (1989). Metabolic alterations in the dorsal prefrontal cortex of autistic patients with normal IQ. *Annals of Neurology, 26,* 438.

Minugh-Purvis, N., & McNamara, K. J. (Eds.). (2002). *Human evolution through developmental change.* Baltimore: Johns Hopkins University Press.

Mix, K. S., Huttenlocher, J., & Levine, S. C. (2002). Multiple cues for quantification in infancy. *Psychological Bulletin, 128,* 278–294.

Miyawaki, T., Goodchild, A. K., & Pilowsky, P. M. (2002). Activation of mu-opioid receptors in rat ventrolateral medulla selectively blocks baroreceptor reflexes while activation of delta opioid receptors blocks somato-sympathetic reflexes. *Neuroscience, 109,* 133–144.

Molfese, D. L., & Molfese, V. J. (1985). Electrophysiological indices of auditory discrimination in newborn infants: The bases for predicting later language development? *Infant Behavior and Development, 8,* 197–211.

Molfese, D. L., Morse, P. A., & Peters, C. J. (1990). Auditory evoked responses to names for different objects: Cross-modal processing as a basis for infant language acquisition. *Developmental Psychology, 26,* 780–795.

Monk, C. S., & Webb, S. J. (2001). Prenatal neurobiological development: Molecular mechanisms and anatomical change. *Developmental Neuropsychology, 19,* 211–236.

Mooney, R., Penn, A. A., Gallego, R., & Shatz, C. J. (1996). Thalamic relay of spontaneous retinal activity prior to vision. *Neuron, 17,* 863–874.

Moore, C., & Corkum, V. (1998). Infant gaze following based on eye direction. *British Journal of Developmental Psychology, 16,* 495–503.

Moore, D. S. (1988). *Auditory and visual integration in very young infants.* Unpublished doctoral dissertation, Harvard University, Cambridge, MA.

Moore, J. K., & Guan, Y. L. (1998). MAP2 expression in developing dendrites of human brainstem auditory neurons. *Journal of Chemical Neuroanatomy, 16,* 1–15.

Moore, J. K., Perazzo, L. M., & Braun, A. (1995). Time course of axonal myelination in the human brainstem auditory pathway. *Hearing Research, 87,* 21–31.

Morrongiello, B. A., Lasenby, J., & Lee, N. (2003). Infants' learning, memory, and generalization of learning for bimodal events. *Journal of Experimental Child Psychology, 84,* 1–19.

Moster, D., Lie, R. T., Irgens, L. M., Bjerkedal, T., & Markestad, T. (2001). The association of Apgar score with subsequent death and cerebral palsy; a population-based study in term infants. *Journal of Pediatrics, 138,* 798–803.

Mrzljak, L., Uylings, H. B., Van Eden, C. G., & Judas, M. (1990). Neuronal development in human prefrontal cortex in prenatal and postnatal stages. *Progress in Brain Research, 85,* 185–222.

Mrzljak, L., Uylings, H. B. H., Kostovic, I., & Van Eden, C. G. (1988). Prenatal development of neurons in the prefrontal cortex. *Journal of Comparative Neurology, 271,* 355–386.

Mrzljak, L., Uylings, H. B. H., Kostovic, I., & Van Eden, C. G. (1992). Prenatal development of neurons in the prefrontal cortex II. *Journal of Comparative Neurology, 316,* 485–486.

Mumme, D. L., & Fernald, A. (2003). The infant as onlooker. *Child Development, 74,* 221–237.

Murayama, K., Meeker, R. B., Murayama, S., & Greenwood, R. S. (1993). Developmental expression of vasopressin in the human hypothalamus: Double-labeling with *in situ* hybridization and immunocytochemistry. *Pediatric Research, 33,* 152–158.

Murdock, G. P. (1945). The common denominator of cultures. In R. Linton (Ed.), *The science of man in the world crisis* (pp. 110–128). New York: Columbia University Press.

Murphy, B. L., Arnsten, A. F. T., Goldman-Rakic, P. S., & Roth, R. H. (1996). Increased dopamine turnover in the prefrontal cortex impairs spatial working memory performance. *Proceedings of the National Academy of Sciences, USA, 1325,* 1329.

Nadarajah, B., & Parnavelas, J. G. (2002). Modes of neuronal migration in the developing cerebral cortex. *Nature Reviews Neuroscience, 3,* 423–432.

Naigles, L. R., & Hoff-Ginsberg, E. (1998). Why are some verbs learned before other verbs? *Journal of Child Language, 25,* 95–125.

Nakagawa, A., Sukigara, M., & Benga, A. (2003). The temporal relationship between reduction of early imitative responses in the development of attention mechanisms. *BMC Neuroscience, 4,* 33–50.

Namy, L. L., & Gentner, D. (2002). Making a silk purse out of two sows' ears. *Journal of Experimental Psychology: General, 131,* 5–15.

Namy, L. L., & Waxman, S. R. (1998). Words and gestures. *Child Development, 69,* 295–308.

Nelson, E. E., Shelton, S. E., & Kalin, N. H. (2003). Individual differences in the responses of naive rhesus monkeys to snakes. *Emotion, 3,* 3–11.

Nelson, K. (1996). Memory development from 4 to 7 years. In A. G. Sameroff & M. M. Haith (Eds.), *The five to seven year shift* (pp. 141–160). Chicago: University of Chicago Press.

Nelson, K. B., Grether, J. K., Croen, L. A., Dambrosia, J. M., Dickens, B. F., Jellife, L. L., et al. (2001). Neuropeptides and neurotrophins in neonatal blood of children with autism or mental retardation. *Annals of Neurology, 49,* 597–606.

Neville, H. J., & Bavelier, D. (1998). Neural organization and plasticity of language. *Current Opinion in Neurobiology, 8,* 254–258.

Newcombe, N. (2002). The nativist-empiricist controversy in the context of recent research on spatial and quantitative development. *Psychological Science, 13,* 395–401.

Newcombe, N., & Fox, N. A. (1994). Infantile amnesia. *Child Development, 65,* 31–40.

Newman, C., Atkinson, J., & Braddick, O. (2001). The development of reaching and looking preferences in infants to objects of different size. *Developmental Psychology, 37,* 561–572.

Nijhout, H. F. (2003). The importance of context in genetics. *American Scientist, 91,* 416–423.

Nolan, E., & Kagan, J. (1980). Recognition of self and self's products in preschool children. *Journal of Genetic Psychology, 137,* 285–294.

Nordenstroom, A., Servin, A., Bohlin, G., Larsson, A., & Wedell, A. (2002). Sex-typed toy play behavior correlates with the degree of parental androgen exposure assessed by CYP21 genotype in girls with congenital adrenal hyperplasia. *Journal of Clinical Endocrinology and Metabolism, 87,* 5119–5124.

Nordin, V., Lekman, A., Johansson, M., & Fredman, P. (1998). Gangliosides in cerebrospinal fluid in children with autism spectrum disorders. *Developmental Medicine and Child Neurology, 40,* 587–594.

Nugent, K., Kagan, J., & Snidman, N. (2002). *Relation of newborn reactivity to four-month temperament.* Unpublished manuscript.

Ohlrich, E. S., & Barnet, A. B. (1972). Auditory evoked responses during the first year of life. *Electroencephalography and Clinical Neurophysiology, 32,* 161–169.

Ohman, A., & Mineka, S. (2003). The malicious serpent. *Current Directions in Psychological Science, 12,* 5–9.

Okabe, S., Hanajima, R., Ohnishi, T., Nishikawa, M., Imabayashi, E., Takano, H., et al. (2003). Functional connectivity revealed by single-photon emission computed tomography (SPECT) during repetitive transcranial magnetic stimulation (rTMS) of the motor cortex. *Clinical Neurophysiology, 114,* 450–457.

Olausson, H., Lamarre, Y., Backlund, H., Morin, C., Wallin, B. G., Starck, G., et al. (2002). Unmyelinated tactile afferents signal touch and project to insular cortex. *Nature Neuroscience, 5,* 900–904.

Oliff, H. S., & Gallardo, K. A. (1999). The effect of nicotine on developing brain catecholamine systems. *Frontiers in Bioscience, 4,* D883–D897.

Oluwatimilehin, T., Hiraoka, T., & Halle, H. M. (2001). Transient interhemispheric neuronal synchrony correlates with object recognition. *Journal of Neuroscience, 21,* 3942–3948.

Oppenheim, R. W. (1999). Cell death during development of the nervous system. *Annual Review of Neuroscience, 14,* 453–501.

O'Rahilly, R., & Müller, F. (1999). *The embryonic human brain* (2nd ed.). New York: Wiley-Liss.

Orme, N. (2001). *Medieval children.* New Haven, CT: Yale University Press.

Ornitz, E. M. (1983). The functional neuroanatomy of infantile autism. *International Journal of Neuroscience, 19,* 85–124.

Ornitz, E. M. (2002). Developmental aspects of neurophysiology. In M. Lewis (Ed.), *Child and adolescent psychiatry* (pp. 60–74). Philadelphia: Lippincott.

Otsuka, Y., & Yamaguchi, M. K. (2003). Infants' perception of illusory contours in static and moving figures. *Journal of Experimental Child Psychology, 86,* 244–251.

Owens, D. F., & Kriegstein, A. (2002). Is there more to GABA than synaptic inhibition? *Nature Reviews Neuroscience, 3,* 715–727.

Pallier, C., Dehaene, S., Poline, J. B., LeBihan, D., Argenti, A. M., & Mehler, J. (2003). Brain imaging of language plasticity in adopted adults. *Cerebral Cortex, 13,* 155–161.

Pandya, D. N., & Kuypers, H. G. J. M. (1969). Cortico-cortical connections in the rhesus monkey. *Brain Research, 13,* 13–36.

Paneth, N. (2001). Cerebral palsy in term infants—Birth or before birth? *Journal of Pediatrics, 138,* 791–792.

Pang, M. Y. C., Lam, T., & Yang, J. F. (2003). Infants adopt their stepping to repeated trip-inducing stimuli. *Journal of Neurophysiology, 90,* 2731–2740.

Patrick, J. (1982). Fetal breathing movements. *Clinical Obstetrics and Gynecology, 25,* 787–803.

Paule, M. G., Rowland, A. S., Ferguson, S. A., Chelonis, J. J., Tannock, R., Swanson, J. M., et al. (2000). Attention deficit/hyperactivity disorder: Characteristics, interventions and models. *Neurotoxicology and Teratology, 22,* 631–651.

Paus, T. (2001). Primate anterior cingulate cortex: Where motor control, drive and cognition interface. *Nature Reviews Neuroscience, 2,* 417–424.

Paz, O. (1999). *Itinerary.* New York: Harcourt Brace.

Pearson, H. (2002). Your destiny, from day one. *Nature, 418,* 14–15.

Peiper, A. (1925). Sinnesempfindungen des kindes vor seiner geburt. *Monatsschrift für Kinderheilkunde, XXIX,* 236–241.

Pelphrey, K. A., Reznick, J. S., Goldman, D., Sasson, N., Morrow, J., Donahoe, A., et al. (2003) (unpublished manuscript). *The development of infant working memory.*

Penfield, W., & Welch, K. (1951). The supplementary motor area of the cerebral cortex. *Archives of Neurology and Psychiatry, 66,* 289–317.

Penn, A. A., & Schatz, C. J. (1999). Brain waves and brain wiring: The role of endogenous and sensory-driven neural activity in development. *Pediatric Research, 45,* 447–458.

Pennisi, E. (2004). The first language. *Science, 303,* 1319–1320.

Persinger, M. A., & LaLonde, C. A. (2002). Hemispheric asymmetry (lateralization) in electroencephalographic activity while viewing familiar and unfamiliar patterns from kimura figures. *International Journal of Neuroscience, 112,* 65–79.

Peterson, B. S. (2003). Conceptual, methodological, and statistical challenges in brain imaging studies of developmentally based psychopathologies. *Development and Psychopathology, 15,* 811–832.

Petitto, L. A. (1992). Modularity and constraints in early lexical acquisition. In M. R. Gunnar & M. Maratsos (Eds.), *Modularity and constraints in language and cognition* (Vol. 25, pp. 25–58). Hillsdale, NJ: Lawrence Erlbaum Associates, Inc.

Petrovich, G. D., Canteras, N. S., & Swanson, L. W. (2001). Combinatorial amygdalar inputs to hippocampal and hypothalamic behavioral systems. *Brain Research, 38,* 247–289.

Piaget, J. (1950). *Psychology of intelligence.* London: Routledge & Kegan Paul.

Pierce, K., Müller, R. A., Ambrose, J., Allen, G., & Courchesne, E. (2001). Face processing occurs outside the fusiform 'face area' in autism: Evidence from functional MRI. *Brain, 124,* 2059–2073.

Ploog, D. (2002). Is the neural basis of vocalization different in non-human primates and Homo sapiens? In T. J. Crow (Ed.), *The speciation of modern homo sapiens* (pp. 121–137). Oxford, England: Oxford University Press.

Poeppel, D., & Hickok, G. (2004). Towards a new functional anatomy of language. *Cognition, 92,* 1–2.

Poremba, A., Malloy, M., Saunders, R. C., Carson, R. E., Herscovitch, P., & Mishkin, M. (2004). Species specific calls evoke asymmetric activity in the monkey's temporal poles. *Nature, 427,* 448–451.

Porter, R. H., & Winberg, J. (1999). Unique salience of maternal breast odors for newborn infants. *Neuroscience and Biobehavioral Reviews, 23,* 439–449.

Posner, M. I., & Petersen, S. E. (1990). The attention systems of the human brain. *Annual Review of Neuroscience, 13,* 25–42.

Povinelli, D. J., & Bering, J. M. (2002). The mentality of apes revisited. *Current Directions in Psychological Science, 11,* 115–119.

Povinelli, D. J., Landry, A. M., Thall, L. A., Clark, B. R., & Castille, C. M. (1999). Development of young children's understanding that the recent past is causally bound to the present. *Developmental Psychology, 35,* 1426–1439.

Prather, M. D., Lavenex, P., Mauldin-Jourdain, M. L., Mason, W. A., Capitanio, J. P., Mendoza, S. P., et al. (2001). Increased social fear and decreased fear of objects in monkeys with neonatal amygdala lesions. *Neuroscience, 106,* 653–658.

Prechtl, H. F. R. (1981). The study of neural development as a perspective of clinical problems. In K. J. Connolly & H. F. R. Prechtl (Eds.), *Maturation and development* (pp. 198–215). London: Heinemann Medical Books.

Prechtl, H. F. R. (1984). *Continuity of neural functions.* Oxford, England: Blackwell.

Prechtl, H. F. R. (1986). New perspectives in early human development. *European Journal of Obstetrics, Gynecology, and Reproductive Biology, 21,* 347–355.

Price, B. H., Daffner, K. R., Stowe, R. M., & Mesulam, M. M. (1990). The compartmental learning disabilities of early frontal lobe damage. *Brain, 113,* 1383–1393.

Quinn, P. C., Bhatt, R. S., Brush, D., Grimes, A., & Sharpnack, H. (2002). Development of form similarity as a gestalt grouping principle in infancy. *Psychological Science, 13,* 320–328.

Rakic, P. (1976). Prenatal genesis of conenctions subserving ocular dominance in the rhesus monkey. *Nature, 261,* 467–471.

Rakic, P. (1988). Specification of cerebral cortical areas. *Science, 241,* 170–176.

Rakic, P. (1995a). A small step for the cell, a giant leap for mankind: A hypothesis of neocortical expansion during evolution. *Trends in Neuroscience, 18,* 383–388.

Rakic, P. (1995b). Radial versus tangential migration of neuronal clones in the developing cerebral cortex. *Proceedings of the National Academy of Sciences, USA, 92,* 11323–11327.

Rakic, P. (Ed.). (2000). *Setting the stage for cognition: Genesis of the primate cerebral cortex.* Cambridge, MA: MIT Press.

Rakic, P., Bourgeois, J. P., Eckenhoff, M. F., Zecevic, N., & Goldman-Rakic, P. S. (1986). Concurrent overproduction of synapses in diverse regions of the primate cerebral cortex. *Science, 232,* 232–235.

Rakic, S., & Zecevic, N. (2000). Programmed cell death in the developing human telencephalon. *European Journal of Neuroscience, 12,* 2721–2734.

Ralston, D. D. (1994). Corticorubral synaptic organization in macaca fascicularis: A study utilizing degeneration, anterograde transport of WGA-HRP, and combined immuno-GABA-Gold Technique and computer-assisted reconstruction. *Journal of Comparative Neurology, 350,* 657–673.

Ramnani, N., & Owen, A. M. (2004). Anterior prefrontal cortex. *Nature Reviews Neuroscience, 5,* 184–194.

Rao, H., Zhou, T., Zhuo, Y., Fan, S., & Chen, L. (2003). Spatiotemporal activation of the two visual pathways in form discrimination and spatial location: A brain mapping study. *Human Brain Mapping, 18,* 79–89.

Rao, S. C., Rainer, G., & Miller, E. K. (1997). Integration of what and where in the primate prefrontal cortex. *Science, 276,* 821–824.

Rapin, I. (1995). Acquired aphasia in children. *Journal of Child Neurology, 10*(X), 267–270.

Rapoport, J. L. (2002). Heritability of ADHD. (Personal communication)

Rapp, D. N., & Samuel, A. G. (2002). A reason to rhyme. *Journal of Experimental Psychology: Learning, Memory, and Cognition, 28,* 564–571.

Raymond, G. V., Bauman, M. L., & Kemper, T. L. (1996). Hippocampus in autism: A Golgi analysis. *Acta Neuropathologica (Berlin), 91,* 117–119.

Reber, P. J., Gitelman, D. R., Parrish, T. B., & Mesulam, M. M. (2003). Dissociating explicit and implicit category knowledge with fMRI. *Journal of Cognitive Neuroscience, 15,* 574–583.

Reichelt, R., Hofmann, D., Födisch, H.-J., Möhler, H., Knapp, M., & Hebebrand, J. (1991). Ontogeny of the benzodiazepine receptor in human brain: Fluorographic, immunochemical, and reversible binding studies. *Journal of Neurochemistry, 57,* 1128–1135.

Ren, Z. G., Porzgen, P. P., Youn, Y. H., & Sieber-Blum, M. (2003). Ubiquitous embryonic expression of the norepinephrine transporter. *Developmental Neuroscience, 25,* 1–13.

Rhodes, G., Geddes, K., Jeffery, L., Dziurawiec, S., & Clark, A. (2002). Are average and symmetric faces attractive to infants? Discrimination and looking preferences. *Perception, 31,* 315–321.

Richards, J. E. (1997). Effects of attention on infants' preference for briefly exposed visual stimuli in the paired comparison recognition memory paradigm. *Developmental Psychology, 33,* 22–31.

Richards, J. E., & Crouse, K. (2000). Extended visual fixation in the early preschool years. *Child Development, 71,* 602–620.

Richards, J. E., & Hunter, S. K. (2002). Testing neural models of the development of infant visual attention. *Developmental Psychobiology, 40,* 226–236.

Riese, M. L. (2003). Newborn temperament and sudden infant death syndrome. *Applied Developmental Psychology, 23*, 643–653.

Rizzo, T. (2001). Habituation technique in study of development of fetal behaviour. *Lancet, 357*, 328–329.

Rizzolatti, G., Fogassi, G., & Gallese, V. (2000). Cortical mechanisms subsuming object grasping and action recognition: A new view on the cortical motor functions. In M. S. Gazzaniga (Ed.), *The new cognitive neurosciences* (2nd ed., pp. 539–582). Cambridge, MA: MIT Press.

Roberts, G. W. (1991). Schizophrenia; a neuropathological perspective. *British Journal of Psychiatry, 158*, 8–17.

Robinson, J. L., Kagan, J., Reznick, J. S., & Corley, R. (1992). The heritability of inhibited and uninhibited behavior: A twin study. *Developmental Psychology, 28*, 1030–1037.

Rochat, P. (1998). Self-perception and action in infancy. *Experimental Brain Research, 123*, 102–109.

Rochat, P., & Senders, S. J. (1991). Active touch in infancy. In M. J. S. Weiss & P. R. Zelazo (Eds.), *Newborn attention* (pp. 412–442). Norwood, NJ: Ablex.

Rochat, P., Striano, T., & Blatt, L. (2002). Differential effect of happy, neutral, and sad still faces on 2, 4, and 6-month-old infants. *Child Development, 11*, 289–303.

Rogoff, B. (1996). Developmental transitions in children's participation in sociocultural activities. In A. G. Sameroff & M. M. Haith (Eds.), *The five to seven year shift* (pp. 273–294). Chicago: University of Chicago Press.

Rogoff, B., Newcombe, N., & Kagan, J. (1974). Planfulness and recognition memory. *Child Development, 45*, 972–977.

Roman, T., Szobot, C., Martins, S., Biederman, J., Rohde, L. A., & Hutz, M. H. (2002). Dopamine transporter gene and response to methylphenidate in attention-deficit/hyperactivity disorder. *Pharmacogenetics, 12*, 497–499.

Rorke, L. B. (1994). A perspective: The role of disordered genetic control of neurogenesis in the pathogenesis of migration disorders. *Journal of Neuropathology and Experimental Neurology, 53*, 105–117.

Rose, S. A., Feldman, J. F., & Jankowski, J. J. (2001). Visual short-term memory in the first year of life. *Developmental Psychology, 37*, 539–549.

Rose, S. A., Feldman, J. F., & Jankowski, J. J. (2003). Infant visual recognition memory. *Developmental Psychology, 39*, 563–571.

Rosenberg, D. R., & Lewis, D. A. (1994). Changes in the dopaminergic innervation of monkey prefrontal cortex during late postnatal development: A tyrosine hydroxylase immunohistochemical study. *Biological Psychiatry, 36*, 272–277.

Rosenblith, J. F., & Sims-Knight, J. E. (1985). *In the beginning*. Monterey, CA: Brooks/Cole.

Rosenhall, U., Nordin, V., Brantberg, K., & Gillberg, C. (2003). Autism and auditory brain stem responses. *Ear and Hearing, 24*, 206–214.

Rosenkranz, J. A., & Grace, A. A. (2002). Dopamine mediated modulation of motor evoked amygdala potentials during Pavlovian conditioning. *Nature, 417*, 282–287.

Ross, C., & Pearlson, G. (1996). Schizophrenia, the heteromodal association neocortex and development: Potential for a neurogenetic approach. *Trends in Neuroscience, 19*, 171–176.

Ross, M. E., & Walsh, C. A. (2001). Human brain malformations and their lessons for neuronal migration. *Annual Review of Neuroscience, 24*, 1041–1070.

Ross-Sheehy, S., Oakes, L. M., & Luck, S. J. (2003). The development of short term memory capacity in infants. *Child Development, 74*, 1807–1822.

Rouselle, L., Palmers, E., & Noel, M. P. (2004). Magnitude comparison in preshoolers: What counts? *Journal of Experimental Child Psychology, 87*, 57–84.

Roy, T. S., Seidler, F. J., & Slotkin, T. A. (2002). Prenatal nicotine exposure evokes alterations of cell structure in hippocampus and somatosensory cortex. *Journal of Pharmacology and Experimental Therapy, 300*, 124–133.

Royston, M. C., & Roberts, G. W. (1995). When neurons go astray. *Current Biology, 5,* 342–344.

Rubenstein, A. J., Kalakanis, L., & Langlois, J. H. (1999). Infant preferences for attractive faces. *Developmental Psychology, 35,* 848–855.

Rubia, K., Overmeyer, S., Taylor, E., Brammer, M., Williams, S. C. R., Simmons, A., et al. (1999). Hypofrontality in attention deficit hyperactivity disorder during higher-order motor control: A study with functional MRI. *American Journal of Psychiatry, 156,* 891–896.

Ruddle, K. (1993). The transmission of traditional ecological knowledge. In J. Inglis (Ed.), *Traditional ecological knowledge* (pp. 17–31). Ottawa, Ontario: The Canadian Museum of Nature.

Ruff, H. A., & Birch, H. G. (1974). Infant visual fixation. *Journal of Experimental Child Psychology, 17,* 460–473.

Rusoft, A. C., & Dubin, M. W. (1977). Development of receptive field properties of retinal ganglion cells in kittens. *Journal of Neurophysiology, 40,* 1184–1198.

Russon, A. E., & Galdikas, B. M. (1995). Constraints on great apes' imitation. *Journal of Comparative Psychology, 109,* 5–17.

Rutter, M., & O'Connor, T. G. (2004). Are there biological programming effects for psychological development? *Developmental Psychology, 40,* 81–94.

Saavedra, S., & Silverman, W. K. (2002). Case study: Disgust and a specific phobia of buttons. *Journal of the American Academy of Child and Adolescent Psychiatry, 41,* 1376–1379.

Sackett, G. P. (1966). Monkeys reared in isolation with pictures as visual input. *Science, 154,* 1468–1472.

Saffran, J. R. (2003). Statistical language learning. *Current Directions in Psychological Science, 12,* 110–114.

Saffran, J. R., Aslin, R. N., & Newport, E. L. (1996). Statistical learning by 8-month-old infants. *Science, 274,* 1926–1928.

Saffran, J. R., & Thiessen, E. D. (2003). Pattern induction by infant language learners. *Developmental Psychology, 39,* 484–494.

Saitoh, O., Karns, C. M., & Courchesne, E. (2001). Development of the hippocampal formation from 2 to 42 years. MRI evidence of smaller area dentata in autism. *Brain, 124,* 1317–1324.

Salamone, J. D., & Correa, M. (2002). Motivational views of reinforcement. *Behavioral Brain Research, 137,* 3–25.

Salum, C., & Roque-da-Silva, A. (2003). Conflict as a determinant of rat behavior in three types of elevated plus maze. *Behavioral Processes, 63,* 87–93.

Samuelson, L. K., & Smith, L. B. (1999). Early noun vocabularies. *Cognition, 73,* 1–33.

Samuelson, L. K., & Smith, L. B. (2000). Grounding development in cognitive processes. *Child Development, 71,* 98–106.

Sandhofer, C. M., & Smith, L. B. (1999). Learning color words involves learning a system of mappings. *Developmental Psychology, 35,* 668–679.

Sandyk, R. (1992). Melatonin and maturation of REM sleep. *International Journal of Neuroscience, 63,* 105–114.

Saxe, R., Carey, S., & Kanwisher, N. (2004). Understanding other minds. In S. T. Fiske, D. L. Schacter, & C. Zahn-Waxler (Eds.), *Annual review of psychology* (Vol. 55, pp. 87–124). Palo Alto, CA: Annual Reviews.

Schaal, B., Marlier, L., & Soussignan, R. (1998). Olfactory function in the human fetus: Evidence from selective neonatal responsiveness to odor of amniotic fluid. *Behavioral Neuroscience, 112,* 1438–1449.

Schack, B., Weiss, S., & Rappelsberger, P. (2003). Cerebral information transfer during word processing. *Human Brain Mapping, 19,* 18–36.

Schadé, J. P., & von Groenigen, W. B. (1961). Structural organization of the human cerebral cortex. *Acta Anatomica, 47,* 74–111.

Schaffer, H. R., Greenwood, A., & Parry, M. H. (1972). The onset of wariness. *Child Development, 43*, 165–175.

Schall, J. D. (2004). On building a bridge between brain and behavior. In S. T. Fiske, D. L. Schacter, & C. Zahn-Waxler (Eds.), *Annual review of psychology* (Vol. 55, pp. 23–50). Palo Alto, CA: Annual Reviews.

Schechtman, V. L., Lee, M. Y., Wilson, A. J., & Harper, R. M. (1996). Dynamics of respiratory patterning in normal infants and infants who subsequently died of the sudden infant death syndrome. *Pediatric Research, 40*, 571–577.

Schendon, H. E., & Kutas, M. (2003). Time course of processes and representations supporting visual object identification and memory. *Journal of Cognitive Neuroscience, 15*, 111–135.

Schiff, M., Duyme, M., Dumaret, A., Stewart, J., Tomkiewicz, S., & Feingold, J. (1978). Intellectual status of working-class children adopted early into upper-middle-class families. *Science, 400*, 1503–1504.

Schlottmann, A., & Surian, L. (1999). Do 9-month-old infants perceive causation-at-a-distance? *Perception, 28*, 1105–1113.

Schmahmann, J. D., & Pandy, D. N. (1997). Anatomic substrates: The cerebrocerebellar system. In J. D. Schmahmann (Ed.), *The cerebellum and cognition* (pp. 31–55). San Diego, CA: Academic.

Schmidt, L. A., Trainor, L. J., & Santesso, D. L. (2003). Development of frontal electroencephalogram (EEG) and heart rate (ECG) responses to affective musical stimuli during the first twelve months of postnatal life. *Brain and Cognition, 52*, 27–32.

Schneider, R. A., & Helms, J. A. (2003). The cellular and molecular origins of beak morphology. *Science, 299*, 565–568.

Schultz, W. (2000). Multiple reward signals in the brain. *Nature Reviews Neuroscience, 1*, 199–207.

Schwartz, C. E., Wright, C., Shin, L. M., Kagan, J., Whalen, P. J., McMullin, K. G., et al. (2003). Differential amygdalar response to novel versus familiar neutral faces. *Biological Psychiatry, 53*, 854–862.

Seeman, P., Bzowej, N. H., Guan, H. C., Bergeron, C., Becker, L. E., Reynolds, G. P., et al. (1987). Human brain dopamine receptors in children and aging adults. *Synapse, 1*, 399–404.

Segal, M., Korkotian, E., & Murphy, D. D. (2000). Dendritic spine formation and pruning: Common cellular mechanisms? *Trends in Neurosciences, 23*, 53–57.

Selemon, L. D., & Goldman, P. S. (1988). Common cortical and subcortical target areas of dorsolateral prefrontal and posterior parietal cortices in the rhesus monkey. *Journal of Neuroscience, 8*, 4049–4068.

Sellers, M. J., Klein, R. E., & Minton, C. (1972). Developmental determinants of attention. *Developmental Psychology, 6*, 185.

Serbin, L. A., Poulin-Doubois, D., & Eichstedt, J. A. (2002). Infants' responses to gender inconsistent events. *Infancy, 3*, 531–542.

Seress, L., & Mrzljak, L. (1992). Postnatal development of mossy cells in the human dentate gyrus: A light microscopic Golgi study. *Hippocampus, 2*, 127–142.

Shafer, V. L., Moor, M. L., Kreuzer, J. A., & Kurtzberg, D. (2000). Maturation of mismatch negativity in school-age children. *Ear and Hearing, 21*, 242–251.

Shamay-Tsoory, S. G., Tomer, R., Berger, B. D., & Aharon-Peretz, J. (2003). Characterization of empathy deficits following pre-frontal brain damage. *Journal of Cognitive Neuroscience, 151*, 324–337.

Shatz, C. J. (1996). Emergence of order in visual system development. *Proceedings of the National Academy of Sciences, USA, 93*, 602–608.

Shaywitz, B. A., Fletcher, J. M., & Shaywitz, S. E. (1995). Defining and classifying learning disabilities and attention-deficit/hyperactivity disorder. *Journal of Child Neurology, 10*, S50–S57.

Shaywitz, B. A., Yager, R. D., & Klopper, J. H. (1976). Selective brain dopamine depletion in developing rats. *Science, 191,* 306.

Shinskey, J. L., & Munakata, Y. (2003). Are infants in the dark about hidden objects? *Developmental Science, 6,* 273–282.

Shoal, G. D., Giancola, P. R., & Kirillova, G. P. (2003). Salivary cortisol, personality, and aggressive behavior in adolescent boys. *Journal of the American Academy of Child and Adolescent Psychiatry, 42,* 1101–1107.

Shweder, R. A., Mahapatra, M., & Miller, J. G. (1987). Culture and moral development. In J. Kagan & S. Lamb (Eds.), *The emergence of morality in young children* (pp. 1–83). Chicago: University of Chicago Press.

Sie, L. T. L., van der Knaap, M. S., Wezel-Meijler, V., & Valk, J. (1997). MRI assessment of myelination of motor and sensory pathways in the brain of preterm and term-born infants. *Neuropediatrics, 28,* 97–105.

Siegler, R. S. (1996). Uni-dimensional thinking, multi-dimensional thinking, and characteristic tendencies of thought. In A. G. Sameroff & M. M. Haith (Eds.), *The five to seven year shift* (pp. 63–84). Chicago: University of Chicago Press.

Simock, G., & Hayne, H. (2003). Age related changes in verbal and nonverbal memory during childhood. *Developmental Psychology, 39,* 805–814.

Simock, G., & Hayne. (2002). Breaking the barrier. *Psychological Science, 13,* 225–231.

Simonati, A., Tosati, C., Rosso, T., Piazzola, E., & Rizzuto, N. (1999). Cell proliferation and death: Morphological evidence during corticogenesis in the developing human brain. *Microscopy Research and Techniques, 45,* 341–352.

Simonds, R. J., & Scheibel, A. B. (1989). The postnatal development of the motor speech area: A preliminary study. *Brain and Language, 37,* 42–58.

Sininger, Y. S., Doyle, K. J., & Moore, J. K. (1999). The case for early identification of hearing loss in children. *Pediatric Clinics of North America, 46,* 1–14.

Slater, A., Morison, V., & Somers, M. (1988). Orientation discrimination and cortical function in the human newborn. *Perception, 17,* 597–602.

Slater, A., von der Schulenburg, C., Brown, E., Badenoch, M., Butterworth, G., Parsons, S., et al. (1998). Newborn infants prefer attractive faces. *Infant Behavior & Development, 21,* 345–354.

Slater, A. M., & Morison, V. (1985). Shape constancy and slant perception at birth. *Perception, 14,* 337–344.

Slater, P., McConnell, S., D'Souza, S. W., Barson, A. J., & Simpson, M. D. C. (1992). Age-related changes in binding to excitatory amino acid uptake site in temporal cortex of human brain. *Developmental Brain Research, 65,* 157–160.

Slotow, R., Vandyk, G., Poule, J., Page, B., & Klacke, A. (2000). Older bull elephants control young males. *Nature, 408,* 425–436.

Smiley, J., Levey, A. I., Ciliax, B. J., & Goldman-Rakic, P. S. (1994). D_1 dopamine receptor immunoreactivity in human and monkey cerebral cortex: Predominant and extrasynaptic localization in dendritic spines. *Proceedings of the National Academy of Sciences, USA, 91,* 5720–5724.

Smiley, J. F., & Goldman-Rakic, P. (1996). Serotonergic axons in monkey prefrontal cerebral cortex synapse predominantly on interneurons as demonstrated by serial section electron microscopy. *Journal of Comparative Neurology, 367,* 431–443.

Smith, A. (1776). *An inquiry into the nature and causes of the wealth of nations.* London: Methuen. (Published in 1904)

Smith, A. M., Bourbonnais, D., & Blanchette, G. (1981). Interaction between forced grasping and a learned precision grip after ablation of the supplementary motor area. *Brain Research, 222,* 395–400.

Smith, L. B. (1995). Self-organizing processes in learning to learn words. In C. A. Nelson (Ed.), *Basic and applied perspectives on learning, cognition, and development* (Vol. 28, pp. 1–32). Mahwah, NJ: Lawrence Erlbaum Associates, Inc.

Smith, L. B., Jones, S. S., & Landau, B. (1996). Naming in young children. *Cognition, 60,* 143–171.

Sparks, B. F., Friedman, S. D., Shaw, D. W., Aylward, E. H., Echelard, D., Artru, A. A., et al. (2002). Brain structural abnormalities in young children with autism spectrum disorder. *Neurology, 59,* 184–192.

Spelke, E. S. (1994). Initial knowledge. *Cognition, 50,* 431–445.

Spencer, J. P., & Schutte, A. R. (2004). Unifying representations and responses. *Psychological Science, 15,* 187–193.

Spencer, T. J., Biederman, J., Wilens, T. E., & Faraone, S. V. (2002). Overview and neuro-biology of attention-deficit/hyperactivity disorder. *Journal of Clinical Psychiatry, 63,* 3–9.

Sperandio, S., de Belle, I., & Bredesen, D. E. (2000). An alternative, nonapoptotic form of programmed cell death. *Proceedings of the National Academy of Sciences, USA, 97,* 14376–14381.

Stams, G. J. M., Juffer, F., & IJzendoorn, M. H. (2002). Maternal sensitivity, infant attachment, and temperament in early childhood predict adjustment in middle childhood. *Developmental Psychology, 38,* 806–821.

State, M. W., Lombroso, P. J., Pauls, D. I., & Leckman, J. (2000). The genetics of childhood psychiatric disorders: A decade of progress. *Journal of the American Academy of Child and Adolescent Psychiatry, 39,* 946–962.

Steele, C. M. (1997). A threat in the air. *American Psychologist, 52,* 613–629.

Stefanacci, L., Clark, R. E., & Zola, S. M. (2003). Selective neurotoxic amygdala lesions in monkeys disrupt reactivity to food and object stimuli and have limited effects on memory. *Behavioral Neuroscience, 117,* 1029–1043.

Stein, V., & Nicoll, R. A. (2003). GABA generates excitement. *Neuron, 37,* 375–378.

Stephan, K. E., Marshall, J. C., Friston, K. J., Rowe, J. B., Ritzl, A., Zilles, K., et al. (2003). Lateralized cognitive processes and lateralized past control in the human brain. *Science, 301,* 384–386.

Stewart, J. W., Bruder, G. E., McGrath, P. J., & Quitkin, F. M. (2003). The age of onset and course of illness defined biologically distinct groups within atypical depression. *Journal of Abnormal Psychology, 112,* 253–267.

Stokstad, E. (2001). New hints into the biological basis of autism. *Science, 294,* 34–37.

Strohman, R. (2002). Maneuvering in the complex path from genotype to phenotype. *Science, 296,* 701–703.

Strome, E. M., Wheler, G. H., Higley, J. D., Loriaux, D. L., Suomi, S. J., & Doudet, J. (2002). Intracerebroventricular corticotropin-releasing factor increases limbic glucose metabolism and has social context-dependent behavioral effects in nonhuman primates. *Proceedings of the National Academy of Sciences, USA, 99,* 15749–15754.

Sullivan, E. V., Pfefferbaum, A., Adalsteinsson, E., Swan, G. E., & Carmelli, D. (2002). Differential rates of regional brain change in callosal and ventricular size: A 4-year longitudinal MRI study of elderly men. *Cerebral Cortex, 12,* 438–445.

Super, C. M., Kagan, J., Morison, F. J., Haith, M. M., & Wieffenbach, J. (1972). Discrepancy and attention in the five-month infant. *Genetic Psychology Monographs, 85,* 305–331.

Swaab, D. F., Goudsmit, E., Kremer, H. P. H., Hofman, M. A., & Ravid, R. (1992). The human hypothalamus in development of sexual diferentiation, aging and Alzheimer disease. *Progress in Brain Research, 91,* 465–472.

Swanson, J., Posner, M., Fusella, J., Wasdell, M., Sommer, T., & Fan, J. (2001). Genes and attention deficit hyperactivity disorder. *Current Psychiatry Reports, 3,* 92–100.

Swanson, J. M., Sergeant, J. A., Taylor, E., Sonuga-Barke, E. J., Jensen, P. S., & Cantwell, D. P. (1998). Attention deficit hyperactivity disorder and hyperkinetic disorder. *Lancet, 351,* 429–433.

Taddio, A., & Katz, J. (1997). Effect of neonatal circumcision on pain response during subsequent routine vaccination. *Lancet, 349,* 599–603.

Taga, G., Ikejiri, T., Tachibana, T., Shimojo, S., Soeda, A., Takeuchi, K., et al. (2002). Visual feature binding in early infancy. *Perception, 31,* 273–286.

Tager-Flusberg, H., & Joseph, R. M. (2002). Identifying neurocognitive phenotypes in autism. *Philosphical Transactions of the Royal Society of London, Series B, 15,* 1–12.

Takahashi, T., Shirane, R., Sato, S., & Yoshimoto, T. (1999). Developmental changes of cerebral blood flow and oxygen metabolism in children. *American Journal of Neuroradiology, 20,* 917–922.

Tan, S. S., Kalloniatis, M., Sturm, K., Tam, P. P. L., Reese, B. E., & Falkner-Jones, B. (1998). Separate progenitors for radial and tangential cell dispersion during development of the cerebral neocortex. *Neuron, 21,* 295–304.

Tanaka, M. (1995). Object sorting in chimpanzees. *Journal of Comparative Psychology, 109,* 151–161.

Taylor, M., J., McCarthy, G., Saliba, E., & Degiovanni, E. (1999). ERP evidence of developmental changes in processing of faces. *Clinical Neurophysiology, 110,* 910–915.

Tervaniemi, M., & Hugdahl, K. (2003). Lateralization of auditory-cortex functions. *Brain Research Reviews, 43,* 231–246.

Thal, D. J., Marchman, V., Stiles, J., Aram, D., Trauner, D., Nass, R., et al. (1991). Early lexical development in children with focal brain injury. *Brain and Language, 40,* 491–527.

Thatcher, R. W. (1992). Cyclical cortical reorganization during early childhood. *Brain and Cognition, 20,* 24–50.

Thierry, G., & Giraud, A. L. (2003). Hemispheric dissociation and access to the human semantic system. *Neuron, 38,* 499–506.

Thomas, A., & Chess, S. (1977). *Temperament and development.* New York: Brunner/Mazel.

Thomas, D. G., & Lykins, M. S. (1995). Event related potential measures of 24-hour retention in five-month-old infants. *Developmental Psychology, 31,* 946–957.

Thomas, D. G., Whitaker, E., Crow, C. D., Little, V., Love, L., Lykins, M. S., et al. (1997). ERP variability as a measure of information storage in infant development. *Developmental Neuropsychology, 13,* 205–232.

Thomasson, M. A., & Teller, D. Y. (2000). Infant color vision. *Vision Research, 40,* 1051–1057.

Thompson, R. H., & Swanson, L. W. (2002). Structural characterization of a hypothalamic visceromotor pattern generator network. *Brain Research Reviews, 41,* 153–202.

Thorndike, E. L. (1907). *The elements of psychology.* New York: A. G. Seiler.

Tomasello, M. (1999). *The cultural origins of human cognition.* Cambridge, MA: Harvard University Press.

Tomasello, M. (2003). *Constructing a language.* Cambridge, MA: Harvard University Press.

Tomasello, M., & Haber, K. (2003). Understanding attention. *Developmental Psychology, 39,* 906–912.

Topal, J., Miklosi, A., Csanyi, V., & Doka, A. (1998). Attachment behavior in dogs (canis familiaris). *Journal of Comparative Psychology, 112,* 219–229.

Touwen, B. (1976). Neurological development in infancy. *Clinics in Developmental Medicine, 58,* 70–72.

Tranel, D., & Eslinger, P. J. (2000). Effects of early onset brain injury on the development of cognition and behavior: introduction to the special issue. *Developmental Neuropsychology, 18,* 273–280.

Trottier, G., Srivastava, L., & Walker, C. D. (1999). Etiology of infantile autism: A review of recent advances in genetic and neurobiological research. *Journal of Psychiatry and Neuroscience, 24,* 103–115.

Tsivilis, D., Otten, L. J., & Rugg, M. D. (2001). Context effects on the neural correlates of recognition memory. *Neuron, 31,* 497–505.

Tsivilis, D., Otten, L. J., & Rugg, M. D. (2003). Repetition effects elicited by objects and their contexts. *Human Brain Mapping, 19,* 145–154.

Tucker, D. M., Luu, P., Desmond, R. E., Harty-Speiser, A., Davey, C., & Flaisch, T. (2003). Corticolimbic mechanisms and emotional decisions. *Emotion, 3,* 127–149.

Turati, C. (2004). Why faces are not special to newborns. *Current Directions in Psychological Science, 13,* 5–8.

Turati, C., & Simion, F. (2002). Newborns' recognition of changing and unchanging aspects of schematic faces. *Journal of Experimental Child Psychology, 83,* 239–261.

Turkheimer, E., Haley, A., Waldron, M., D'Onofrio, B., & Gottesman, I. I. (2003). Socioeconomic status modifies heritability of I.Q. in young children. *Psychological Science, 14,* 623–628.

Ulanovsky, N., Las, L., & Nelken, I. (2003). Processing of low-probability sounds by cortical neurons. *Nature Neuroscience, 6,* 391–398.

Uylings, H. B. M. (2001). The human cerebral cortex in development. In A. F. Kalverboer & A. Gramsbergen (Eds.), *Handbook of brain and behaviour in human development* (pp. 63–80). London: Kluwer Academic.

Vaccarino, F. M. (2000). Stem cells and neuronal progenitors and their diversity in the CNS: Are time and place important? *The Neuroscientist, 6,* 338–352.

Valdizan, J. R., Abril-Villalba, B., Mendez-Garcia, M., Sana-Capdevilla, O., Pablo, M. J., Peralta, P., et al. (2003). Cognitive evoked potentials in autistic children. *Revista de Neurologia, 36,* 425–428.

Valenstein, E. S., Cox, V. C., & Kakolewski, J. W. (1970). Reexamination of the role of the hypothalamus in motivation. *Psychological Review, 77,* 16–31.

van der Kooy, D., & Weiss, S. (2000). Why stem cells? *Science, 287,* 1439–1441.

van Praag, H., Kempermann, G., & Gage, F. H. (2000). Neural consequences of environmental enrichment. *Nature Reviews Neuroscience, 1,* 191–198.

Vandenbergh, J. G. (2003). Prenatal hormone exposure and sexual variation. *American Scientist, 91,* 218–225.

Varendi, H., Porter, R. H., & Winberg, J. (1996). Attractiveness of amniotic fluid odor: Evidence of prenatal olfactory learning? *Acta Paediatrica, 85,* 1223–1227.

Vargha-Khadem, F., Watkins, K., Alcook, K., Fletcher, P., & Passingham, R. (1995). Praxis and nonverbal cognitive deficits in a large family with a genetically transmitted speech and language disorder. *Proceedings of the National Academy of Sciences, USA, 92,* 930–933.

Vargha-Khadem, F., Watkins, K. E., Price, C. J., Ashburner, J., Alcock, K. J., Connelly, A., et al. (1998). Neural basis of an inherited speech and language disorder. *Proceedings of the National Academy of Sciences, USA, 95,* 12695–12700.

Vervaecke, H., DeVries, H., & Van Elsacker, L. (1999). An experimental evaluation of the consistency of competitive ability and agnostic dominance in different social contexts in captive bonobos. *Behavior Genetics, 136,* 423–442.

Vicari, S., Albertoni, A., & Chilosi, A. M. (2000). Plasticity and reorganization during language development in children with early brain injury. *Cortex, 36,* 31–46.

Vining, E. P., Feeman, J. M., Pillias, D. J., Uematsu, S., Carson, B. S., Brandt, J., et al. (1997). Why would you remove half a brain? *Pediatrics, 100,* 163–171.

Vitalis, T., Alvarez, C., Chen, K., Shih, J. C., Gaspar, P., & Cases, O. (2003). Developmental expression pattern of monoamine oxidases in sensory organs and neural crest derivatives. *Journal of Comparative Neurology, 464,* 392–403.

Vogel, G. (2002). Missized mutants help identify organ tailors. *Science, 297,* 328.

Volkow, N. D., Fowler, J. S., Wang, G. J., Ding, Y. S., & Gatley, S. J. (2002). Role of dopamine in the therapeutic and reinforcing effects of methylphenidate in humans: Results from imaging studies. *European Neuropsychopharmacology, 12,* 557–566.

Volpe, J. (1995). *Neurology of the newborn* (3rd ed.). Philadelphia: Saunders.

Wadhwa, S., & Bijlani, V. (1988). Cytodifferentiation and developing neuronal circuitry in the human lateral geniculate nucleus. *International Journal of Developmental Neuroscience, 6,* 59–77.

Waller, G., Watkins, B., Potterton, C., Niederman, M., Sellings, J., Willoughby, K., et al. (2002). Pattern of birth in adults with anorexia nervosa. *Journal of Nervous and Mental Disease, 190,* 752–756.

Walsh, C., & Cepko, C. (1992). Widespread dispersion of neuronal clones across functional regions of the cerebral cortex. *Science, 255,* 434–440.

Wang, H., & Wessendorf, M. W. (2002). Mu and delta opioid receptor mRNAs are expressed in periaqueductal brain neurons projecting to the rostral ventromedial medulla. *Neuroscience, 109,* 619–634.

Warrington, E. K., & McCarthy, R. A. (1994). Multiple meaning systems in the brain: A case for visual semantics. *Neuropsychologia, 21,* 1465–1473.

Webb, S. J., & Nelson, C. A. (2001). Perceptual priming for upright and inverted faces in infants and adults. *Journal of Experimental Child Psychology, 79,* 1–22.

Weinberger, N. M. (2003). The nucleus basalis and memory codes. *Neurobiology of Learning and Memory, 80,* 268–284.

Weinstock, M. (1997). Does prenatal stress impair coping and regulation of hypothalamic-pituitary-adrenal axis? *Neuroscience and Biobehavioral Reviews, 21,* 1–10.

Welge-Lussen, A., Wille, C., Renner, B., & Kobal, G. (2003). Test–retest reliability of chemosensory evoked potentials. *Journal of Clinical Neurophysiology, 20,* 135–142.

Weliky, M., & Katz, L. C. (1999). Correlational structure of spontaneous neuronal activity in the developing lateral geniculate nucleus in vivo. *Science, 285,* 599–604.

Werker, J. F., & Tees, R. L. (1983). Developmental changes across childhood in the perception of non-native speech sounds. *Canadian Journal of Psychology, 37,* 278–286.

Westberg, L., Melke, J., Landen, M., Nilsson, S., Baghaei, F., Rosmond, R., et al. (2003). Association between dinucleotide repeat polymorphism of the estrogen receptor alpha gene and personality traits in women. *Molecular Psychiatry, 8,* 118–122.

White, S. H. (1996). The child's entry into the age of reason. In A. G. Sameroff & M. M. Haith (Eds.), *The five to seven year shift* (pp. 17–32). Chicago: University of Chicago Press.

White, S. H., & Pillemer, D. B. (1979). Childhood amnesia and the development of a socially accessible memory system. In J. F. Kihlstrom & F. J. Evans (Eds.), *Functional disorders of memory* (pp. 29–73). Hillsdale, NJ: Lawrence Erlbaum Associates, Inc.

White, T., & Andreasen, N. C. (2002). Brain volumes and surface morphology in monozygotic twins. *Cerebral Cortex, 12,* 486–493.

Whiting, B. B., & Whiting, J. W. M. (1975). *Children of six cultures.* Cambridge, MA: Harvard University Press.

Whitney, D., Goltz, H. C., Thomas, C. G., Gati, J. S., Menon, R. S., & Goodale, M. A. (2003). Flexible retinopy. *Science, 302,* 878–881.

Wiesel, T. N. (1982). Postnatal development of the visual cortex and the influence of environment. *Nature, 299,* 583–591.

Wiesel, T. N., & Hubel, D. H. (1965). Extent of recovery from the effects of visual deprivation in kittens. *Journal of Neurophysiology, 28,* 1060–1072.

Wiesendanger, M., & Wise, S. P. (1992). Current issues concerning the functional organization of motor cortical areas in non-human primates. *Advances in Neurology, 57,* 117–133.

Williams, G. V., & Goldman-Rakic, P. S. (1995). Modulation of memory fields by dopamine D1 receptors in prefrontal cortex. *Nature, 376,* 572–575.

Wilson, E. O. (1999). *Consilience.* New York: Vintage.

Wilson, F. A., & Rolls, E. T. (1993). The effect of stimulus novelty and familiarity on neuronal activity in the amygdala of monkeys performing recognition memory tasks. *Experimental Brain Research, 93,* 367–382.

Winberg, J. (1998). Olfaction and human neonatal behaviour: Clinical implications. *Acta Paediatrica, 87,* 6–10.

Winkler, I., Schroger, E., & Cowan, N. (2001). The role of large-scale memory organization in the mismatch negativity event-related brain potential. *Journal of Cognitive Neuroscience, 13,* 59–71.

Witter, M. P. (1993). Organization of the entorhinal-hippocampal system: A review of current anatomical data. *Hippocampus, 3,* 33–44.

Wood, H. (2002). About-face. *Nature Reviews Neuroscience, 3,* 254.

Woodward, A. L. (1998). Infants selectively encode the goal object of an actor's reach. *Cognition, 69,* 1–34.

Woodward, A. L., & Hayne, K. L. (1999). Infants' learning about words and sounds in relation to objects. *Child Development, 70,* 65–77.

Worobey, J., & Lewis, M. (1989). Individual differences in the reactivity of young infants. *Developmental Psychology, 25,* 663–667.

Wulfeck, B. B., Bates, E., & Krupa-Kwiatkowski, M. (2004). Grammaticality sensitivity in children with early focal injury and children with specific language impairment. *Brain and Language, 88,* 215–228.

Xiang, H., Lin, C., Ma, X., Zhang, Z. B. J. M., Weng, X., & Gao, J. H. (2000). Involvement of the cerebellum in semantic distinctions. *Human Brain Mapping, 18,* 208–214.

Xu, F. (2003). Numerosity discrimination in infants. *Cognition, 89,* 1315–1325.

Yakovlev, P. I., & Lecours, A. R. (1967). The myelogenetic cycles of regional maturation of the brain. In A. Minkowski (Ed.), *Regional development of the brain in early life* (pp. 3–70). Oxford, England: Blackwell.

Yamaguchi, K., Goto, N., & Yamamoto, T. Y. (1989). Development of human cerebellar nuclei. *Acta Anatomica, 136,* 61–68.

Yamakoshi, M. M., Tomonaga, M., Tanaka, M., & Matsuzawa, T. (2003). Preference for human direct gaze in infant chimpanzees (pan troglodytes). *Cognition, 89,* B53–B64.

Yang, T. T., Menon, V., Reid, A. J., Gotlib, I. H., & Reiss, A. L. (2003). Amygdalar activation associated with happy facial expressions in adolescents. *Journal of the American Academy of Child and Adolescent Psychiatry, 42,* 979–985.

Yaniv, D., Desmedt, A., Jaffard, R., & Richter-Levin, G. (2004). The amygdala and appraisal processes. *Brain Research Reviews, 44,* 179–186.

Yilmazer-Hanke, D. M., Roskoden, Y., Zilles, K., & Schwegler, H. (2003). Anxiety related behavior and densities of glutamate, GABA, acetylcholine and serotonin receptors in the amygdala of seven inbred mouse strains. *Behavioural Brain Research, 145,* 145–159.

Yoshida, H., & Smith, L. B. (2003). Known and novel noun extensions. *Child Development, 74,* 564–577.

Young, S. K., Fox, N. A., & Zahn-Waxler, C. (1999). The relation between temperament and empathy in 2-year-olds. *Developmental Psychology, 35,* 1189–1197.

Yu, M. C. (1993). An immunohistochemical study of neuropeptide Y positive sites in the developing human hippocampal formation. *Developmental Brain Research, 72,* 277–281.

Yuill, N., & Pearson, A. (1998). Development of bases for trait attribution. *Developmental Psychology, 34,* 575–586.

Zahn-Waxler, C., Robinson, J. L., & Emde, R. N. (1992). The development of empathy in twins. *Developmental Psychology, 28,* 1038–1047.

Zalc, B., & Fields, R. D. (2000). Do action potentials regulate myelination? *The Neuroscientist, 6,* 5–13.

Zecevic, N., Bourgeois, J.-P., & Rakic, R. (1989). Changes in synaptic density in motor cortex of rhesus monkey during fetal and postnatal life. *Developmental Brain Research, 50,* 11–32.

Zecevic, N., & Rakic, P. (1991). Synaptogenesis in monkey somatosensory cortex. *Cerebral Cortex, 1,* 510–523.

Zentner, M. R., & Kagan, J. (1996). Perception of music by infants. *Nature, 29,* 383.

Zilles, K., & Rehkämper, O. (1994). *Funktionelle Neuroanatomie* (2nd ed.). Berlin, Germany: Springer-Lehrbuch.

Zilles, K., Schlaug, G., Matelli, M., Luppino, G., & Schleicher, A. (1995). Mapping of human and macaque sensorimotor areas by integrating architectonic, transmitter receptor, MRI and PET data. *Journal of Anatomy, 187,* 515–537.

Zilles, K., Werners, R., Buesching, U., & Schleicher, A. (1986). Ontogenesis of the laminar structure in areas 17 and 18 of the human visual cortex. *Anatomy and Embryology, 174,* 339–353.

Zoghbi, H. Y. (2003). Postnatal neurodevelopmental disorders. *Science, 302,* 826–830.

Zubieta, J. K., Ketter, T. A., Bueller, J. A., Xu, Y., Kilbourn, M. R., Young, E. A., et al. (2003). Regulation of human affective responses by anterior cingulate and limbic mu-opioid neurotransmission. *Archives of General Psychiatry, 60,* 1145–1153.

Author Index

N

O

Subject Index

Note. Page numbers in *italics* refer to figures; those in **boldface** refer to tables.

A

Acetylcholine, 179, 210
Alcohol, effect on fetal breathing, 51
Alertness, in newborns, 61
American Sign Language, 154
Ammon's horn, in autism, 182
Amygdala
  in autism, 183–184
  provocation of, 123–128, **123**
  in reaction to novelty, 121–123, *122*
  in temperament prediction, 139–142
Animal behavior, compared to human, 6–7
A not B task, 108–110, *109*, 189
Anterior commissure, 210
Anticipation, 190
Apoptosis, 39
Arcuate, 211
Arousal, in newborns, 61, 105–106
Associations, establishing, 20–23
Atomoxetine, 216–217
Attachment, temperament and, 146–147
Attachment bond, 146
Attention Deficit Hyperactivity Disorder
  (ADHD), 214–217
Attentiveness. *See* Discrepant event proc-
  essing
Auditory input, effects of, 65–67
Auditory system
  in 8 to 12 month infants, 77–78

in newborns, 70–71, 77
  prenatal, 52–55, *54*
Authority figures, social categories and,
  203
Autism, 179–185, **180**

B

Babbling, in language acquisition, 151–152
Babinski, 82
Balance scale task, 207–208, *208*
Basal ganglia, in language acquisition, 164
Basolateral area, 121
Behavior. *See* Psychological outcomes
Beliefs, 249–251
Birth defects, social categories and, 204
Birth to 8 weeks. *See* Newborns
Blastula, 34
Brain activity, localization of, 232–234
Brain development. *See also specific develop-
  mental phases*
  conceptualizing, 4–9
  phases of, 16–18, 24–30
  psychological outcomes and, 1–4,
    220–225
    context effect on, 9–12, 225–230
    technology effect on, 230–232
Brain states, defined, 1
Brain weight, 208